PICASSO

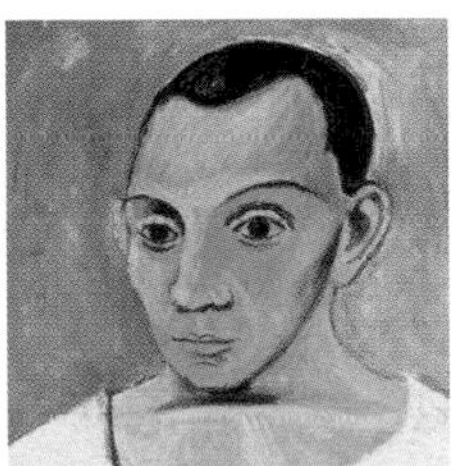

Publisher and Creative Director: Nick Wells
Picture Research: Melinda Révész
Project Editor: Sonya Newland
Designer: Robert Walster
Production: Chris Herbert & Claire Walker

Special thanks to: Vic Newland

FLAME TREE PUBLISHING
Crabtree Hall, Crabtree Lane
Fulham, London, SW6 6TY
United Kingdom

www.flametreepublishing.com

First published 2006

07 08 10 09 06

1 3 5 7 9 10 8 6 4 2

Flame Tree is part of the Foundry Creative Media Company Limited

Produced for Flame Tree Publishing by
BIG BLU LTD
mail@bigbludesign.co.uk

The CIP record for this book is available from the British Library.

ISBN 1 84451 291 6

Printed in China

PICASSO

Author: Mike O'Mahony Foreword: Pepe Karmel

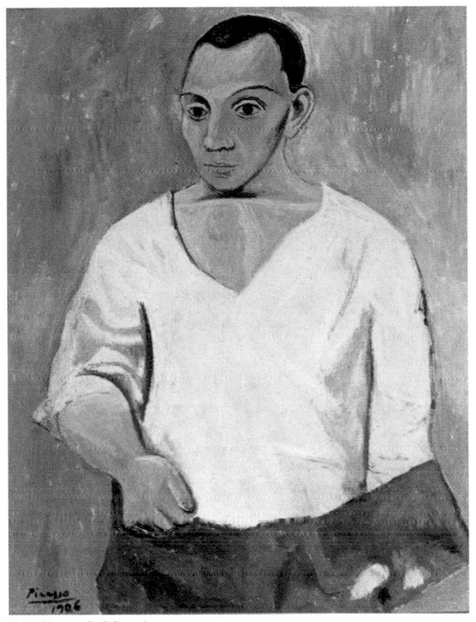
Pablo Picasso, *Self-Portrait*

**FLAME TREE
PUBLISHING**

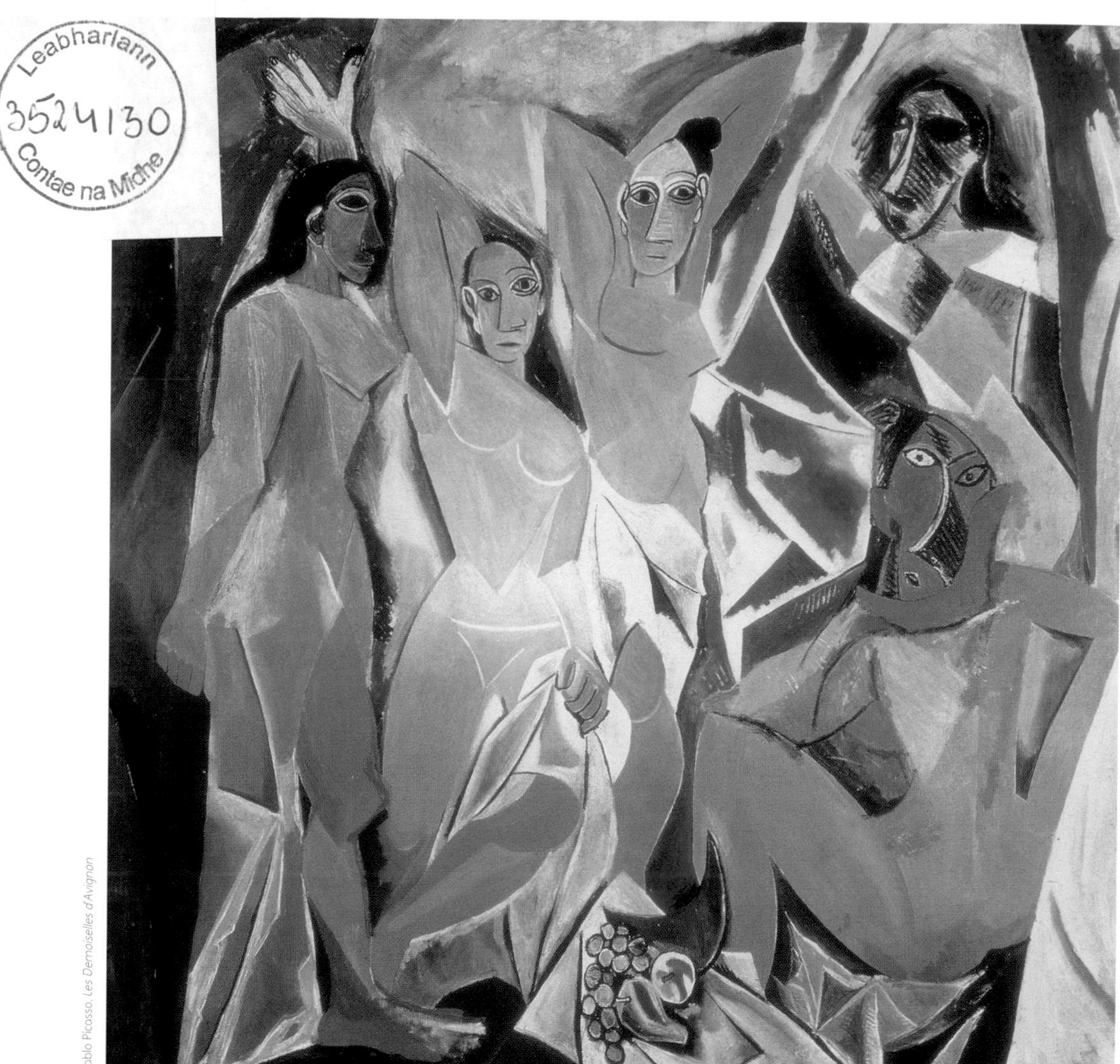

Pablo Picasso, *Les Demoiselles d'Avignon*

Contents

How To Use This Book 8
Foreword 10
Introduction 12

Life 20

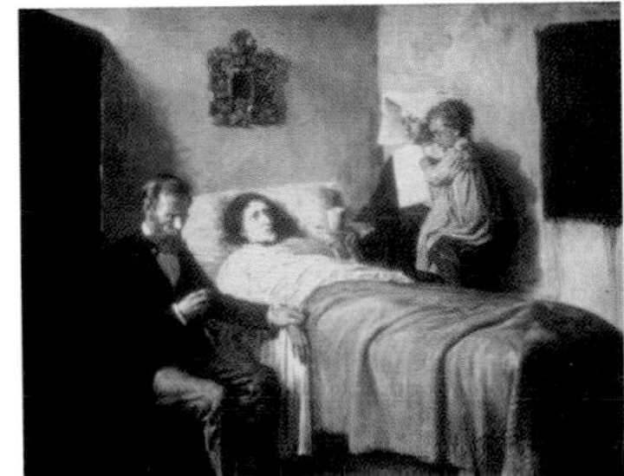
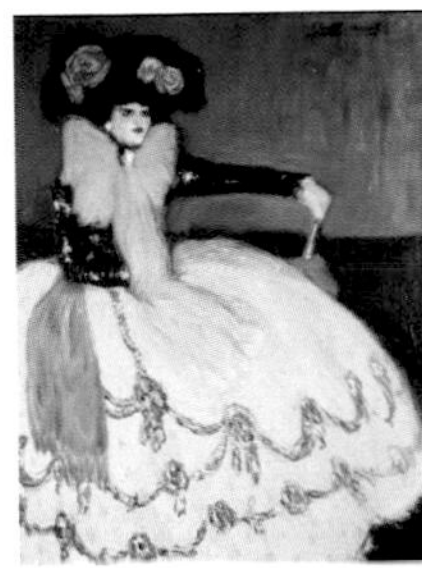
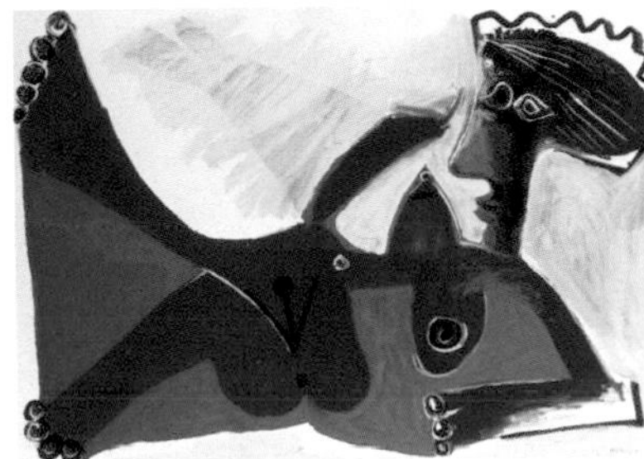

Pablo Picasso, *Science and Charity*; *Woman in Blue*; *Reclining Nude*

Society 114

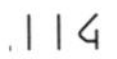

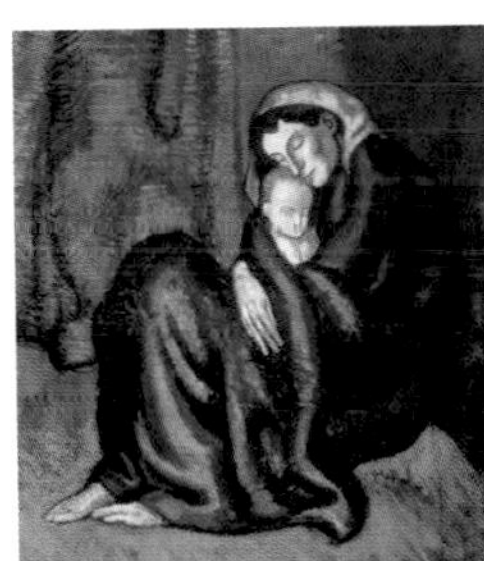
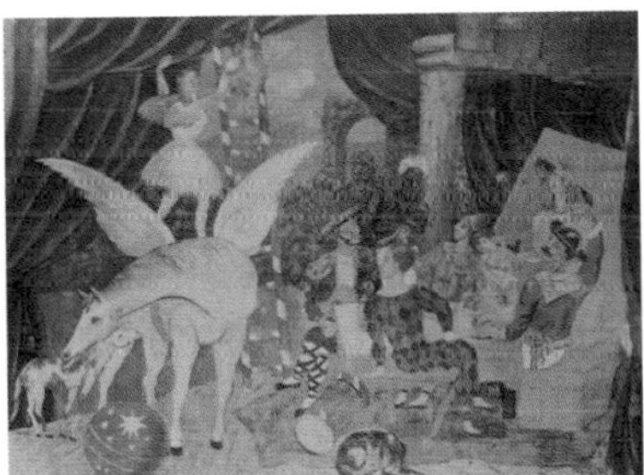
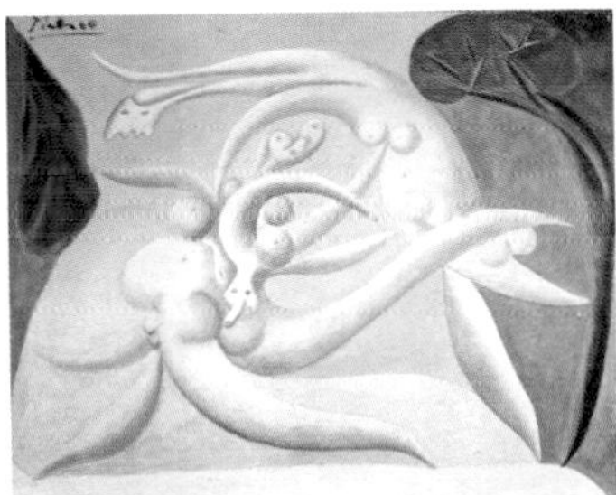

Pablo Picasso, *Mother and Child*; Theatre Curtain for *Parade*; *Circus Scene*

Places 198

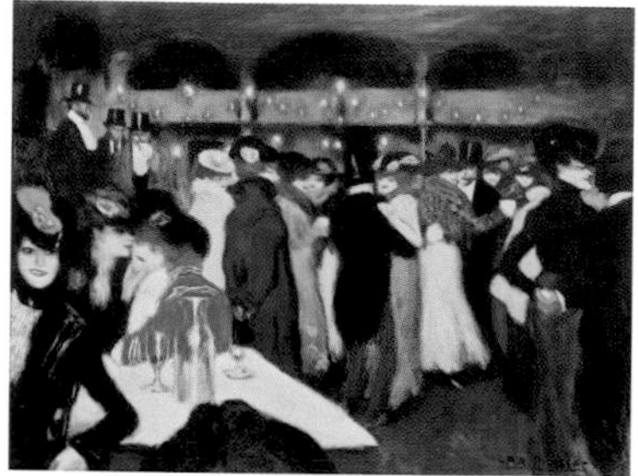
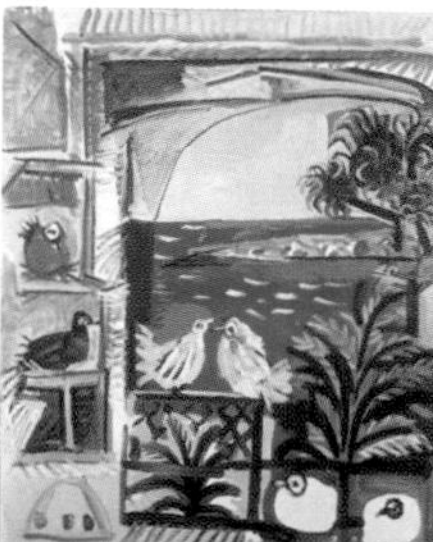
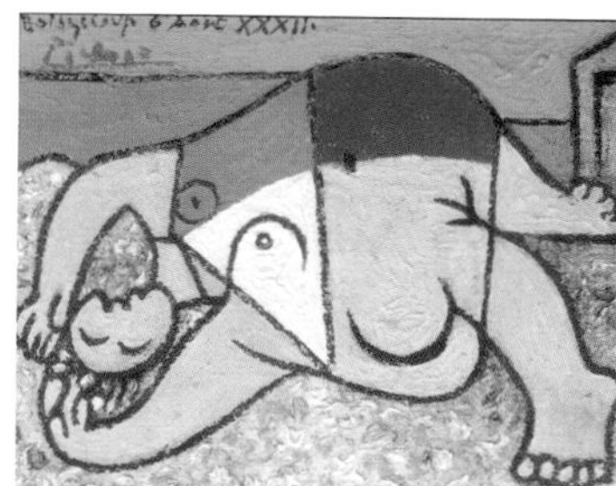

Pablo Picasso, *Le Moulin de la Galette; The Pigeons, Cannes; Woman Lying on the Beach*

Influences 258

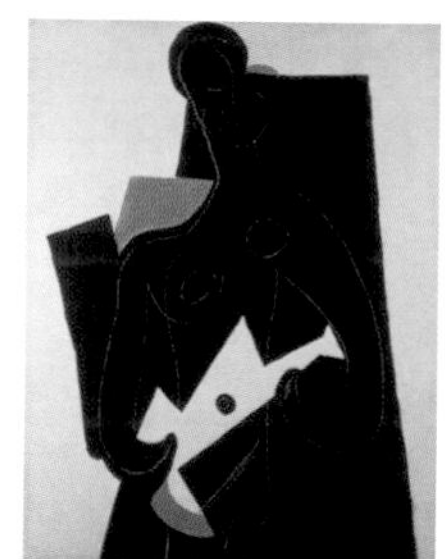
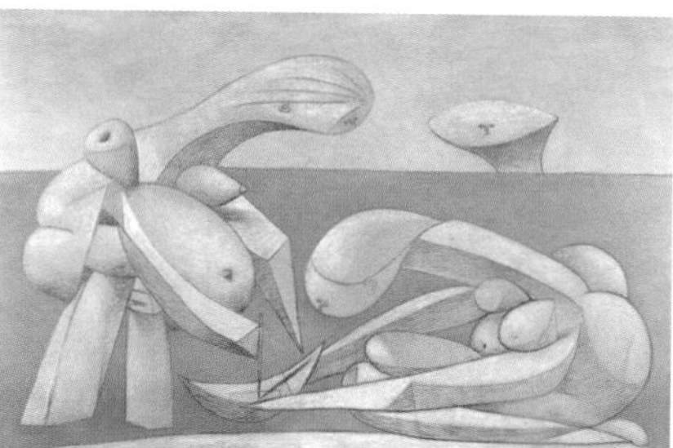
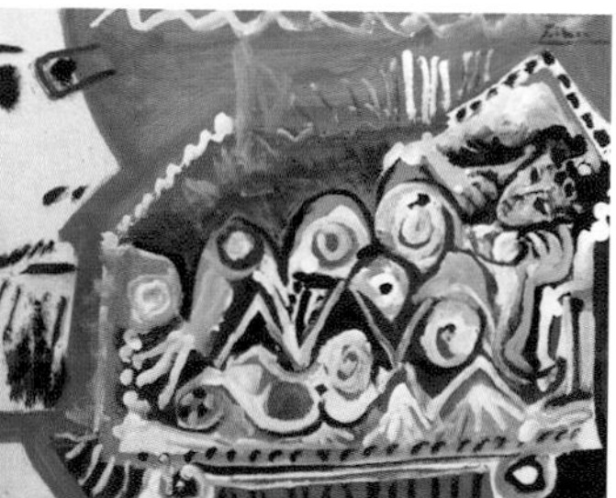

Pablo Picasso, *Woman with a Guitar; On the Beach (Bathing); Lying Nude with Head of a Man in Profile*

Styles & Techniques 296

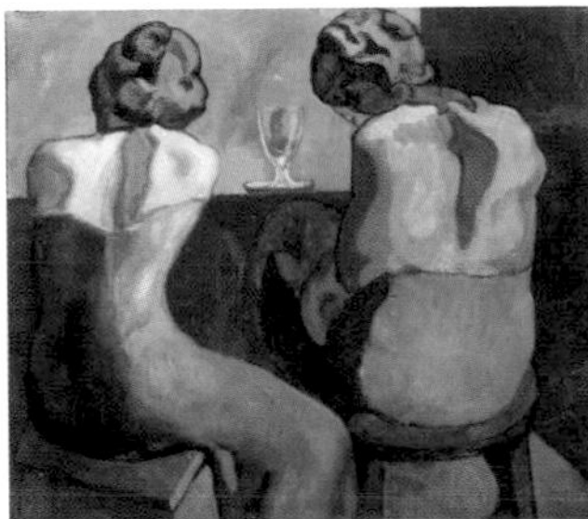
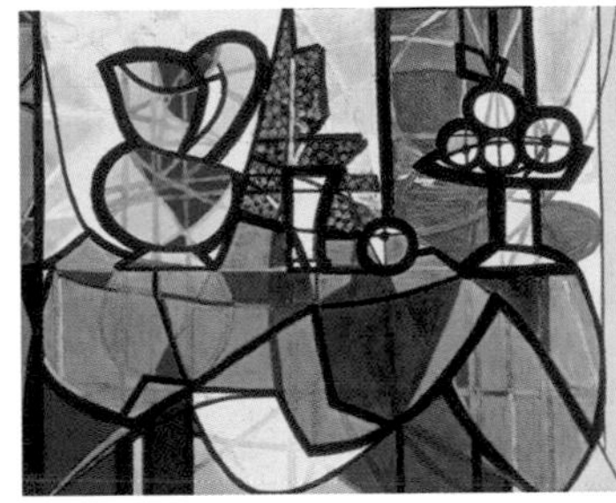
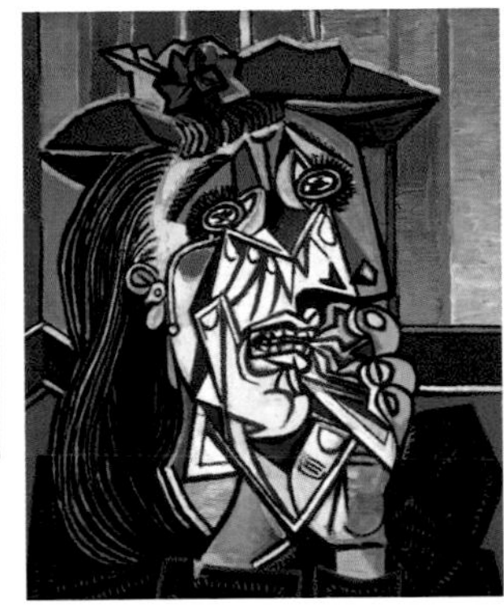

Pablo Picasso, *Two Women at a Bar; Still Life with Pitcher and Bowl of Fruit; Weeping Woman*

Biographies & Further Reading 378

Index by Work 380

General Index 382

How To Use This Book

The reader is encouraged to use this book in a variety of ways, each of which caters for a range of interests, knowledge and users.

- The book is organized into five sections: **Life**, **Society**, **Places**, **Influences** and **Styles & Techniques**.
- **Life** provides a snapshot of how Picasso's work developed during the course of his career, showing the different styles he used and discussing how different people and events in his life affected his work.
- **Society** shows how Picasso's work reflects contemporaneous society, and how events in the wider world of the time were a source of inspiration for him.
- **Places** looks at the work Picasso created in the different places he lived and travelled.
- **Influences** reveals Picasso's sources of inspiration and the artists who were, in turn, inspired by his work.
- **Styles & Techniques** delves into the different techniques Picasso used to produce his pieces, from painting to collage and sculpture, and the varying styles that characterized the different periods of his career.

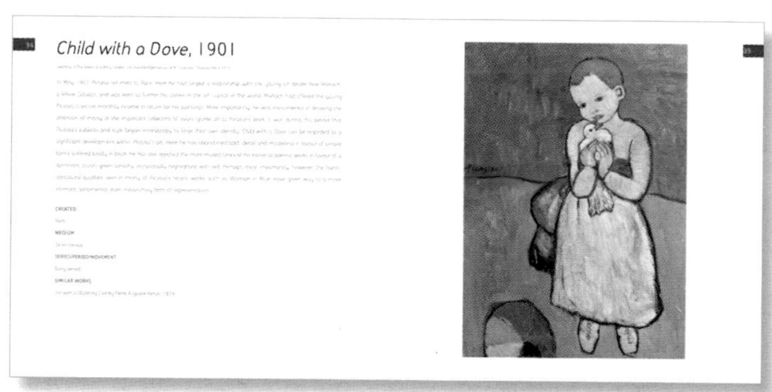

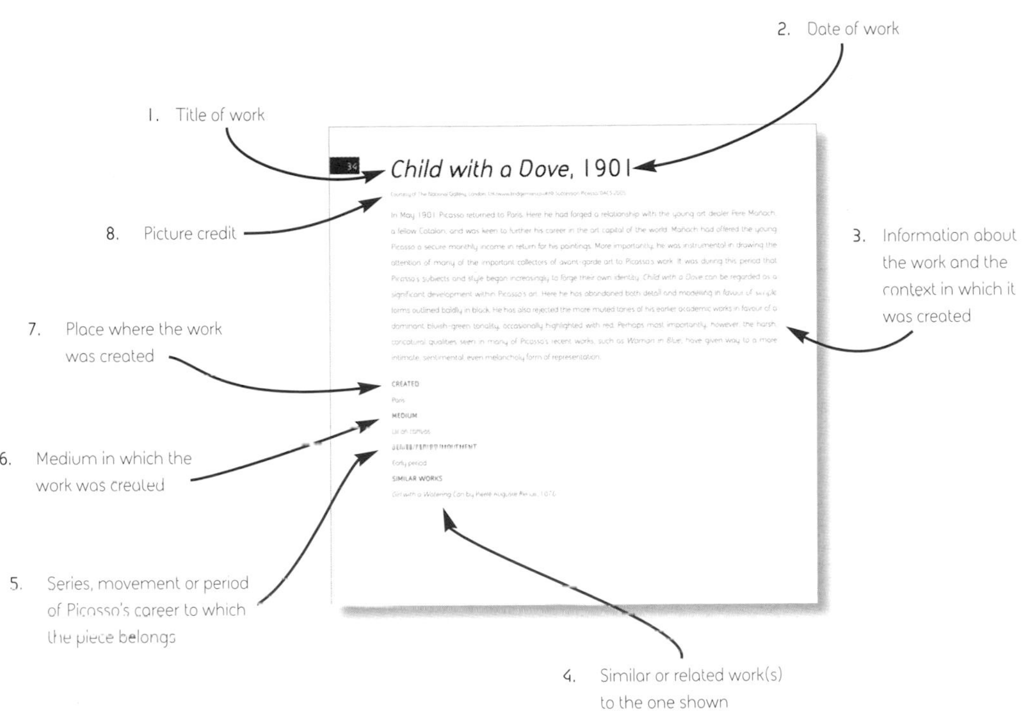
2. Date of work
1. Title of work
34
Child with a Dove, 1901
8. Picture credit
3. Information about the work and the context in which it was created
7. Place where the work was created
CREATED
MEDIUM
6. Medium in which the work was created
SIMILAR WORKS
5. Series, movement or period of Picasso's career to which the piece belongs
4. Similar or related work(s) to the one shown

Foreword

Born in 1881, the son of a provincial Spanish art teacher, Picasso was not a likely candidate to become the greatest artistic innovator of his era. It is true that, from an early age, he displayed a striking talent for drawing and painting. But the great innovators of modern art – like Paul Cézanne, Edvard Munch or Jackson Pollock – are often clumsy and ungifted. Instead of talent, they have genius; incapable of making conventional art, they reinvent art to suit their gifts. By all rights, Picasso should have become a minor artist, a fashionable illustrator or a decorative painter. But something happened to change his fate. In 1905, an expatriate American, Leo Stein, bought one of his paintings, and in the art collection of Stein's extended family – Gertrude, Michael and Sarah – he discovered the work of Paul Cézanne and Henri Matisse. The encounter galvanized Picasso. In 1907 he painted *Les Demoiselles d'Avignon*; by 1909 he was a recognized leader of the Parisian avant-garde; and for the next 40 years he was the most influential artist in the world.

In *Les Demoiselles d'Avignon* Picasso confronted – and forced his contemporaries to confront – the powerful currents of terror and desire that ran beneath the surface of civilized society. Like the paintings of the German Expressionists, the formal language of *Les Demoiselles* was marked by deliberate crudity and simplification. The picture shocked even Picasso's most adventurous contemporaries. Despite this rejection, he did not return to a more conventional, naturalistic style. Instead, he took the simplified forms of *Les Demoiselles* and refined them into a new, quasi-abstract style. He reduced real bodies and real objects to a series of geometric shapes, and then combined these geometric shapes into an overall pattern that covered the canvas like the interlocking pieces of a jigsaw puzzle.

Picasso's new style immediately began to attract followers, first and foremost the painter Georges Braque. In a creative dialogue that lasted seven years, from 1908 to 1914, Picasso and Braque developed the style known as Cubism. It was the greatest revolution in Western art since the Renaissance. Translating three-dimensional form into a sequence of overlapping planes, Cubism broke down the distinction between solid form and empty space. It suggested depth by piling up forms that advanced toward the viewer, instead of receding into the distance according to the mathematical formulas of perspective. Instead of imitating natural appearances, Cubism evoked the identities of things and people by scattering cartoon-like marks (an eye, a moustache, the scroll of a violin) across the planes that were locked into place by a grid of vertical and horizontal lines, parallel to the borders of the picture.

For Picasso, Cubism was a delirious game, a way of describing reality by signs and circumlocutions. For artists such as Piet Mondrian and Kasimir Malevich, however, Cubism pointed to the possibility of an art freed from the responsibility of representing the real world. From constructivism down through the hard-edged abstraction of the 1960s, the language of Cubism was recycled by twentieth-century painters and sculptors. If Picasso had retired in 1914 his work up to that point would already have established him as the most influential artist of the twentieth century.

Far from retiring, however, Picasso plunged into a dizzying succession of artistic experiments. For a decade he worked on two parallel tracks, extending the range of Cubism while inventing a new kind of naturalism that evoked the great tradition of Greek and Roman art without actually imitating it. Picasso's Neoclassical pictures of the early 1920s offered an elegy to the pleasures of marriage and family life, reflecting a blissful era in his own existence. Then, as his personal life grew darker and more complicated, he transformed the evolving language of Cubism into a vehicle for the passions. Desire and rage coursed through his new paintings, expressed by interlacing lines suggesting the curves of breasts and buttocks, and jagged edges suggesting teeth and knives. Picasso's compulsive reinvention of the visual world inspired the Surrealists, who saw his work as the expression of a hallucinatory alternative reality. Picasso's symbolism was rooted in his melodramatic private life, but he put it to public use in his great anti-war painting, *Guernica*, of 1937.

After the Second World War, the rise of Abstract Expressionism, then Pop Art and Minimalism, seemed to consign Picasso to the status of a modern Old Master and his work grew less and less relevant to contemporary art. By 2004, a poll taken in conjunction with the Tate Gallery's Turner Prize revealed that a majority of art experts considered Marcel Duchamp's *Fountain* of 1917 – a urinal bought at a plumbing supply store and exhibited unaltered – more important than either Picasso's *Guernica* or *Les Demoiselles d'Avignon*. Duchamp's Dadaist insistence on the absurdity of life and art speaks more loudly to contemporary artists than does Picasso's passion or inventiveness. It should be remembered, however, that Dada itself grew out of Cubism. Specifically, it was Picasso's invention of collage – the incorporation of found materials and images – that provided the model for Duchamp's invention of the 'ready-made'. Artists today use everyday objects to construct parables of modern life. But if we can make sense of – and even enjoy – their complex allegories, it is in large part because Pablo Picasso taught us to read and enjoy an art of signs.

Pepe Karmel, *2005*

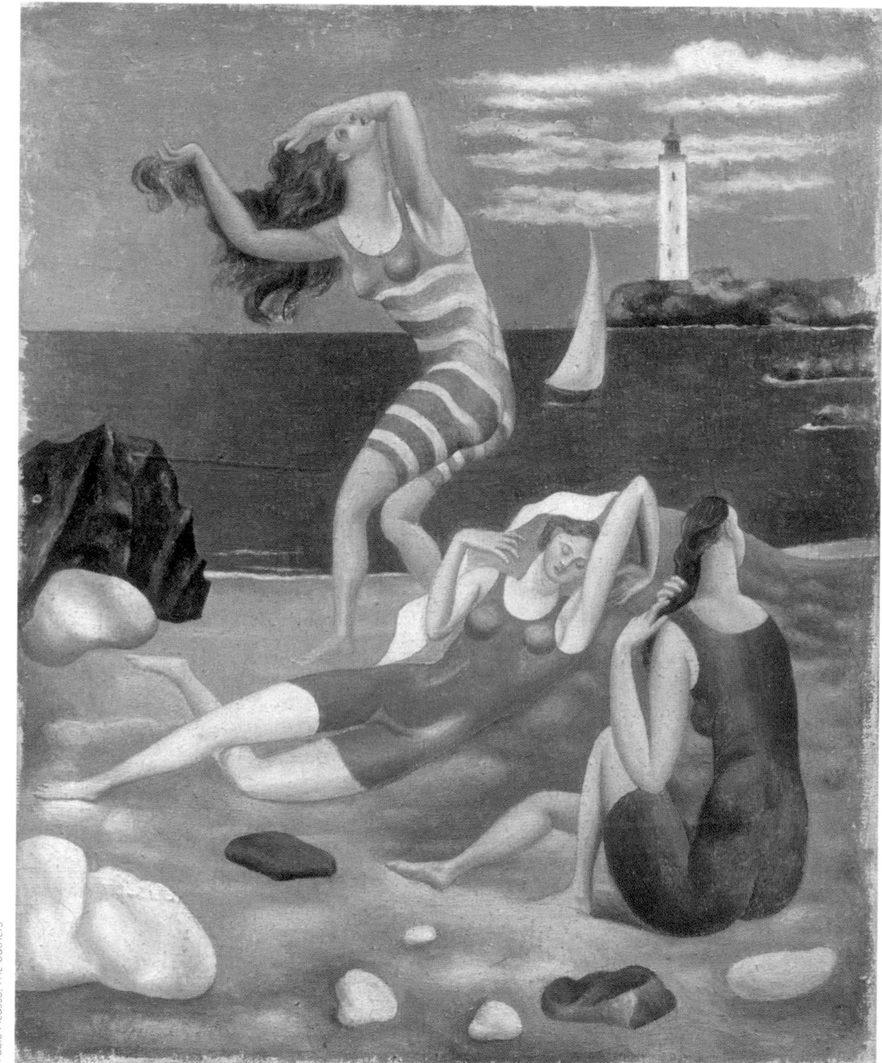

Pablo Picasso, *The Bathers*

Introduction

Few would dispute Pablo Picasso's reputation as one of the pre-eminent artists of the twentieth century. Indeed, the thousands of drawings, paintings, prints, sculptures and ceramics that remain to us are a testament to the sheer scope of his visual imagination and his capacity for artistic innovation – so much so that it seems almost inconceivable that this could be the product of a single individual and a single lifetime. Picasso certainly lived a long and highly active life, and his artistic production spanned the best part of 80 of the 91 years that he walked this earth. Yet, it is not just the volume of his output that matters. More importantly, it is the constantly changing nature of his work, his capacity to express himself and his epoch in a multitude of ever-changing ways that best characterizes Picasso's remarkable achievement.

Picasso stood at the forefront of the major artistic innovations of the twentieth century. His early forays into Symbolism, seen in his 'blue' and 'rose' periods of the first decade of the century, forged one of the most compelling visual vocabularies with which to chart the bohemian existence of turn-of-the-century Paris, whilst his amalgamation of the influences of Paul Cézanne (1839–1906) and African masks resulted in an entirely new and exciting means to represent space. Together with Georges Braque (1882–1963) he was responsible for the invention of Cubism, one of the most radical breaks with art of the past, and yet he was also a leading figure in the return to a more traditional, Neoclassical style in the last years of the First World War. Even here, however, he endowed this traditional approach to painting with a vision uniquely his own. He dabbled in Surrealism in the 1920s and 1930s without ever committing himself to the movement. Nonetheless, his Surrealist-inspired paintings and sculptures remain amongst the most intriguing works of the period and opened the gates for other Surrealists to follow. And when he turned his attention to political subjects, such as the bombing of Guernica during the Spanish Civil War, the occupation of Paris by German troops during the Second World War, or the political tensions inspired by the Cold War, he virtually reinvented the concept of contemporary history painting. Even in his old age, when he started producing works based on Old Master paintings, the sheer formal inventiveness of his art not only resulted in highly creative works, but also enabled us to see afresh what previously had seemed so familiar.

Nor was Picasso restricted in the materials he used. His innovations in painting were matched by his practical reinvention of sculpture in 1912, abandoning the age-old notion of modelling and carving, and introducing construction, the building up of a sculpture from component parts. Moreover, his use of a variety of everyday materials in his two- and three-dimensional works, including old newsprint, wallpaper, broom-handles and even bicycle saddles and toy cars, has transformed the very notion of what constitutes artistic practice.

Throughout his life, Picasso remained an enigmatic figure, an individual constantly reinventing himself as much as his art. In addition to the self-portraits he produced at various stages of his life, he also introduced stock characters such as the harlequin and the minotaur into his works – characters that stood, metaphorically, for the artist himself. Yet the duality of their identity, symbolic of both good and evil, only serves to retain the enigma, never really allowing the viewer any closer to the real Picasso. He also maintained a dual identity as an intensely Spanish artist, yet one who spent the majority of his adult life living in France. Here he was constantly on the move. In Paris he occupied a variety of studios and homes in different parts of the city, and spent most of his summers in the south, on the French Riviera. Even in his old age he lived in an assortment of villas and chateaux dotted throughout the south of France, never fully settling in any of them.

Picasso's domestic life was also in constant flux, as his relationships with the numerous women in his life grew, faded, collapsed and started over. Yet all of this provided an impetus and a background for the constant changes in his work. Indeed, his entire body of art has often been read as a form of autobiography and, at times, it is easy to link his choice of subject matter and stylistic handling to events in his own life. Thus the despair evident within his early blue-period works seems inextricably linked to his initial isolation in Paris, whilst the more ordered and harmonious Neoclassical works of 1917–22 coincided with the happiest days of his marriage to the Russian dancer Olga Khokhlova and the birth of his first child, Paulo. Similarly, the sensual, curvaceous and radiantly coloured forms evident in his portraits of Marie-Thérèse Walter were produced during the early 1930s when Picasso was conducting a secret affair with this young woman, and can be contrasted with the dark, austere and altogether more sinister works he created in Paris during the 1940s, when his relationships with the women in his life were on a less secure footing. Finally, the colourful, exuberant and joyous forms of his late-1940s Mediterranean scenes were undoubtedly inspired by his newfound happiness, living with the young painter Françoise Gilot and their two children, whilst the more brutally painted late self-portraits, with their anxiety-inducing distortions, thickly encrusted surfaces and muddy tones, were notably executed when Picasso was staring his own mortality directly in the face.

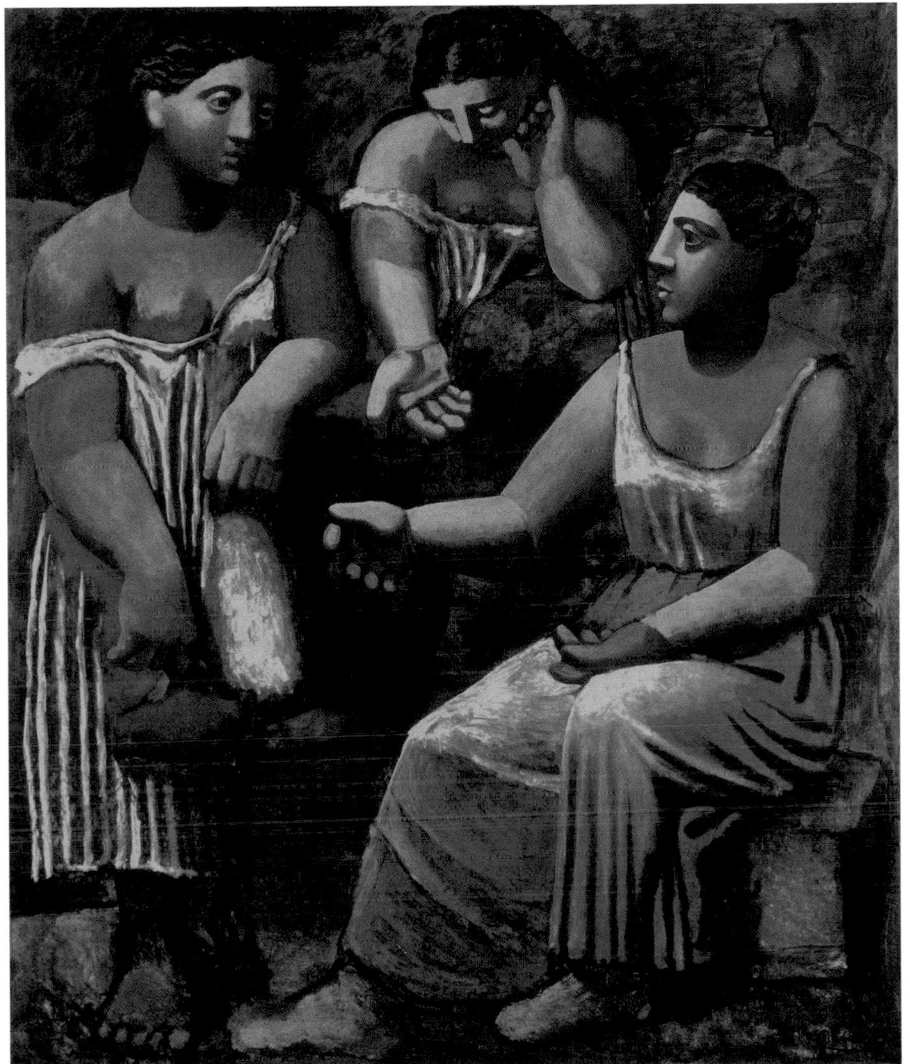

Pablo Picasso, *Three Women at the Spring*

Yet to reduce Picasso's works simply to these personal influences would be to exclude a number of other crucial factors. Picasso did not live his life in isolation from the major political events of the twentieth century. Indeed, his work very much addresses the wider social and historical events he witnessed and experienced first-hand. The class conflicts and political tensions of turn-of-the-century Barcelona – widely known as a hot-bed of anarchism and revolution – certainly inspired Picasso's interests in the poor and dispossessed, as well as encouraging him to reject the conventional academic training he had received as a student. Moreover, many of the technological innovations of the late nineteenth and early twentieth centuries left their mark on the artist. New inventions such as radiotelegraphy and cinema, developments in high-speed travel with the expansion of new motorcars, and new scientific discoveries, such as X-rays, all challenged previous ideas regarding time and space. As a consequence of this, Picasso's Cubist innovations were as much a part of a wider social and philosophical exploration of how time and space might be conceived and represented in light of these changing factors. Picasso also lived through two World Wars, global events that brought death and destruction on a previously unimaginable scale and changed the nature of international relations. Picasso never shied away from the big questions generated by such events, a factor attested to by his famous anti-war icon of 1937, *Guernica*, and his decision to join the Communist Party in 1944. All these wider social factors inevitably left their mark on Picasso's work and, indeed, it was his willingness to grapple with the major issues of his epoch that has made his work so complex and so enduring.

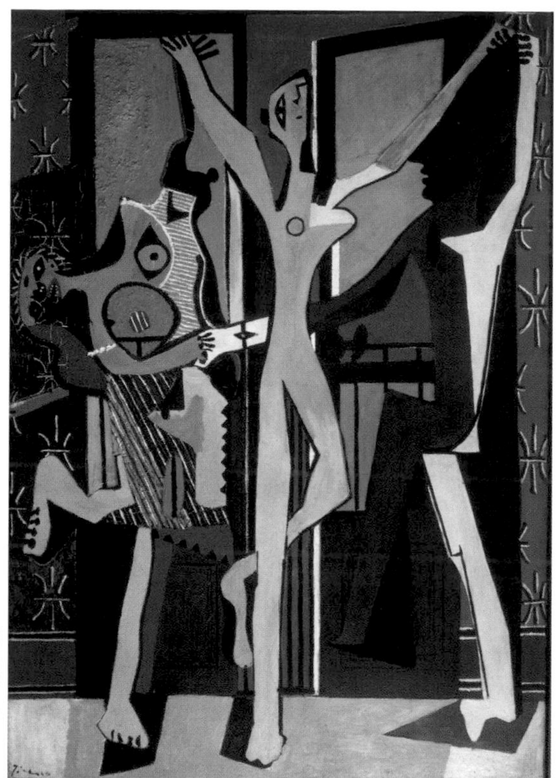

Pablo Picasso, *Three Dancers*

Many of Picasso's works can now be seen in the major museums of the world, from his native Spain and adopted France, to Great Britain, the United States and beyond.

International exhibitions are also regularly held, covering all stages of Picasso's career and all aspects of his work, from his earliest scribbles to his last crayon drawings, from his experiments with fragments of newsprint to his ceramics and monumental sculptures. Few other artists can boast four major museums dedicated solely to their work, yet Paris, Barcelona, Antibes and, most recently, Málaga, are all now home to Picasso Museums. Picasso's works have also been widely reproduced in hundreds of books offering a range of differing interpretations of the artist's work. We are even able to watch the artist at work thanks to a documentary film, *The Mystery of Picasso*, made in 1955 by the French filmmaker Georges Clouzot, and the artist's life has been dramatized in a 1996 Hollywood feature-film entitled *Surviving Picasso*, and starring Anthony Hopkins in the title role. While all this serves to bring us just a little closer to the artist and his work, it can never give us definitive answers. Indeed, it is the endless possibilities of Picasso's works, their ability to resist simple classification and to open up options for wider interpretation, that draws us back again and again to re-explore their many qualities. Picasso rarely painted with a preconceived notion of what the end result should be. Rather, as he stated in the mid 1930s, 'A picture is not thought out and settled beforehand. While it is being done it changes as one's thoughts change. And when it is finished it still goes on changing, according to the state of mind of whoever is looking at it.' Picasso's works will continue to live, to grow, to develop, to go on 'changing' as new generations discover, explore and engage with the work of this extraordinary artist.

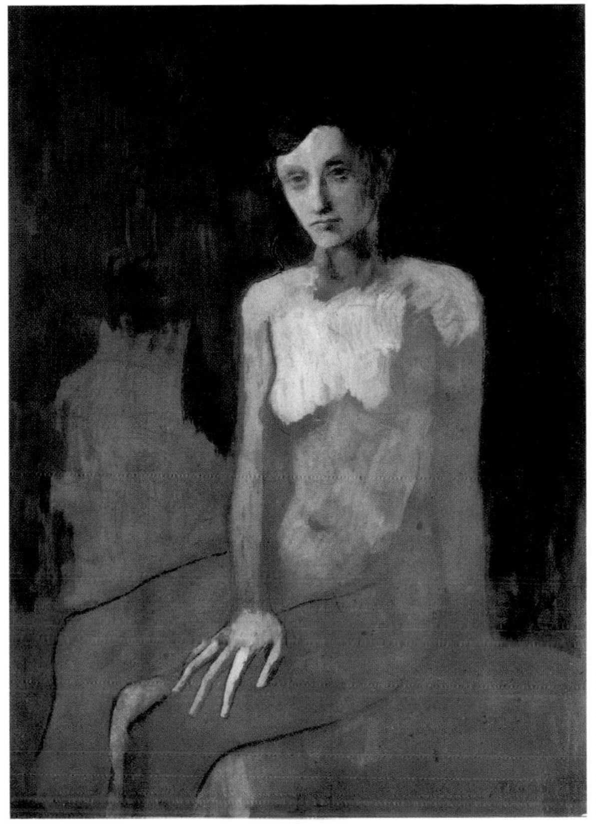

Pablo Picasso, *Seated Nude*

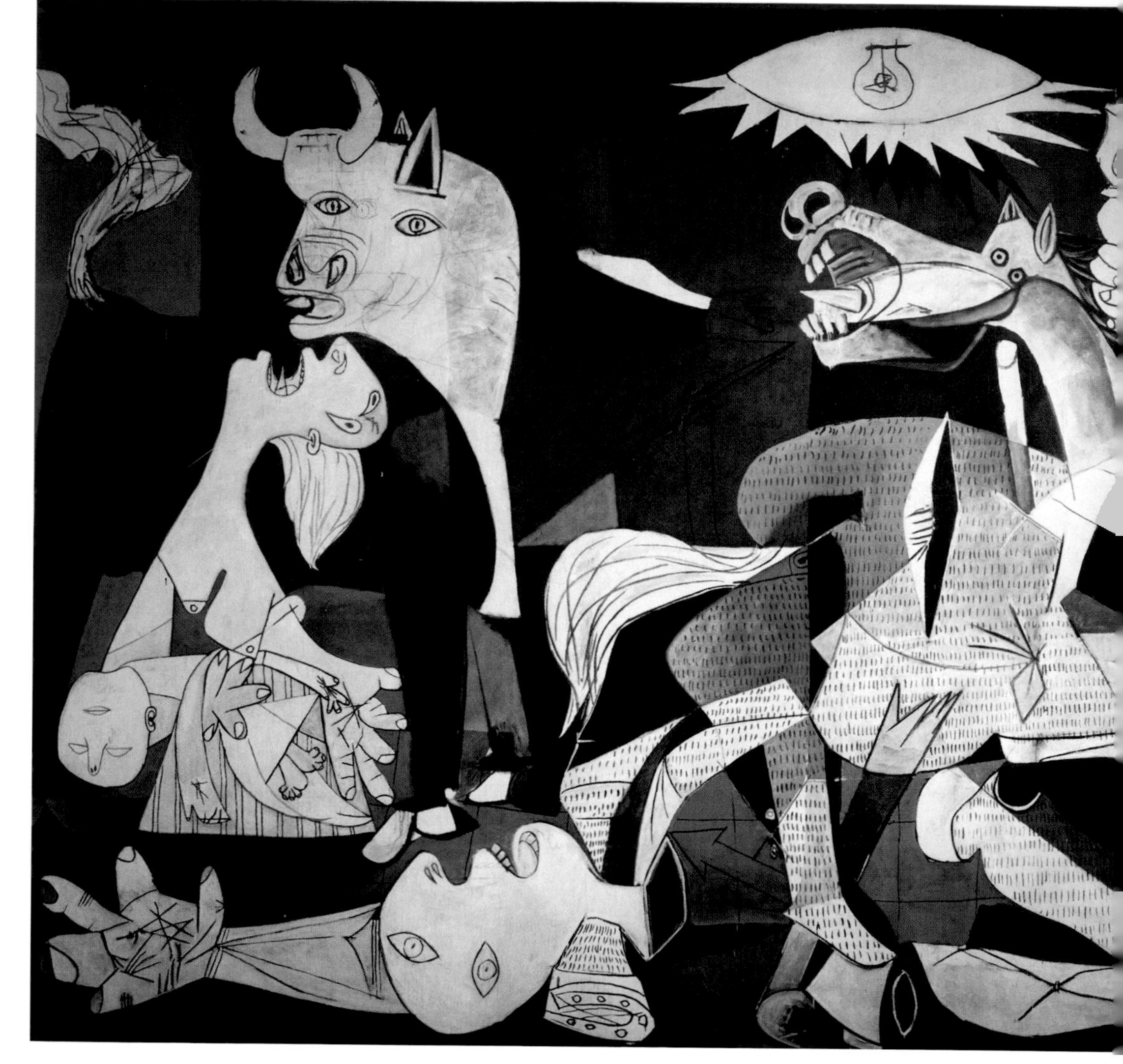

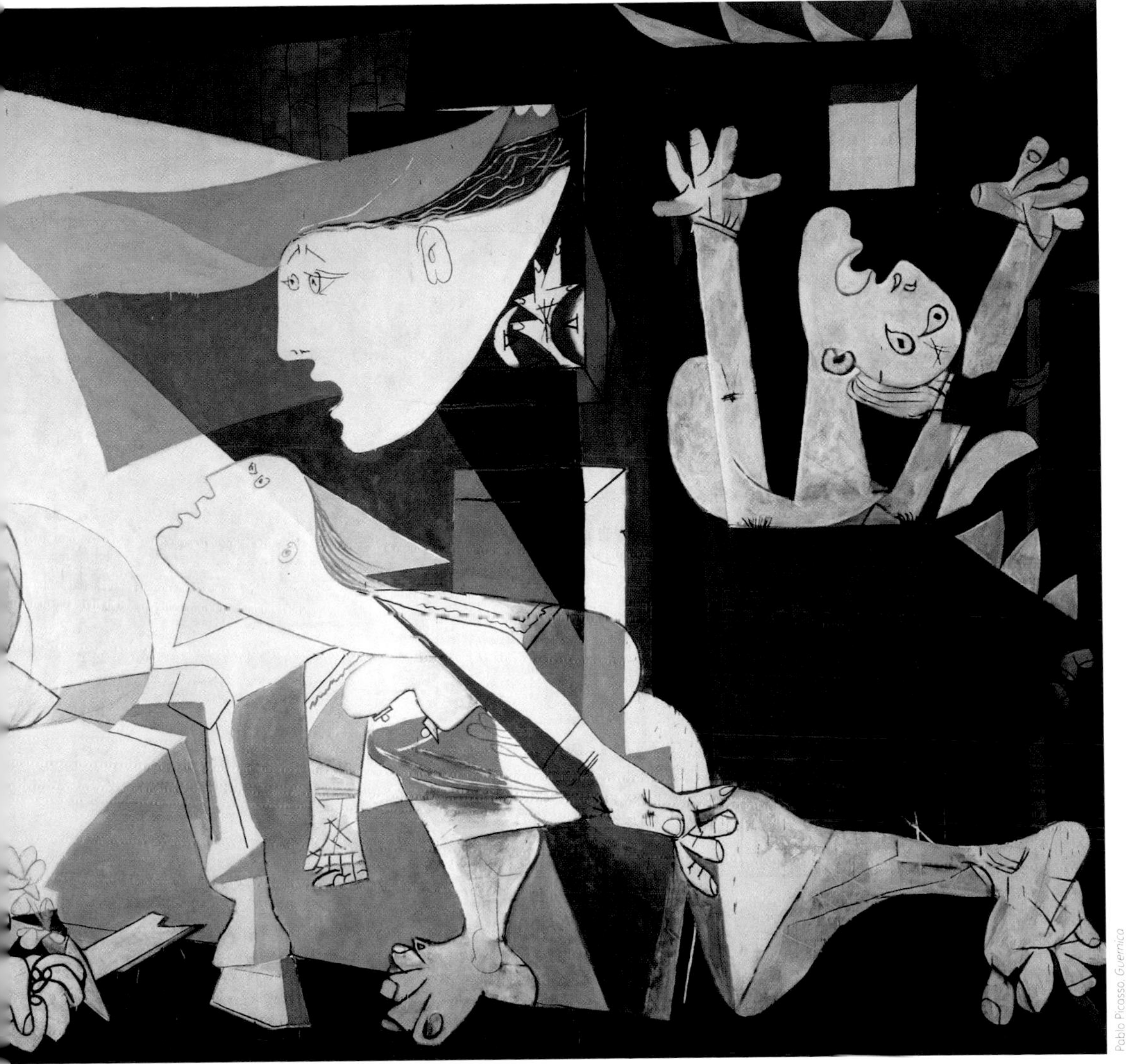

Pablo Picasso, *Guernica*

Picasso

Life

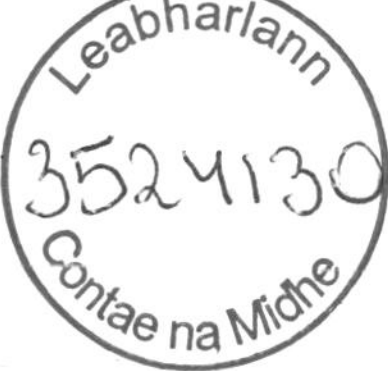

The Artist's Father, 1896

Picasso's talent as an artist developed at a remarkably early age and, like most children, he was encouraged to draw whilst still very young. However, by the age of eight he had produced his first oil painting and at just 11 years old he was attending a specialist art school in La Coruña in northern Spain. It was here that the young Picasso's precocious talent was nurtured, not least by his father José Ruiz Blasco, an academic painter who taught at the school. The young Picasso was schooled in the conventional academic manner, and although he was soon to reject what he perceived to be the strictures and limitations of such training, there can be little doubt that this education provided a strong foundation for much of his later work. Indeed, Picasso's skills as a draughtsman were rarely surpassed. In this early work, Picasso has portrayed his father as a dignified and noble individual seen in three-quarter profile. In keeping with his academic training, the work is executed in muted earth tones, with great attention paid to the details of the sitter's facial features.

CREATED

Barcelona

MEDIUM

Oil on canvas

SERIES/PERIOD/MOVEMENT

Early period

SIMILAR WORKS

Maria Picasso Lopez, the Artist's Mother by Picasso, 1896

Pablo Picasso *Born* 1881 Málaga, Spain

Died 1973

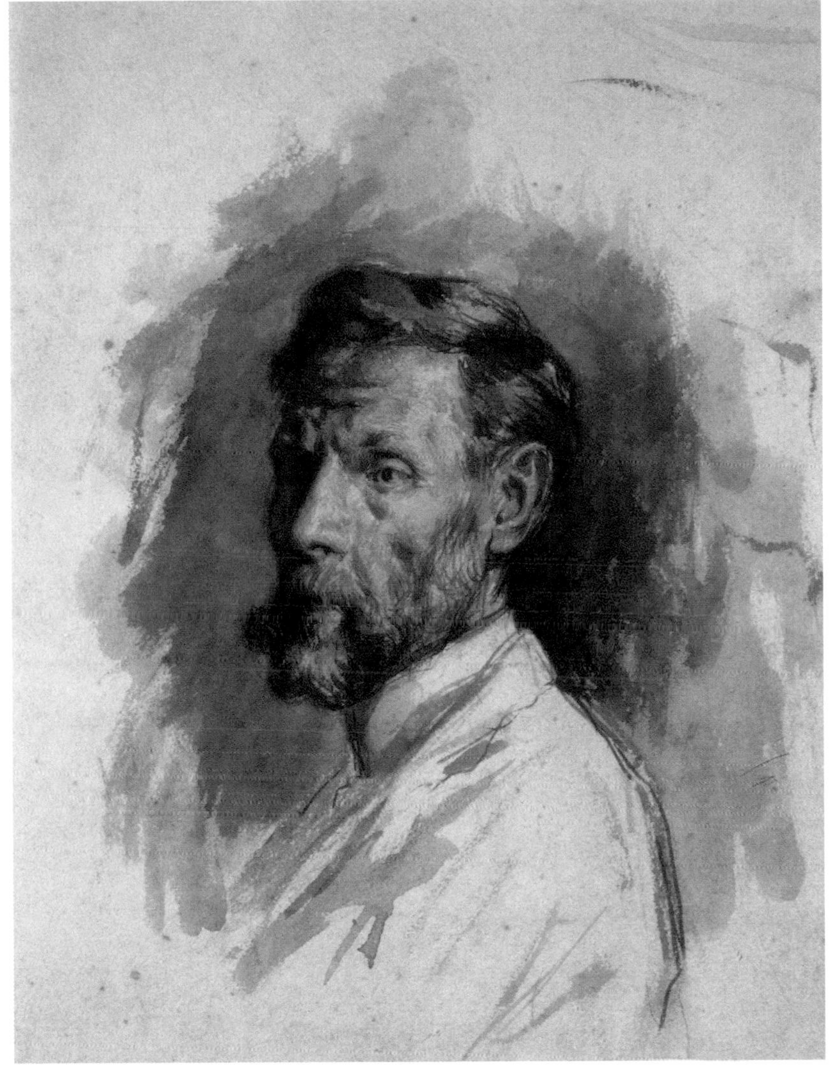

Maria Picasso Lopez, the Artist's Mother, 1896

There can be no doubt that Picasso's father played a vital role in encouraging the artistic training of the youngster. However, Picasso's mother was also a very important part of his early life, and it was from her that he inherited both his surname and his physical appearance. Picasso's parents hailed from Málaga, the small southern Spanish town into which he was born in 1881 and where he was to spend the first 10 years of his life. It seems clear that Picasso's family was always supportive of his artistic ambitions and, indeed, preserved many of his youthful works, which now form a key part of the collection of the Museo Picasso in Barcelona. Moreover, that close family bond is also reflected in the fact that Picasso regularly used members of his immediate family as models during his formative teenage years. Here Picasso has produced a tender pastel portrait of his mother in soft, gentle colours. Picasso's portraits of both his parents are a remarkable achievement for a boy still just 15 years of age.

CREATED

Barcelona

MEDIUM

Pastel on paper

SERIES/PERIOD/MOVEMENT

Early period

SIMILAR WORKS

The Artist's Father by Picasso, 1896

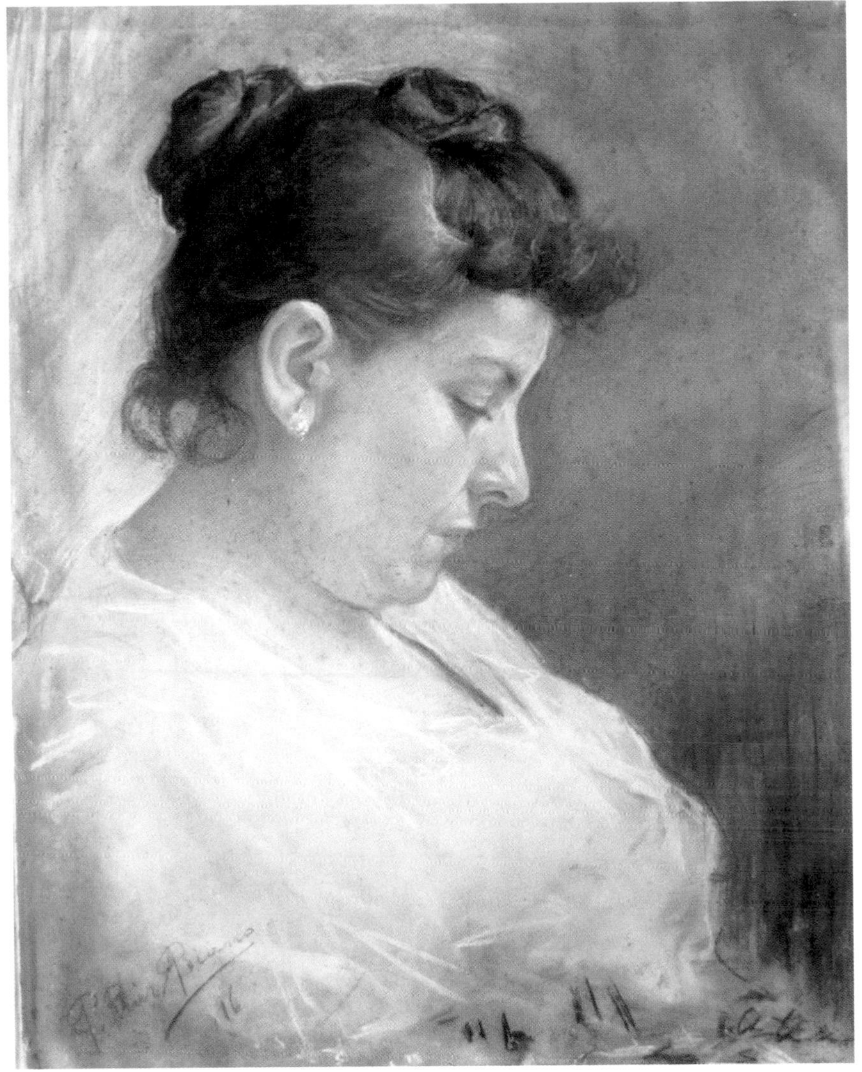

Self-Portrait, 1896

In 1895, Picasso's family moved from La Coruña to Barcelona. Here the young Picasso soon entered the advanced class of La Lonja School of Art, despite being much younger than his contemporaries. In addition to using his parents as models, Picasso also began to produce self-portraits during his youth. One of the earliest of these dates from 1896 and shows the still-boyish artist in his mid teens. The portrait is again executed in the conventional academic manner, its sketch-like, unfinished quality betraying its status as a training exercise. Picasso here appears as a serious-minded and conscientious art student, his close-cropped hair, upright posture and neatly arranged artist's smock revealing a growing awareness of, and pride in, his own appearance. At the same time, Picasso shows his knowledge of artistic precedents, not least of all the self-portraits of the Dutch seventeenth-century painter Rembrandt (1606–69). Here the use of sharp, direct light adds drama to the composition and emphasizes an aspect of Picasso's appearance that will dominate many of his later self-portraits – namely his dark eyes and impenetrable stare.

CREATED

Barcelona

MEDIUM

Oil on canvas

SERIES/PERIOD/MOVEMENT

Early period

SIMILAR WORKS

Self-Portrait by Henri de Toulouse-Lautrec, 1882–83

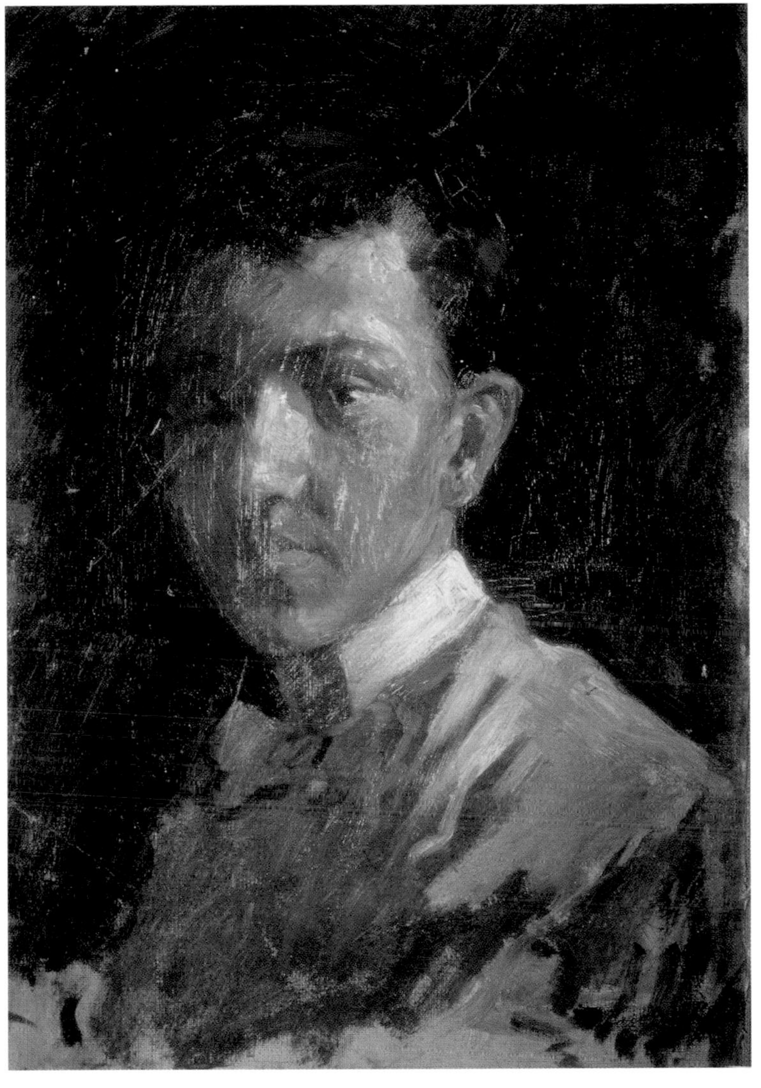

First Communion, 1896

While attending La Lonja School of Art Picasso produced his first large-scale oil painting, entitled *First Communion*. The work was exhibited at a major exhibition in Barcelona and attracted the attention of the local press. It conforms to many of the expectations of academic painting at the end of the nineteenth century, emphasizing a dramatic moment in the youth of a Catholic girl as she kneels before the altar, about to take her first communion and thus make the symbolic transition from childhood to adulthood. Picasso has highlighted this sense of passage by linking the bright white of the young girl's communion dress to the white of the altar cloth and the candlelight that illuminates the whole scene. It is perhaps no coincidence here that Picasso focused upon a moment of transition. The fact that Picasso's own father modelled for the male figure in this work adds another important dimension to the work, which equally marks Picasso's own symbolic transition from artistic childhood to adulthood, as his work entered the public domain for the first time.

CREATED

Barcelona

MEDIUM

Oil on canvas

SERIES/PERIOD/MOVEMENT

Early period

SIMILAR WORKS

Science and Charity by Picasso, 1897

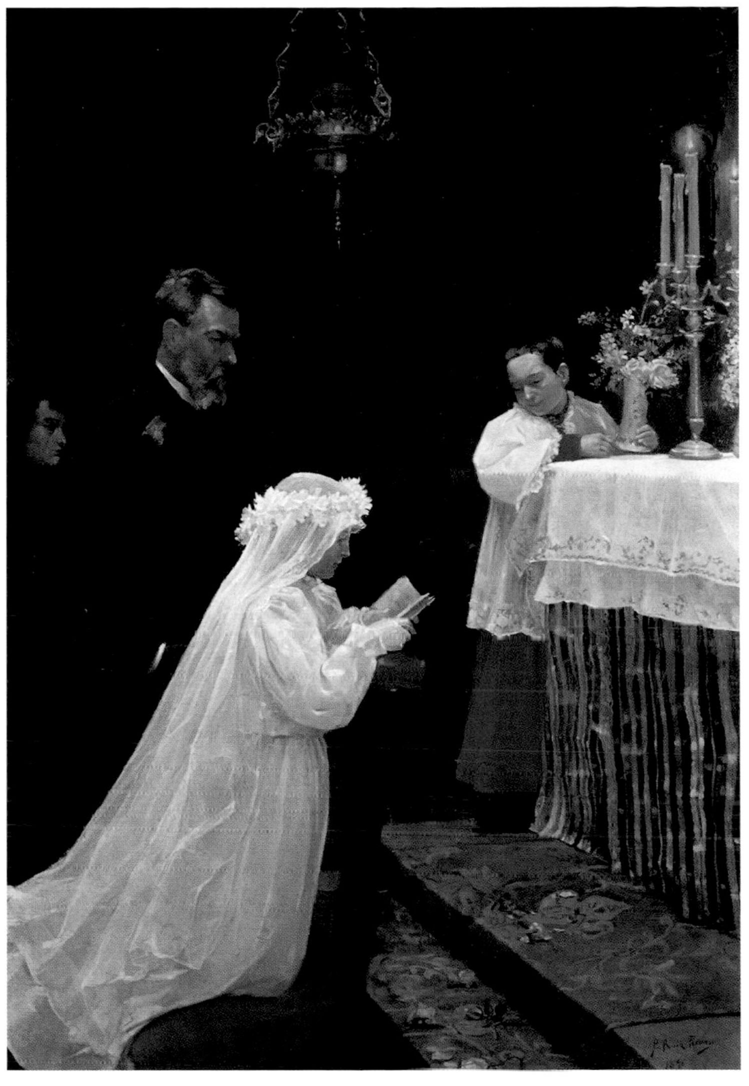

Science and Charity, 1897

Picasso's second major oil painting, *Science and Charity*, proved to be even more of a success than *First Communion*, gaining an honourable mention in a national exhibition in Madrid, and winning a gold medal in an art competition in his home town of Málaga. Notably, Picasso's father was to make another appearance, this time modelling for the doctor in a scene exploring illness and impending death. The continuing presence of Picasso's father in the artist's early works has often been linked to an incident Picasso recorded later in life. When he was just 14 years of age, Picasso's father asked for his assistance in producing a painting of a pigeon. When the father recognized the superiority of his son's work he reportedly handed over his palette and brushes, stating that he would never paint again. This dramatic rendering of Picasso's artistic relationship with his father is almost certainly apocryphal, exaggerated for dramatic effect. Nonetheless, it reveals the vital presence of Picasso's father during this formative period of his career.

CREATED

Barcelona

MEDIUM

Oil on canvas

SERIES/PERIOD/MOVEMENT

Early period

SIMILAR WORKS

The Doctor by Luke Fildes, 1891

First Communion by Picasso, 1896

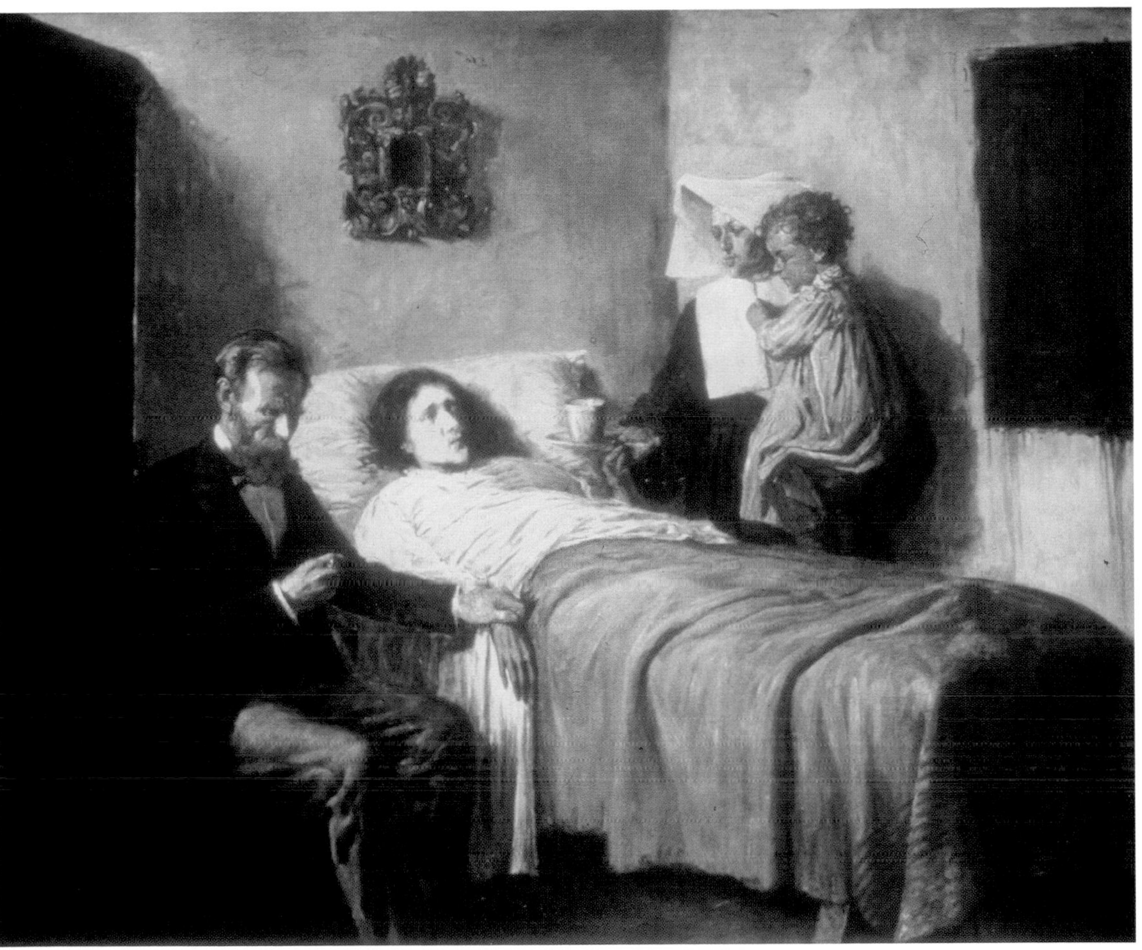

Woman in Blue, 1901

The success of *Science and Charity* boosted Picasso's reputation, and in 1897 he moved to Madrid to study at the prestigious Royal Academy of San Fernando. It was here that he first began to rebel against his middle-class background and his artistic training. Picasso was far from impressed with the education provided him in Madrid, although he did regularly visit the Prado to produce copies after the Old Masters. Within a year, though, he had abandoned his studies altogether. Following a bout of scarlet fever in 1898, Picasso spent much of his time amongst the Bohemian community of Barcelona. In 1900, however, he made his first expedition to Paris, a trip that was to transform his life and career. In Paris, Picasso discovered the work of Henri de Toulouse-Lautrec (1864–1901) and produced a number of works in Lautrec's sometimes harsh, caricatural manner. *Woman in Blue* was painted in Madrid shortly after Picasso's return to Spain in 1901. However, it encapsulates this transition in Picasso's work, drawing upon the artificiality of modern urban fashions, by highlighting the excess of make-up and the exaggerated scale of the woman's hat and dress.

CREATED

Madrid

MEDIUM

Oil on canvas

SERIES/PERIOD/MOVEMENT

Early period

SIMILAR WORKS

Woman with a Black Boa by Henri de Toulouse-Lautrec, 1892

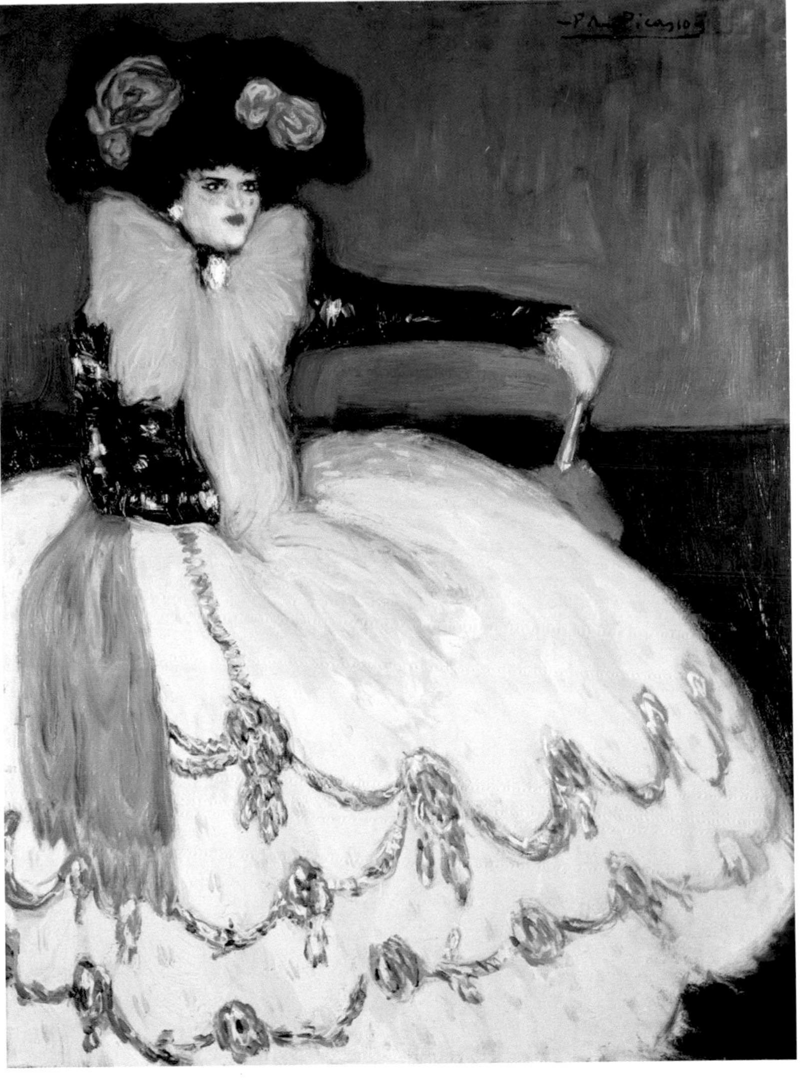
-P R Picasso 01

Child with a Dove, 1901

In May 1901 Picasso returned to Paris. Here he had forged a relationship with the young art dealer Pere Mañach, a fellow Catalan, and was keen to further his career in the art capital of the world. Mañach had offered the young Picasso a secure monthly income in return for his paintings. More importantly, he was instrumental in drawing the attention of many of the important collectors of avant-garde art to Picasso's work. It was during this period that Picasso's subject-matter and style began increasingly to forge their own identity. *Child with a Dove* can be regarded as a significant development within Picasso's art. He has abandoned both detail and modelling in favour of simple forms outlined boldly in black. He has also rejected the more muted tones of his earlier academic works in favour of a dominant bluish-green tonality, occasionally highlighted with red. Perhaps most importantly, however, the harsh, caricatural qualities seen in many of Picasso's recent works, such as *Woman in Blue*, have given way to a more intimate, sentimental, even melancholy form of representation.

CREATED

Paris

MEDIUM

Oil on canvas

SERIES/PERIOD/MOVEMENT

Early period

SIMILAR WORKS

Girl with a Watering Can by Pierre Auguste Renoir, 1876

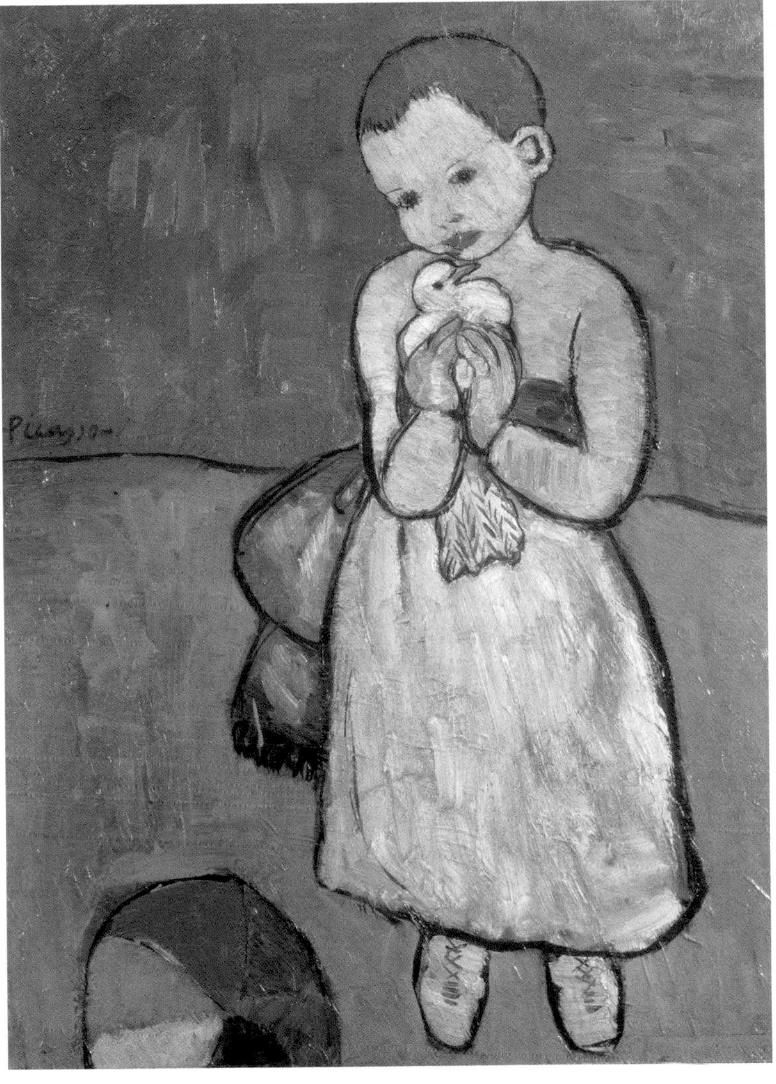

Self-Portrait in a Top Hat, 1901

The summer of 1901 saw Picasso's first major triumph in Paris, when his work was displayed at a one-man show in the gallery of the dealer Ambroise Vollard. The exhibition was widely discussed in the press and proved to be both a critical and financial success, a major achievement for an artist still just 19 years of age. Perhaps as a consequence of this growing reputation, Picasso began to produce many more self-portraits, frequently emphasizing the very different sides of his own character. In this oil sketch, *Self-Portrait in a Top Hat*, Picasso has represented himself as a man-about-town, enjoying the entertainments of turn-of-the century Paris. He is dressed in elegant eveningwear, and gazes self-consciously out towards the viewer. The semi-clad women who form a backdrop, presumably prostitutes from one of Paris's more salubrious night-spots, appear as little more than trophies, reflecting the fashionable and material success of the young artist. However, this lifestyle was to be short-lived. As Picasso stated shortly after the show closed, 'I really had a lot of money but it didn't last long'.

CREATED

Paris

MEDIUM

Oil on canvas

SERIES/PERIOD/MOVEMENT

Early period

SIMILAR WORKS

M. Delaporte at the Jardin de Paris by Henri de Toulouse-Lautrec, 1893

Portrait of Gustave Coquiot by Picasso, 1901

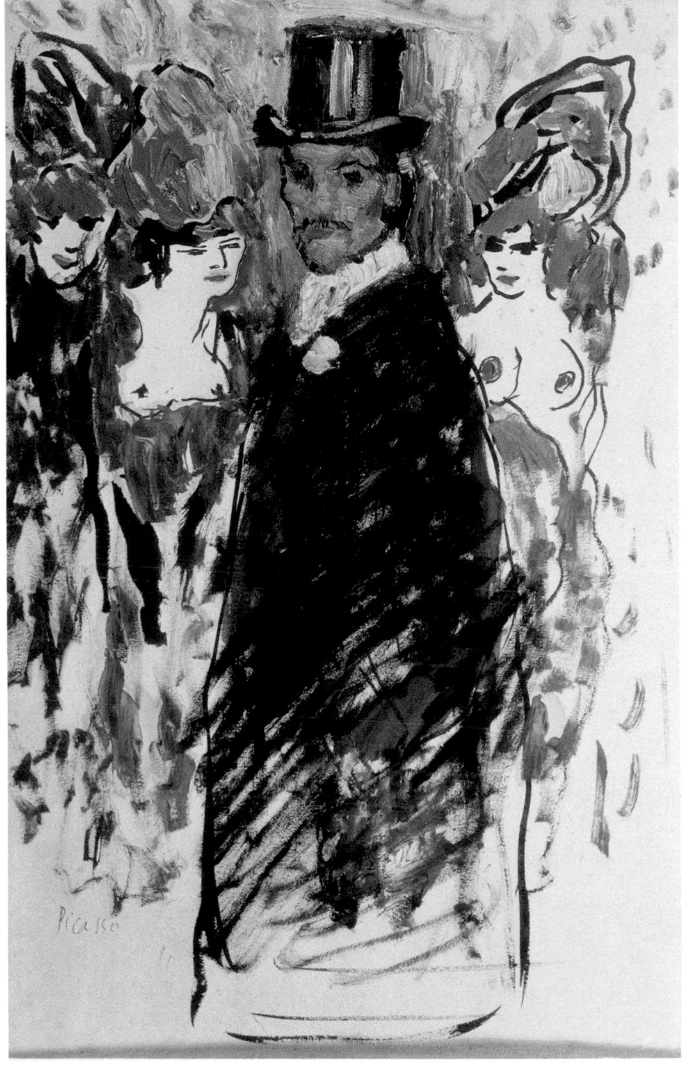
Picasso

Self-Portrait, 1901

Picasso's other self-portraits of 1901 could scarcely be more of a contrast to *Self-Portrait in a Top Hat*. One of the most emotionally intense of these works is the self-portrait produced in an expressionist manner, reminiscent of the Norwegian painter Edvard Munch (1863–1944). The surface of this work is sketchy with rapidly applied brushstrokes. Other areas, particularly in the lower right, have hardly been painted at all. This might suggest that the work is incomplete. However, Picasso has added his signature, confirming that he regarded the work as finished. Here, all the emphasis is on Picasso's face as it emerges from a gloom-laden background. The light falls directly upon his features, flattening all the contours and emphasizing his large, staring eyes, which confront the spectator directly. This gaze seems manic, almost possessed, as if the artist is in the thrall of some spiritual power or hallucinatory state. Here Picasso has underplayed the technical skills of the artist, suggesting that his talent lies more in the power of his gaze, in his status as a visionary.

CREATED

Paris

MEDIUM

Oil on cardboard

SERIES/PERIOD/MOVEMENT

Early period

SIMILAR WORKS

Self-Portrait by Edvard Munch, 1895

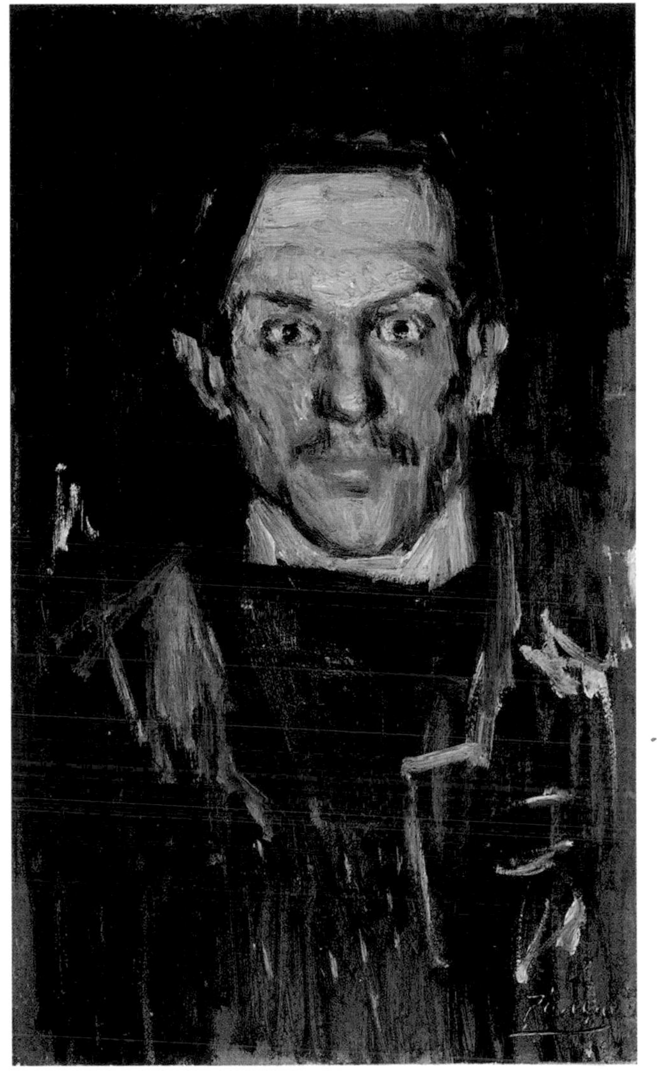

Self-Portrait, 1901

The remarkable series of self-portraits produced by Picasso in 1901 culminated in this striking work. Here Picasso has abandoned all reference to material wealth or heightened emotional intensity, to focus instead upon desolation, isolation and alienation. The work owes a considerable debt to the late self-portraits of Vincent van Gogh (1853–90), particularly his *Self-Portrait with Bandaged Ear*. Picasso has represented himself as cold, emaciated and alone, the huge overcoat, buttoned up around the neck, the prominent cheekbones and the bluish, sickly pallor all contributing to a sense of the artist as an outcast, rejected by society. Moreover, his wearied expression belies the still-teenage youth of the artist. Yet this is clearly not simply a document recording his material status. Rather, it strives to emphasize his own self-perception as alienated – an outsider in a foreign land. The overall blue tonality here deployed by Picasso to highlight this sense of despair and misery was, in the course of the next few years, to become a dominant feature of what has subsequently been termed Picasso's 'blue period'.

CREATED

Paris

MEDIUM

Oil on canvas

SERIES/PERIOD/MOVEMENT

Blue period

SIMILAR WORKS

Self-Portrait with Bandaged Ear by Vincent van Gogh, 1889

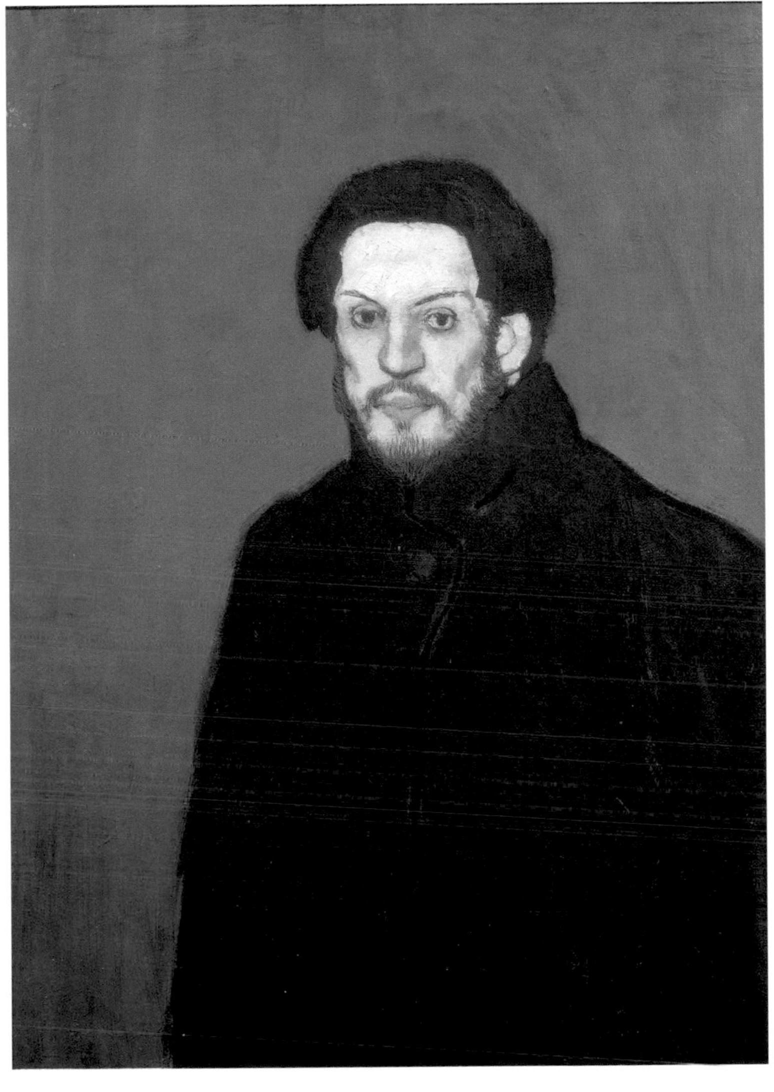

Portrait of Jaime Sabartés Y Gual, 1901

Picasso was frequently surrounded by a coterie of friends whilst in Paris, despite his self-representation as a lonely, isolated individual. Among these were many from his native Spain, including his lifelong compatriot Jaime Sabartés. Picasso and Sabartés had been students together in Barcelona in the 1890s, and in 1901 Picasso invited his friend to join him in Paris. Sabartés was initially reluctant to leave Spain, but he travelled to Paris in October of that year. Later in life Sabartés recorded an important event during that period. One evening he visited the Café La Lorraine, intending to meet up with Picasso and other friends. Sabartés arrived early and sat at a table with a glass of beer, alone, awaiting his friends' arrival. Renowned as being rather short-sighted, Sabartés did not initially notice Picasso on his arrival. Consequently, Picasso noted the melancholy expression of his friend sitting alone at the café table. Within the next couple of days Picasso produced this image of Sabartés, again using a dominant blue tonality to emphasize a mood of loneliness and isolation.

CREATED

Paris

MEDIUM

Oil on canvas

SERIES/PERIOD/MOVEMENT

Blue period

SIMILAR WORKS

In a Café (The Absinthe Drinker) by Edgar Degas, 1875–76

At the Café by Paul Gauguin, 1888

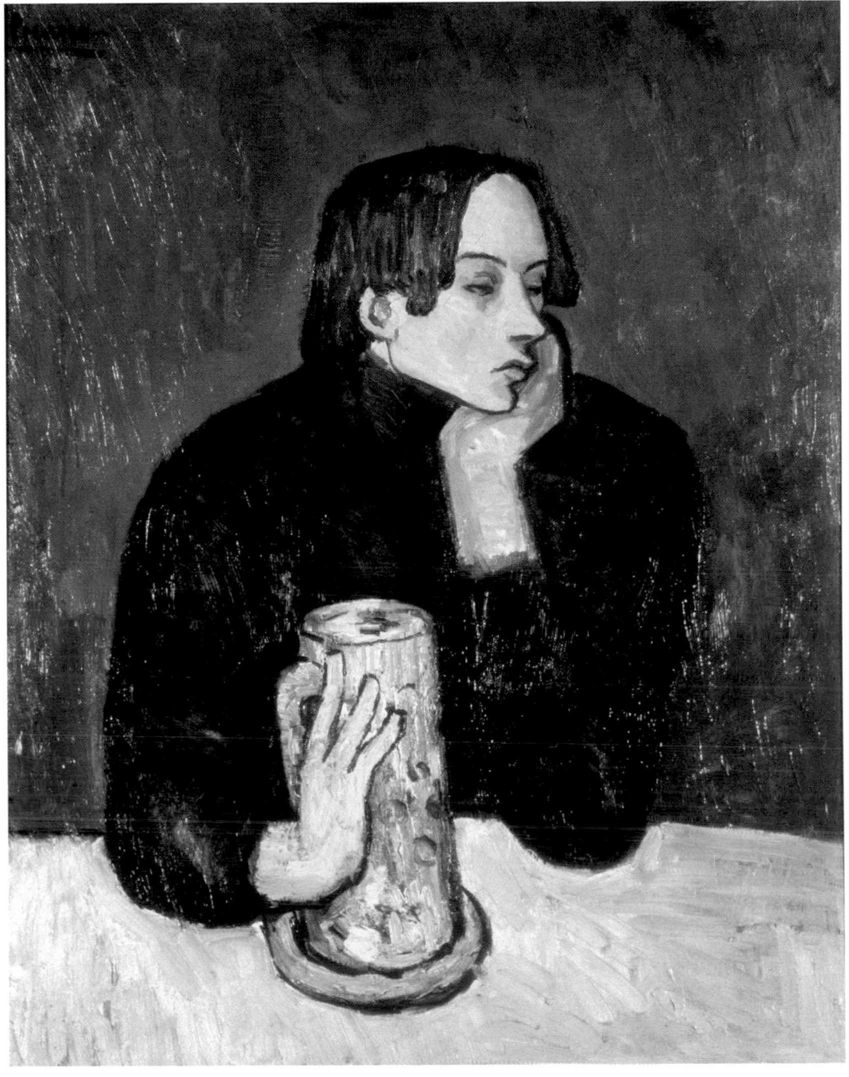

Portrait of Mateu Fernandez de Soto, 1901

Mateu Fernandez de Soto was a Catalan artist and a key member of Picasso's close circle of friends. De Soto was a sculptor and in 1899 had shared a studio with Picasso in Barcelona. A quiet, reserved and serious-minded individual, he particularly reminded Picasso of the images of scholarly monks painted by the Spanish artist El Greco (1541–1614). In October 1901, de Soto moved to Paris and took a room with Sabartés in the Hotel des Ecoles in the fashionable Latin Quarter. By early winter, however, his financial resources had dried up and he moved into Picasso's studio. It was during his stay that Picasso produced this compelling portrait of his friend. Physically, de Soto was described as small, pale and shabby. Picasso, however, has given his subject gravitas by focusing on his head and shoulders, and paying particular attention to the thoughtful and purposeful gaze of the sitter. This portrait clearly meant a great deal to Picasso, and is one of the few paintings of this period that Picasso kept all his life.

CREATED

Paris

MEDIUM

Oil on canvas

SERIES/PERIOD/MOVEMENT

Blue period

SIMILAR WORKS

Portrait of Fray Hortensio Felix Paravicino by El Greco, 1609

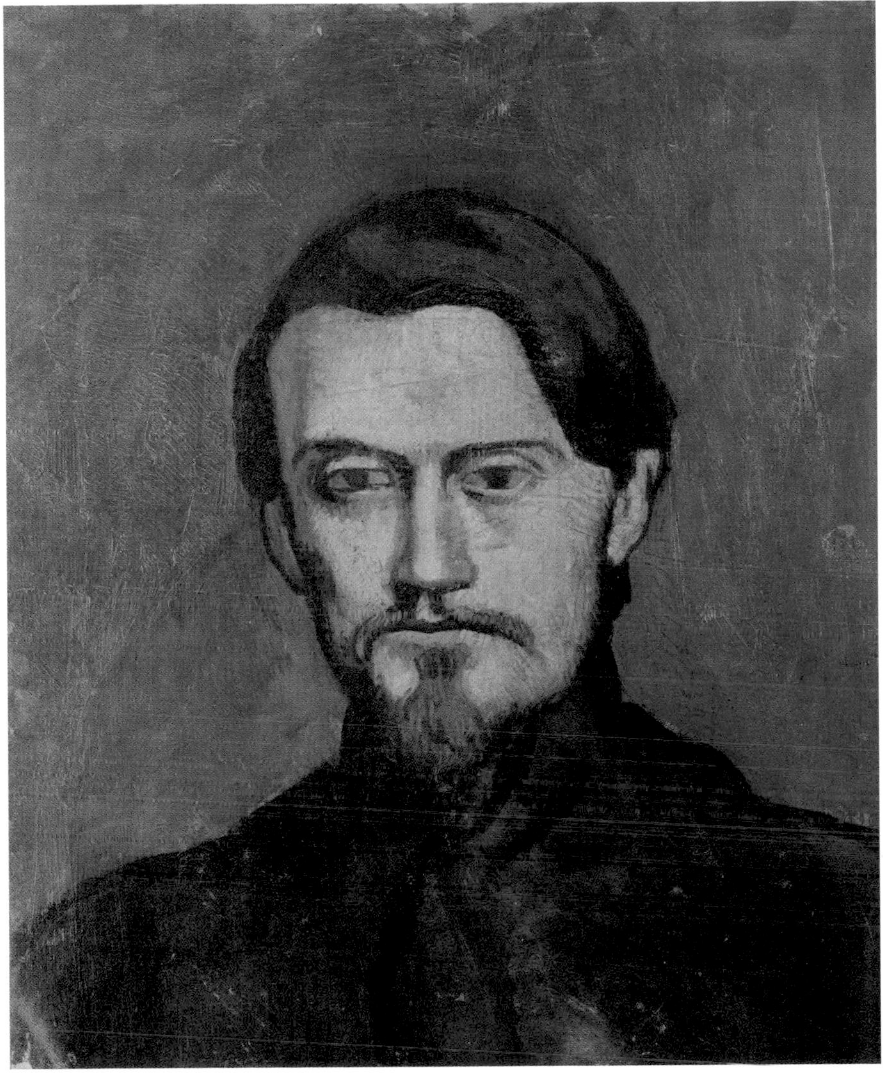

The Absinthe Drinker (Portrait of Angel Fernandez de Soto), 1903

In the winter of 1901 Picasso decided to leave Paris and return to Barcelona, possibly as a consequence of financial difficulties. His contract with the art dealer Mañach was broken at this time. Back in Barcelona Picasso soon took up with his old friends, including Angel Fernandez de Soto, brother of the sculptor Mateu, whom Picasso had painted whilst in Paris. By all accounts, Angel was a very different character from his brother. In contrast to Mateu's serious-mindedness, Angel was frivolous and frequently dressed like a dandy, despite his meagre income. Angel certainly had pretensions to being a painter, and shared his Barcelona studio with Picasso on two occasions. However, it seems that he scarcely took painting seriously and was more interested in the society of fellow artists. Indeed, Picasso described his friend as 'an amusing wastrel'. In this portrait, Picasso has captured both the youthful confidence and indolence of his friend, seated at a café table and glancing somewhat condescendingly towards the viewer. With his heavy-lidded eyes and slightly sneering mouth, de Soto is presented as the epitome of the young bohemian.

CREATED

Barcelona

MEDIUM

Oil on canvas

SERIES/PERIOD/MOVEMENT

Blue period

SIMILAR WORKS

M. Boileau at the Café by Henri de Toulouse-Lautrec, 1893

Portrait of Mateu Fernandez de Soto by Picasso, 1901

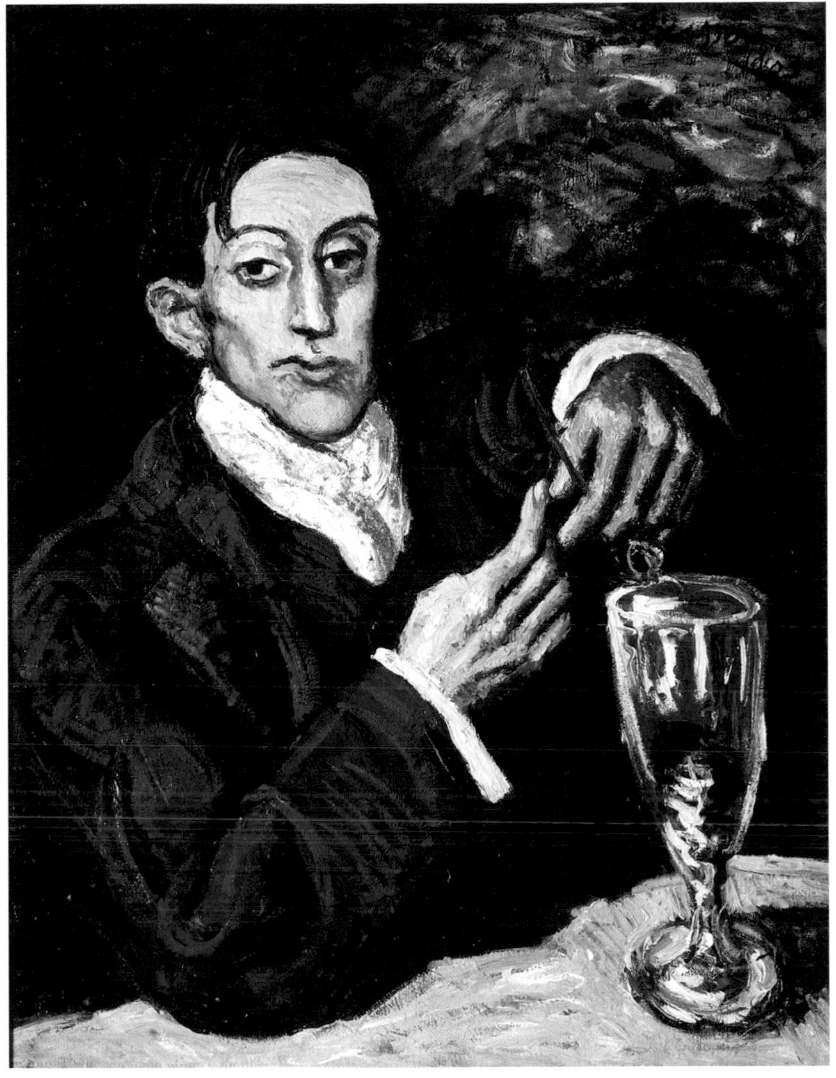

Life, 1903

In this classic work of his 'blue period' Picasso revisited a particularly painful moment in his life – the death of his close friend from Barcelona, Carlos Casagemas. Two years earlier Casagemas had committed suicide in Paris, having been rejected by a model with whom he had fallen in love. Picasso was deeply affected by this tragedy. However, *Life* is not a literal depiction of the incident. Rather, Picasso has meditated upon a wider sense of unrequited love, loss and death. Here, two lovers stand in an ambiguous space. The man, representing Casagemas, glances towards a mother cradling a small child. Two pictures in the background, representing another pair of lovers and a lonely man in a crouched position, suggest that the scene is set in an artist's studio. Yet it remains far from clear why these figures have gathered together, and they seem lost in their own thoughts. Here Picasso has used a stark setting and the isolation and disjointedness of the figures to emphasize a sense of tragedy and hopelessness.

CREATED

Barcelona

MEDIUM

Oil on canvas

SERIES/PERIOD/MOVEMENT

Blue period

SIMILAR WORKS

Where do we come from? Who are we? Where are we going? by Paul Gauguin, 1897

The Burial of Casagemas by Picasso, 1901

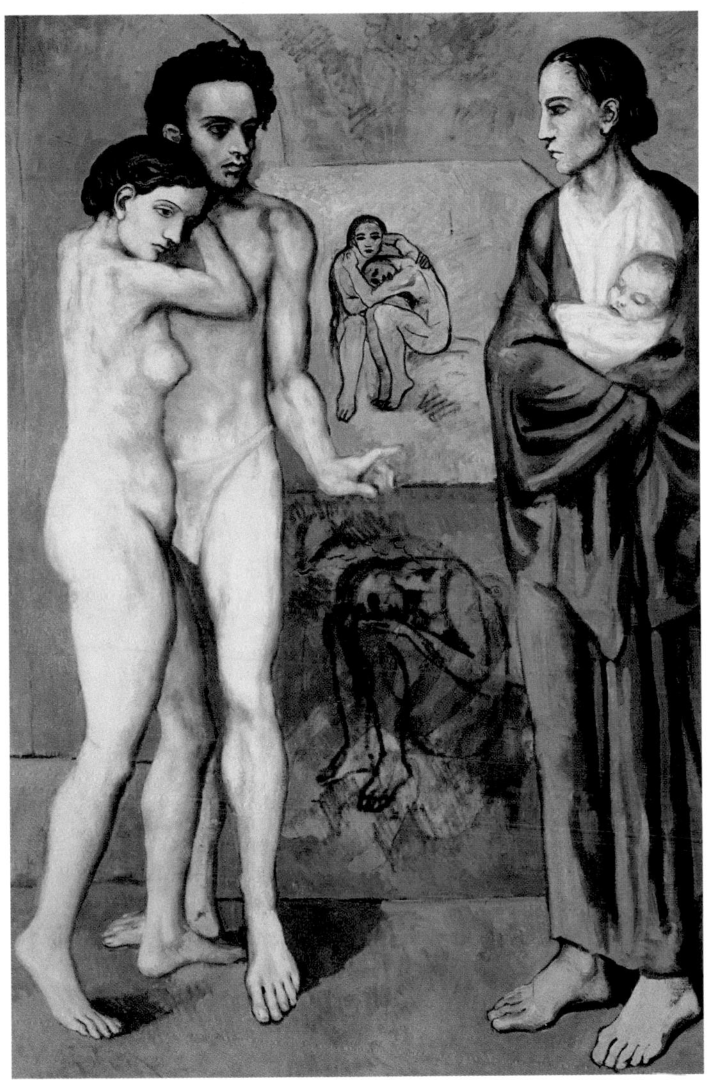

La Celestine (Carlota Valdivia), 1904

Courtesy of Musee Picasso, Paris, France, Giraudon/www.bridgeman.co.uk/© Succession Picasso/DACS 2005

Throughout 1902 and 1903 Picasso spent most of his time in Barcelona, making one trip to Paris in the winter of 1902. In Barcelona he continued to develop his 'blue-period' works, including one of the more highly finished paintings, entitled *La Celestine*. The title is taken from a fifteenth-century Spanish novel, recounting a story of love, betrayal and ultimate tragedy. What is perhaps most striking here, however, is Picasso's tender and sympathetic rendering of the sitter, Carlota Valdivia, a brothel-keeper who worked on the same street on which Picasso's studio was situated. Picasso does not shy away from the signs of age, the facial hair growing on the woman's chin, or the sitter's affliction, most notably the loss of an eye. Rather, his overt emphasis on these aspects of Valdivia's appearance adds a sense of dignity and honesty to this powerful portrayal of a real-life character. At the same time, Picasso uses the literary title and the costume of a Spanish mantilla to allude to traditional Spanish culture and to refer back to the work of his Spanish predecessors, Francisco de Goya (1746–1828) and Diego Velazquez (1599–1660).

CREATED

Barcelona

MEDIUM

Oil on canvas

SERIES/PERIOD/MOVEMENT

Blue period

SIMILAR WORKS

The Dwarf Don Sebastián de Morra by Diego Velazquez, 1645

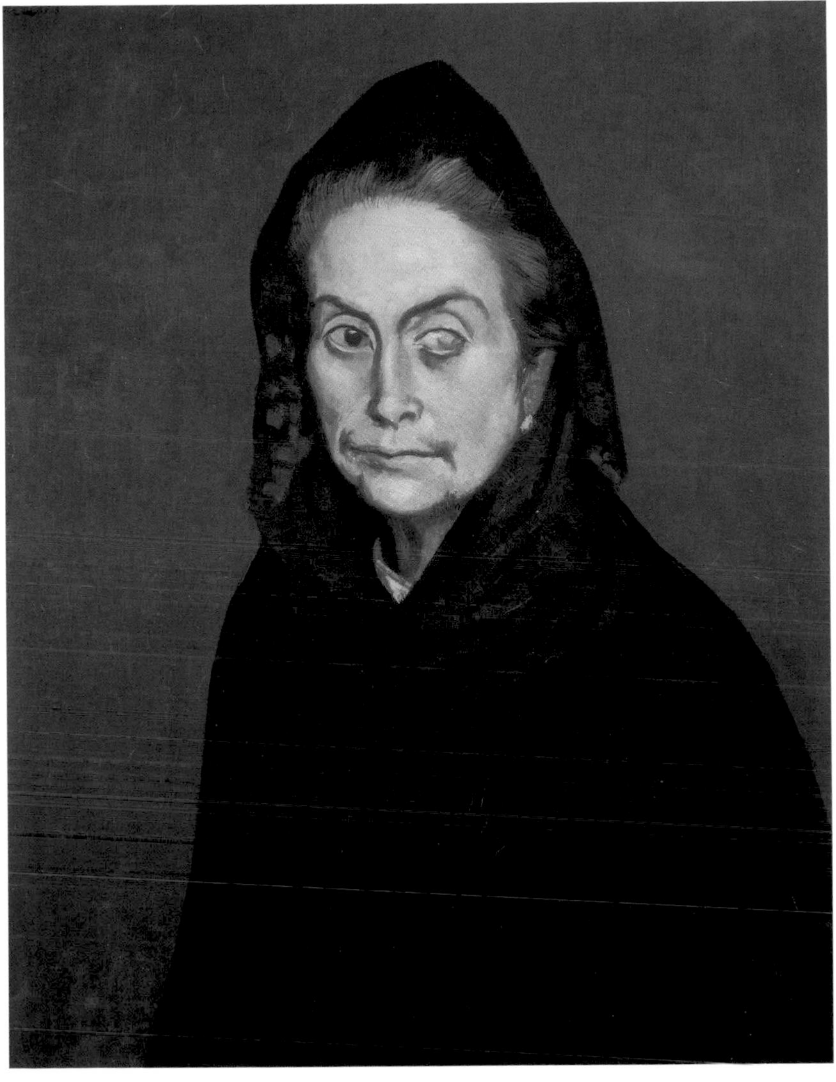

The Frugal Repast, 1904

In April 1904 Picasso moved to Paris for the fourth time in as many years. This time, however, he remained a resident of France for the rest of his life. Still short of money, Picasso rented an inexpensive, run-down studio in the Rue Ravignan in Montmartre. The building was popularly known as the 'bateau-lavoir', as it bore a remarkable similarity to the wooden laundry-boats operating on the river Seine. Here Picasso produced his first major etching, a work entitled *The Frugal Repast*. Despite its absence of colour, this piece is perhaps the culminating work of Picasso's 'blue period'. The image intensifies the sense of abject poverty in turn-of-the-century Paris. Here we are presented with a couple seated at a table. In front of them stands an empty plate, a small chunk of bread and a notably large bottle of wine. The emaciated bodies of the characters represented – and not least of all their elongated, skeletal hands – seem barely able to support their own weight. Poverty is thus exemplified while alcohol is presented as the sole solace in desperate lives.

CREATED

Paris

MEDIUM

Etching on paper

SERIES/PERIOD/MOVEMENT

Blue period

SIMILAR WORKS

In a Café (The Absinthe Drinker) by Edgar Degas, 1875–76

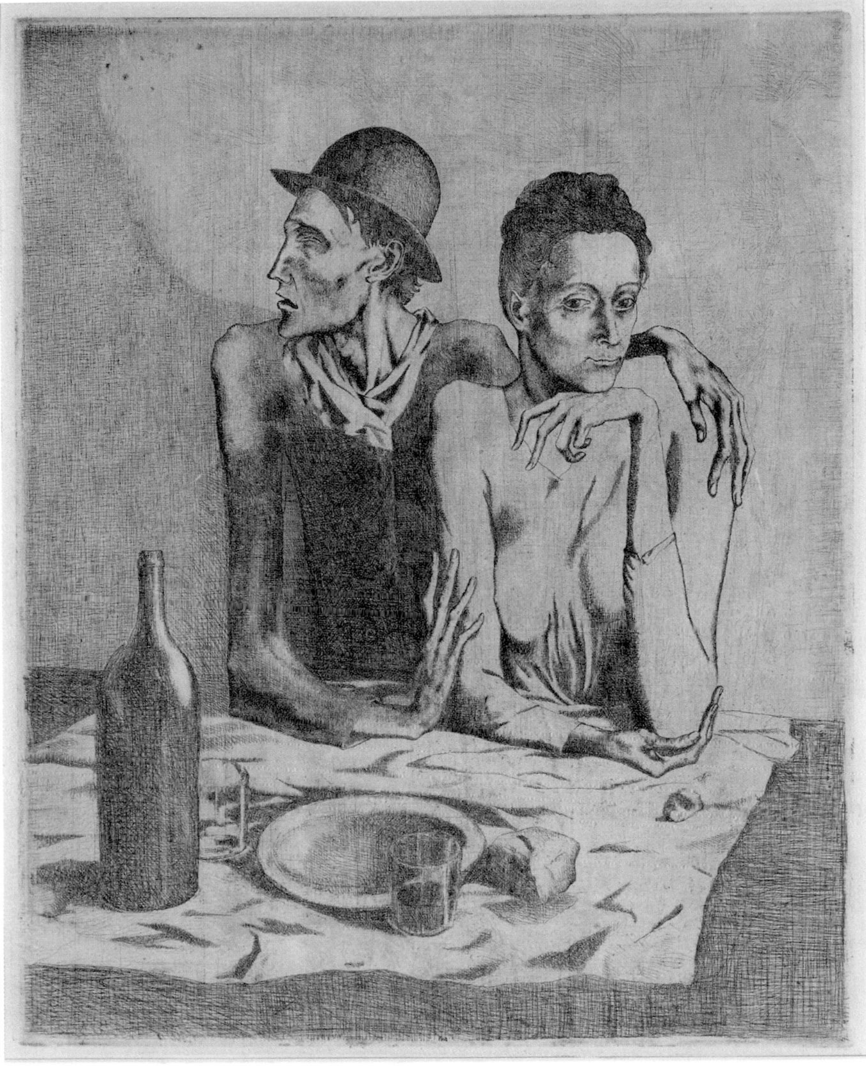

Portrait of Gertrude Stein, 1906

Finally settled in Paris, Picasso's mood started to change. In August 1904 he began a long affair with the model Fernande Olivier, whom he met at the 'bateau-lavoir'. During this period the mood of Picasso's works also began to change. The sombre blue of the earlier works gradually gave way to the brighter pink tonality that characterized his 'rose period'. In subject matter too, the desolate characters of the 'blue period' gave way to street performers and musicians, partly influenced by his regular visits to the Médrano Circus in Montmartre. In 1905 Picasso was introduced to the American art collector Gertrude Stein. Shortly afterwards he offered to paint a portrait of Stein and, over the next few months, she regularly visited Picasso's studio to pose. The resulting portrait marked a changing point in Picasso's art. The pink tonality of his 'rose period' is still much in evidence. However, Picasso now introduced a new monumentality into his work, derived partly from the work of the nineteenth-century French painter Jean Auguste Dominique Ingres (1780–1867), but also owing a great deal to Picasso's recent discovery of ancient Iberian sculpture.

CREATED

Paris

MEDIUM

Oil on canvas

SERIES/PERIOD/MOVEMENT

Proto-Cubist period

SIMILAR WORKS

Iberian sculpted busts from the Louvre

Self-Portrait by Picasso, 1906

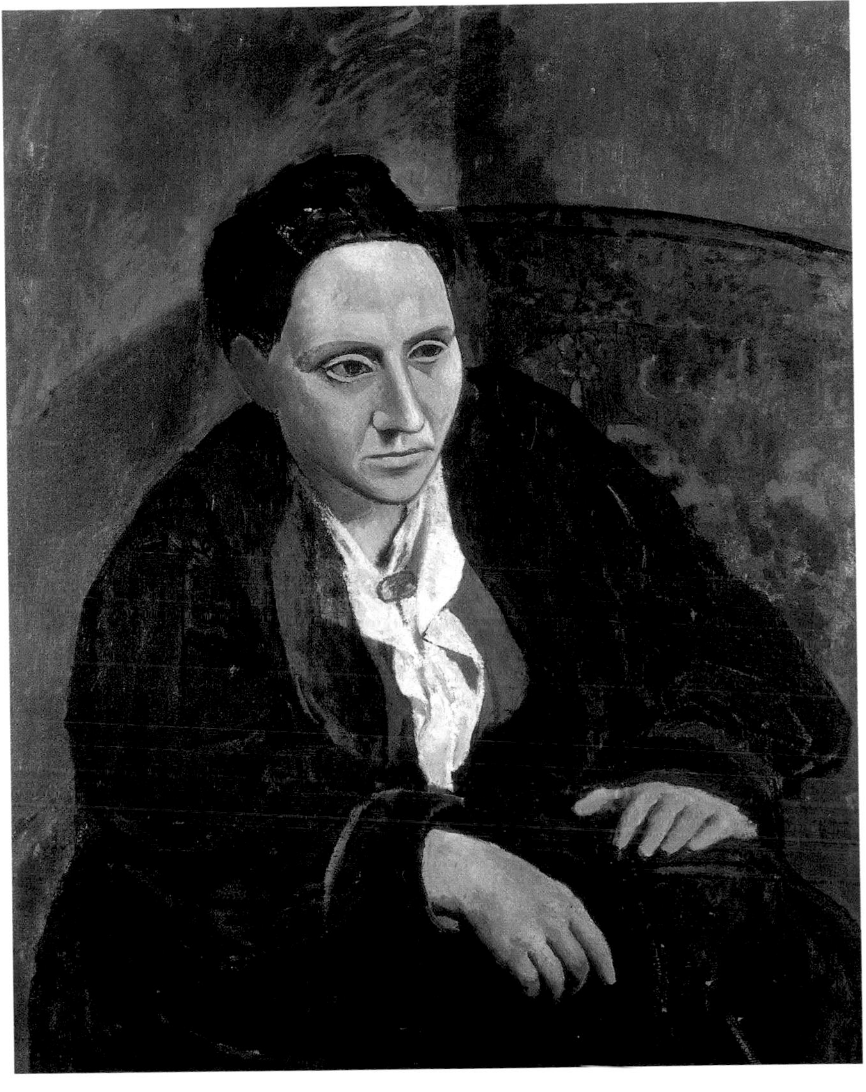

Self-Portrait, 1906

In the midst of working on his *Portrait of Gertrude Stein*, Picasso escaped Paris for a short trip back to his native Spain. It was also at this time that he became increasingly interested in a series of Iberian sculptures recently put on display in the Louvre. The sculptures are notable for their simple, monumental forms and their large, clearly defined features. It was this simplification that had inspired Picasso's portrait of Stein and, over the next few months, he was to experiment with this in a number of self-portraits. The summer of 1906 proved to be particularly hot and sultry. Confined to the stifling atmosphere of his studio, Picasso often worked stripped to the waist. In this *Self-Portrait*, Picasso has represented himself in such a condition. Perhaps most interestingly, he has reduced his facial features to simple, black outlines emphasizing large, lozenge-shaped eyes, a pronounced nose and prominent ear. These features coincide largely with the style of the Iberian heads so admired by Picasso.

CREATED

Paris

MEDIUM

Oil on canvas

SERIES/PERIOD/MOVEMENT

Proto-Cubist period

SIMILAR WORKS

Portrait of Gertrude Stein by Picasso, 1906

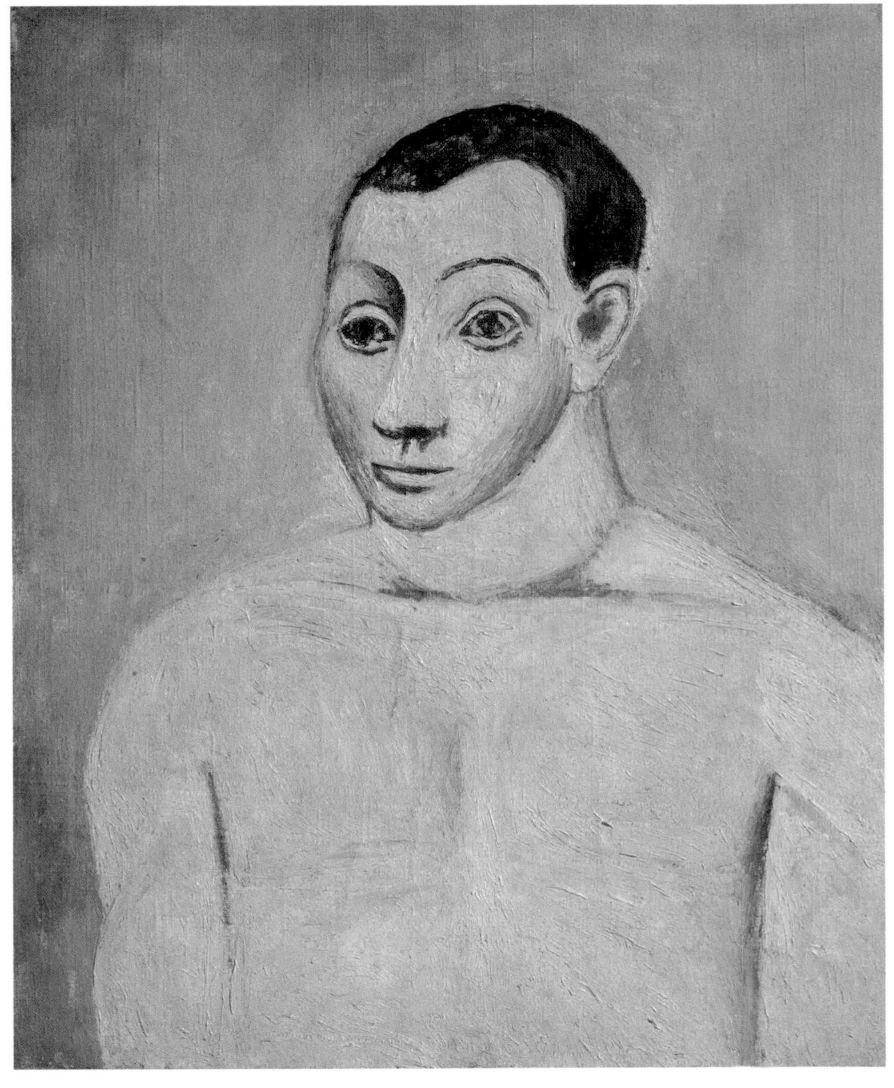

Self-Portrait, 1906

Courtesy of Philadelphia Museum of Art, Pennsylvania, PA, USA/www.bridgeman.co.uk/© Succession Picasso/DACS 2005

Now in his mid-twenties, and having re-established his reputation, Picasso's confidence was growing. Recently his work had been acquired not only by Gertrude Stein, but also by a number of foreign collectors, including the German Wilhelm Uhde and the Russian Sergei Shchukin. Picasso's star was clearly in the ascendancy once more. This confidence is aptly expressed in his *Self-Portrait* of 1906, the culmination of the many self-portraits he had been working on during the summer. Here Picasso has presented himself at work, casually dressed in an under-shirt and carrying a palette. His monumental form is stripped to the bare essentials, and his physique fills the frame as if bursting with youthful energy. It is notable that Picasso has not represented a brush in his right hand. This, instead, is formed into a fist. Attention is rather focused upon his deep and penetrating gaze, as if by the power of his look alone he can capture and control the world around him. This portrait represents a significant shift towards Picasso's mature work.

CREATED

Paris

MEDIUM

Oil on canvas

SERIES/PERIOD/MOVEMENT

Proto-Cubist period

SIMILAR WORKS

Portrait of Gertrude Stein by Picasso, 1906

Self-Portrait by Picasso, 1906

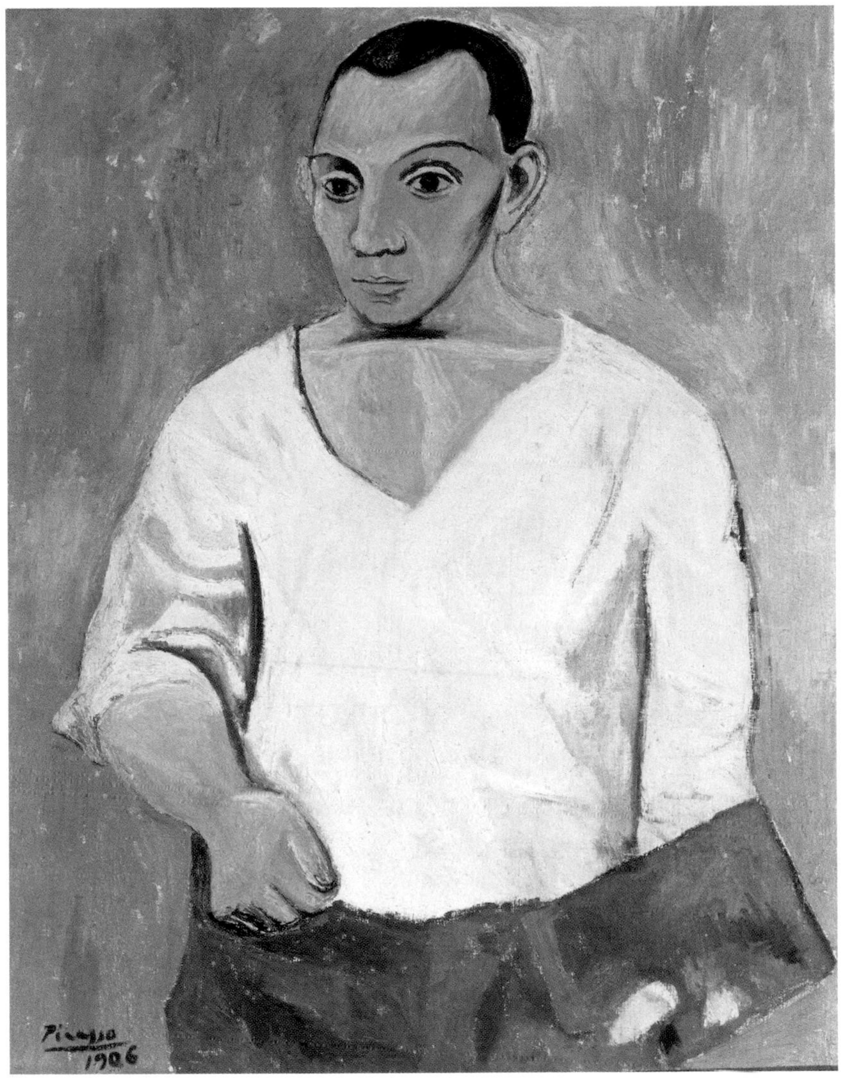
Picasso
1906

Self-Portrait, 1907

The year 1907 is rightly regarded as groundbreaking, not only for Picasso but also for the entire history of twentieth-century art. It was in this year that Picasso's art took a huge leap forward, not least of all with his large-scale painting *Les Demoiselles d'Avignon*. Whilst Picasso was working on the numerous sketches for this major work, he also produced a smaller self-portrait that reveals the direction in which his work was now heading. Here Picasso has represented himself in a herringbone coat and white collar, but all attention is focused upon his face and significantly enlarged eyes. The self-confidence of previous self-portraits has here metamorphosed into a manic stare. Some art historians have linked this intense image to early silent cinema and, in particular, its use of close-up and intense emotional expression to characterize the melodrama being enacted. Picasso was certainly a devotee of the cinema and regularly attended movies. However, this work also anticipates the disintegration of conventional representations of space that was to occupy Picasso over the next few years, culminating in the emergence of Cubism.

CREATED

Paris

MEDIUM

Oil on canvas

SERIES/PERIOD/MOVEMENT

Proto-Cubist period

SIMILAR WORKS

African Masks on display at the Trocadero in Paris

Portrait of André Derain by Maurice Vlaminck, 1905

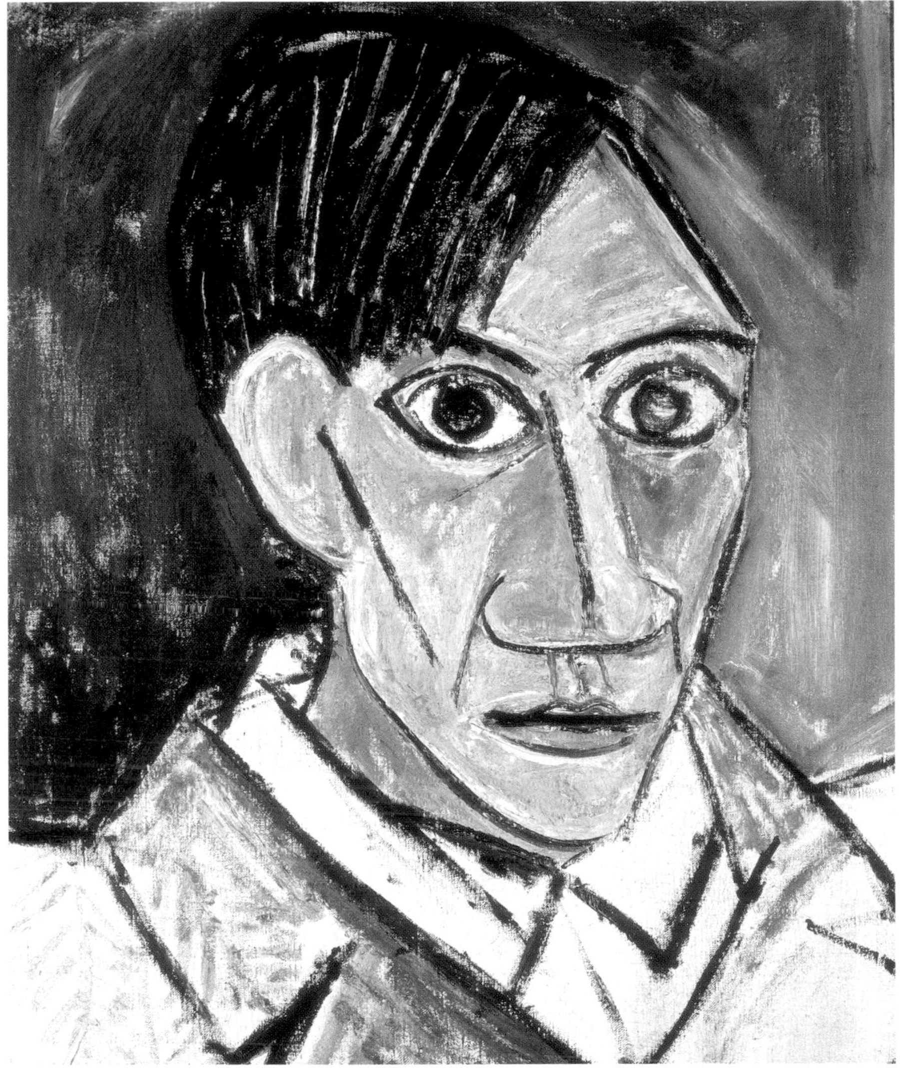

Friendship, 1908

One of the great controversies of Picasso's early years revolves around the question of when he first encountered masks from the African continent. Picasso himself later claimed that this happened after he had painted *Les Demoiselles d'Avignon* in 1907, but this is widely disputed. What is clear is that Picasso's awareness of these cultural artefacts, then described as 'primitive', had a significant impact upon his art. However, Picasso combined this interest with other influences, most notably the late paintings of bathers by Paul Cézanne (1839–1906), which were exhibited in Paris in 1907, a year after the artist's death. *Friendship* is one of the many works produced by Picasso at this time that focuses upon bather figures. The work seems to combine both the mask-like asymmetrical facial features, possibly derived from African masks, with the bodily distortions that characterize Cézanne's late bathers. The dark tonality of the flesh and the simplification of forms make these figures ambiguous in terms of both race and gender, while the outlines of the figures themselves can only just be distinguished from the background space they inhabit.

CREATED

Paris

MEDIUM

Oil on canvas

SERIES/PERIOD/MOVEMENT

Proto-Cubist period

SIMILAR WORKS

Three Female Bathers by Paul Cézanne, 1875–77

Large Nude by Georges Braque, 1908

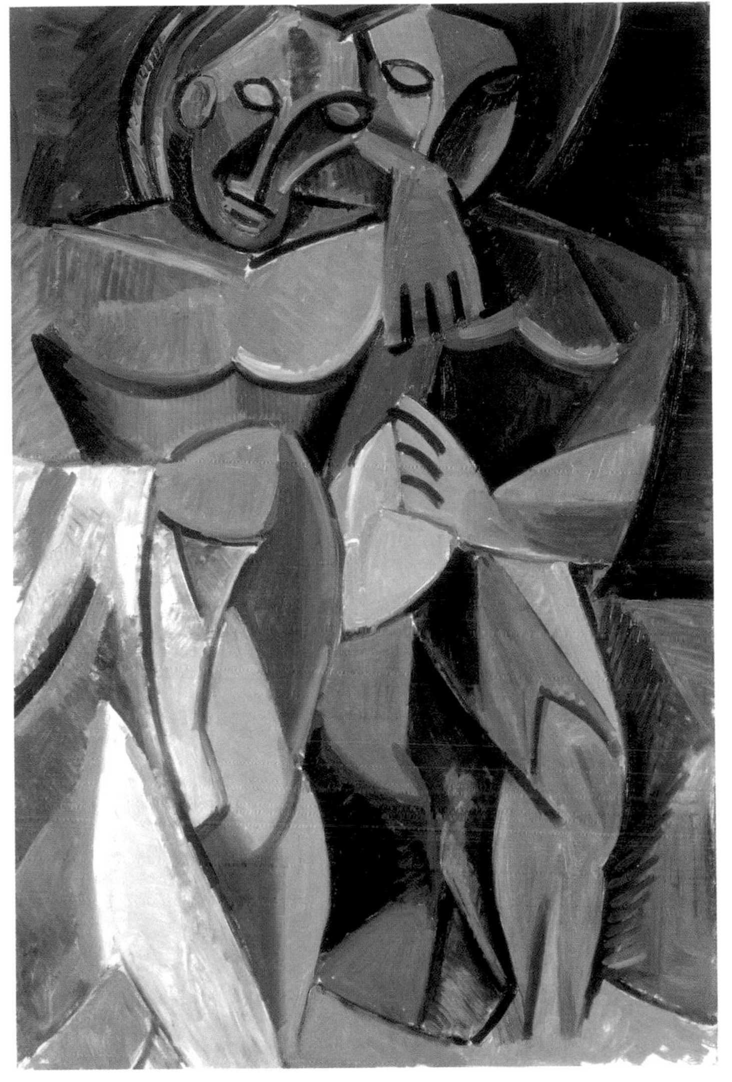

Houses on the Hill (Horta de Ebro), 1909

Picasso first met fellow painter Georges Braque (1882–1963) in 1907. Both were passionate admirers of Cézanne and, over the next few years, they experimented together to develop the art form that came to be called Cubism. Both Picasso and Braque gradually rejected the conventional single viewpoint that had dominated painting since the Renaissance, producing works that revealed objects as if seen from several viewpoints simultaneously. They also adopted a palette of muted greens, ochres and greys, derived in part from Cézanne, which served to emphasize the formal qualities of their work. In the summer of 1909, Picasso travelled to Horta de Ebro in his native Spain, and here produced a series of landscapes that adopted this newly emerging style. His *Houses on the Hill (Horta de Ebro)* provides a good example of this. Here Picasso has turned this view of a group of houses perched at the top of a hill into an agglomeration of geometrical forms, with all detailing such as windows, removed. The topography of the scene has also been freely rearranged to emphasize further that this landscape has been produced from many distinct viewpoints.

CREATED

Horta de Ebro

MEDIUM

Oil on canvas

SERIES/PERIOD/MOVEMENT

Early Cubist period

SIMILAR WORKS

Houses at L'Estaque by Paul Cézanne, 1879–82

Houses at L'Estaque by Georges Braque, 1908

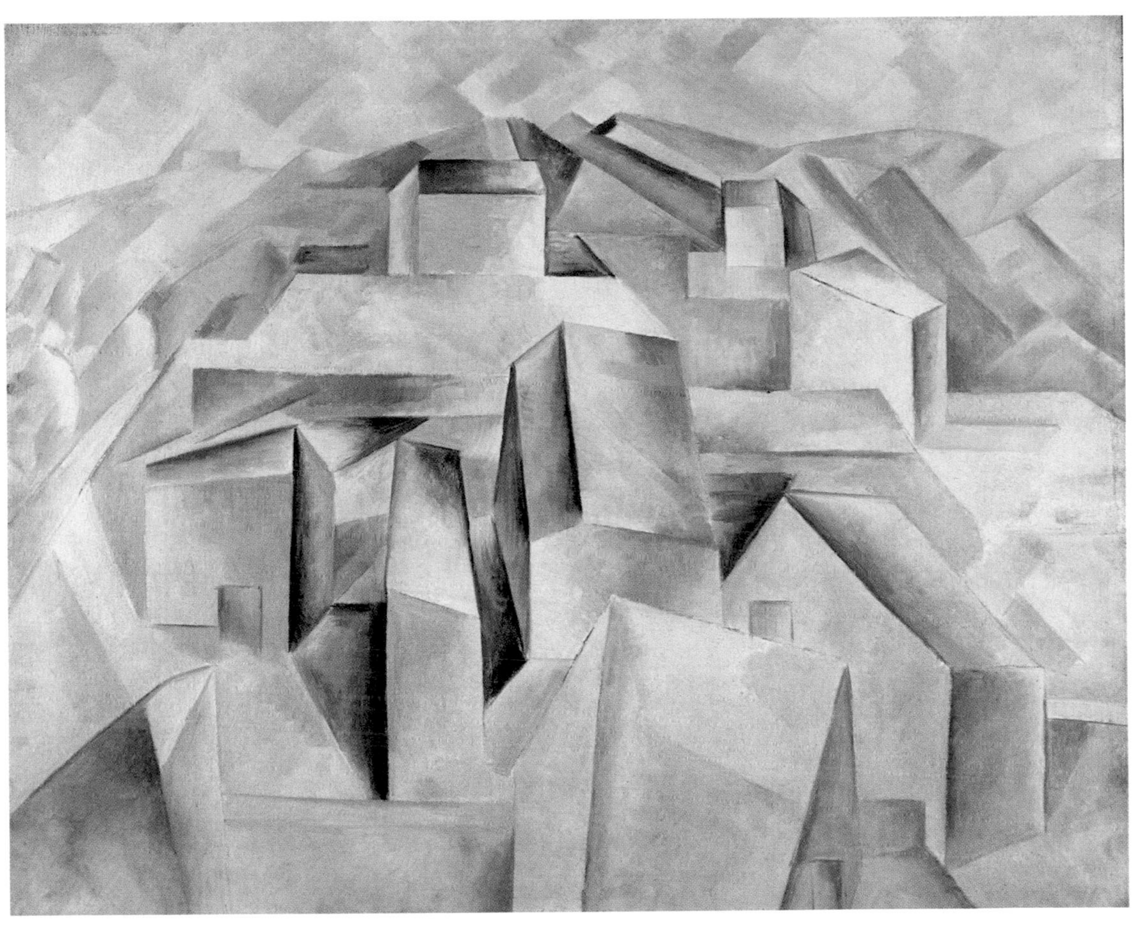

Portrait of Ambroise Vollard, 1910

By 1910, the break-up of form that increasingly characterized Picasso's early Cubism reached a new level, with a series of portraits representing important art dealers who were supporting his career. The first of these to be completed was a portrait of Vollard, the dealer who had staged Picasso's first exhibition in Paris in 1901. Vollard was fond of having his portrait painted and had, in recent years, been painted by both Pierre Auguste Renoir (1841–1919) and Cézanne. Picasso, by all accounts, was happy to join this established band, and produced a remarkable painting that captures the sheer physical presence of the sitter, despite the disintegration of the formal structure of the work. Here, Vollard's bulldog-like head emerges clearly from the framework of facetted lines and shapes that defines the space he inhabits. The closed eyes suggest that Vollard might well be taking a nap whilst sitting for Picasso, although there is no evidence that this was actually the case. Despite this, Vollard still appears as a blunt, formidable character, a factor borne out by many descriptions of this influential art dealer.

CREATED

Paris

MEDIUM

Oil on canvas

SERIES/PERIOD/MOVEMENT

Cubist period

SIMILAR WORKS

Portrait of Ambroise Vollard by Paul Cézanne, 1899

Portrait of Ambroise Vollard by Pierre Auguste Renoir, 1908

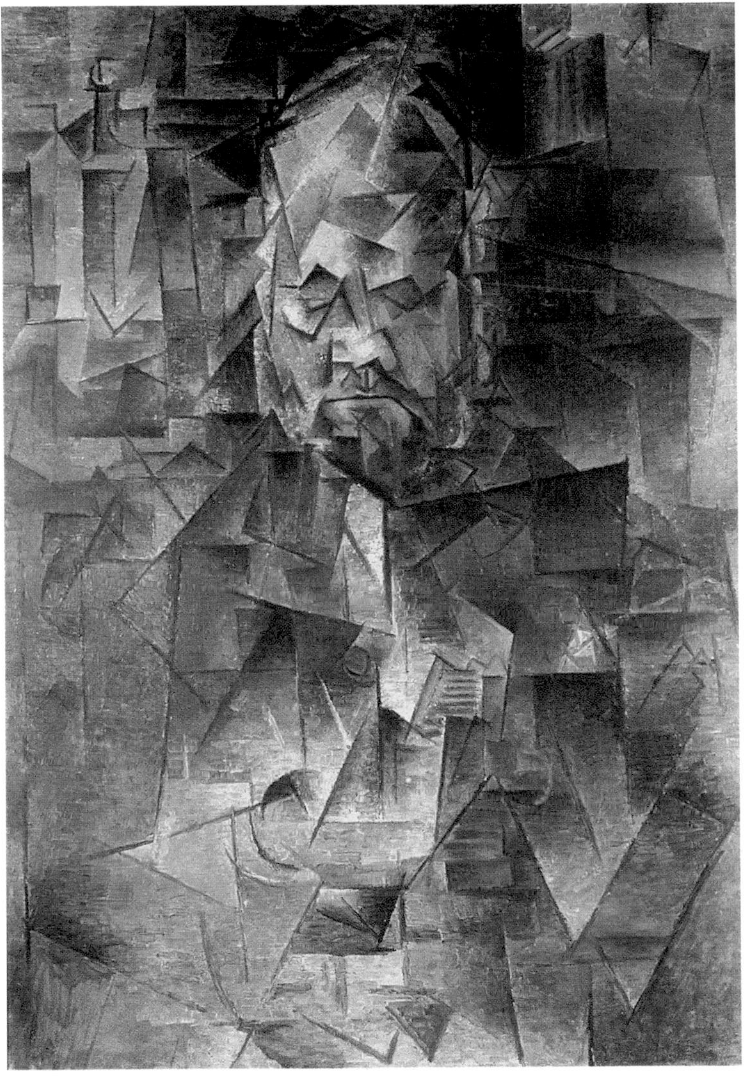

Portrait of Daniel-Henry Kahnweiler, 1910

Shortly after completing his portrait of Vollard, Picasso turned his attention to another influential dealer, Daniel-Henry Kahnweiler. Hailing originally from Germany, Kahnweiler had begun to make inroads into the Parisian art market, and at this time he was beginning to buy works by Picasso. Not long after this portrait was painted, Kahnweiler offered Picasso an exclusive contract that secured the artist's financial security until the outbreak of the First World War. This portrait represents a further incursion into the break-up of form to the point at which the sitter seems barely discernible. Kahnweiler's face can just about be picked out in the upper-right of the image, identifiable mainly by the inclusion of a wave of hair and a simple line to suggest a moustache. Two similar lines in the lower centre of the image register his watch chain, whilst his clasped hands can be seen at bottom-centre. Interestingly, Picasso included an African mask in the top-left, though this is barely discernible. From this point onwards, Cubism would rapidly develop into an even more experimental and challenging art form.

CREATED

Paris

MEDIUM

Oil on canvas

SERIES/PERIOD/MOVEMENT

Cubist period

SIMILAR WORKS

Portrait of Ambroise Vollard by Picasso, 1910

Portrait of Picasso by Juan Gris, 1912

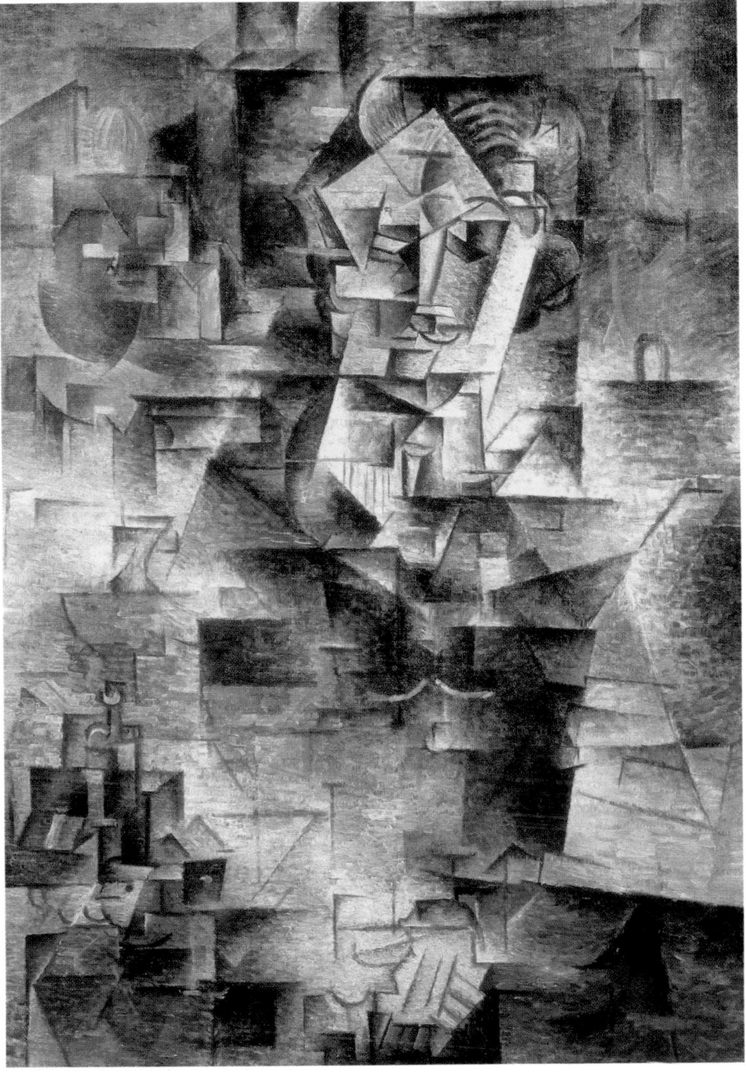

Violin and Sheet Music, 1912

Between 1910 and 1914 Picasso and Braque continued to produce experimental works. In 1912, they began to introduce fragments of text and, indeed, fragments of the real world in the form of collaged elements such as newspaper cuttings, sheet music and bottle labels. This new collage technique challenged the very nature of what was conventionally understood to be a work of art. In *Violin and Sheet Music* Picasso pasted together various pieces of coloured paper, cut into fragmented forms that suggest parts of musical instruments. In this way he and Braque were formulating a new visual language that suggested the popular culture of the music hall and cafés they regularly frequented. This was a time of enormous success for Picasso and his reputation grew at a meteoric pace. His personal life, however, remained turbulent. By 1911 his relationship with Fernande was on the rocks and he started a new relationship with Eva Gouel (also known as Marcelle Humbert), whom he affectionately nicknamed 'ma jolie'. Tragically Eva was to die in the winter of 1915, precipitating another moment of crisis in the artist's life.

CREATED

Paris

MEDIUM

Gouache, coloured paper and musical score, pasted on to cardboard

SERIES/PERIOD/MOVEMENT

Cubist period

SIMILAR WORKS

Violin and Pipe (le Quotidien) by Georges Braque, 1913

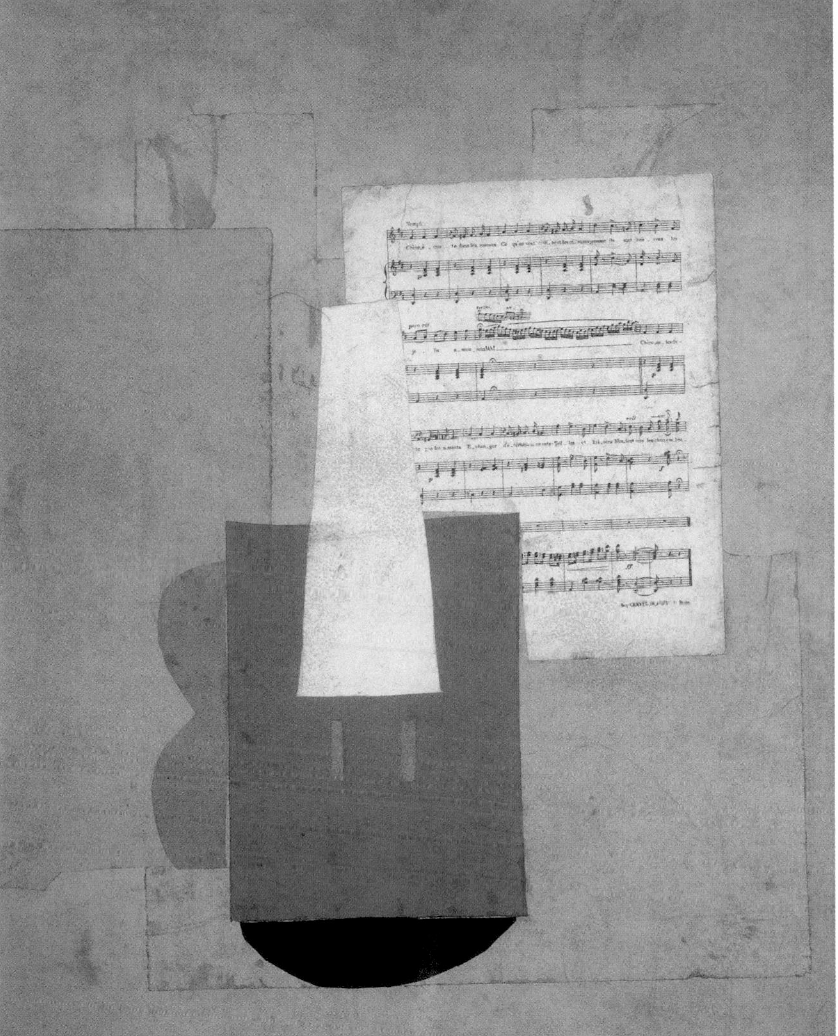

Portrait of Olga in an Armchair, 1917

The outbreak of war in 1914 inevitably had a huge impact upon Picasso's personal life and his career. While fellow artists such as Braque and André Derain (1880–1954) went off to fight, Picasso, as a Spanish citizen, chose not to serve. The war also brought about a significant change in the art market, not least because many of the foreign collectors who had gathered in Paris were forced to return to their native lands. Moreover, Cubism – despite being a movement whose birth was intimately connected with Paris and its avant-garde milieu – was increasingly attacked as a foreign import. Ever adaptable, Picasso developed a new style during the war, one that drew heavily upon the work of Ingres. In 1917 he adopted this highly meticulous style to produce a portrait of Olga Khokhlova, a dancer whom he had recently met through his contacts with Sergei Diaghilev's (1872–1929) Ballets Russes. In this portrait, Picasso has quoted directly from one of Ingres' most famous works, his *Portrait of Madame Moitessier*. The *Portrait of Olga* was to mark a new stage in Picasso's art and life.

CREATED

Montrouge

MEDIUM

Oil on canvas

SERIES/PERIOD/MOVEMENT

Neoclassical period

SIMILAR WORKS

Portrait of Madame Moitessier by Jean Auguste Dominique Ingres, 1856

Paulo as a Harlequin by Picasso, 1924

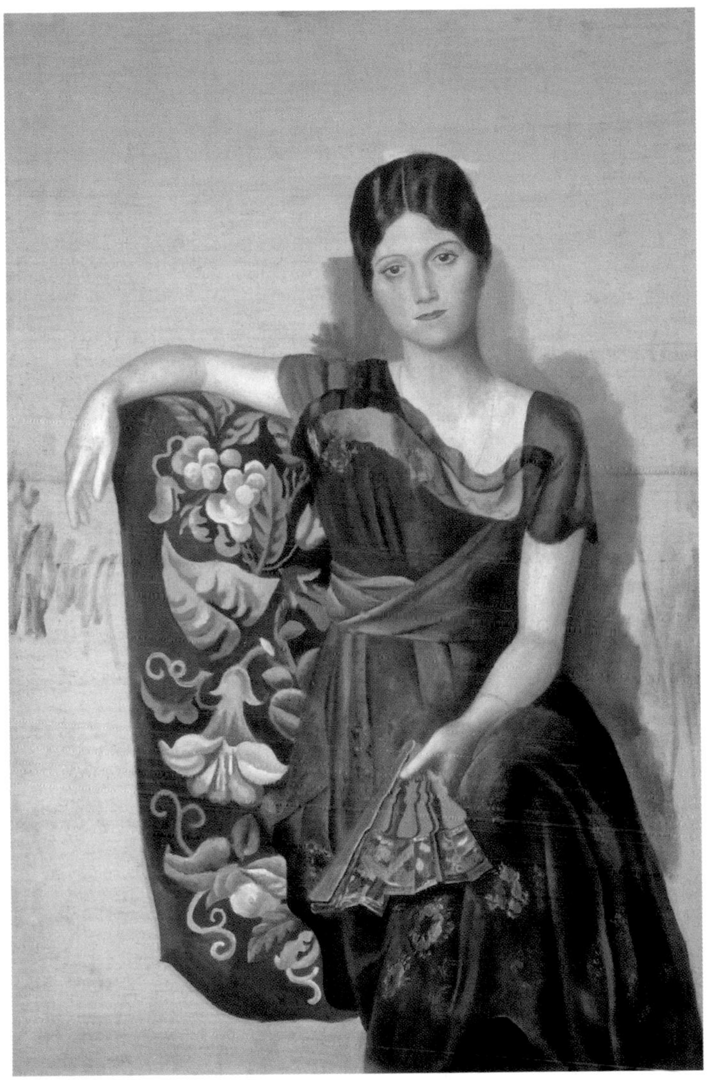

Vera Nemchinova and Felix Fernandez Dancing, 1919

In the summer of 1918 Picasso married Olga, and for the next few years his career was to be closely associated with the theatrical world from which she hailed. The Ballets Russes had been staging annual performances in Paris since 1909, and in 1916 the writer Jean Cocteau (1889–63) persuaded Picasso to produce stage and costume designs for a Ballets Russes performance entitled *Parade*. This collaboration gave Picasso the opportunity to return to the theme of performers and dancers that had dominated his earlier 'rose period' and, indeed, the figure of the harlequin played a dominant role in his works of this period. Picasso had adopted a more academic style during the war and now placed a great deal of emphasis on drawing. Working in a tight, linear style, he produced a series of portraits of his friends, as well as the musicians, writers and performers associated with the Ballets Russes. This drawing, showing dancers at a Ballets Russes rehearsal, reveals Picasso's new emphasis on figuration and linear rhythm, and demonstrates a significant departure from his earlier Cubist works.

CREATED

London

MEDIUM

Pencil on paper

SERIES/PERIOD/MOVEMENT

Neoclassical period

SIMILAR WORKS

Dancer Exercising at the Barre by Edgar Degas, *c.* 1885

Costume Designs for the Ballets Russes by Leon Bakst, *c.* 1910–14

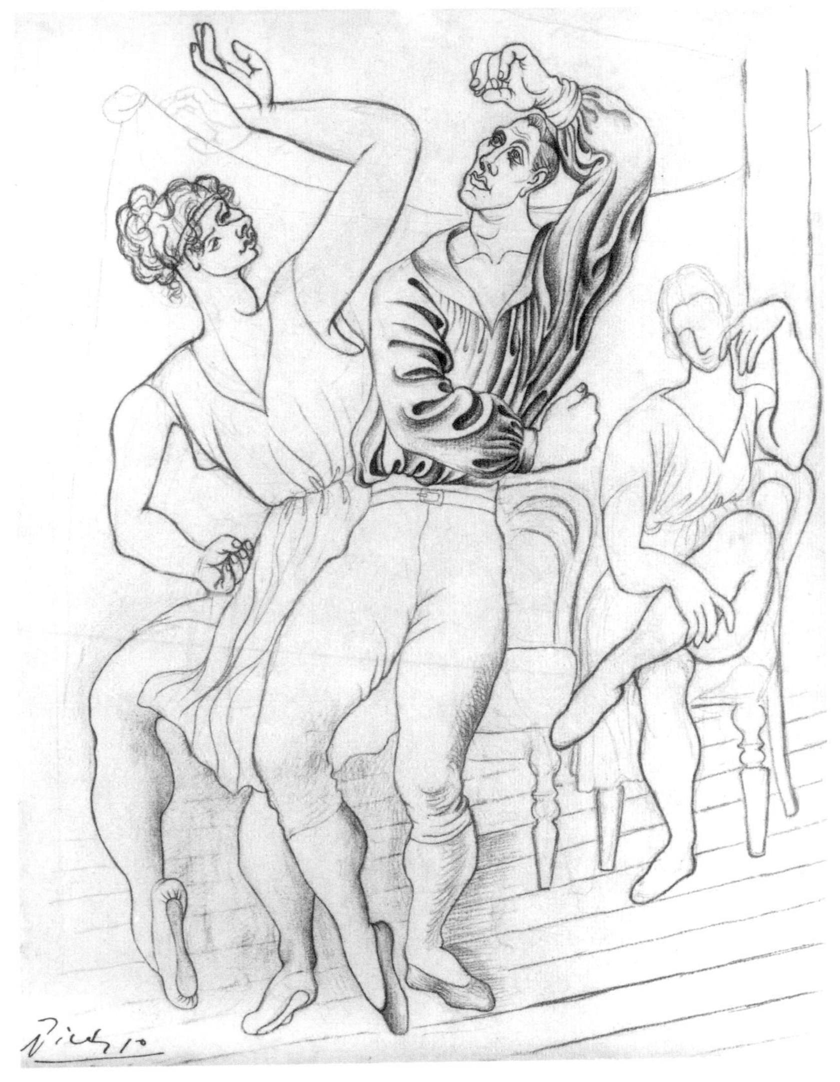

Erik Satie, 1920

In the early post-war years Picasso continued to produce pencil portraits of the musicians and performers with whom he was collaborating. Despite the fact that many were based upon photographs, these drawings manage to capture the unique personality of the individuals represented. Picasso first met the French pianist and composer Erik Satie (1866–1925) in 1917, when both were working with Cocteau on the production of *Parade*. He was again to collaborate with Satie seven years later, for the Ballets Russes production of *Mercure*. Like Picasso, Satie had come to Paris in his youth and spent much of his time in the bohemian cafés of Montmartre. Satie's career, however, did not really take off until later in life, when he gained a reputation as a radical composer – largely as a result of his collaborative work with Picasso and Cocteau. Here Picasso has once again used the linear drawing style derived from Ingres. However, he has exaggerated the size of Satie's hands, as if to emphasize their importance to the pianist. Notably he has also distorted their shape to symbolize the unconventionality of Satie's compositions.

CREATED

Paris

MEDIUM

Pencil and charcoal on paper

SERIES/PERIOD/MOVEMENT

Neoclassical period

SIMILAR WORKS

Pencil Study for the Portrait of M. Bertin by Jean Auguste Dominique Ingres

Portrait of Igor Stravinsky by Picasso, 1920

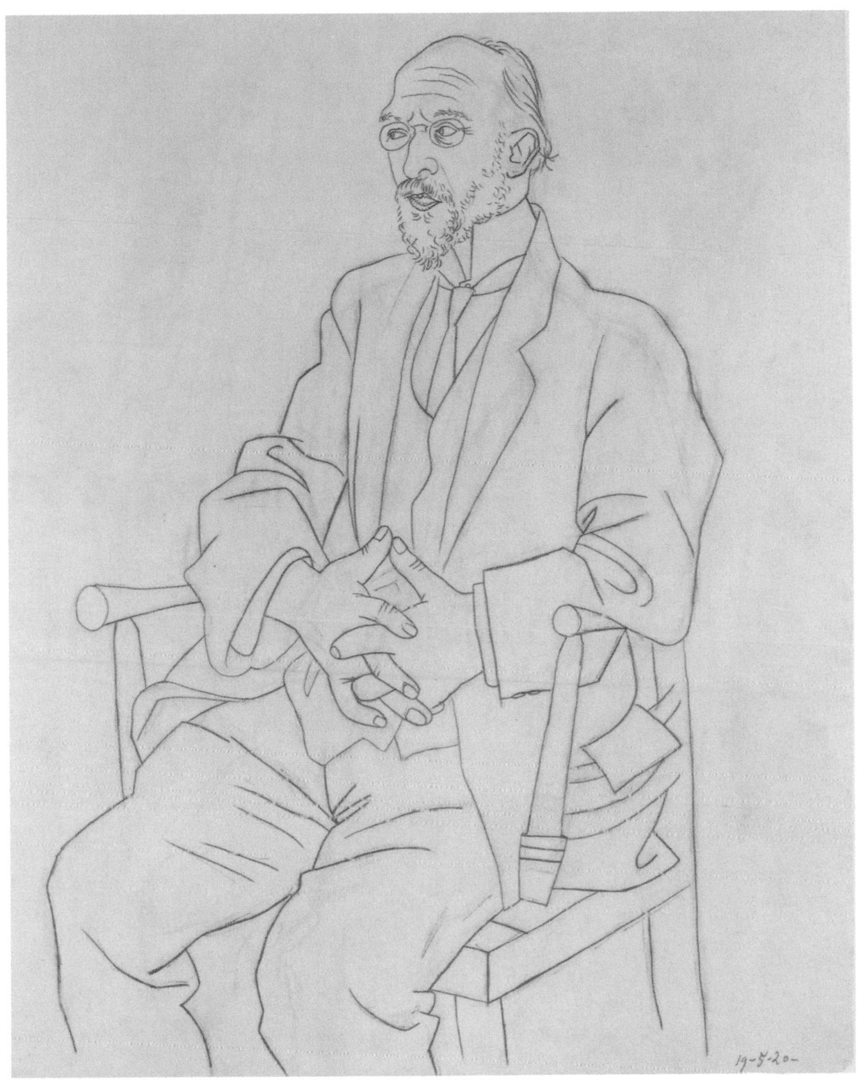
19-5-20-

Woman in a Red Petticoat, 1922

Throughout the early 1920s Picasso's life seemed to be on a relatively sound footing. His marriage to Olga appeared to bring social and domestic contentment, and the Picassos regularly attended the many fashionable soirées of Parisian society. The couple lived a genteel existence, moving between Paris and the southern French resorts of Biarritz and Juan-les-Pins. In 1921 the birth of their first child, Paulo, also contributed to a sense of order and stability in Picasso's life. His career, too, was advancing well. In addition to numerous theatrical commissions, Picasso's work was being widely exhibited. This stability was also reflected in many of Picasso's paintings – and can be seen in the development of his Neoclassical works. For example, the idealized and monumental forms evident in his *Woman in a Red Petticoat* clearly derive from antique statuary. Here the woman is represented at a natural spring, or source. Such scenes, emphasizing bathing, cleansing or gathering water, were closely related to classical subject-matter, and formed a key aspect of Picasso's work during this period.

CREATED

Dinard or Paris

MEDIUM

Oil on canvas

SERIES/PERIOD/MOVEMENT

Neoclassical period

SIMILAR WORKS

The Mediterranean by Aristide Maillol, 1905

Three Women at the Spring by Picasso, 1921

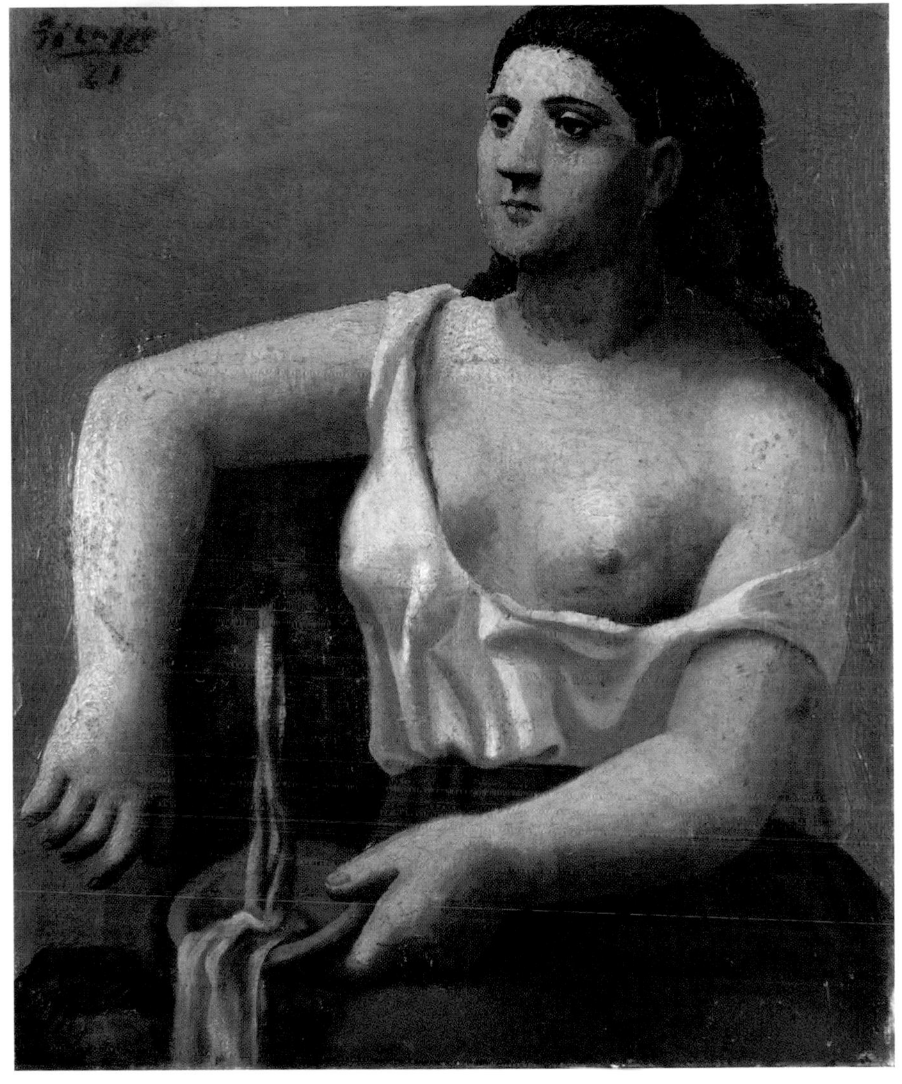

Paulo as a Harlequin, 1924

The birth of Paulo marked the beginning of one of the artist's most prolific periods of activity. Over the next few years Picasso produced a vast panoply of works – some in a Cubist style, others in the Neoclassical style that he had adopted during the First World War. In 1924 Picasso painted one of his best-known portraits of his now three-year-old son in the costume of a harlequin. The work has notably been left unfinished. The background is not defined and the legs of the chair have been only lightly sketched in. These lines also reveal how Picasso has moved Paulo's leg at least twice, shifting the composition from that of a standing figure to a seated one. In this way, the portrait of Paulo directly echoes Picasso's earlier 1917 portrait of Paulo's mother, Olga, in an armchair. Both are represented seated, and both works are similarly unfinished. In many ways these two images represent the importance of Picasso's family to him at this stage in his life. Indeed, Picasso kept the portraits of Paulo with him for the rest of his life.

CREATED

Paris

MEDIUM

Oil on canvas

SERIES/PERIOD/MOVEMENT

Neoclassical period

SIMILAR WORKS

Portrait of Olga in an Armchair by Picasso, 1917

Harlequin and Pierrot by André Derain 1924

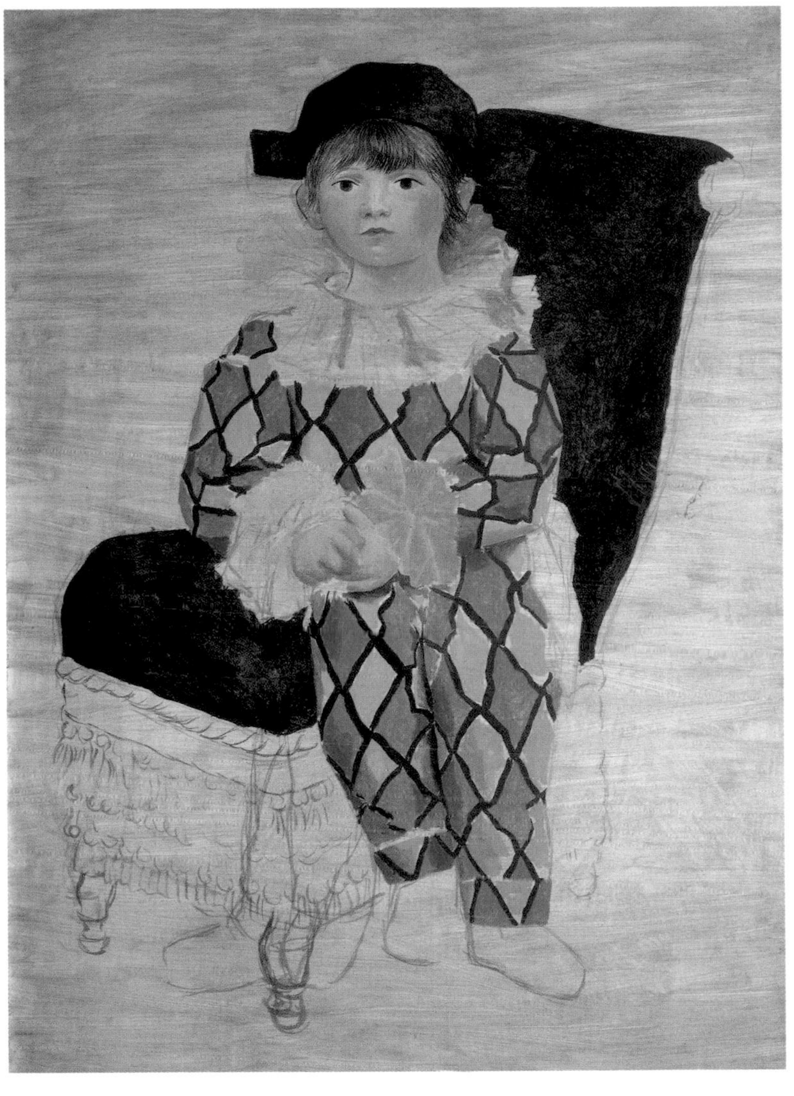

Three Dancers, 1925

In the spring of 1925 Picasso began work on a major canvas that suggests a significant change of mood in his life and work. In *Three Dancers*, Picasso has abandoned the more harmonious and balanced style of his recent Neoclassical work in favour of a more aggressive, fragmented and violent representation. In terms of subject matter Picasso has retained a focus on theatrical performers. His dancers, however, are treated more like monsters, whose jagged and distorted forms confront and threaten the spectator. Several factors may well have contributed to this shift in Picasso's work. For example, he had recently heard of the tragic death of Ramon Pichot, a fellow Catalan painter whom Picasso had known in his youth. Picasso was later to state that the inclusion of a black silhouette in the upper right of the canvas was in homage to Pichot. However, the artist's emphasis on monstrous female forms, dancing maniacally in a claustrophobic interior, seems also to allude to the impending breakdown of his marriage and his rejection of both the theatricality and domesticity that had characterized his life with Olga.

CREATED

Paris

MEDIUM

Oil on canvas

SERIES/PERIOD/MOVEMENT

Surrealist period

SIMILAR WORKS

Dance by Henri Matisse, 1909–10

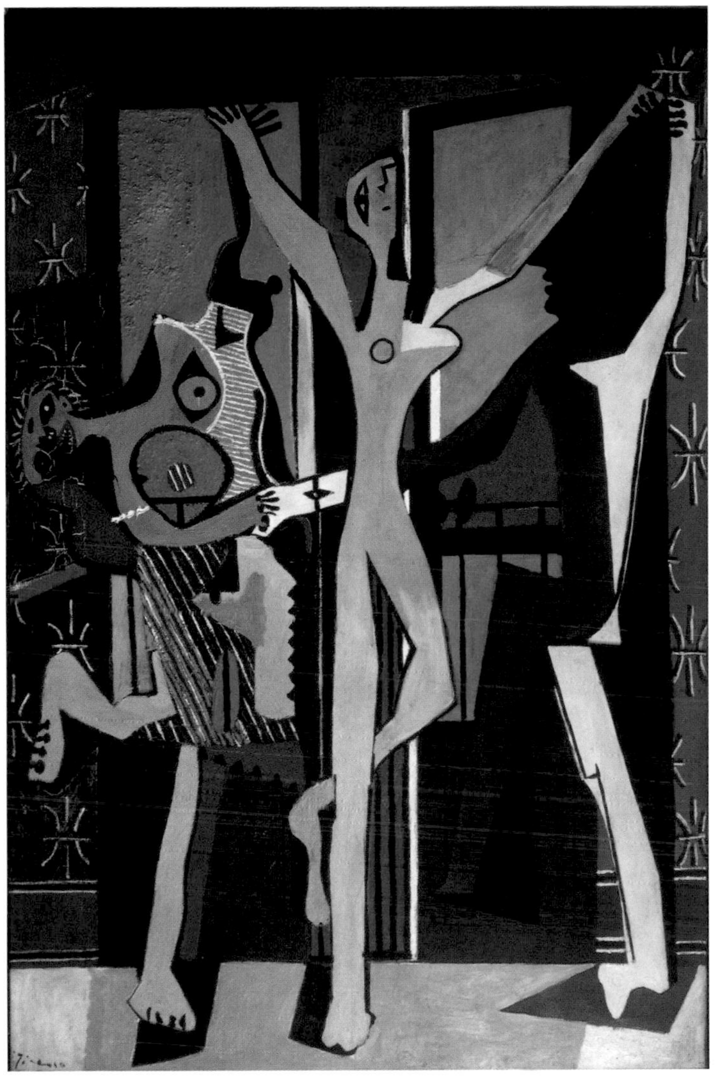

Bathers, 1928

From early in his relationship with Olga, Picasso had taken to spending the summer months at the coast, sometimes at Dinard in Brittany, but mostly on the French Riviera at St Raphael, Cap d'Antibes and Juan-les-Pins. Here he produced dozens of images of bathers by the shore. Sometimes these were represented as modern figures in fashionable bathing costumes, and at other times as antique figures from classical mythology. Picasso adopted a number of different styles for these works. In line with the Neoclassical style that characterized much of his work in the early post-war period, many of these were monumental in form and reminiscent of antique statuary. By the mid-1920s, however, he also produced a series of bathers using the fragmented and distorted forms typical of the figures in *Three Dancers* (1925). The peculiar bathers represented in this image – metamorphic creatures seemingly constructed from non-organic geometric forms – reveal Picasso's newfound interest in the sculptural quality of his work. Here Picasso was largely inspired by his friendship and collaboration with the Spanish sculptor Julio González (1876–1942).

CREATED

Dinard

MEDIUM

Oil on canvas

SERIES/PERIOD/MOVEMENT

Surrealist period

SIMILAR WORKS

Hector and Andromache by Giorgio de Chirico, 1917

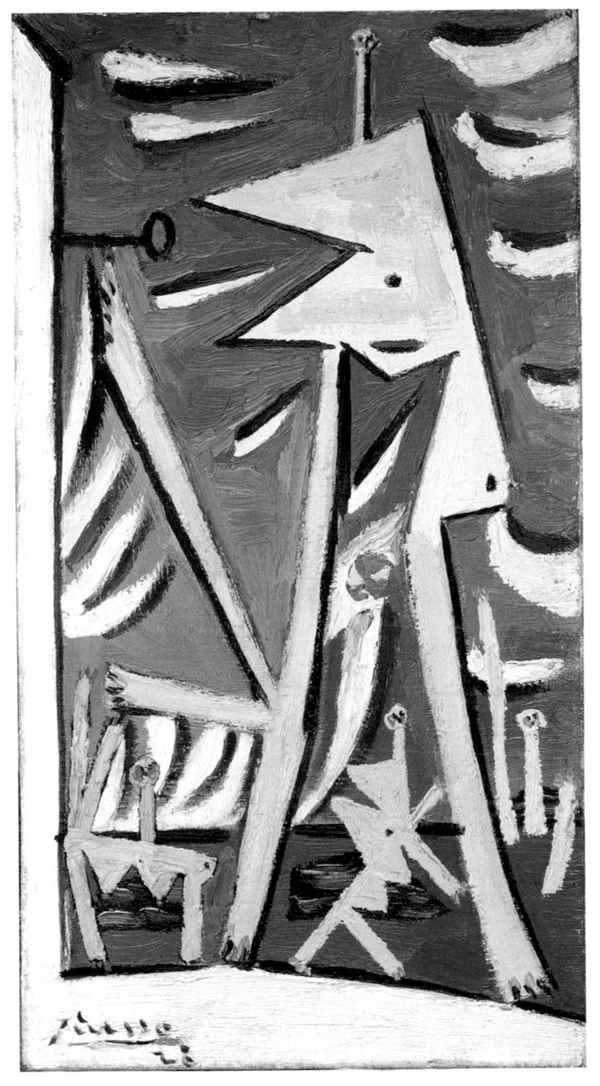

The Sculptor, 1931

Throughout his life, Picasso produced a vast array of sculptures in a variety of media. These began with his Cubist sculptures of the period 1910–14. After this Picasso abandoned the art for a while, only beginning again in the late 1920s, with a series of wire constructions based upon simple line drawings produced in three dimensions. Around this time Picasso established a new sculpture studio in Boisgeloup, 65 km (40 miles) north of Paris, and began to produce a series of sculptures, many of monumental proportions reminiscent of monolithic figures. Picasso's interest in sculpture at this time can also be traced in a number of etchings, drawings and paintings he produced based upon the theme of the sculptor in his studio. In this work, Picasso has represented the sculptor – probably himself – in a studio setting, contemplating his own works. Two sculptures are also included in the composition: a large bust of a woman staring down at the sculptor; and, in the background, a nude figure, constructed from sensual rounded forms, caressing a tube-like element mounted on a plinth. Here, sensuality and sexuality pervade the sculptor's sense of reverie.

CREATED

Paris

MEDIUM

Oil on panel

SERIES/PERIOD/MOVEMENT

Surrealist period

SIMILAR WORKS

The Artist's Studio by Gustave Courbet, 1855

The Artist's Studio by Frédéric Bazille, 1870

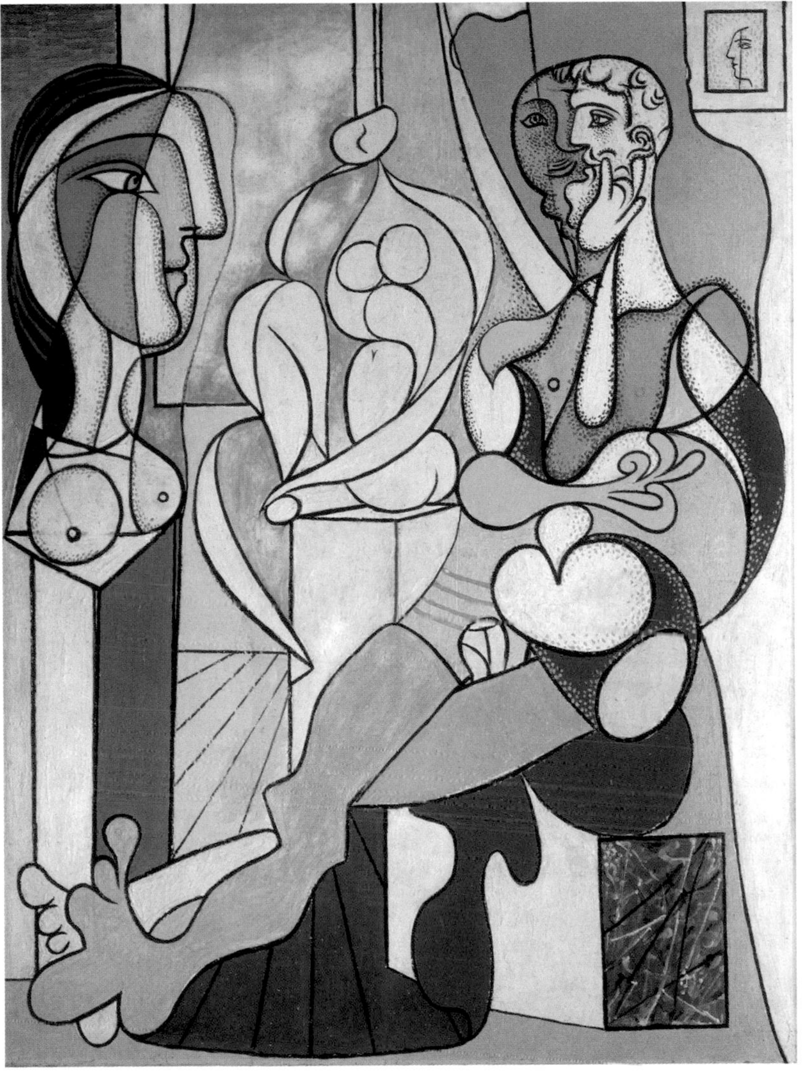

Woman with a Flower, 1932

There is some dispute regarding exactly when Picasso first met Marie-Thérèse Walter, a woman nearly 30 years his junior. What is clear is that she had become his mistress by 1927 and was to feature in many of his works over the next decade or so. At first, Picasso kept this relationship secret from his family. However, he started to use Marie-Thérèse as a model early on, and it is she who appears in the painting *Woman with a Flower*. Many of Picasso's images of Marie-Thérèse, including this one, reveal a new departure in Picasso's art. Here the artist has constructed the female body from an assemblage of soft, curvaceous, organic forms, as if a being has metamorphosed from these strange components. Picasso's emphasis on metamorphosis was doubtless inspired in part by his familiarity with Surrealism at this time. The Surrealists celebrated Picasso and regarded his work as highly important, though Picasso always distanced himself from them as a group. Nonetheless, the dialogue between Picasso and the emerging Surrealists is here very much in evidence.

CREATED

Boisgeloup

MEDIUM

Oil on canvas

SERIES/PERIOD/MOVEMENT

Surrealist period

SIMILAR WORKS

Reading by Picasso, 1932

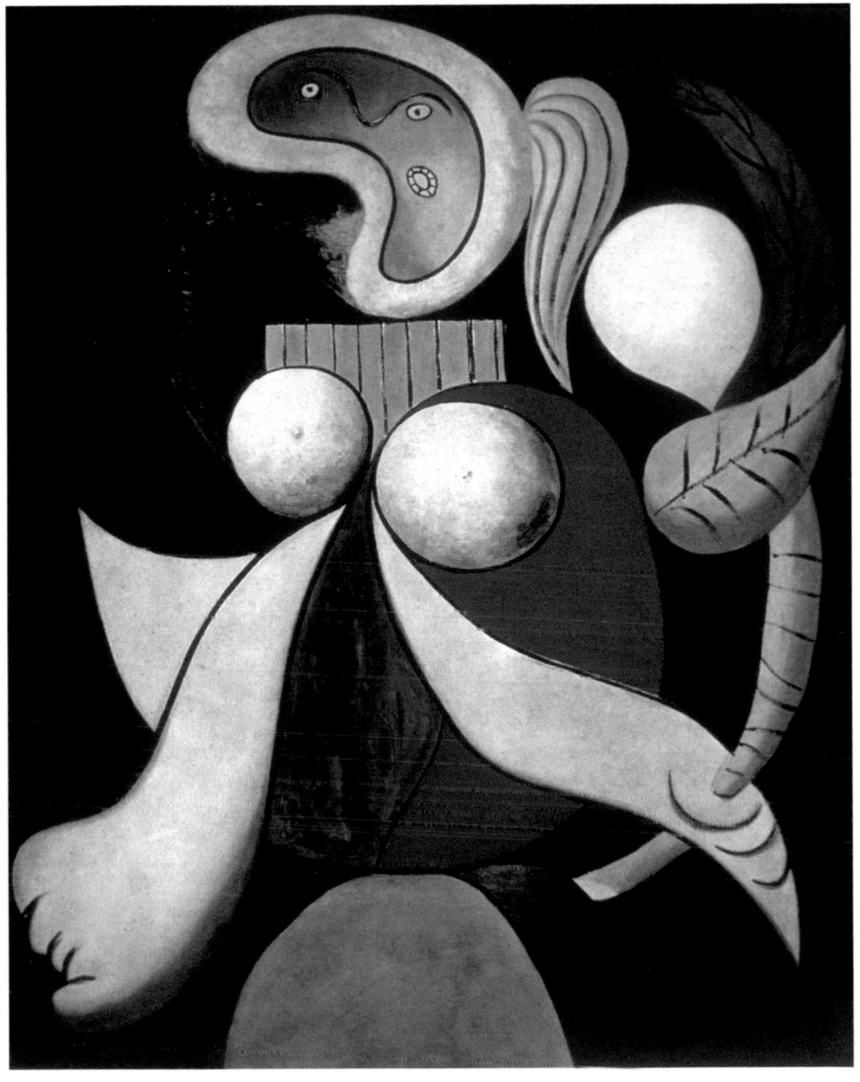

Portrait of Marie-Thérèse, 1936

In 1930, although still living with Olga and Paulo, Picasso acquired a Parisian flat for his mistress Marie-Thérèse. He continued to see her regularly and, in many respects, she can be regarded as the artist's muse throughout this period. She was to feature prominently in many of his paintings of seated and recumbent women during the late 1920s and 1930s, as well as being the model for many of the sculptures he produced, including a series of monumental busts, one of which appears in the painting *The Sculptor* (1931). The portrait shown here is unusually detailed in its emphasis on Marie-Thérèse's facial features. It focuses upon the youthful serenity of the sitter, highlighting her poise and grace. This was a typical feature of many of Picasso's paintings of his mistress, many of which show her at ease, sleeping or dreaming, and celebrate her beauty and sensuality by adopting soft, curvaceous forms and bright optimistic colours.

CREATED

Paris or Juan-les-Pins

MEDIUM

Pen, ink and grey wash on paper

SERIES/PERIOD/MOVEMENT

Surrealist period

SIMILAR WORKS

Lorette's Sister by Henri Matisse, 1916–17

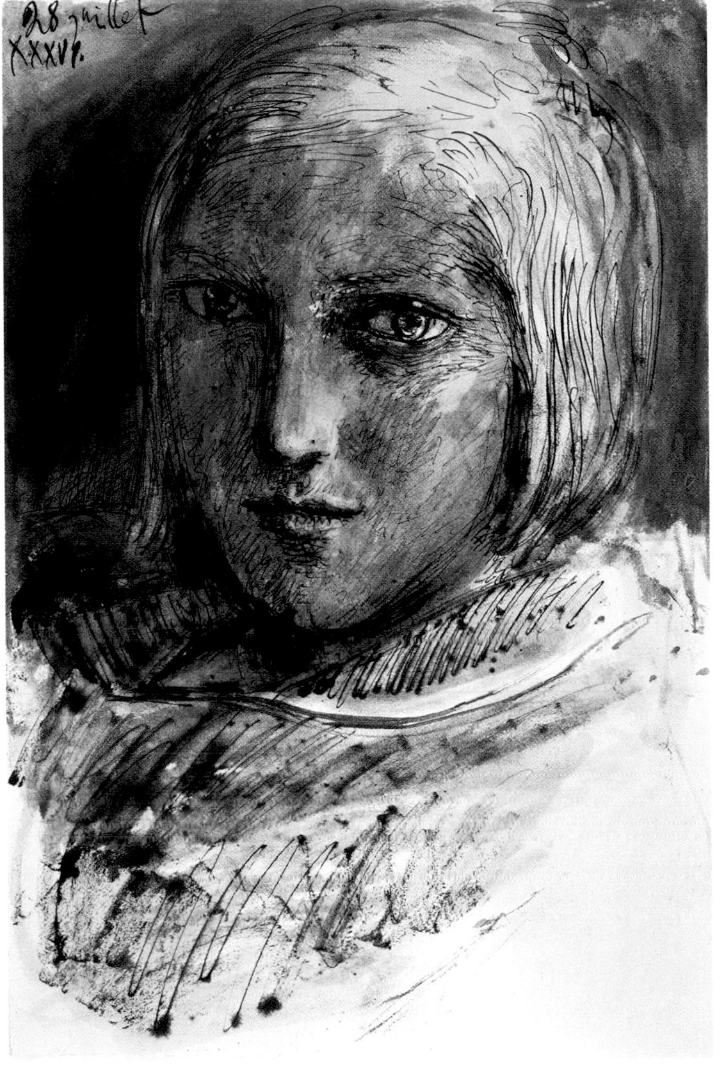
28 juillet
XXXVI.

Minotaur and Dead Mare in Front of a Cave, 1936

Picasso included a number of etchings representing the sculptor's studio in a series of 100 prints commissioned by the dealer Vollard and subsequently known as the Vollard Suite. Picasso worked on this series between 1930 and 1937, during which time his marriage finally collapsed. In addition to the sculptor's studio etchings, the Vollard Suite also saw the introduction of a figure that was to feature extensively in Picasso's work during the 1930s – the minotaur. This mythological creature, half-bull, half-human, represented for Picasso the co-existence of good and evil, the primitive and the civilized, in humanity. Notably, this was something that Picasso particularly valued in the Spanish tradition of the bullfight, and in 1934 he travelled throughout his native Spain to witness the sport he loved. In this image, Picasso has represented the minotaur emerging from a cave, carrying the body of a dead horse. Here he was clearly making an allusion to the contest to the death that characterizes bullfights. At the same time, however, he has brought together the violence of the struggle with the tenderness with which the victor bears the body of his victim.

CREATED

Juan-les-Pins

MEDIUM

Gouache and India ink on paper

SERIES/PERIOD/MOVEMENT

Surrealist period

SIMILAR WORKS

Covers for the Surrealist Journal *Minotaure* by Albert Skira, 1933–38

Guernica by Picasso, 1937

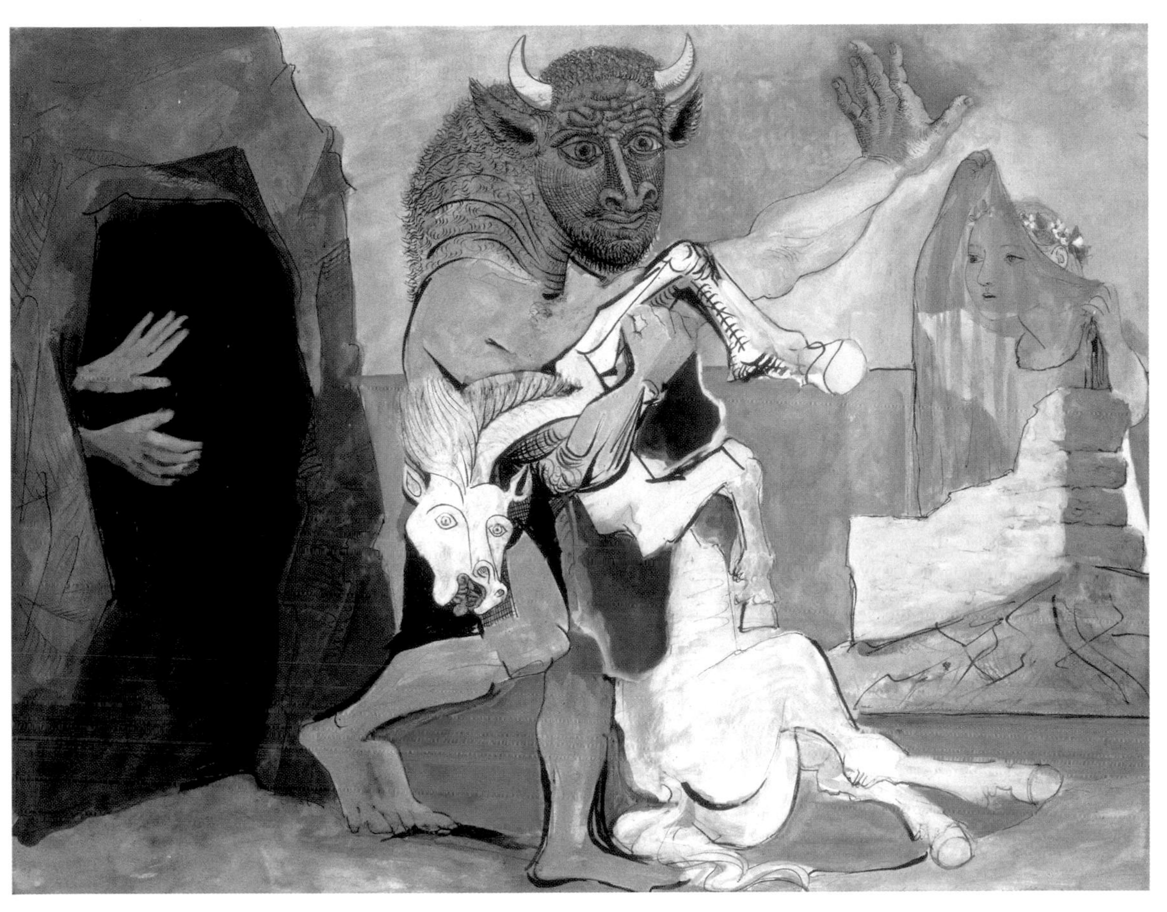

Portrait of Maya with her Doll, 1938

In 1935 Marie-Thérèse became pregnant and gave birth to a daughter, Maya. Shortly after this Picasso finally left Olga to move in with his mistress and new child. This precipitated another stormy period in his personal life, a factor further exacerbated by political events. In 1936 the Spanish Civil War began and Picasso felt himself swept up in the momentous events of the epoch. That year Spanish Republicans declared Picasso the new director of the Prado, Spain's national art gallery, even though the collection had been removed for safekeeping and Picasso was unable to travel to Spain. In 1937 Picasso also committed himself to the Republican cause by painting *Guernica*, his famous attack on the atrocities perpetrated by the Spanish Nationalists under General Franco. With Europe in political turmoil, Picasso turned to a more domestic subject, representing his daughter Maya much as he had earlier painted Paulo. However, far from focusing on calm and tranquillity, Picasso has adopted the distortions of his more recent works. Even the doll lying lifelessly in Maya's arms recalls the dead child carried by one of the victims in *Guernica*.

CREATED

Paris

MEDIUM

Oil on canvas

SERIES/PERIOD/MOVEMENT

Surrealist period

SIMILAR WORKS

Child with Doll by Henri Rousseau, 1904–05

Paulo as a Harlequin by Picasso, 1924

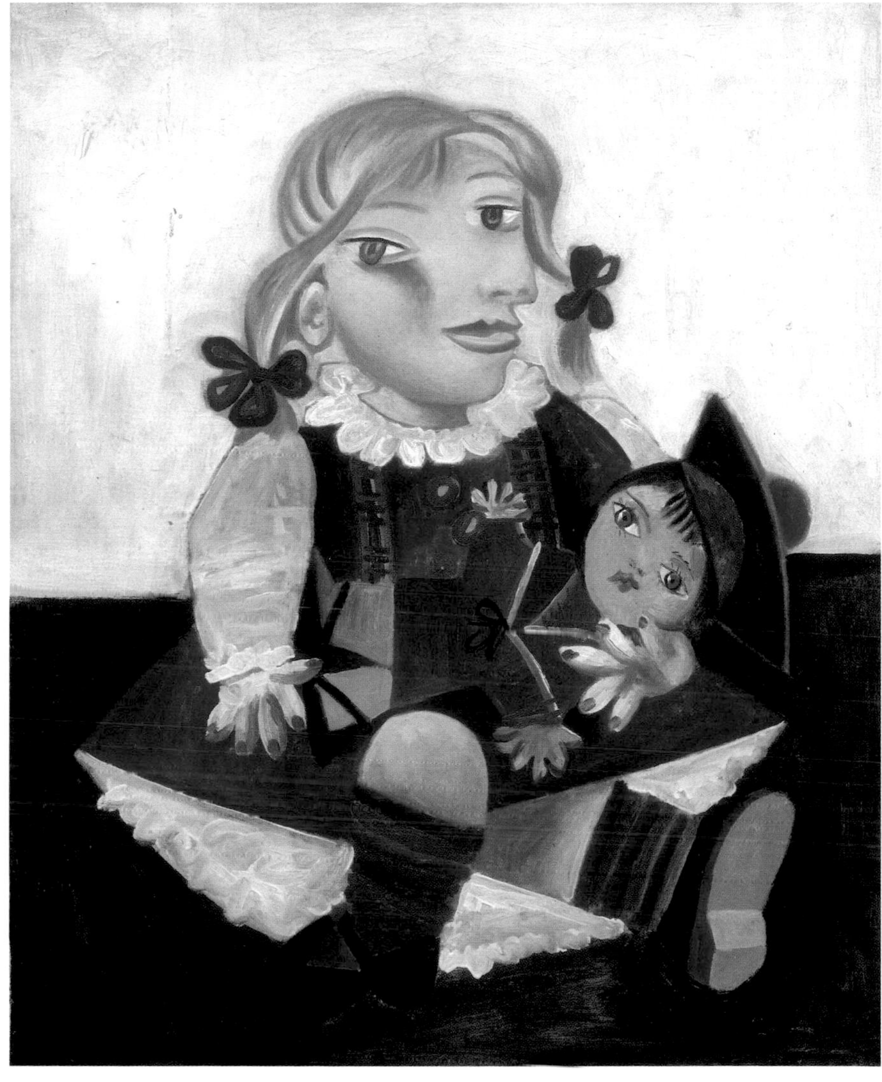

Paloma in Blue, 1952

When the Second World War began in 1939 Picasso entered another period of great uncertainty. Unlike many fellow artists, Picasso remained in Paris during the occupation of the city by German forces. Protected by his wealth and fame, he survived the war reasonably securely, although the occupying forces did ban him from exhibiting his work. In 1943, Picasso met a young painter, Françoise Gilot; she soon became his mistress and mother to two more of his children. In 1947 she gave birth to Picasso's second son, Claude. Two years later a daughter, Paloma, was born. The name, which means 'dove' in Spanish, was highly significant for Picasso. In 1949, the year of Paloma's birth, he produced a lithograph representing a dove. The subject-matter clearly recalled the artist's relationship with his father, so renowned as a painter of pigeons and doves, as well as echoing Picasso's own youthful works, such as *Child with a Dove*. However, Picasso's new dove was to acquire worldwide fame when it was adopted as the motif for the World Peace Congress, organized by the Communist Party.

CREATED

Vallauris

MEDIUM

Oil on plywood

SERIES/PERIOD/MOVEMENT

Post-War Communist period

SIMILAR WORKS

Girl in a Blue Armchair by Mary Cassatt, 1878

Portrait of Maya with her Doll by Picasso, 1938

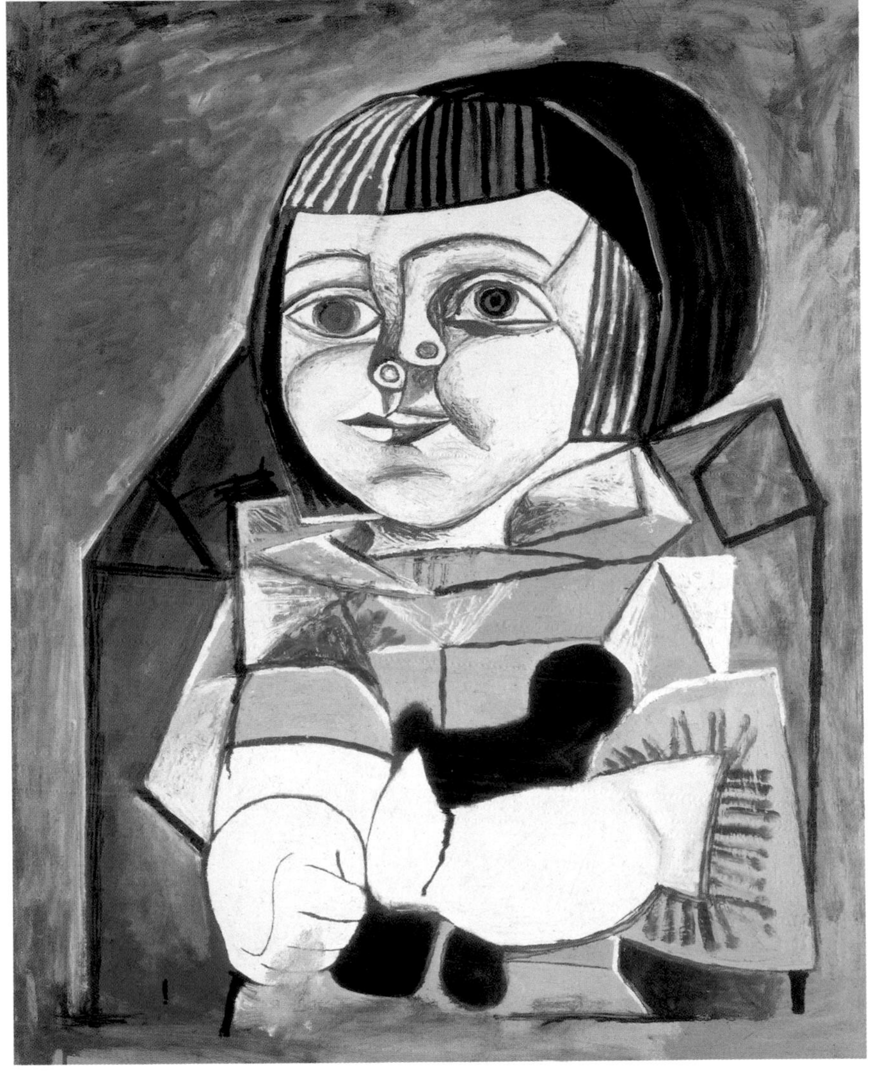

Claude Drawing Françoise and Paloma, 1954

In 1948 Picasso moved to Vallauris in the south of France. Here, he turned his hand to a new medium – ceramics. Unsurprisingly Picasso's work in this medium was highly innovative and he was soon exhibiting his ceramic work in Paris. In 1952 Picasso also executed a pair of murals entitled *War* and *Peace*, installed in a deconsecrated chapel in Vallauris. By 1954, following a well-established pattern, Picasso's relationship with Françoise began to break down. Once again, the artist inscribed these changing circumstances in his private life into his works. At first glance, this painting of his son Claude drawing his mother Françoise and sister Paloma might seem to be an image of domestic contentment. However, it is notable that the two children, distinguished from the background by blocks of blue and green colour, are involved in their own thoughts while Françoise, reduced to a mere outline in white, has almost entirely disappeared. Within a few weeks of the completion of this portrait, Françoise and the children left Vallauris – and Picasso – for Paris.

CREATED

Vallauris

MEDIUM

Oil on canvas

SERIES/PERIOD/MOVEMENT

Post-War Communist period

SIMILAR WORKS

The Bellilli Family by Edgar Degas, 1859–60

The Family of the Artist by Pierre Auguste Renoir, 1896

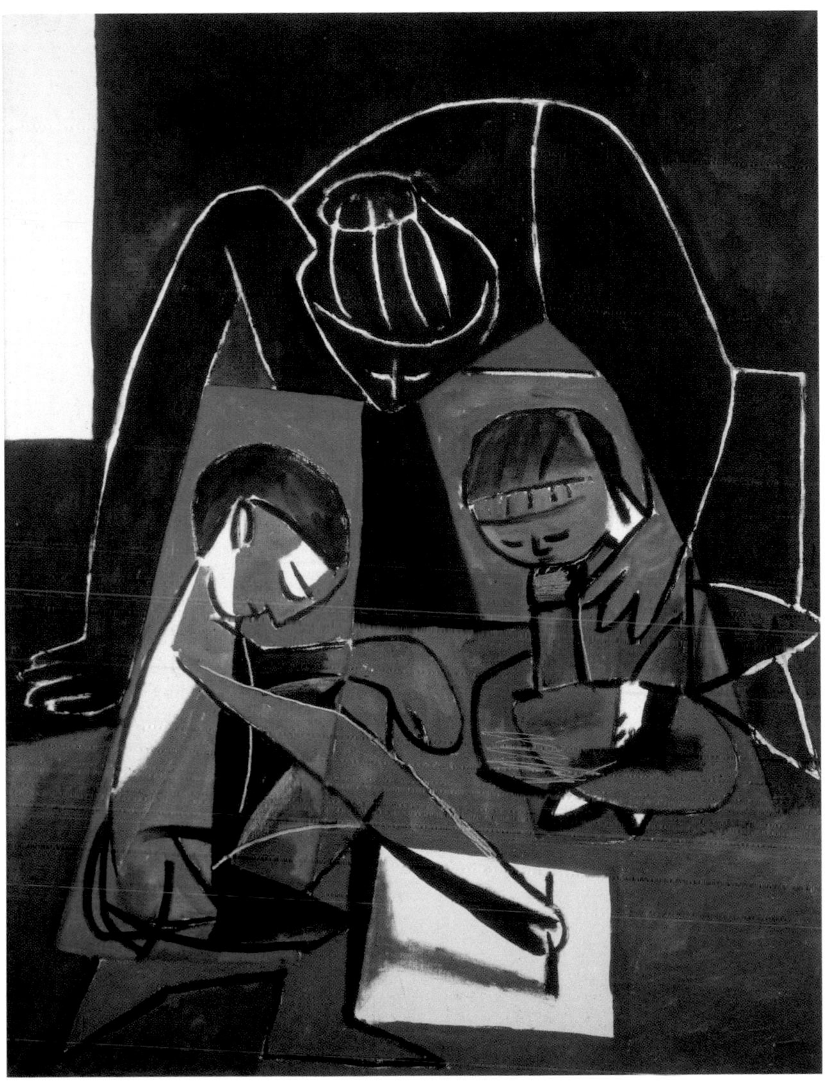

Portrait of the Artist's Wife, Jacqueline Kneeling, 1954

The year 1954 was a depressing one for Picasso. Several of his long-time friends, including the writers Maurice Raynal and Paul Eluard, and the painter Henri Matisse (1869–1954) had recently died. His relationship with Françoise had fallen apart. The departure of Françoise and the children left Picasso alone, but a new woman, Jacqueline Roque, soon emerged on the scene. Now in his seventies, Picasso began what was to be his last major relationship. In 1954 Jacqueline moved in with Picasso and the couple married seven years later. In 1955 Picasso and Jacqueline acquired a new home called 'La Californie', situated on a hill in Cannes overlooking the Golfe Juan. Here Picasso embarked on a feverish period of painting. Jacqueline was to become one of the major subjects of this period, and he painted his new partner over and over again. Here we see Jacqueline in profile, seated with her knees tucked up to her chest. The elongated neck, simple striped dress and sandals give the sitter the air of a classical goddess.

CREATED

Vallauris

MEDIUM

Oil on canvas

SERIES/PERIOD/MOVEMENT

Late period

SIMILAR WORKS

Woman Holding her Feet by Aristide Maillol, 1905

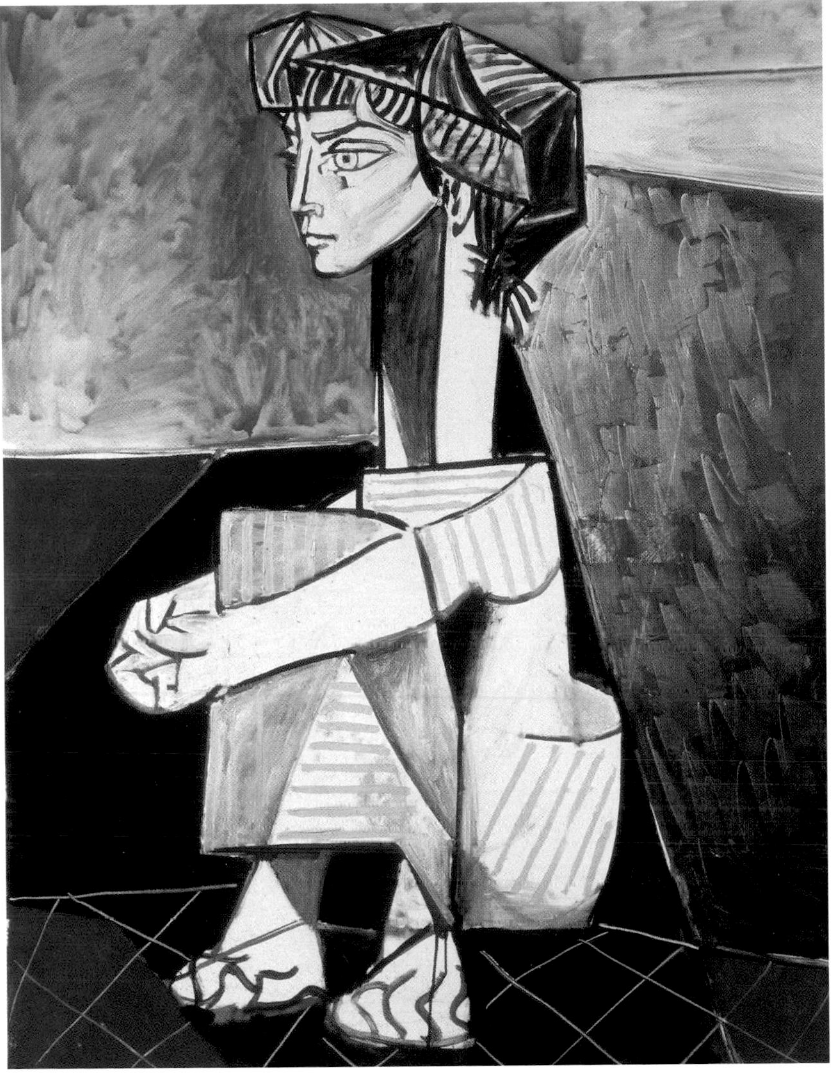

The Women of Algiers, after Delacroix, 1955

Jacqueline made frequent appearances in a series of paintings Picasso executed in the mid-1950s. Between December 1954 and February 1955 he produced 15 works, all inspired by the famous painting *The Women of Algiers* (1834) by Eugène Delacroix (1798–1863). The variations are only loosely based on the original work, and Picasso notably incorporated many of his Cubist-inspired distortions into his pieces. In this version Jacqueline appears several times – as a standing and a reclining nude in the right half of the canvas, and dressed in oriental costume but with breasts bared, as in Delacroix's original work. Picasso's emphasis on Jacqueline as an odalisque could also be construed as a homage to his friend and fellow painter Matisse, who had recently died. Matisse was well known for his representations of women as odalisques, dressed in exotic costumes. Picasso later stated, 'When Matisse died, he bequeathed to me his odalisques'. It might also be regarded as no coincidence that Picasso's focus on Delacroix's Algerian women came at the time of the Algerian crisis in French politics.

CREATED

Paris

MEDIUM

Oil on canvas

SERIES/PERIOD/MOVEMENT

Late period

SIMILAR WORKS

The Women of Algiers by Eugène Delacroix, 1834

Odalisques by Henri Matisse, 1928

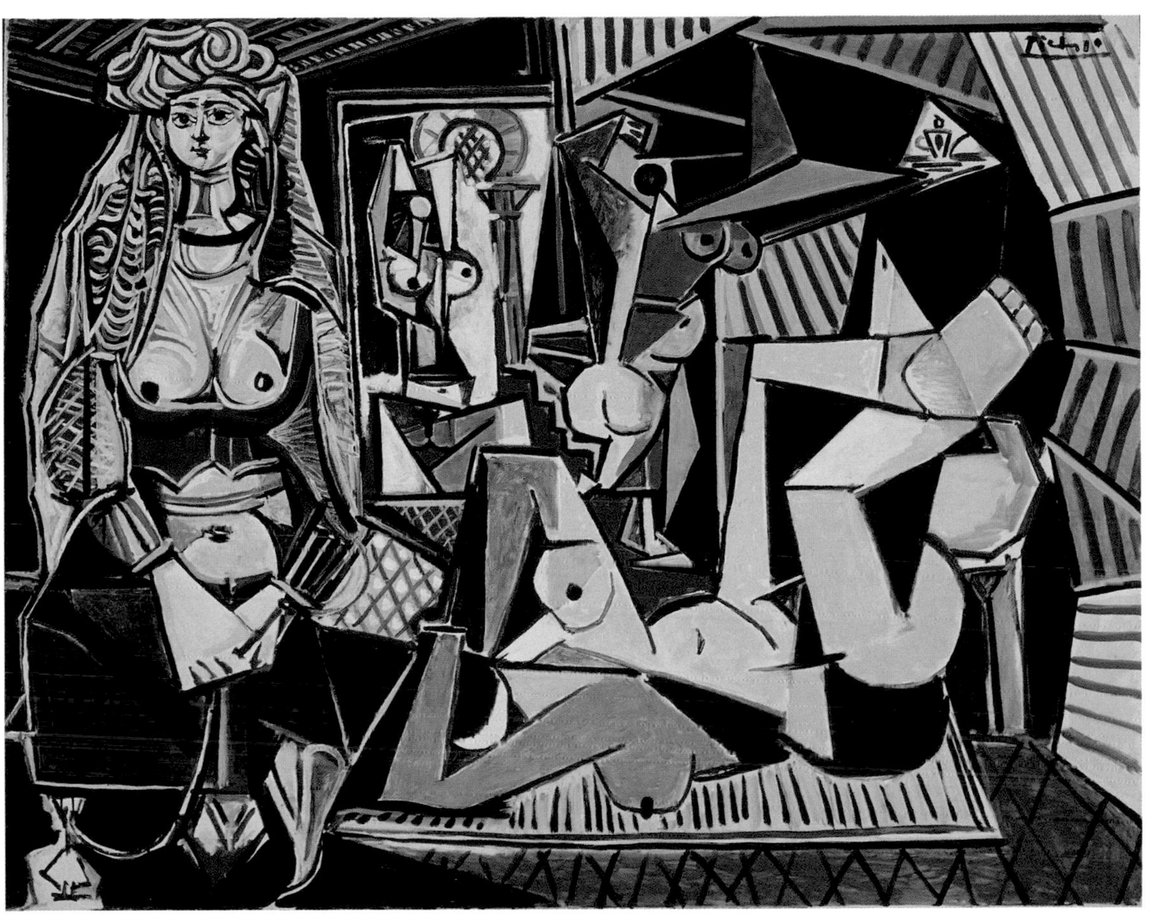

Las Meninas No. 1, 1957

Delacroix's *Women of Algiers* was by no means the only Old-Master painting that Picasso chose to revisit in his old age. In 1957 he turned his attention to Velazquez's *Las Meninas* (1656), producing over 50 variations on the work. Later still he produced multiple images based upon Edouard Manet's (1832–83) *Déjeuner sur l'herbe* (1863) and Jacques-Louis David's (1748–1825) *Rape of the Sabines* (1794–99). Velazquez's *Las Meninas*, in many ways, provided the ideal model for Picasso to reinvent. Not only did Velazquez hail from Picasso's native Spain, but also the work focused on the subject of the painter and his model, one that had resonated in Picasso's work throughout his career. Some of the *Las Meninas* variations adopted the bright colours and Cubist-inspired distortions of his 1930s figures. This one, the first of the series, is executed using a monochrome palette to recall the muted tones of Velazquez's original work. All the main figures are included, right down to the dog in the right foreground. The left-hand side is dominated by the image of the artist – here with a Cubist-style simultaneous full-face and profile.

CREATED

Cannes

MEDIUM

Oil on canvas

SERIES/PERIOD/MOVEMENT

Late period

SIMILAR WORKS

Las Meninas by Diego Velazquez, 1636

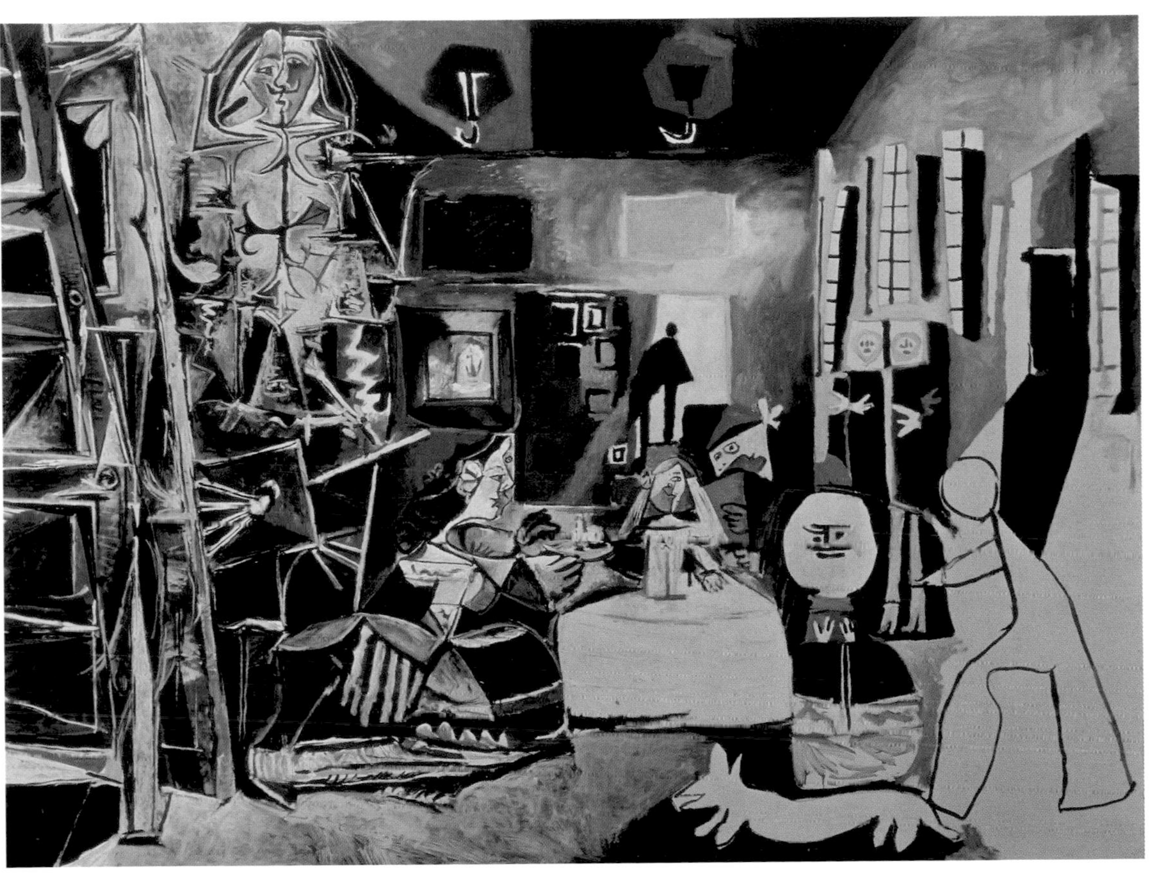

Bullfight, 1959 (published in *Toros y Toreros*, 1961)

Throughout the late 1950s and early 1960s Picasso's attention was increasingly drawn to his native Spain. No longer able – or in fact willing – to return to the country still run by the Fascist dictator General Franco, Picasso conjured up images of his homeland in his works. In addition to reintroducing the bull into a number of his paintings and sculptures, he also produced illustrations for two books, *La Tauromaquia* ('The Art of Bullfighting') published in 1957, and *Toros y Toreros* ('Bulls and Toreadors') published in 1961. Both celebrated the traditional Spanish bullfight. In this particular rendering, for the latter publication, the for-once victorious bull has succeeded in goring its tormentor and has thrown both the horse and rider into the air. Picasso's passion for bullfighting is evidenced by the frequency with which he attended such events in the main arenas of the south of France, at Arles and Fréjus. The artist later confessed that many of his bullfighting scenes were produced on Sundays when he was unable to attend the festivals he regarded as such a key part of his Spanish cultural identity.

CREATED

Mougins

MEDIUM

India ink and coloured crayon on paper

SERIES/PERIOD/MOVEMENT

Late period

SIMILAR WORKS

The Bullfight by Francisco de Goya, 1816

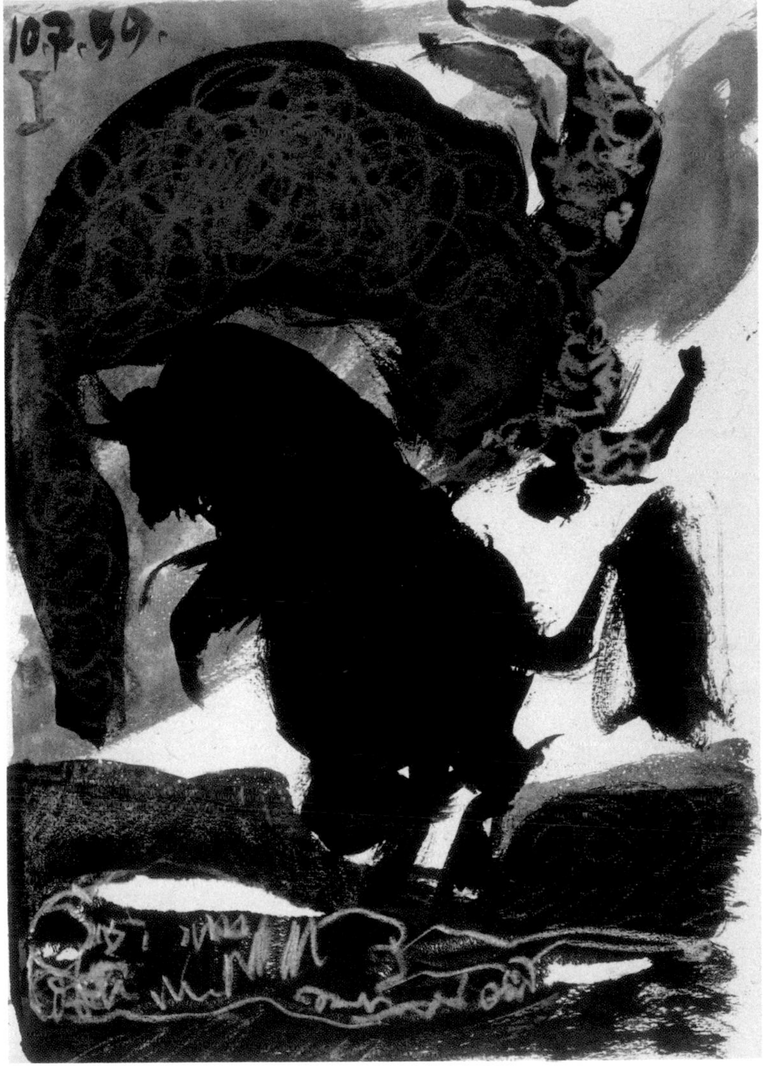
10.7.59.
I

Bust of a Seated Woman, 1960

Courtesy of Private Collection, Giraudon/www.bridgeman.co.uk/© Succession Picasso/DACS 2005

By 1960 Picasso was well established as the grand old man of modern art. Now approaching his eightieth birthday, he had recently been celebrated with major exhibitions in the United States and Europe, and had been commissioned to complete a mural for the UNESCO building in Paris. Ever creative, he also began a series of sculptures using sheet metal, thus engaging once more with an entirely new medium. He also continued to paint female nudes – such as this *Bust of a Seated Woman*, based upon Jacqueline – in a variety of styles. In 1961 he and Jacqueline were married and, in the next year alone, Picasso produced over 70 portraits of his new wife. High honours continued to follow. In 1962 he was awarded the Lenin Peace Prize for the second time; he had been an earlier recipient of the award in 1950. The following year saw the opening of the Museo Picasso in Barcelona, later to house many works donated by Picasso's family. However, the same year witnessed the death of two of his close friends, Braque and Cocteau, which deeply saddened the aging artist.

CREATED

Vauvenargues

MEDIUM

Oil on canvas

SERIES/PERIOD/MOVEMENT

Late period

SIMILAR WORKS

Bust of a Woman by Pierre Auguste Renoir, 1873–75

Female Nude by Amedeo Modigliani, 1916

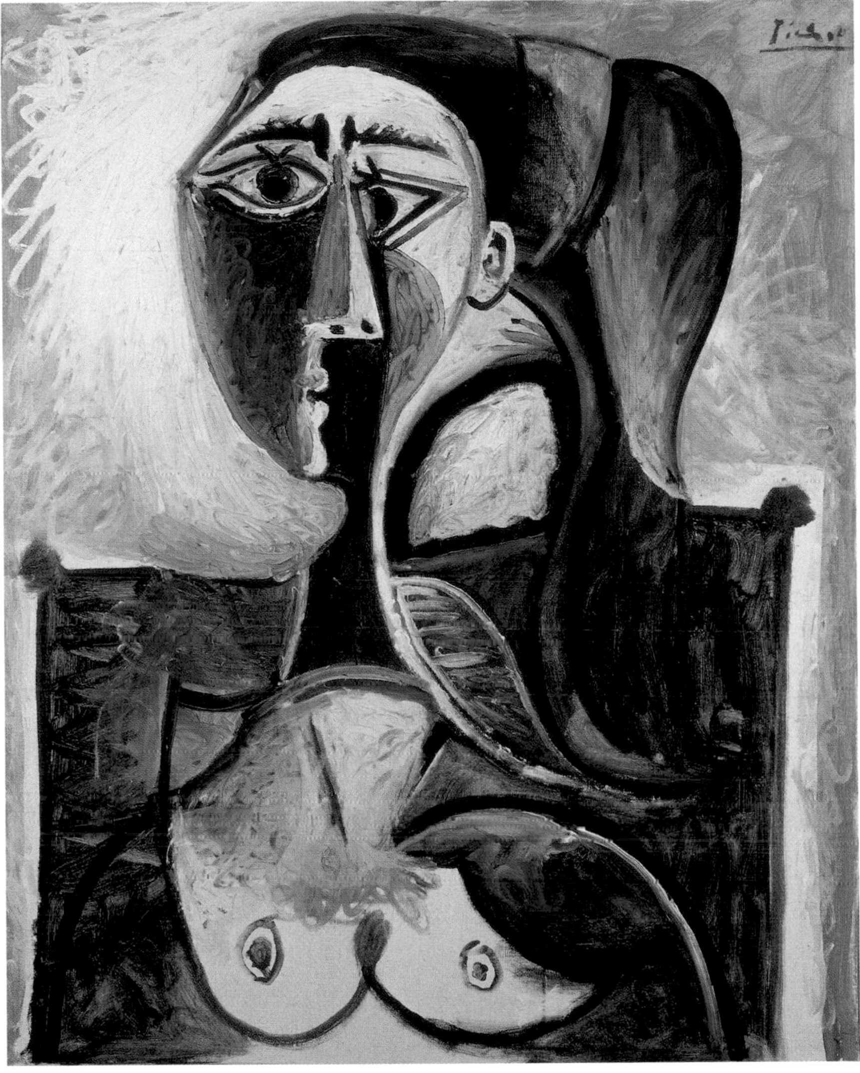

Reclining Nude, 1968

Picasso remained remarkably fit and agile well into his old age. In 1965, however, at the grand old age of 83, Picasso made what was to be his last trip to Paris. Two years later he was still confrontational enough to refuse the Legion d'Honneur offered to him by the French state. Picasso never returned to his native Spain, having refused to set foot on Spanish soil while the country remained under the Fascist dictatorship of General Franco. However, in 1968 he did donate a large number of his *Las Meninas* works to the Museo Picasso in Barcelona, though he was never to see the museum himself. Picasso's output barely diminished at this time. In 1968 he produced a large number of etchings and gouaches, many of a highly erotic nature. Amongst these is this sketch of a reclining nude. Here the figure is represented as if clothed in a red dress. The transparency of the material, however, reveals Picasso's continuing fascination with the naked female form and his explicit emphasis on the sexual organs.

CREATED

Mougins

MEDIUM

Gouache on paper

SERIES/PERIOD/MOVEMENT

Late period

SIMILAR WORKS

Large Reclining Nude by Henri Matisse, 1935

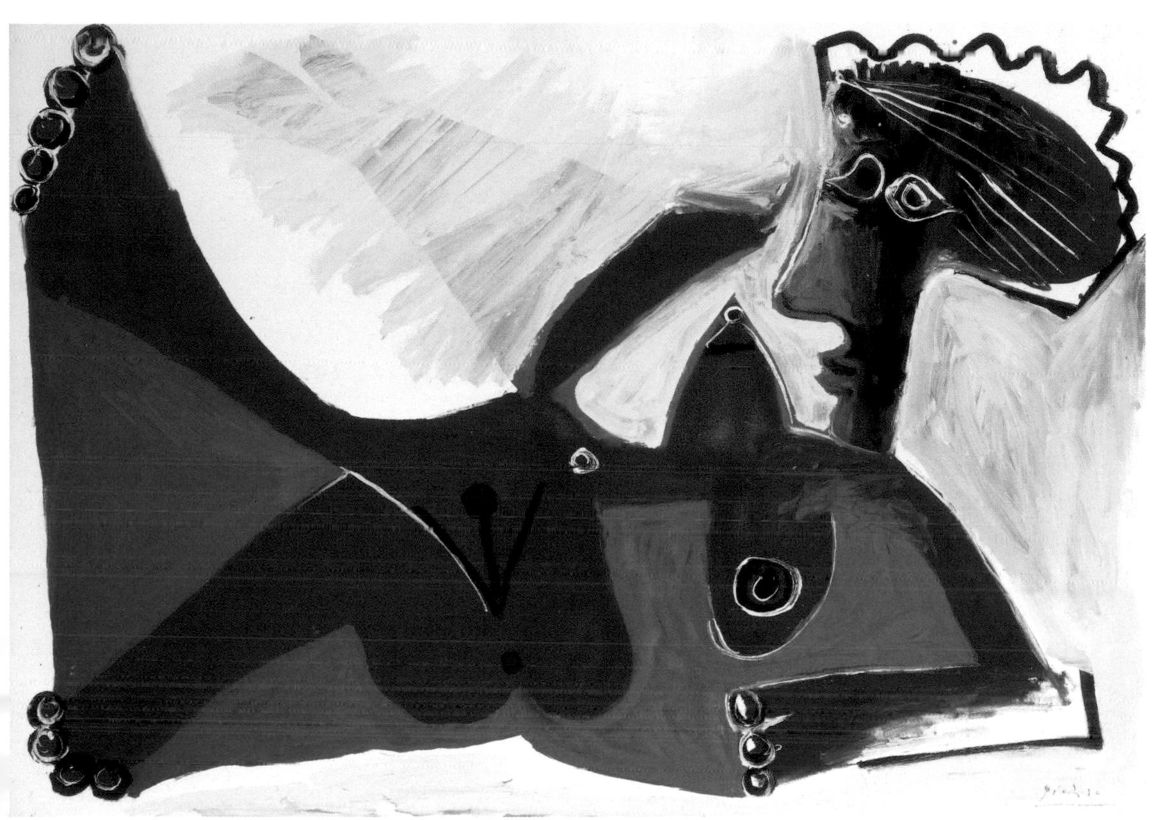

Flautist and Child (Fatherhood), 1971

In October 1971 Picasso celebrated his ninetieth birthday. Despite the inevitable frailties brought on by old age he remained active, producing a large number of drawings and oil paintings. Among these late works is *Flautist and Child (Fatherhood)*, an enigmatic painting that introduces a reference back to childhood. Here a bearded figure, dressed in the costume of a cavalier, stands beside a young child. In his right hand he carries a flute, although the musical instrument is held more like a pen or brush. It seems far from clear here what the relationship between the older man and the younger child might be. However, the child notably leans forward towards the instrument, thus suggesting the process of passing skill on from one generation to the next. Is Picasso, towards the end of his life, recalling the artistic education he received at the hands of his father? Picasso continued to produce both drawings and paintings right up to his final days. He died in April 1973, aged 91, and was buried in the grounds of the Chateau at Vauvenargues, near the foot of Monte Sainte-Victoire.

CREATED

Mougins

MEDIUM

Oil on canvas

SERIES/PERIOD/MOVEMENT

Late period

SIMILAR WORKS

Young Flute Player by Judith Leyster, *c.* 1630–35

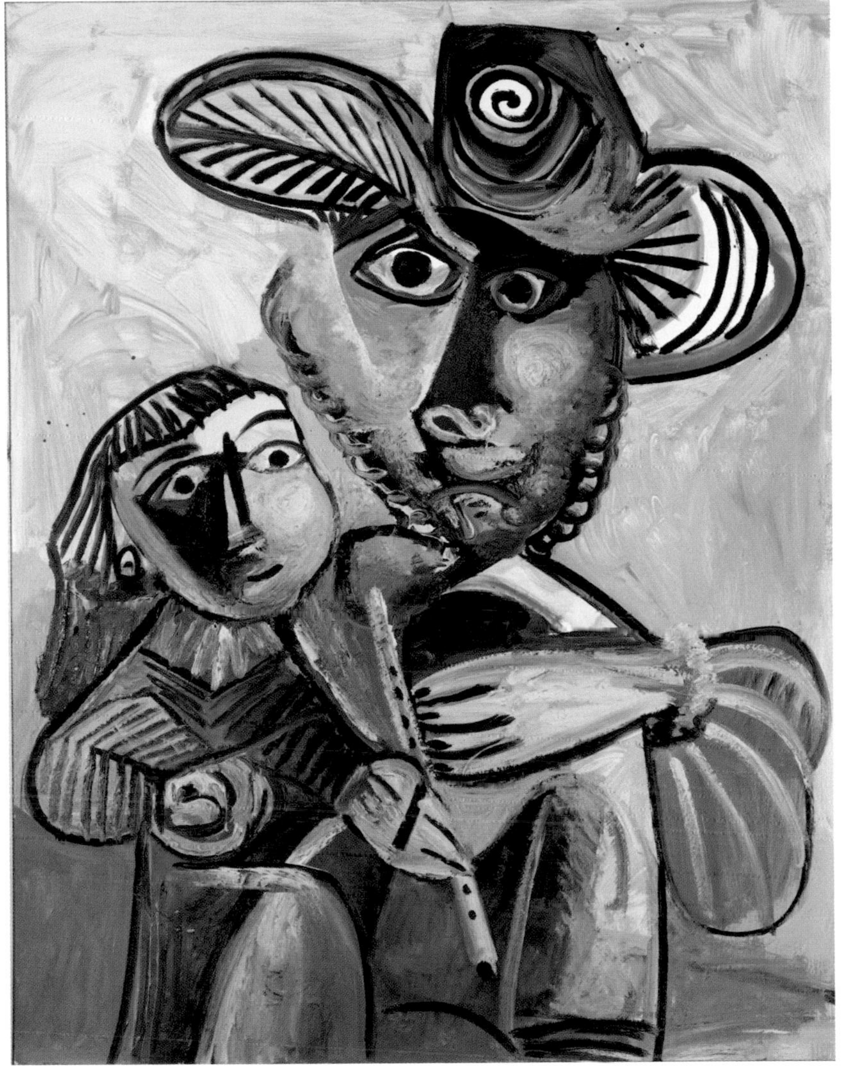

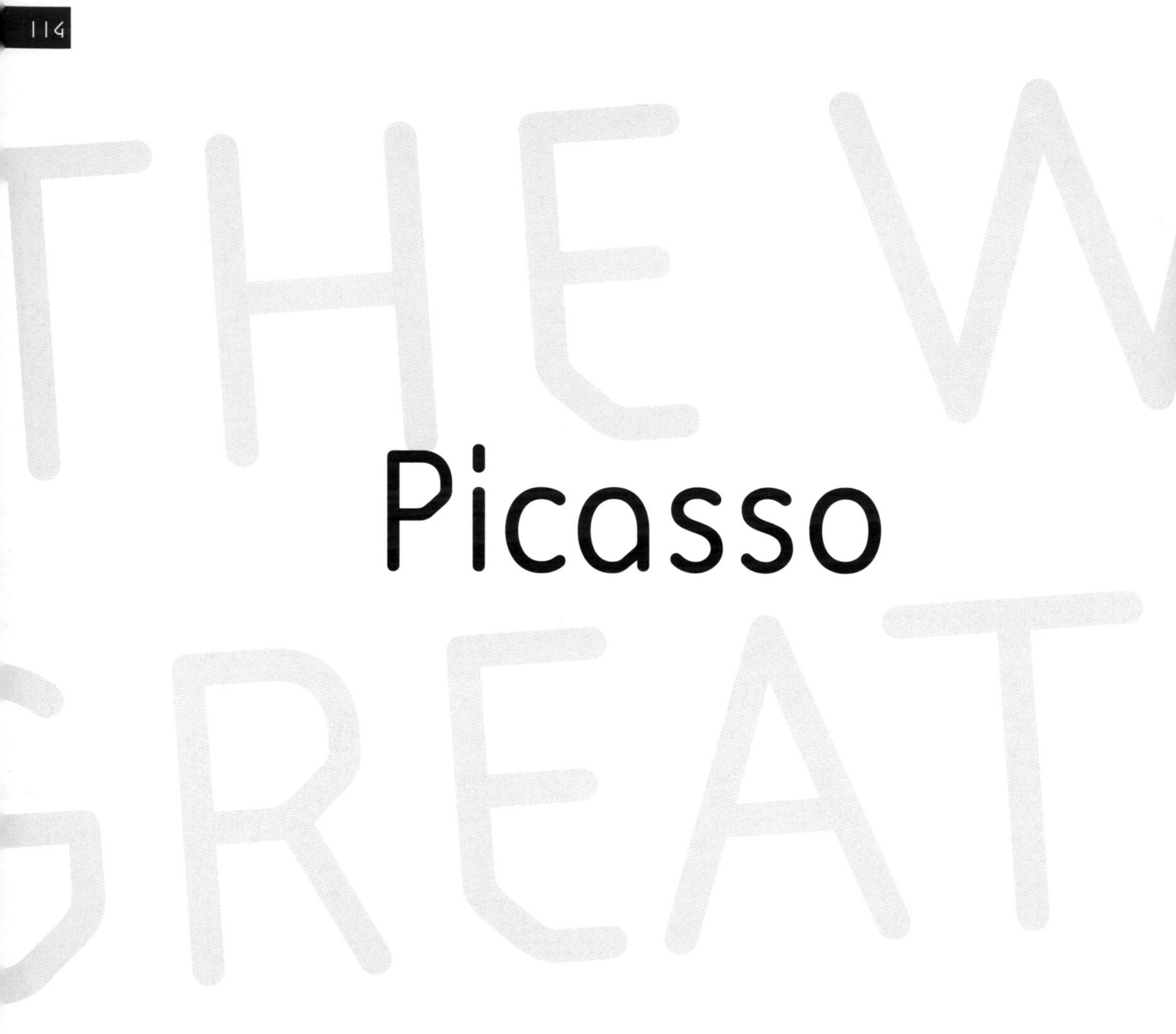

Picasso

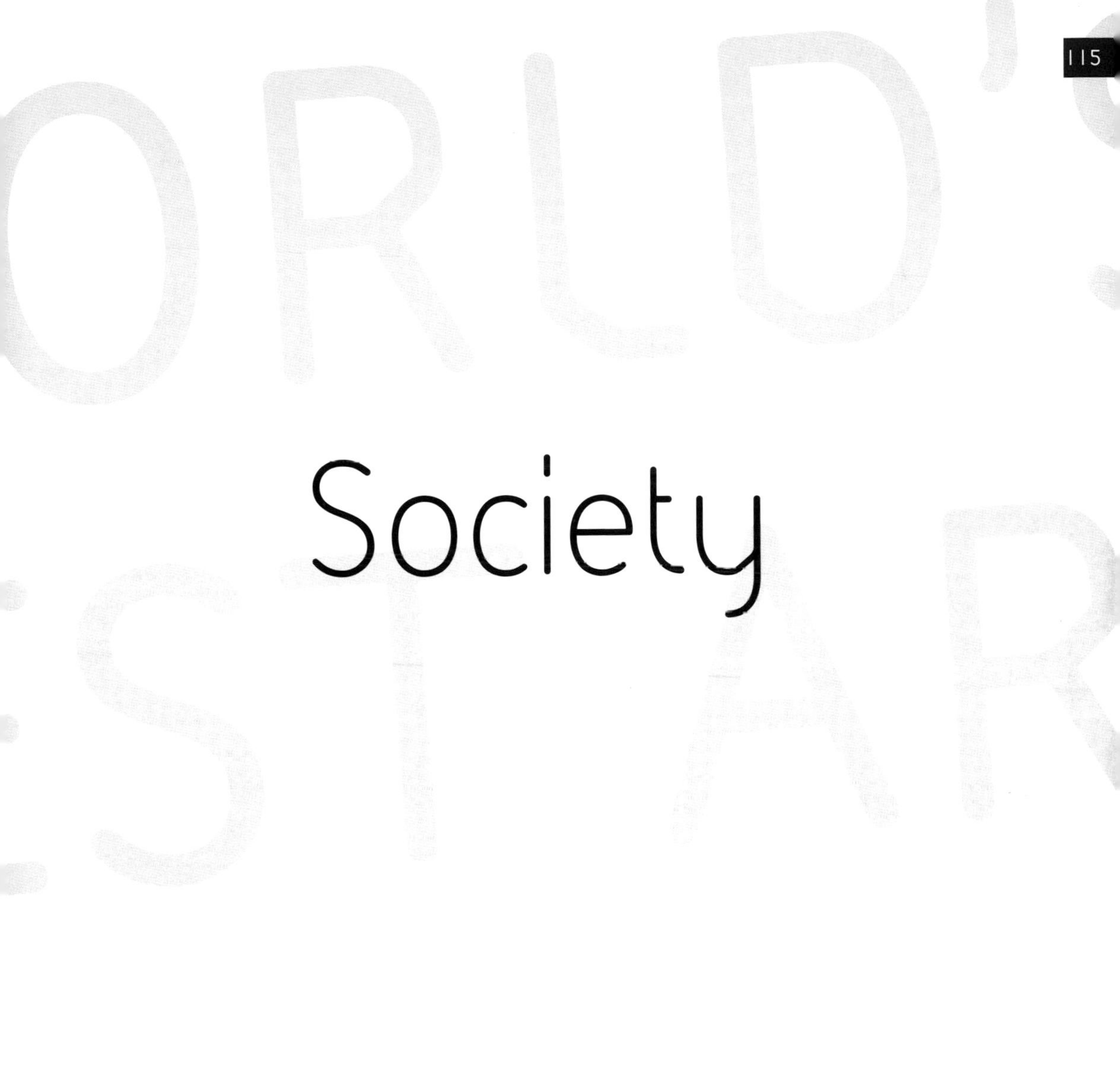

Society

The Saltimbanques or *Harlequin and his Companion*, 1901

Picasso's interest in social outcasts such as street performers, or saltimbanques, dated from his days as a student in Barcelona. At the turn of the century, Barcelona was the principal city of Catalonia in northern Spain. This thriving industrial centre was rapidly transforming as rural populations migrated to the city, thus bringing together a mixture of classes and political opinions. In this climate Barcelona soon became renowned as a centre of anarchism. Picasso met many Catalan intellectuals and dissidents at the Four Cats Café, which he regularly frequented and where he was made well aware of left-wing politics. Having witnessed first-hand the urban poverty brought about by industrialization, Picasso and his friends were largely sympathetic to these left-wing views. After his first trip to Paris in 1900, Picasso took up the issue of the alienated and dispossessed of the city in his work. Street performers, such as the figure of the harlequin, represented for Picasso the dark side of the city and would feature prominently in his work over the next few years.

CREATED

Paris

MEDIUM

Oil on canvas

SERIES/PERIOD/MOVEMENT

Early period

SIMILAR WORKS

Wandering Saltimbanques by Honoré Daumier, *c.* 1847–50

Pierrot and Harlequin by Paul Cézanne, 1888

Pablo Picasso *Born* 1881 Málaga, Spain

Died 1973

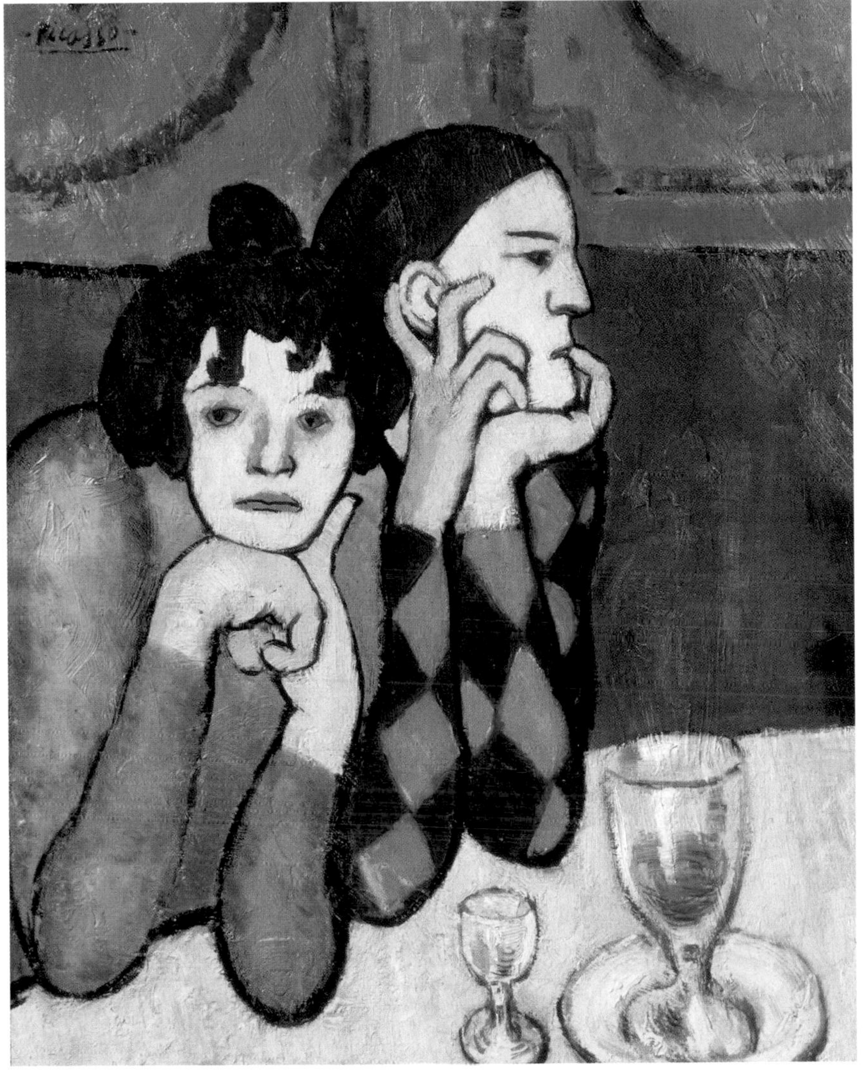

Woman with a Chignon, 1901

When Picasso first went to Paris he gravitated to the north of the city, to Montmartre. At this time the area had an established reputation as the bohemian quarter. For years it had been a magnet for artists and intellectuals, particularly those that could not afford the more expensive rents in the city centre. It was widely regarded as a dangerous but enticing area. Life in Montmartre was largely centred upon the numerous cafés and cabarets, where friends gathered to discuss art and politics, to consume alcohol and, frequently, to meet up with prostitutes. Many nineteenth-century artists, most notably Henri de Toulouse-Lautrec (1864–1901), had built their reputations upon their knowledge of the seamier side of Montmartre, and Picasso worked very much within this tradition. *Woman with a Chignon* focuses upon a woman seated alone in a café, seemingly waiting and gazing towards the spectator. The representation seems to allude to prostitution. However, Picasso does not show his woman as enticing or appealing. Instead, he has emphasized the boredom and drudgery of the profession and the ill-effects it has upon the individual.

CREATED

Paris

MEDIUM

Oil on canvas

SERIES/PERIOD/MOVEMENT

Early period

SIMILAR WORKS

In a Café (The Absinthe Drinker) by Edgar Degas, 1875–76

Interior of a Café by Edouard Manet, 1880

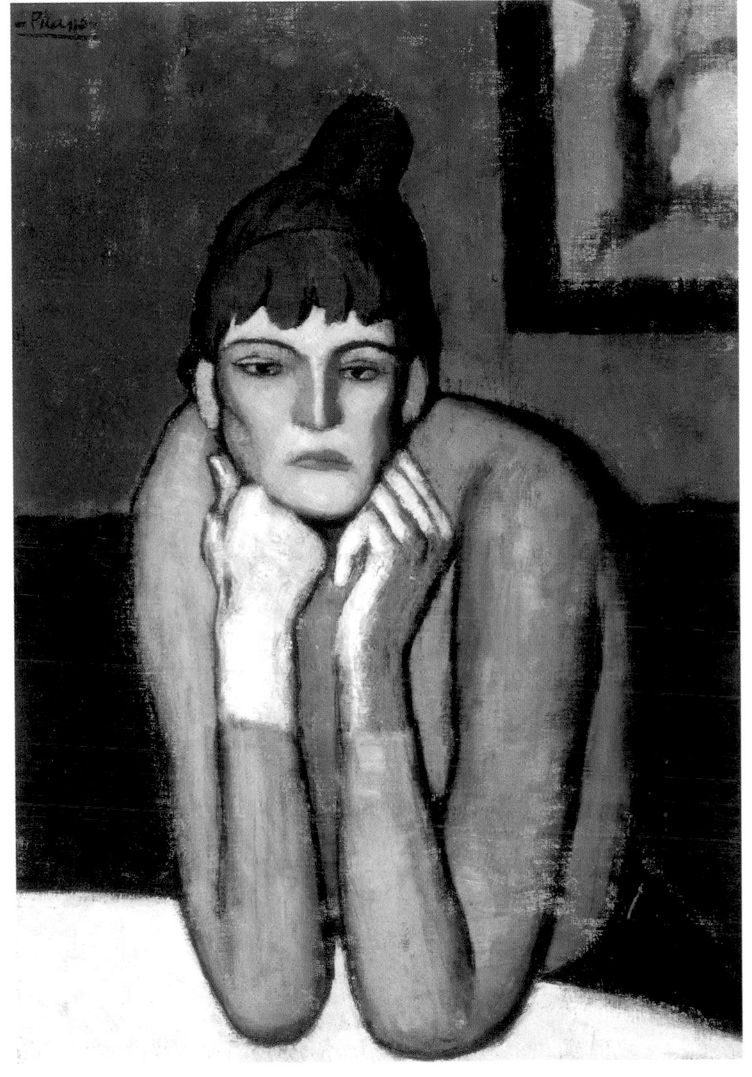

The Absinthe Drinker, 1901

Picasso's emphasis on social deprivation did not only have its origins in the work of other artists. Literature and drama – from the novels of Emile Zola (1840–1902) to the plays of Henrik Ibsen (1828–1906) – had highlighted the darker sides of society. One major concern of the era was the ill-effects of alcoholism, particularly among the working classes. Picasso's *The Absinthe Drinker* certainly shows awareness of this issue. The work represents a woman seated at a café table, with a siphon and glass before her. The lurid green colour of the drink confirms that this is absinthe, a wormwood-flavoured liqueur that had become popular during the late nineteenth century. Picasso's image represents a woman seemingly drinking alone. Her elongated limbs and extended fingers clutch at her own body as she sits staring into space, lost in her own world. The ambiguous costume and harshly defined features, exaggerated by the cruel light of the café, make the figure seem almost masculine, and only the hairstyle identifies this figure as female. Here, the consumption of absinthe is explicitly associated with a mood of hopelessness and destitution.

CREATED

Paris

MEDIUM

Oil on canvas

SERIES/PERIOD/MOVEMENT

Early period

SIMILAR WORKS

Plum Brandy by Edouard Manet, 1877

Portrait of Jaime Sabartés Y Gual by Picasso, 1901

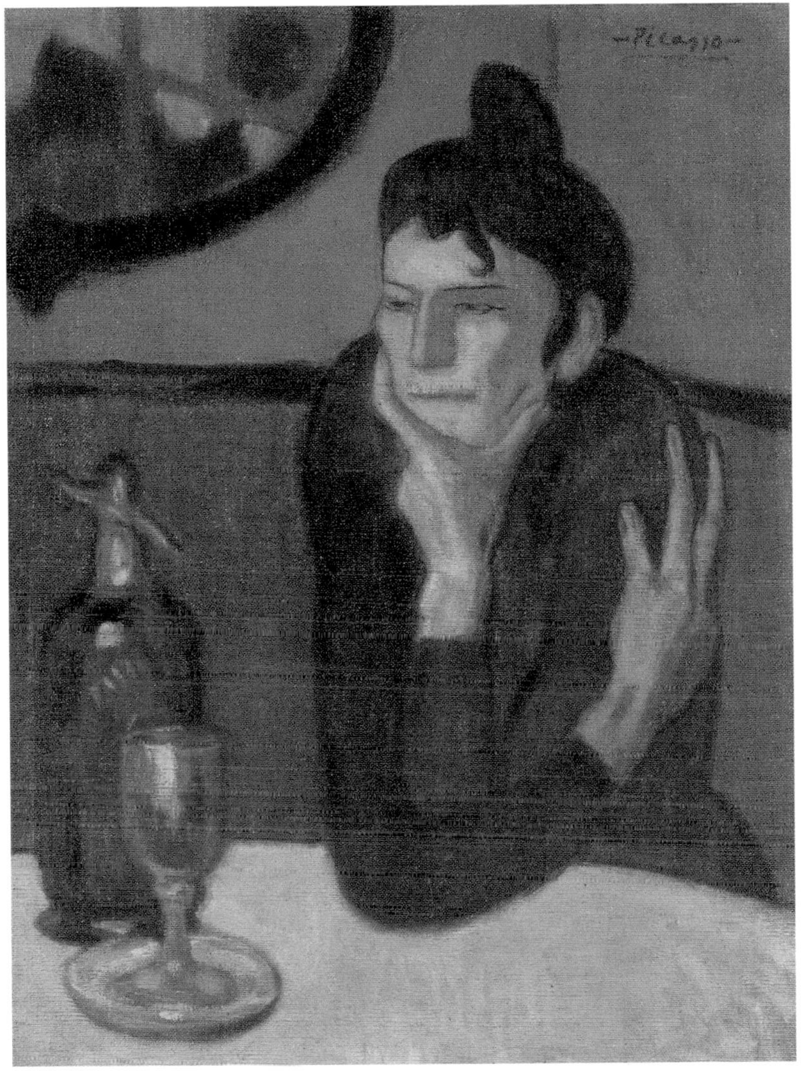
Picasso

Portrait of Gustave Coquiot, 1901

Picasso's portrait of Gustave Coquiot was produced on his second trip to Paris in 1901. As a writer, Coquiot agreed to provide a favourable review of Picasso's exhibition at Vollard's gallery, and Picasso provided the portrait as 'recompense'. In many ways Coquiot was an appropriate choice of reviewer. He regularly wrote about the more risqué side of Montmartre life, and the cafés and cabarets frequented by both artists and prostitutes. Picasso's portrait of Coquiot captures the mood of this world. Coquiot himself is dressed in white tie and tails – the uniform of the bourgeoisie at leisure. His immaculate moustache and goatee beard betray his concern for his own appearance. Coquiot occupies an ambiguous space, however, that could be defined as a nightclub, or indeed one of the countless brothels of Montmartre. Women stretch languorously and seductively behind Coquiot's head, as if they are the visual articulation of his lurid thoughts. The portrait aptly captures the social milieu of turn-of-the-century Paris, with its class divisions and decadent pleasures.

CREATED

Paris

MEDIUM

Oil on canvas

SERIES/PERIOD/MOVEMENT

Early period

SIMILAR WORKS

M. Boileau at the Café by Henri de Toulouse-Lautrec, 1893

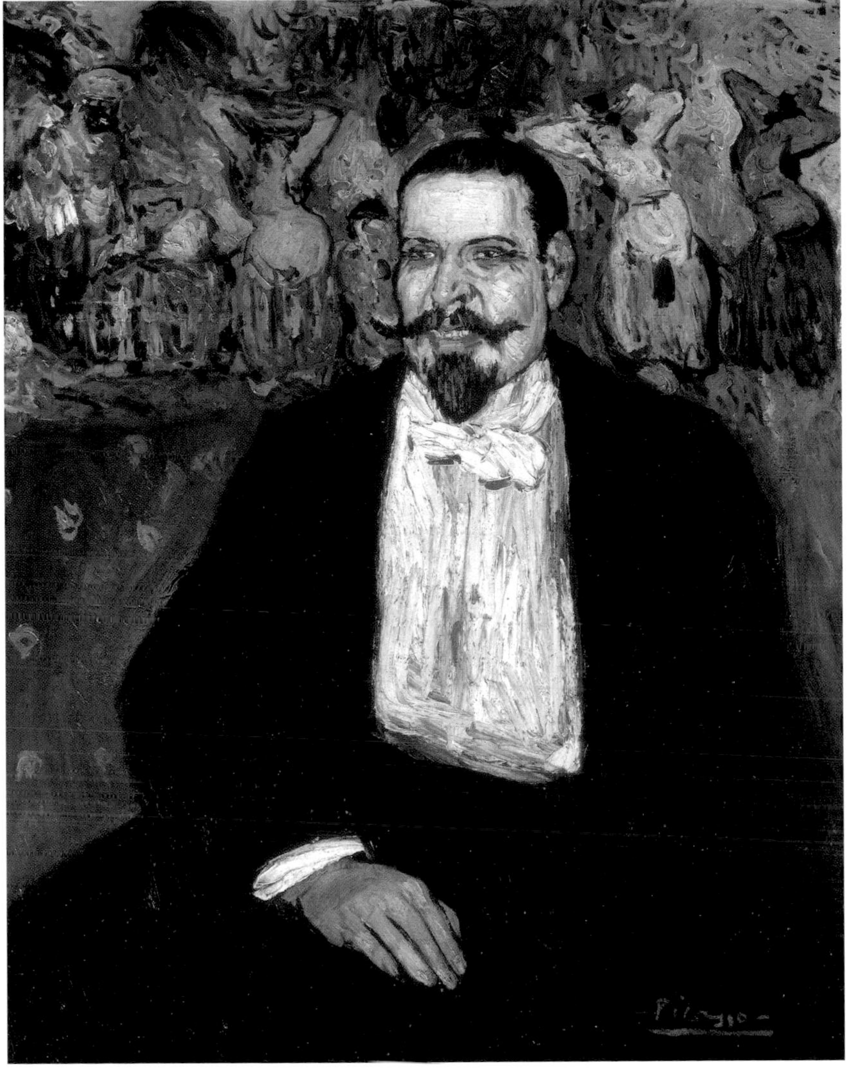

Mother and Child, c. 1901

In the late summer of 1901 Picasso visited the women's prison of Saint-Lazare. His first-hand experience of this squalid environment informed the poverty-induced melancholy of many of his 'blue-period' works. The prison was, in some respects, the product of the social circumstances of turn-of-the-century Paris. Desperate poverty had induced extensive prostitution, which in turn caused the spread of venereal diseases. This inevitably led to further desperate poverty and many of the inmates at the Saint-Lazare prison were ex-prostitutes suffering from such diseases. The prison, well known in its day, had become the subject of both artists and writers, and even appeared in the lyrics of popular songs sung in the cafés and cabarets of Montmartre. Picasso's *Mother and Child* depicts an aspect of such incarceration that particularly disturbed the artist – the presence of children in the prison. The mother, identifiable as a Saint-Lazare inmate by her white bonnet, is represented as an abject figure whose attenuated form conveys a sense of overall despair. However, Picasso has allowed a sense of hope to permeate the work, through his obvious allusion to the Madonna and Child.

CREATED

Paris

MEDIUM

Oil on canvas

SERIES/PERIOD/MOVEMENT

Blue period

SIMILAR WORKS

Madonna and Child by Raphael, 1505

Mother and Child by Picasso, 1921

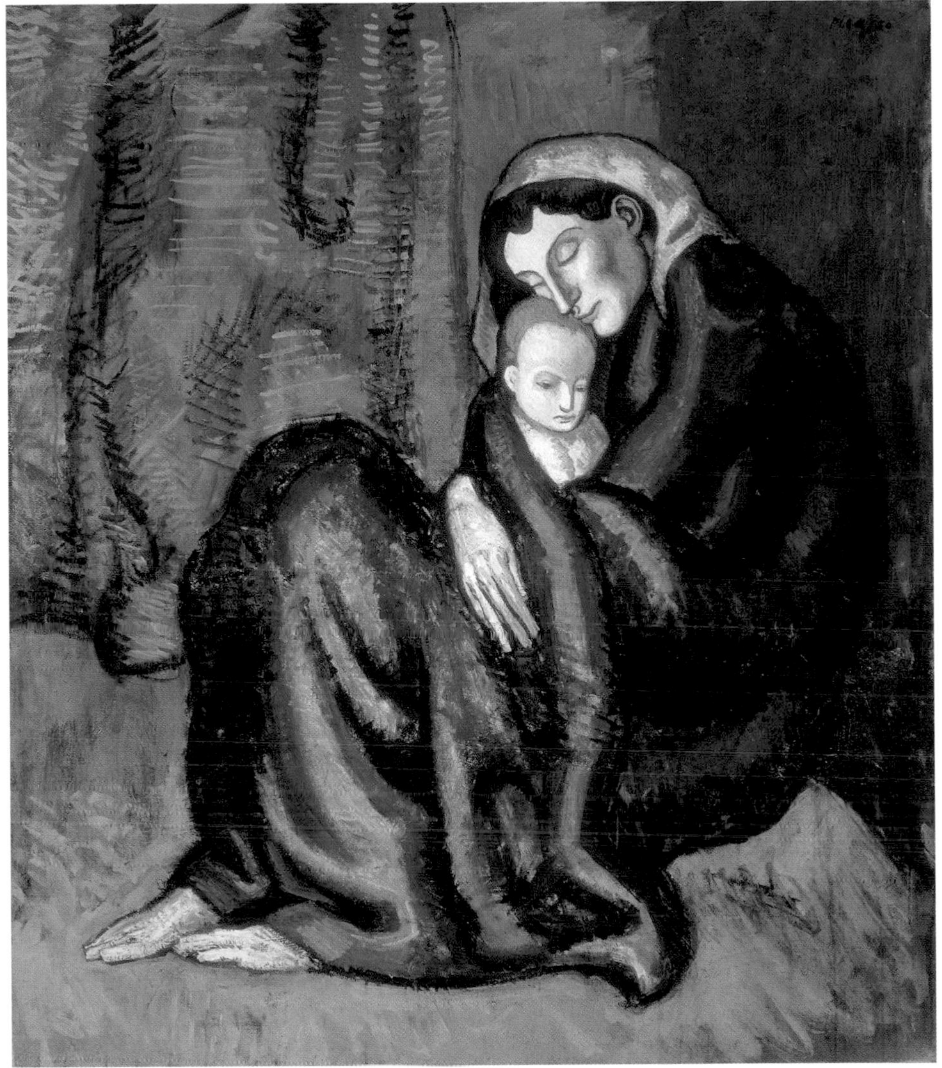

The Soup, 1902

Despite his initial success at the Vollard exhibition in 1901, Picasso's funds soon dried up. It was not unusual for the artist to go hungry during this period in Paris, but his own circumstances only heightened his awareness of the desperate poverty that frequently surrounded him. Back in Barcelona in 1902 Picasso produced the painting entitled *The Soup*. Once again he drew upon his experiences in visiting the women's prison of Saint-Lazare. However, he also harked back to a visit he had made to the Pantheon to see the murals, completed five years earlier by the French Symbolist painter Pierre Puvis de Chavannes (1824–98). One of Puvis' scenes from the life of St Geneviève notably represented a starving woman being assisted in the street. Picasso sketched this scene, which probably influenced his decision to paint a similar moment. *The Soup*, however, is intriguingly ambiguous. Is the older woman, physically weighed down by her destitution, giving the soup to the small child or receiving it from her? Either way, Picasso centres the act of charity upon the basic need for nourishment.

CREATED

Barcelona

MEDIUM

Oil on canvas

SERIES/PERIOD/MOVEMENT

Blue period

SIMILAR WORKS

Scene from the Life of St Geneviève in the Pantheon in Paris by Pierre Puvis de Chavannes, 1874–78

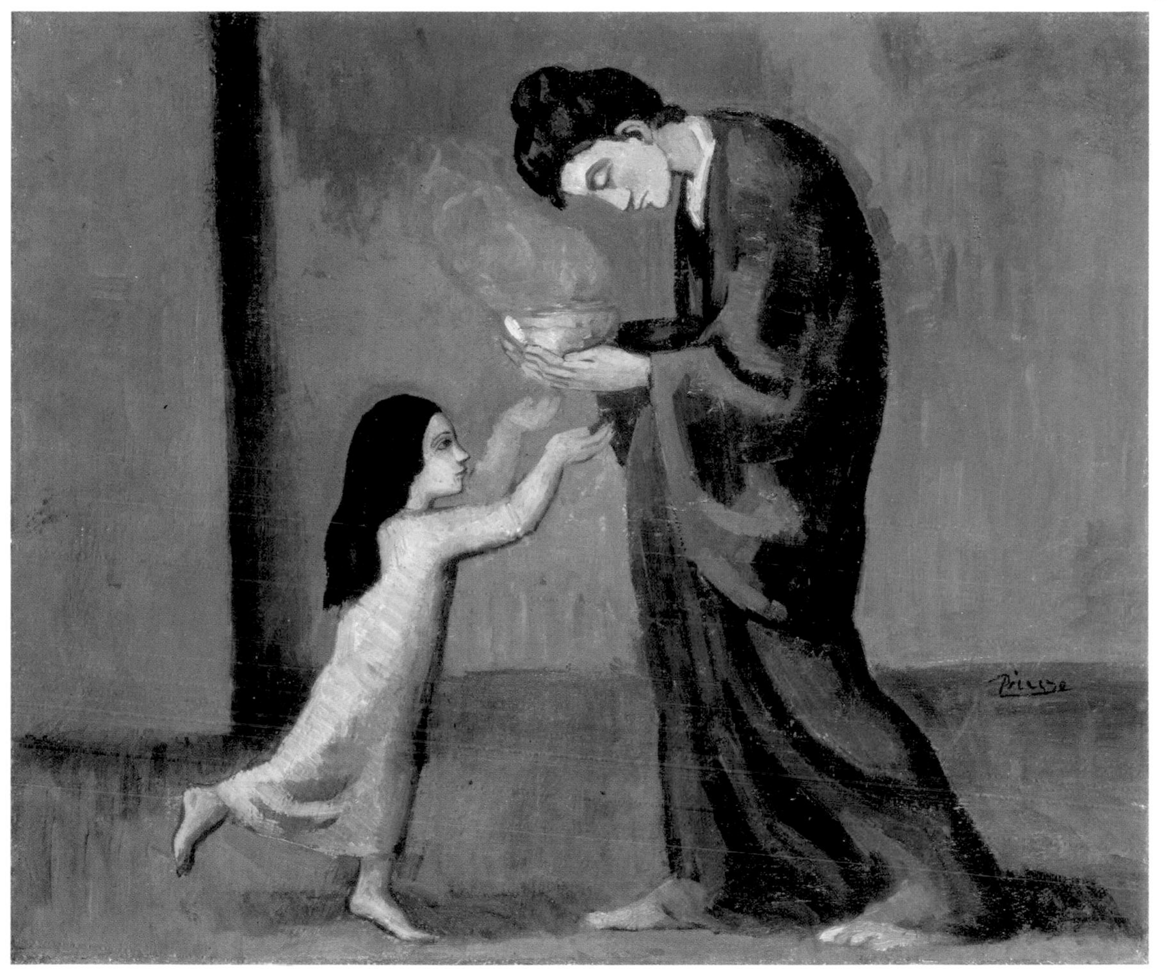

The Old Guitarist, 1903

Like many of his 'blue-period' works, *The Old Guitarist* was produced back in Barcelona but drew upon Picasso's experiences of the poverty and hardship that he both experienced and witnessed in Paris. It is, perhaps, hard to imagine Picasso producing these starkly cold images in the midst of a Spanish summer, but here Picasso was expressing some of the anxieties that plagued his life. *The Old Guitarist*, which represents a gaunt figure with notably sunken eyes, can be considered as one of a series of works produced at this time that specifically address the subject of blindness. Others include *The Blind Beggar* and *The Blind Man's Meal*. This obsession may be linked to the deteriorating sight of Picasso's own father at this time, but could equally betray the artist's anxieties about contracting syphilis, which was known to cause blindness. Picasso's portrait of the one-eyed brothel keeper Carlota Valdivia, produced the following year, could provide further evidence of this concern, widely held amongst the bohemian community of Montmartre.

CREATED

Barcelona

MEDIUM

Oil on wood

SERIES/PERIOD/MOVEMENT

Blue period

SIMILAR WORKS

The Guitar Player by Edouard Manet, 1860

Gypsy with a Mandolin by Jean Baptiste Camille Corot, 1874

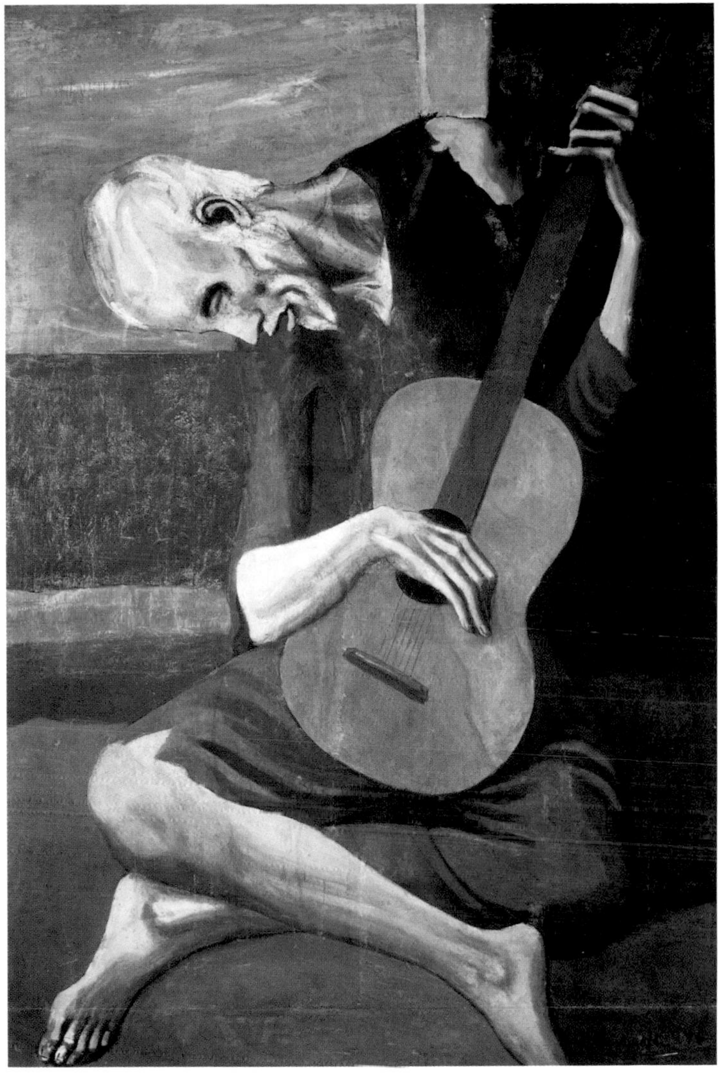

Les Misérables, 1904

Courtesy of Private Collection/www.bridgeman.co.uk/© Succession Picasso/DACS 2005

In 1904, when Picasso finally moved permanently to Paris, he continued to produce works emphasizing the loneliness, isolation and alienation of urban poverty. However, works such as *Les Misérables* now focused upon couples rather than individuals. These images seem to offer a little more hope than many of the works of his 'blue period', emphasizing dependency and companionship. This can also be seen in his etching produced around the same time entitled *The Frugal Repast*. Picasso's personal circumstances may have contributed to this less isolated vision, not least his new life at the Montmartre studio known as the 'bateau-lavoir'. Here Picasso initially shared a single room with two other men, sleeping on the floor – though such cramped accommodation was scarcely unusual. It was also at this time that Picasso started a long-term relationship with his first great love, the model Fernande Olivier, a factor that may have contributed to the growing emphasis on couples in his work, such as the pair so tenderly represented here.

CREATED

Paris

MEDIUM

Oil on canvas

SERIES/PERIOD/MOVEMENT

Blue period

SIMILAR WORKS

In a Café (The Absinthe Drinker) by Edgar Degas, 1875–76

The Frugal Repast by Picasso, 1904

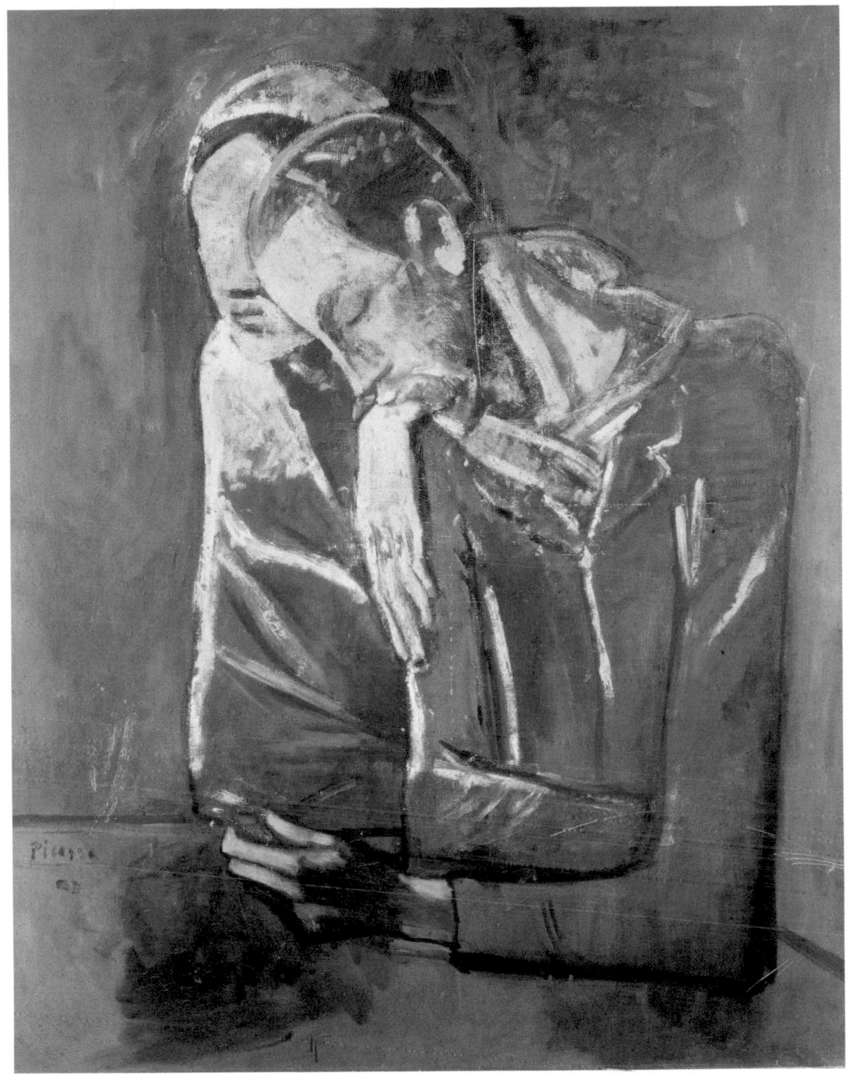
Picasso

Portrait of Suzanne Bloch, 1904

Picasso's interest in portraying musicians and actors stemmed largely from his early visits to Paris at the turn of the century. Shortly after his Vollard exhibition of 1901, he was asked to produce a series of portrait drawings of many of the female cabaret performers of the day, including the dancer Jane Avril. The project, however, never came to fruition. Picasso's inspiration here was Toulouse-Lautrec, whose numerous portraits of Montmartre cabaret stars – including Avril, La Goulue and Yvette Guilbert – were widely known. The close relationship between artists and performers, many of whom lived cheek by jowl in Montmartre, meant that the former were frequently called upon to produce promotional material for the latter. In 1904, Picasso's close friend, the poet Max Jacob (1876–1944), introduced him to Henri Bloch and his sister Suzanne, both professional musicians. Henri had commissioned Picasso to produce a portrait of Suzanne, a well-known opera singer, in exchange for free tickets to musical events. This watercolour of Suzanne is far from being highly personalized – or flattering. Rather, the sitter is harshly caricatured in a style reminiscent of Toulouse-Lautrec.

CREATED

Paris

MEDIUM

Watercolour on paper

SERIES/PERIOD/MOVEMENT

Blue period

SIMILAR WORKS

Jane Avril Entering the Moulin Rouge by Henri de Toulouse-Lautrec, *c.* 1892

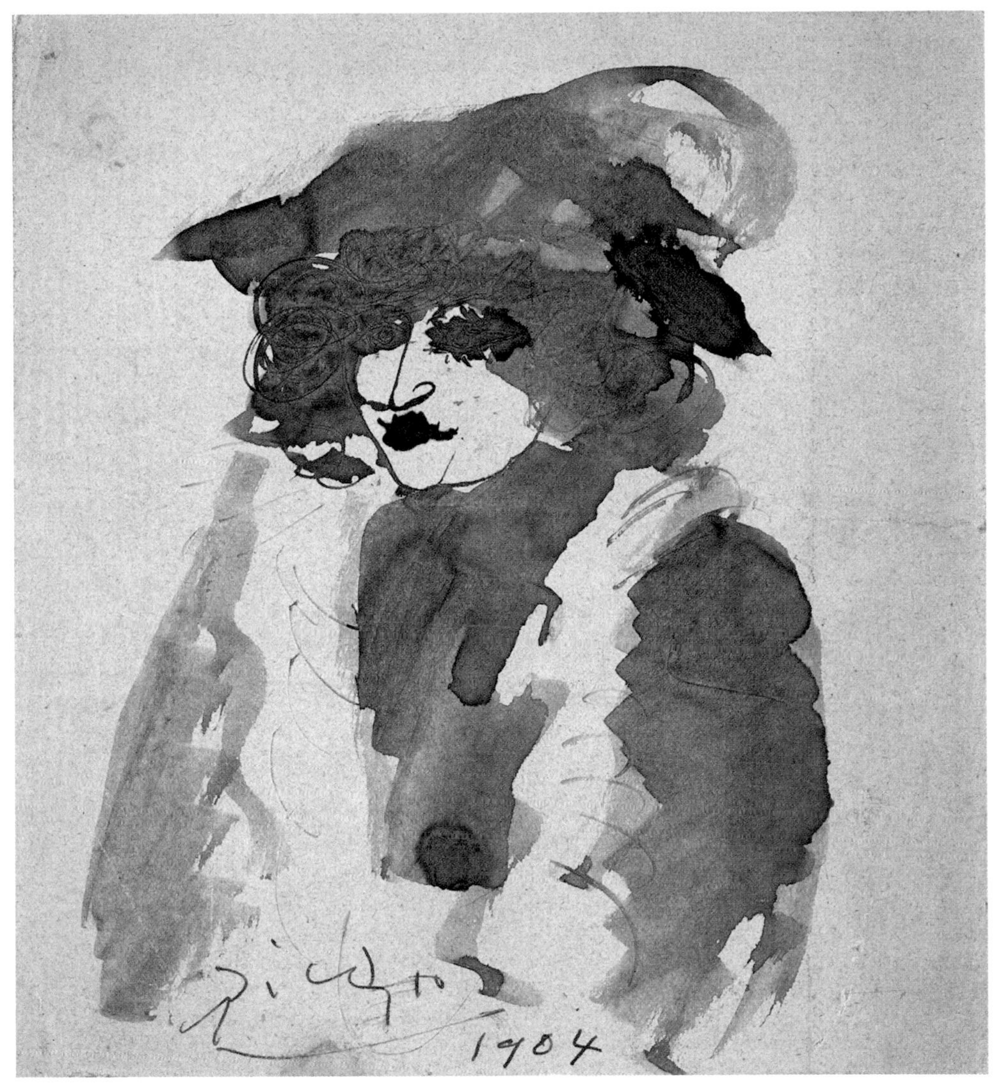
Picasso
1904

The Family of Saltimbanques, 1905

'I liked the clowns best of all.... They could invent their own outfits, their own characters, do anything they fancied.' Thus stated Picasso, referring to one of his favourite Montmartre haunts, the Médrano Circus. Picasso had shown great interest in street and circus performers from the time of his first visit to Paris. In 1905, he produced a large-scale canvas, entitled *The Family of Saltimbanques*, representing a group of such performers. This is a sketch for the finished work. Many French painters, including the Le Nain brothers, Louis (*c.* 1593–1648) and Antoine (*c.* 1588–1648), Jean-Antoine Watteau (1684–1721) and Honoré Daumier (1808–79), had earlier depicted such characters. The biggest influence on Picasso, however, was Edouard Manet's (1832–83) *The Old Musician*, first produced in 1862, but later exhibited at the Salon d'Autumne the same year that Picasso produced this work. Picasso drew extensively on his visits to the circus. However, he does not focus on the performances themselves. Instead he shows the characters as social outcasts. Nonetheless, *The Family of Saltimbanques* marks a shift in Picasso's work. Now a brighter palette and a more lyrical romanticism has replaced the despondency of the 'blue period'.

CREATED

Paris

MEDIUM

Gouache on cardboard

SERIES/PERIOD/MOVEMENT

Rose period

SIMILAR WORKS

Wandering Saltimbanques by Honoré Daumier, *c.* 1847–50

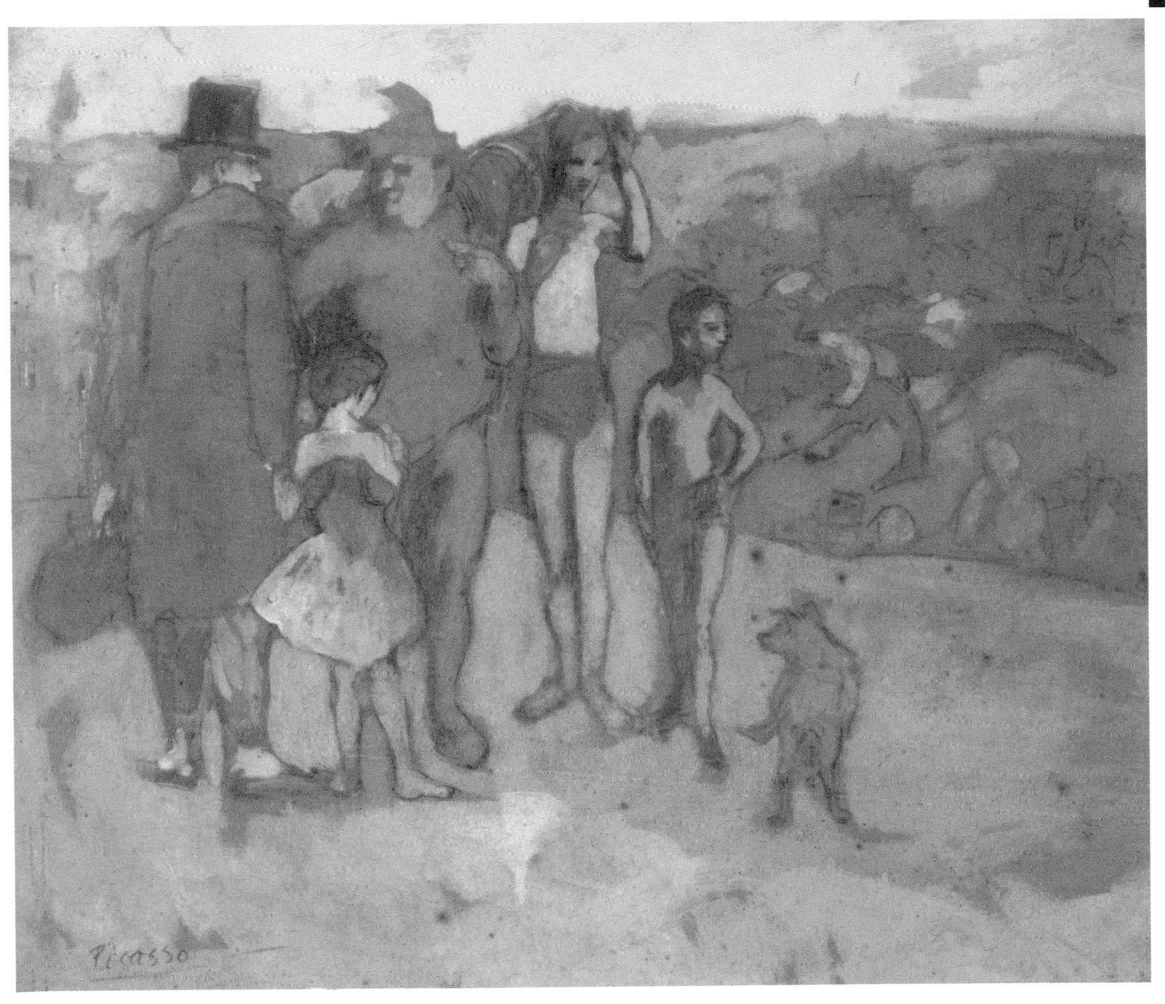
Picasso

Les Demoiselles d'Avignon, 1907

Les Demoiselles d'Avignon marked a significant shift in Picasso's career, bringing to an end the early experimentation in romantic subject-matter and heralding the arrival of Cubism. Nonetheless the work is very much the product of Picasso's early experiences, not least of all of his awareness of prostitution both in Barcelona and Paris. The painting is a confrontational representation of a group of prostitutes displaying themselves to a potential customer. One of the most striking features of the work is the distinction between the faces of the three figures on the left and the two on the right. For the latter, it is clear that Picasso was influenced by the forms of African masks he had recently seen. However, the contrast between the conventionally alluring faces on the left and the fragmented, asymmetrical and distorted features on the right seems to confound our understanding of the scene. Is Picasso perhaps revealing his anxieties about the possible ill-effects of prostitution and disease? His first-hand knowledge of the physical deformities brought on by syphilis, seen on his visits to the women's prison of Saint-Lazare, may well have suggested this to the artist.

CREATED

Paris

MEDIUM

Oil on canvas

SERIES/PERIOD/MOVEMENT

Proto-Cubist period

SIMILAR WORKS

African Masks on display at the Trocadero in Paris

Large Nude by Georges Braque, 1908

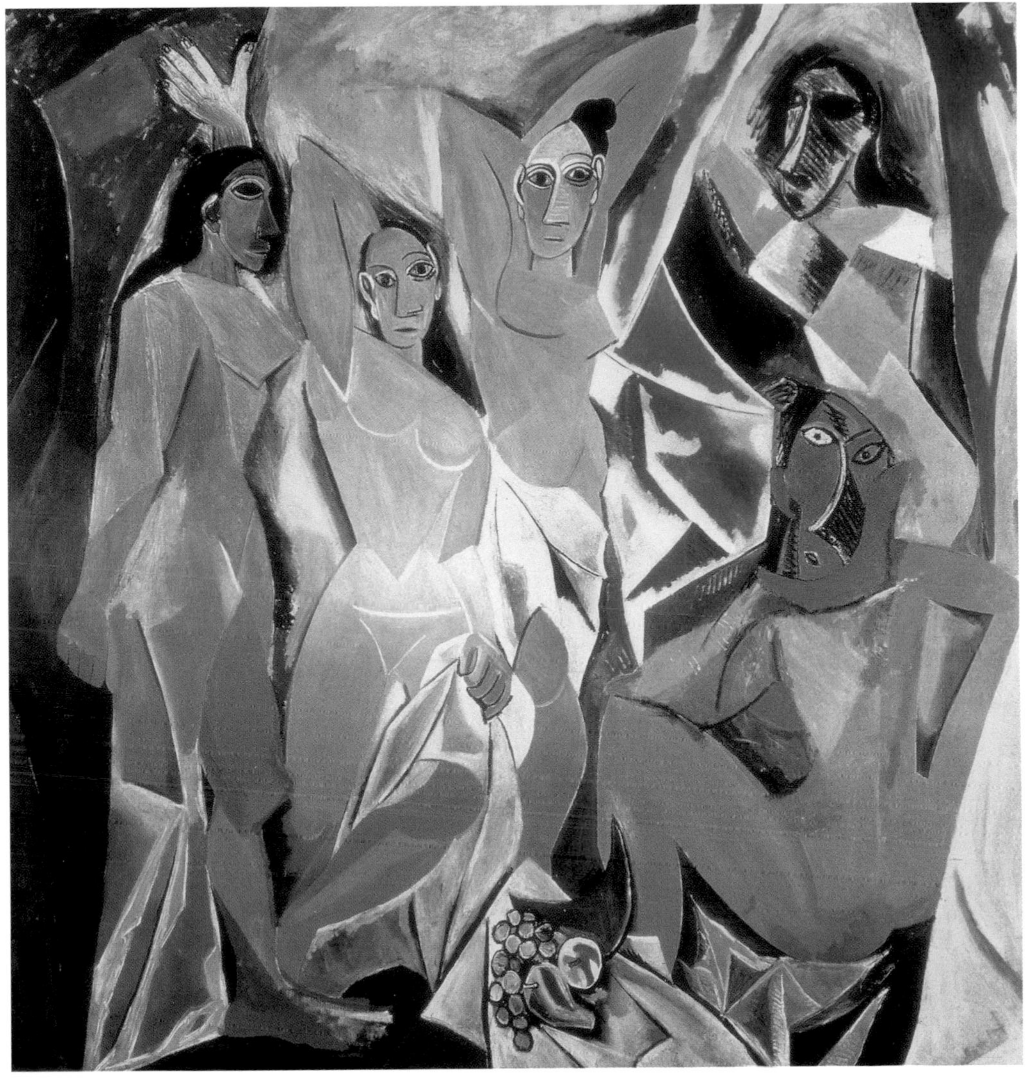

The Offering, 1908

The formal treatment of *Les Demoiselles d'Avignon* had been largely inspired by Picasso's newfound interest in sculptural forms – particularly those associated with so-called 'primitivism'. The term is today rightly regarded as somewhat problematic. In the early twentieth century, however, it was a catch-all phrase that was equally applied to the art of the past, such as the Iberian heads in the Louvre that had inspired Picasso's recent work, or to contemporary African and Oceanic art. In particular, 'primitivism' signified carving, and it is clear from many of Picasso's works of this time that he was much interested in the non-western carved masks and figures that were on display in the Trocadero, Paris's Museum of Ethnography, or available for purchase in the local flea markets. France's position as a major colonial power had certainly facilitated access to such artefacts. In this work, the simplified, mask-like facial features of the two figures in the foreground, and the schematic body of the female in the centre of the image, are clearly derived from Picasso's knowledge of these so-called 'primitive' objects.

CREATED

Paris

MEDIUM

Gouache on paper

SERIES/PERIOD/MOVEMENT

Proto-Cubist period

SIMILAR WORKS

A Modern Olympia by Paul Cézanne, *c.* 1873–74

Les Demoiselles d'Avignon by Picasso, 1907

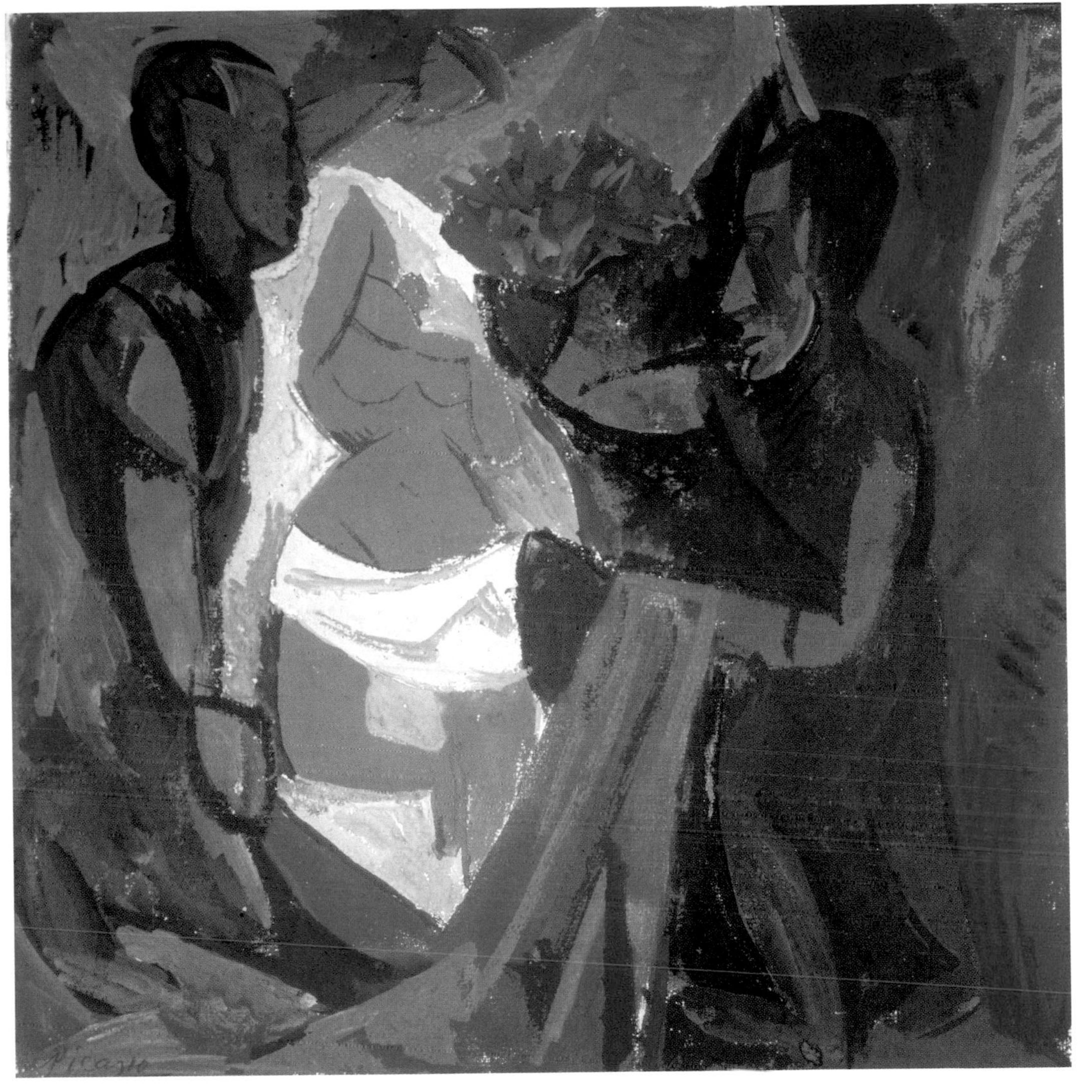

Woman Farmer (half-length), 1908

Picasso's sculptural interests, and particularly his fascination with African masks, are perhaps made most apparent in his representation of a farmer's wife, produced whilst on vacation at La Rue-des-Bois in the summer of 1908. Picasso and Fernande visited this sleepy French village, north of Paris, to escape the heat of the city. Here they rented a quiet farmhouse run by a widow named Marie-Louise Putman. Picasso was fascinated by the sheer physical presence of the woman, who was over six feet tall. He produced a series of drawings and paintings of Madame Putman, including this head-and-shoulders portrait. Picasso has reduced the facial features to simple shapes indicating hair, eyebrows, eyes, ears and a nose. He has omitted a mouth altogether. This mask-like face reduces the individual to the bare essentials of form, as if the peasant woman herself has been carved out of wood from the forest in which she lives. Here, the so-called 'primitivism' of African masks has been matched to the 'primitive' life of the French rural population, as perceived by the artist.

CREATED

La Rue-des-Bois

MEDIUM

Oil on canvas

SERIES/PERIOD/MOVEMENT

Proto-Cubist period

SIMILAR WORKS

African Masks on display at the Trocadero in Paris

Farmer's Wife by Picasso, 1908

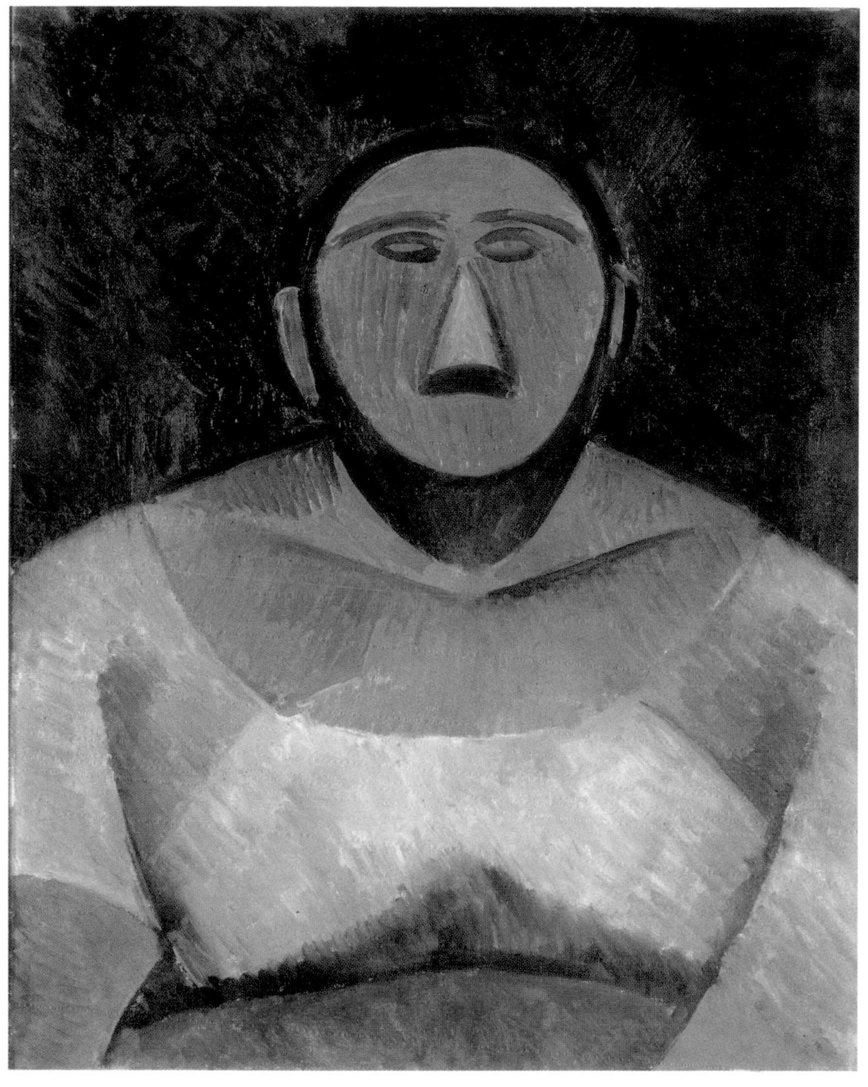

Violin, Pipe, Glass and Anchor, Souvenir of Le Havre, 1912

In the summer of 1912 Picasso took a trip to Le Havre with his close friend, the artist and co-founder of Cubism, Georges Braque (1882–1963). The previous year, Braque had introduced written letters into his groundbreaking work entitled *The Portuguese* (1909), a practice that Picasso was soon to adopt. Although relatively little is known about the trip, Picasso produced a number of works on his return to Paris that allude both to Braque and to the trip. Amongst these, *Violin, Pipe, Glass and Anchor* includes a host of visual and textual references to Le Havre. These include fragments of an anchor and a clay pipe (a popular tourist souvenir) and, amongst numerous other fragments of words, references to AVRE (for Le Havre) and FLEUR (for Honfleur, a nearby coastal resort). While these inclusions clearly relate to Picasso's personal experiences, it should not be assumed that the artist here set out to convey a prescribed meaning to the work, readily intelligible to the spectator. Instead, such works set out to explore new possibilities to represent such experiences in visual form.

CREATED

Sorgues or Paris

MEDIUM

Oil on canvas

SERIES/PERIOD/MOVEMENT

Cubist period

SIMILAR WORKS

The Portuguese by Georges Braque, 1911

Ma Jolie by Picasso, 1911

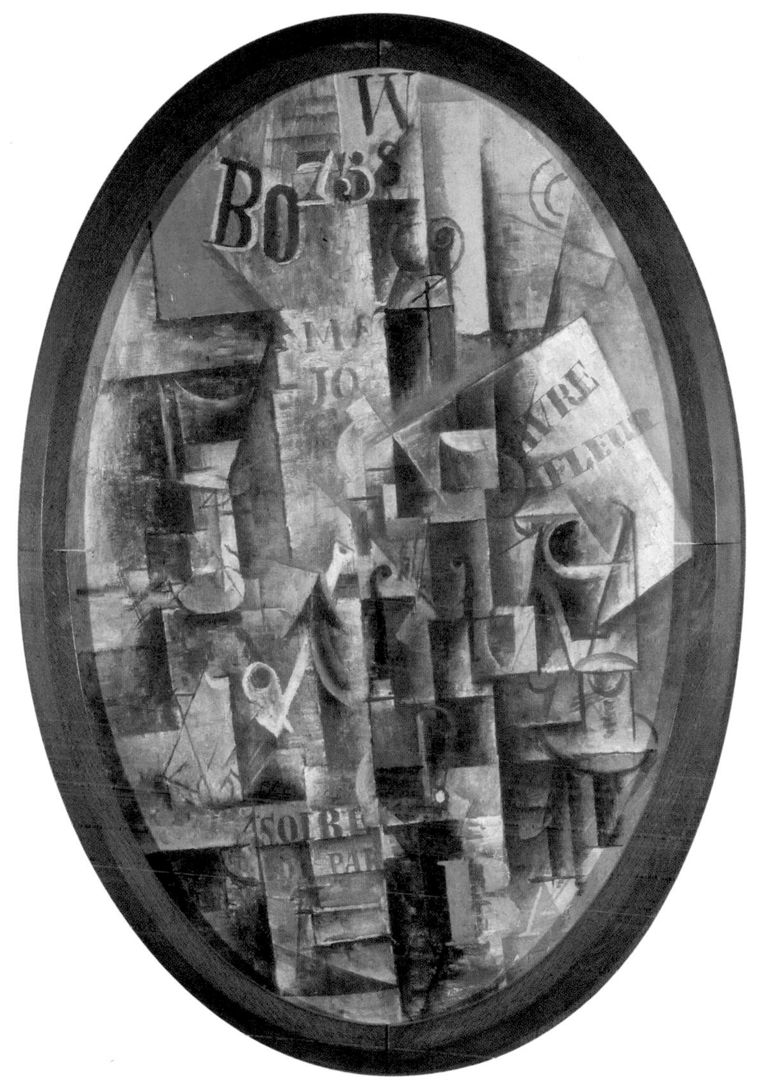
W
BO
MA
JO
AVRE
FLEUR
SOIRE
PAR

Bottle, Cup and Newspaper, 1912

Picasso's Cubist experiments, like those of Braque, completely overturned conventional modes of visual representation. Their various artistic strategies included: the use of multiple viewpoints, examining an object simultaneously from several different positions; representing fragmented forms to stand for the whole – hence a violin f-hole could signify the violin itself; and the inclusion of collaged elements, such as newsprint. In effect, Picasso and Braque were inventing a whole new vocabulary made up of visual signs. It is noteworthy that this coincided with wider investigations into the process of how language itself operated, not least of all in the work of Ferdinand de Saussure (1857–1913), widely regarded as the founder of Semiotics. Saussure's principal argument – that language is arbitrary – is intriguingly explored in Picasso's collages, such as *Bottle, Cup and Newspaper*. Here Picasso deliberately truncates the word 'Journal' (meaning 'newspaper') to 'Jou' (suggesting instead 'game'). The meaning of the word, and the fragment of newsprint on which it appears thus becomes destabilized and open to multiple meanings. In this way Picasso highlights its arbitrariness as a sign, reinforcing Saussure's views.

CREATED

Paris

MEDIUM

Pasted paper, charcoal and pencil on paper

SERIES/PERIOD/MOVEMENT

Cubist period

SIMILAR WORKS

Violin and Pipe (le Quotidien) by Georges Braque, 1913

Still Life on a Table (Gillette) by Georges Braque, 1914

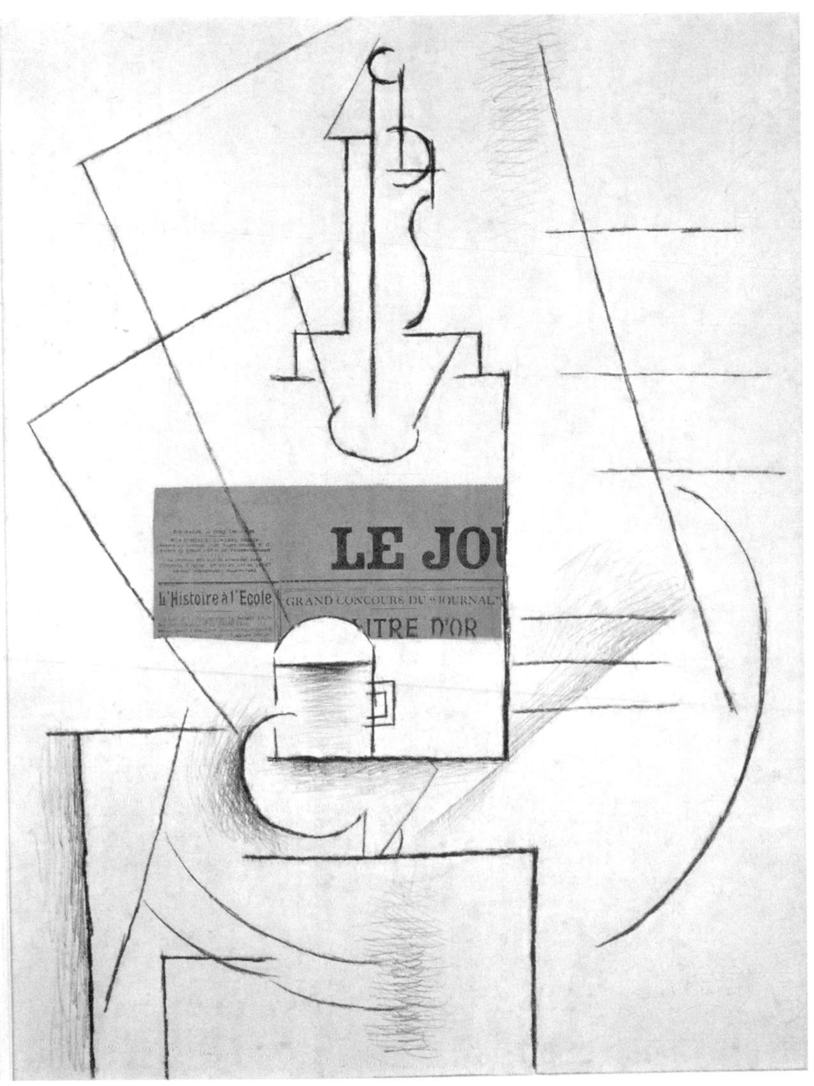
LE JOU
L'Histoire à l'Ecole
GRAND CONCOURS DU JOURNAL
ITRE D'OR

Violin in a Café, 1913

The Cubist use of multiple viewpoints had great significance for many of the wider philosophical questions being explored at the time. Late nineteenth-century technological innovations – such as the invention of the telephone and the motorcar, the development of high-speed photography and the discovery of X-rays – had radically changed the way that the physical world was perceived. Writers such as Marcel Proust (1871–1922) and James Joyce (1882–1941) had abandoned conventional literary narratives in their novels, and philosophers such as Henri Bergson (1859–1941) had argued that time and memory should not be conceived as a progression of static moments, one following the other. Through memory, Bergson argued, the past and the present coexisted simultaneously. His complex theories were widely popularized in the early twentieth century and Picasso was certainly aware of his views. Indeed, his breaking down and reconstruction of an object in works such as *Violin in a Café*, suggested an entirely new way of conceiving of an object in space – one that rejected the conventional notion of painting as the representation of a single view, captured in a single moment in time.

CREATED

Paris

MEDIUM

Oil on canvas

SERIES/PERIOD/MOVEMENT

Cubist period

SIMILAR WORKS

Clarinet and Bottle of Rum on a Mantelpiece by Georges Braque, 1911

Violin and Pipe (le Quotidien) by Georges Braque, 1913

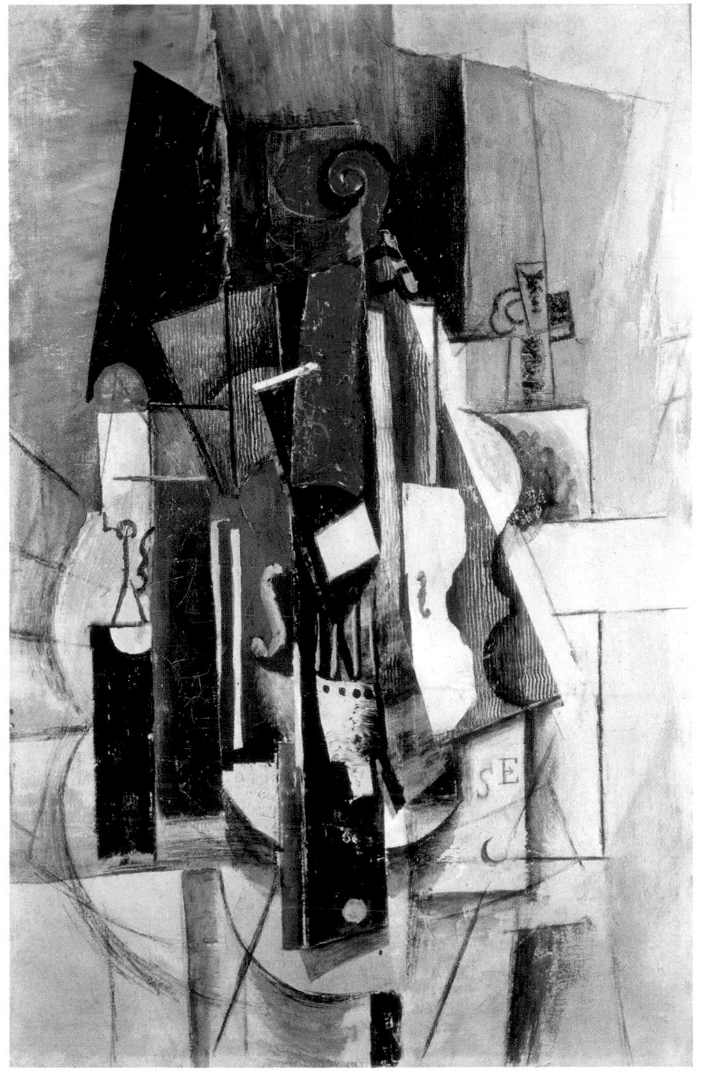
SE

Theatre Curtain for *Parade*, c. 1917

The tragic events of the First World War effectively brought to an end many of the radical artistic experiments generated by Cubism. Picasso remained a non-combatant throughout the war, protected from conscription by his Spanish citizenship. However, avant-garde practices, including Cubism, initially fell out of favour, not least of all as many of those who had supported Cubism, such as Picasso's German art dealer Daniel-Henry Kahnweiler, had been forced into exile. In this climate Picasso's art inevitably changed. One of the catalysts for this change was the writer Jean Cocteau (1889–63), who recruited Picasso into a theatrical venture he was planning. Through Cocteau, Picasso was introduced to the Russian theatrical troupe, the Ballets Russes, starting a collaboration that was highly fruitful for years to come. Picasso's entrée into this milieu came with his curtain design for the production of *Parade*, an avant-garde theatrical extravaganza that opened in Paris in May 1917. Although *Parade* proved to be a highly controversial production, Picasso's design reflected his move back towards the more romantic representation of street performers that had characterized his earlier work.

CREATED

Rome or Paris

MEDIUM

Lithograph on paper

SERIES/PERIOD/MOVEMENT

Neoclassical period

SIMILAR WORKS

Stage set for the Ballets Russes performance of *Sheherazade* by Leon Bakst, 1909

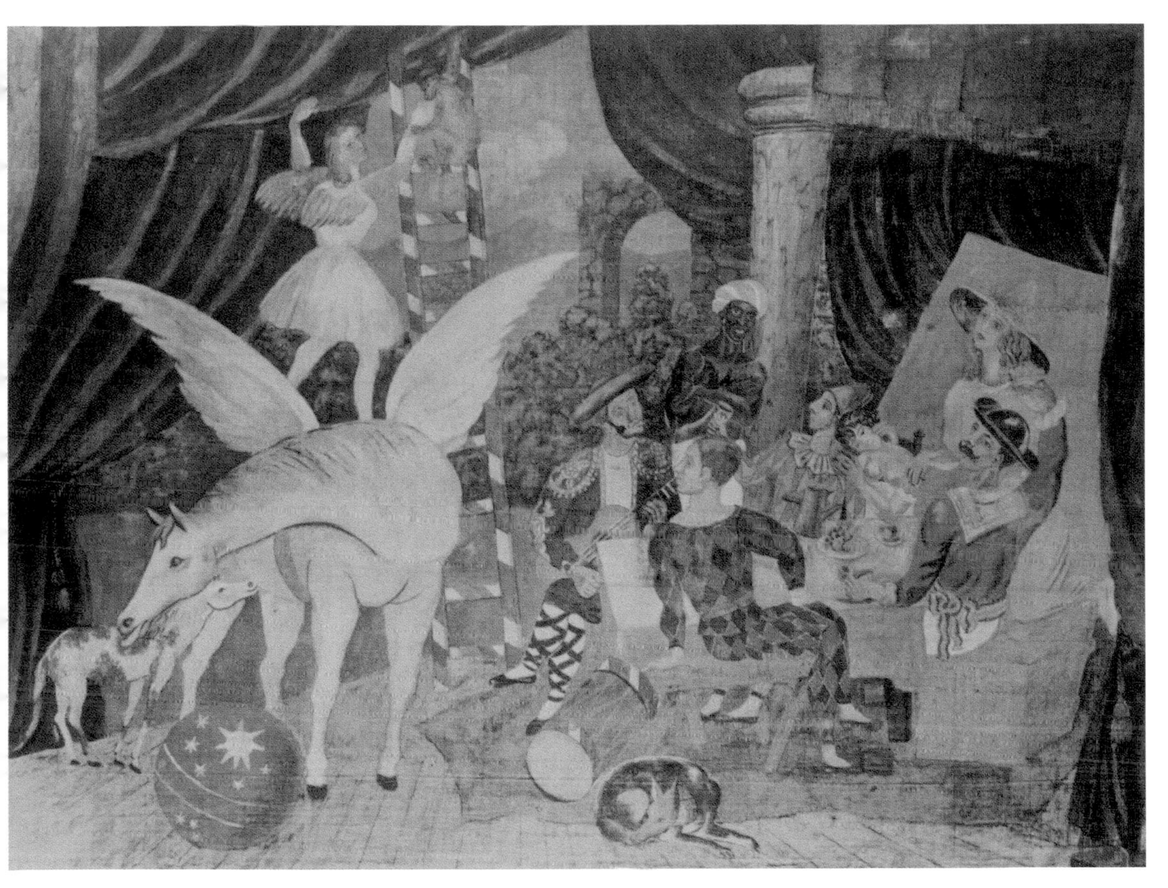

Three Women at the Spring, 1921

Courtesy of Museum of Modern Art, New York, USA/www.bridgeman.co.uk/© Succession Picasso/DACS 2005

In times of conflict and anxiety, nations frequently fall back upon traditional, conservative values, and in the wake of the First World War, France was no exception. A return to the classicism of the past was increasingly promoted as the only way forward for the country. Order and stability replaced innovation and experimentation as core social values, and the artists who seemed most to stand for these values were artists of the past, such as Nicolas Poussin (1594–1665), Claude Lorraine (1600–82) and Jean Auguste Dominique Ingres (1780–1867). It was, therefore, these artists who were increasingly promoted as ideal models for contemporary French culture. In this way, Picasso's adoption of a Neoclassical style in the latter years of the First World War can be regarded as a response to these wider concerns. The end of the conflict also brought about a renewed sense of optimism and hope for the future. *Three Women at the Spring* epitomizes these classical values. The timeless, Arcadian subject matter, and figures derived from antique statues, are composed in a highly ordered, carefully balanced manner. Even the folds in the costumes resemble the fluted columns of Ancient Greek temples.

CREATED

Fontainebleau

MEDIUM

Oil on canvas

SERIES/PERIOD/MOVEMENT

Neoclassical period

SIMILAR WORKS

Young Girls by the Seashore by Pierre Puvis de Chavannes, 1879

The Mediterranean by Aristide Maillol, 1905

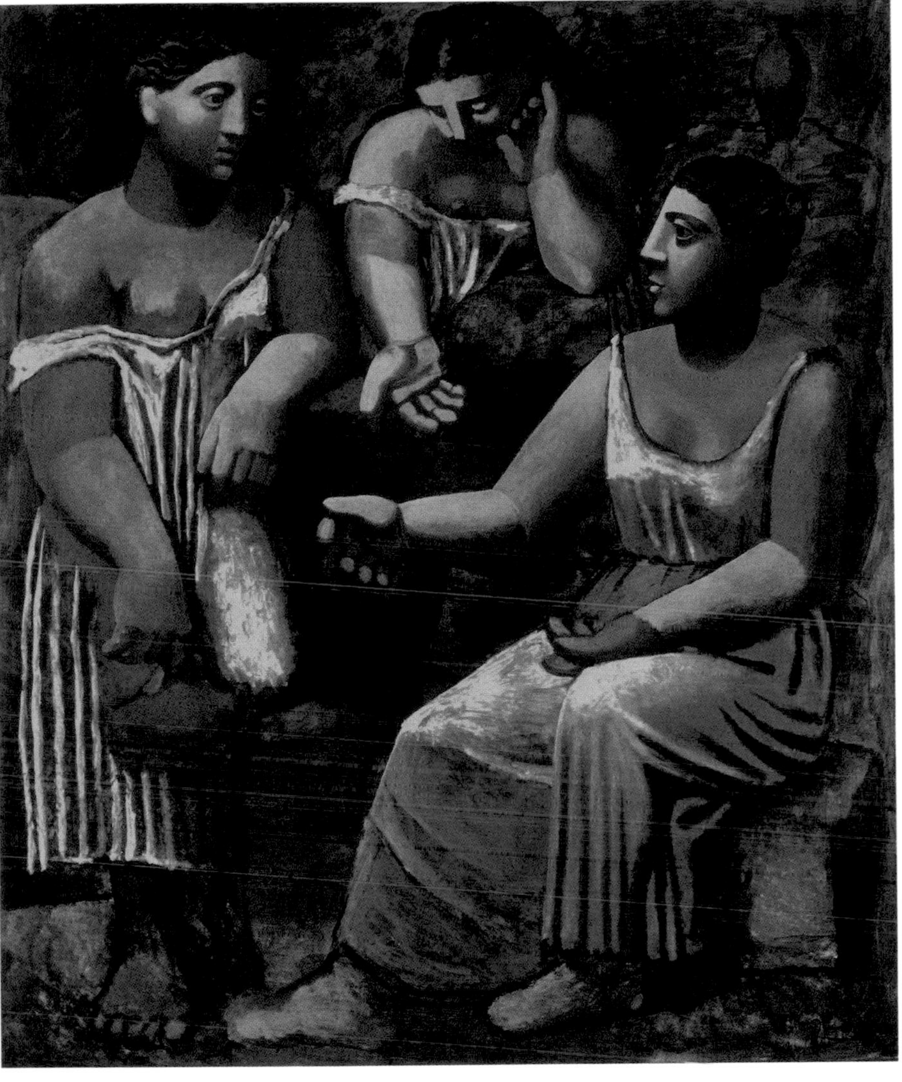

Three Musicians, 1921

In 1921, the same year that he created his Neoclassical painting *Three Women at the Spring*, Picasso produced another large-scale work, this time in a Cubist style. The painting, *Three Musicians*, attempts to reconcile the experimentation of pre-war Cubism with the new subject matter and compositional order of post-war Neoclassicism. Some historians have argued that *Three Musicians* is a deeply autobiographical work, in which Picasso was nostalgically recalling his youthful days at the 'bateau-lavoir'. Indeed, it is claimed that the three figures represent Picasso and his two poet friends Guillaume Apollinaire (1880–1918) and Max Jacob. However, the work is more than just a paean to the past. At a time when pre-war Cubism was still largely out of favour, Picasso's simultaneous adoption of a Cubist vocabulary with the traditional subject matter typical of post-war French painting, can be read as an attempt to bring together what was more widely seen as two opposing styles. Picasso, as ever, remained an enigmatic artist whose works could not be conveniently categorized or pigeonholed.

CREATED

Fontainebleau

MEDIUM

Oil on canvas

SERIES/PERIOD/MOVEMENT

Surrealist period

SIMILAR WORKS

Big City (triptych) by Otto Dix, 1927–28

Three Musicians by Fernand Léger, 1944

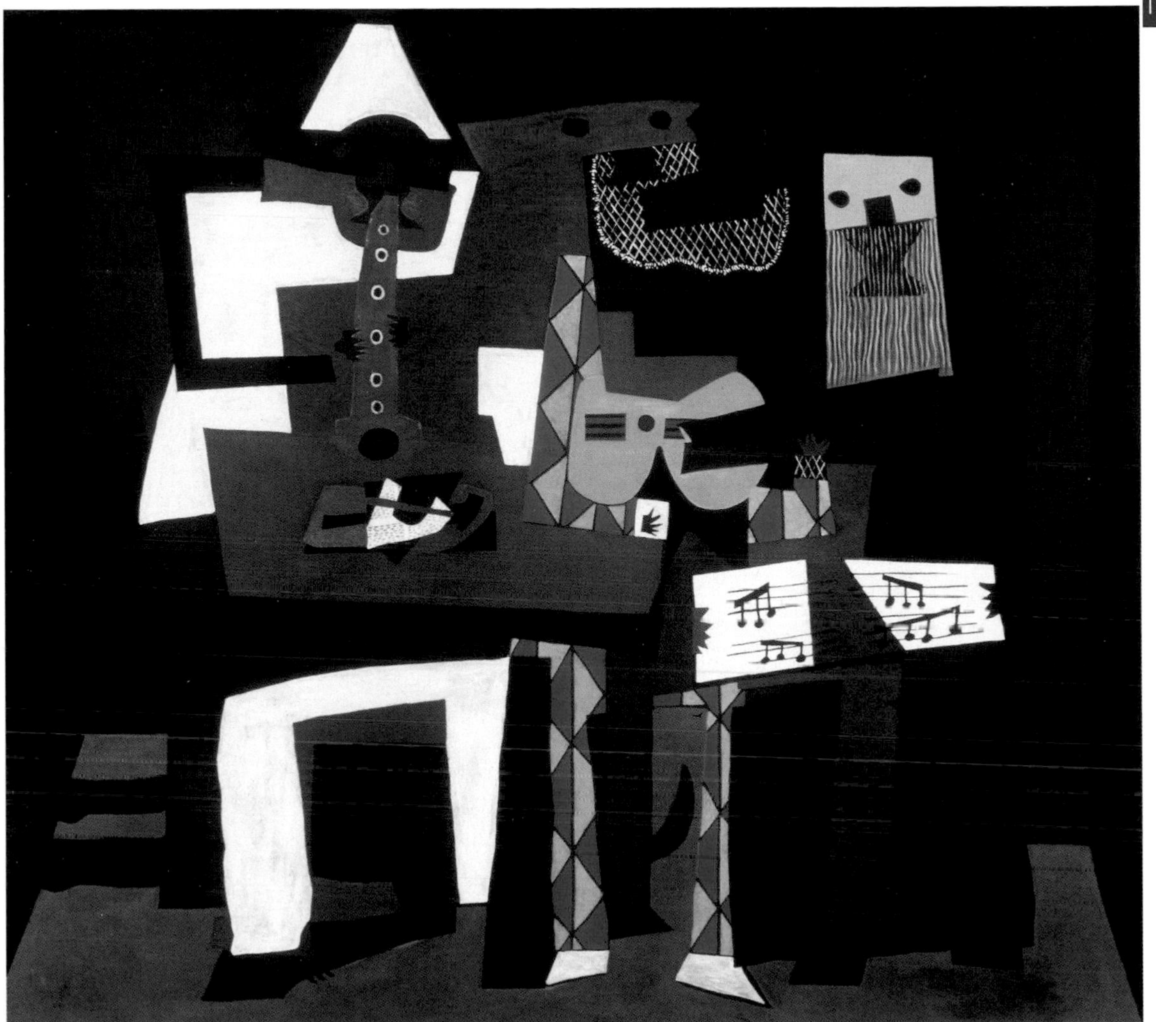

The Crucifixion, 1930

Although raised in Catholic Spain and endowed with a great knowledge of the history of western art, Picasso rarely tackled explicitly religious subjects. However, in 1929 he produced a series of sketches for a major work on the crucifixion theme, largely inspired by Mathias Grünewald's (*c.* 1470/80–1528) gruesome, sixteenth-century crucifixion from the central panel of the *Isenheim Altarpiece*. In the end, Picasso's *The Crucifixion* was produced on a relatively small scale. Nonetheless, it incorporates all the principal characters present in traditional crucifixion scenes, including the centurion lancing Christ's body, the soldiers playing dice at the foot of the cross, and the two thieves whose bodies have been dumped unceremoniously in the left foreground. The whole scene is executed in lurid, acid yellows and reds. However, the figure of Christ himself is portrayed in black and white, as if to emphasize the starkness of the tragedy. This abandoning of colour to intensify the horror of the scene reappeared later in one of Picasso's most famous social-conscience works – his representation of the atrocities brought about by the bombing of Guernica during the Spanish Civil War.

CREATED

Paris

MEDIUM

Oil on plywood

SERIES/PERIOD/MOVEMENT

Surrealist period

SIMILAR WORKS

The Isenheim Altarpiece by Matthias Grünewald, 1515

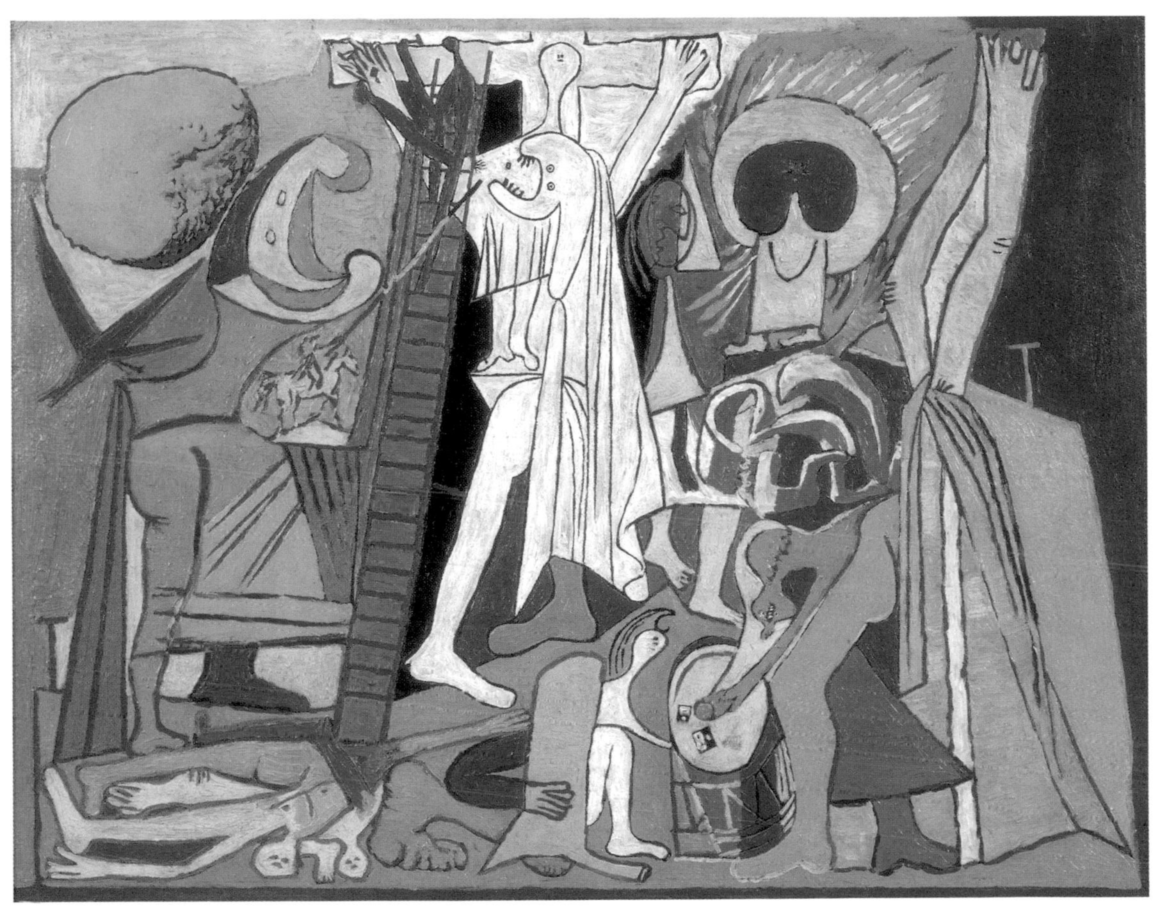

The Acrobat, 1930

The emergence of Surrealism in the mid 1920s left its mark on Picasso's work. Surrealism first entered the public domain with the publication of André Breton's (1896–1966) *Manifesto of Surrealism* in 1924. The Surrealists were greatly interested in art produced by ancient civilizations, by non-western artists, and by children and the insane. In particular, the Surrealist painter Joan Mirò (1893–1983), a fellow Spaniard and close friend of Picasso, combined the influence of both children's drawings and Neolithic cave paintings, many of which had been recently discovered. Mirò's work often introduced unusual hieroglyphic forms to represent figures in a quasi-abstract manner. Throughout the late 1920s Picasso similarly used a strict linear style to create amorphous forms that seemed to metamorphose into beings before the viewer's eyes. In *The Acrobat*, Picasso has produced such a strange hieroglyphic form that, with the addition of a few simple lines to indicate fingers, toes, an eyebrow and an ear, suddenly becomes identifiable as a human form, contorted into the kind of postures practised by acrobats in the circus so beloved by Picasso.

CREATED

Paris

MEDIUM

Oil on canvas

SERIES/PERIOD/MOVEMENT

Surrealist period

SIMILAR WORKS

Person Throwing a Stone at a Bird by Joan Mirò, 1926

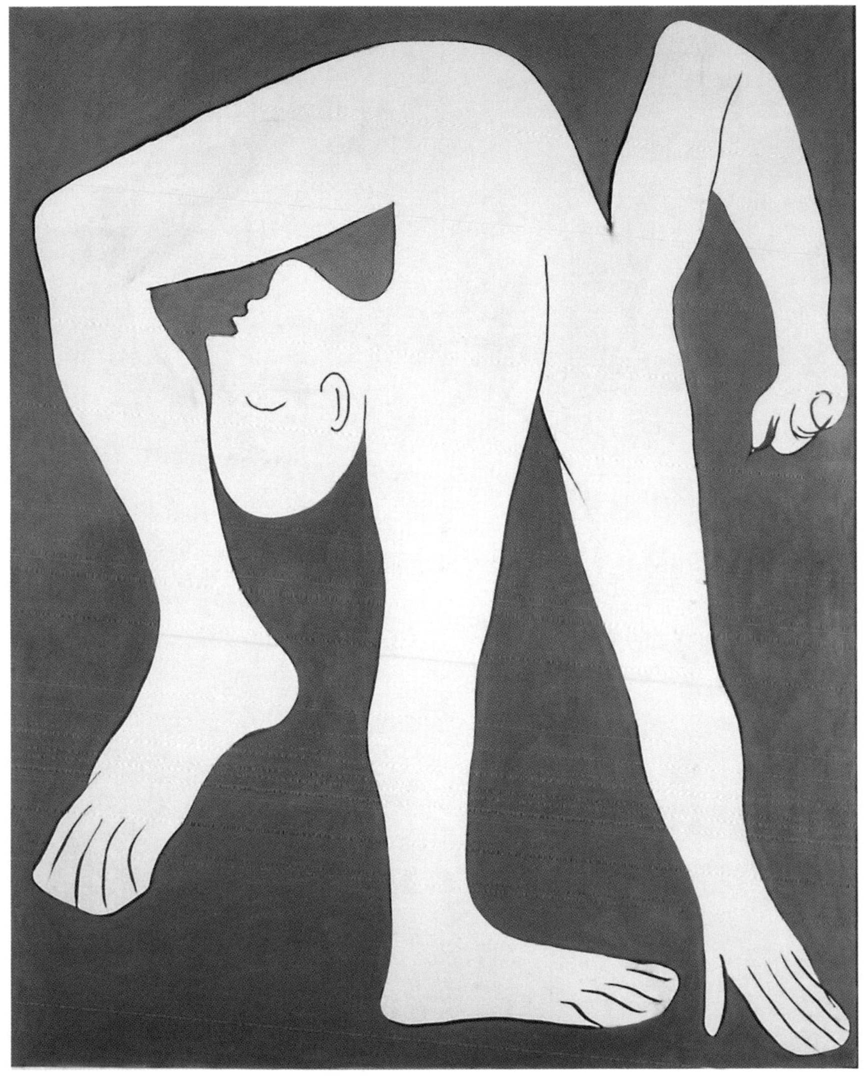

Circus Scene, 1934

Many of Picasso's more hieroglyphic works, such as *The Acrobat*, adopted a strictly two-dimensional linear style, reminiscent of children's drawings and cave paintings. However, he also represented these metamorphic creatures – partly inspired by Surrealism – in a more highly modelled form, frequently placing them within a stage-like setting. A key example of this is his *Circus Scene* of 1934. Here strange forms, seemingly derived from plant-forms or aquatic creatures, float amorphously as if in slow-moving water. However, references to heads, breasts and buttocks suggest that these forms are human. Their long, tendril-like limbs interconnect and brush tenderly against other parts of the bodies. The soft, pastel shades of the work contribute further to the sensual nature of this work. However, the two reddish forms that frame this space, suggest stage wings, while the more clearly defined white ground suggests a stage itself. Within this stage context, these forms metamorphose into human dancers or acrobats, captured in the midst of a beautiful, choreographed performance. Here Picasso has combined the Surrealist emphasis on metamorphosis with his love of theatricality.

CREATED

Paris

MEDIUM

Oil on canvas

SERIES/PERIOD/MOVEMENT

Surrealist period

SIMILAR WORKS

The Horde by Max Ernst, 1927

Gradiva by André Masson, 1939

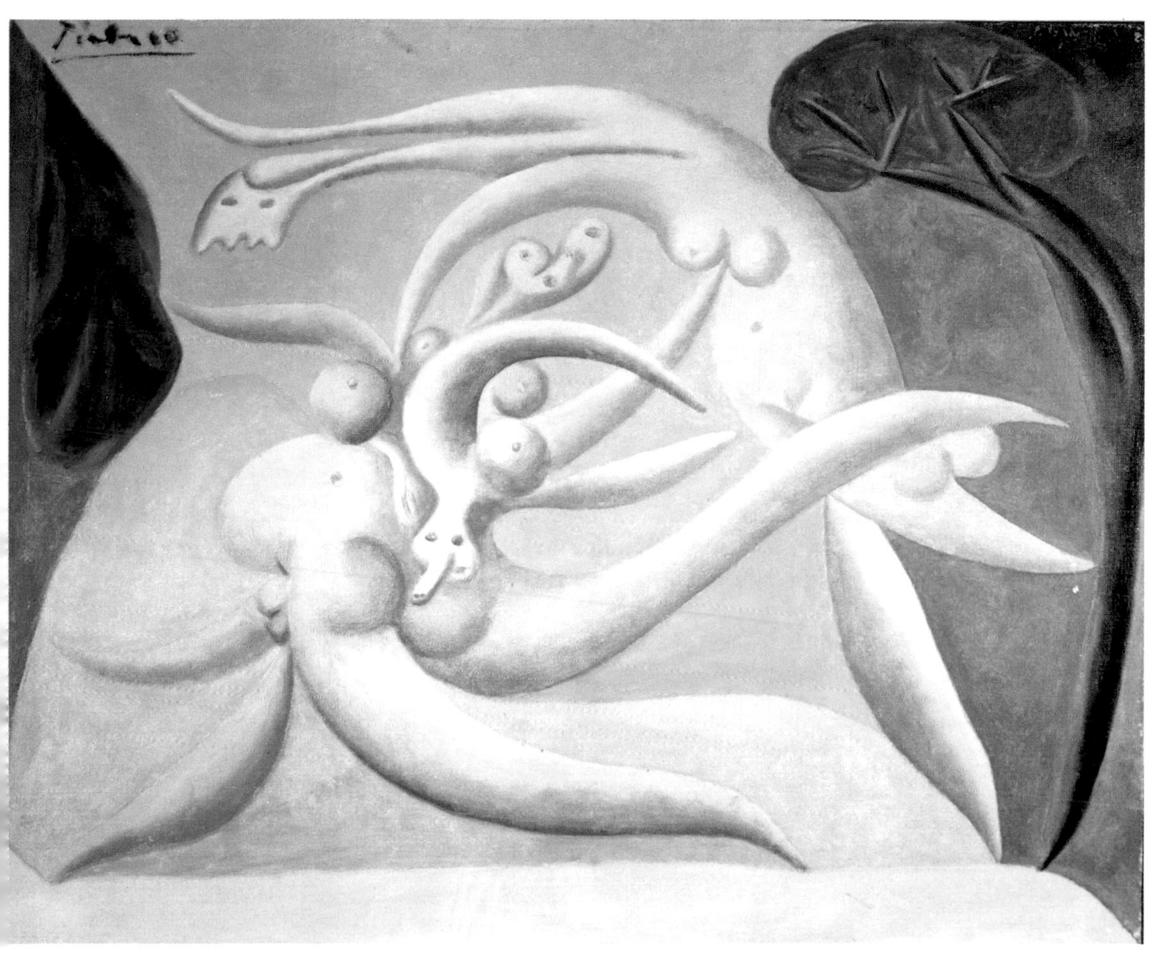

Bullfighting, 1934

In 1934 Picasso returned to Spain for the first time in many years. Little did he know that this would be the last time he would visit his native country. Together with Olga and Paulo, he visited Barcelona, Madrid, San Sebastien and Toledo, attending several bullfights on the way. The experience certainly inspired Picasso to produce a series of works representing the brutal conflict that took place in the bullring. For Picasso, the struggle between the toreador and the bull symbolized the co-existence of nobility and brutality in human nature. Indeed it was at this time that Picasso began to develop his series of works on the theme of the minotaur – the mythological creature, half-man, half-bull, that Picasso frequently used to symbolize his own personality. Picasso's increasing emphasis on the fight to the death enacted in the bullring might also be read as a heightened awareness of the increasing division in Europe and fear of military conflict in the wake of the accession to power in Germany of Adolf Hitler's National Socialist Party.

CREATED

Boisgeloup

MEDIUM

Oil on canvas

SERIES/PERIOD/MOVEMENT

Surrealist period

SIMILAR WORKS

The Bullfight by Francisco de Goya, 1816

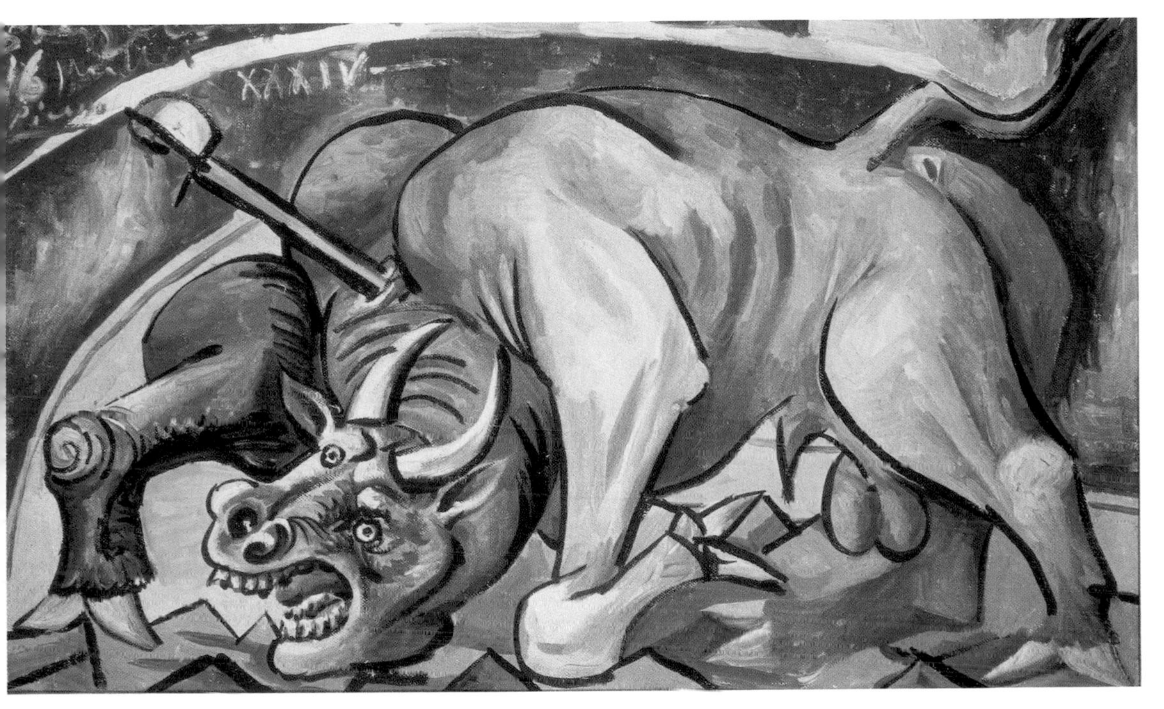
XXXIV

Guernica, 1937

Courtesy of Museo Nacional Centro de Arte Reina Sofia, Madrid, Spain/www.bridgeman.co.uk/© Succession Picasso/DACS 2005

The outbreak of the Spanish Civil War in 1936 effectively exiled Picasso, an avowed Republican supporter. Against the mighty onslaught of General Franco's Nationalist forces, the Republican government continued to seek international support, and here Picasso became one of their key propaganda weapons. In 1937 he was commissioned to produce a mural-sized work for the Paris International Exhibition. The resulting piece, entitled *Guernica*, represents a scene of violence and devastation perpetrated upon a civilian population. It refers specifically to the bombing of the Basque town of Guernica by Nationalist forces earlier that year. In this work Picasso did not present the bombing literally. Rather, he introduced a series of characters, including a mother carrying a dead child, a horse with spear piercing its side and a fallen warrior. The whole is executed in monochrome to emphasize the starkness of the tragedy represented and to allude to the newspaper and newsreel media through which this event was brought to the world's attention. Picasso's *Guernica* has subsequently become one of the most famous artistic icons of anti-war sentiment.

CREATED

Paris

MEDIUM

Oil on canvas

SERIES/PERIOD/MOVEMENT

Surrealist period

SIMILAR WORKS

Disasters of War series of etchings by Francisco de Goya, 1810–20

Massacre in Korea by Picasso, 1951

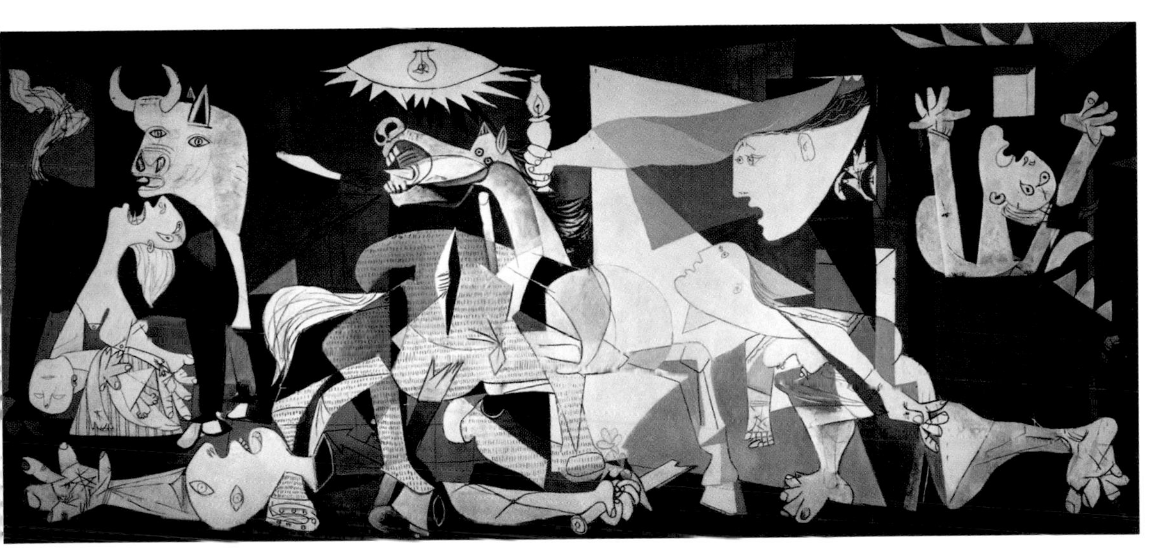

Death's Head, c. 1941

When war was declared in September 1939, few doubted the German intention to invade France, and many of those who had publicly spoken against Fascism fled the country. When Picasso produced *Guernica* for the Spanish Republican government, his political sympathies were openly expressed. All of this makes it more surprising that the artist decided to remain in Paris throughout the German occupation from 1940 to 1944, when many other artists went into exile. There is much debate surrounding Picasso's wartime experiences. Some have declared the artist a hero of the Resistance, while others have accused him of collaboration. What is clear is that Picasso spent most of these years confined to his studio, officially banned from exhibiting by the Nazis. Despite these strictures, however, he continued to produce a vast number of works. In the midst of such destruction it is hardly surprising that Picasso introduced both implicit and explicit references to death and destruction in his art. This small sculpture, with its scarred and pitted surface, epitomizes this – simultaneously resembling a piece of metal shrapnel and a human skull.

CREATED

Paris

MEDIUM

Bronze and copper

SERIES/PERIOD/MOVEMENT

Second World War period

SIMILAR WORKS

Pyramid of Skulls by Paul Cézanne, *c.* 1901

Horse's Skull on Blue by Georgia O'Keeffe, 1930

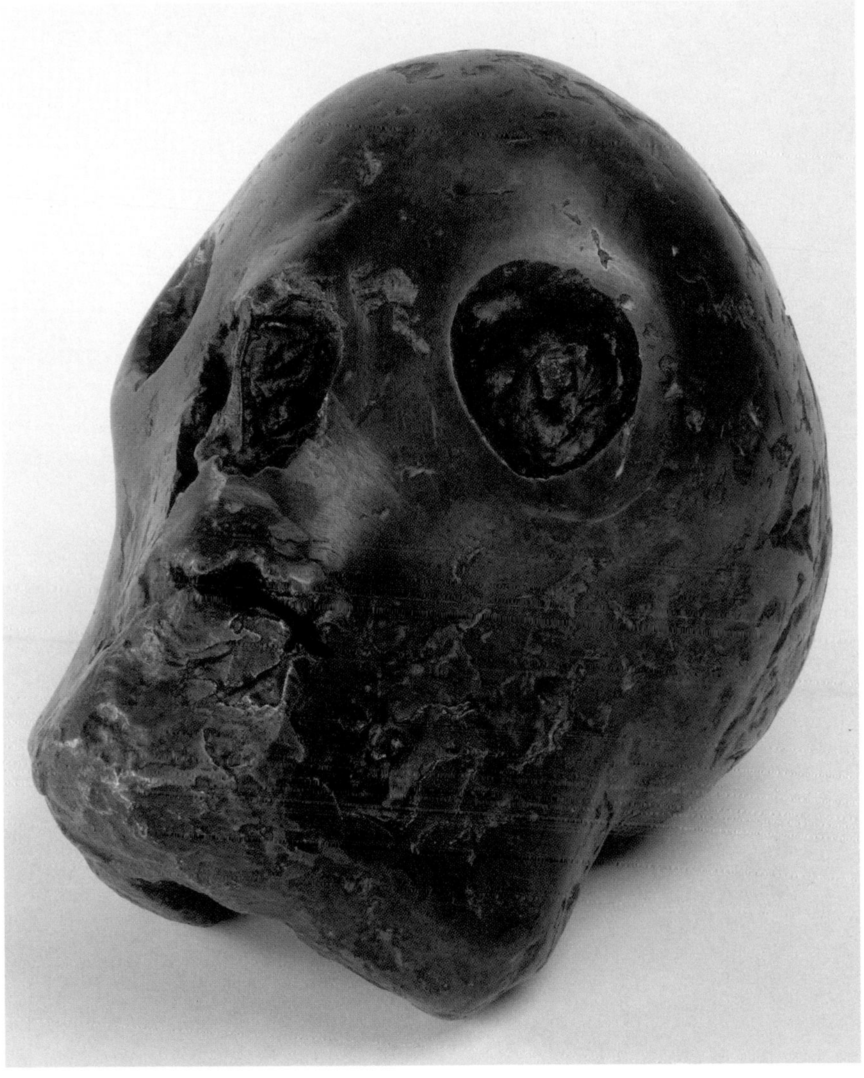

Man with a Sheep, 1943

Man with a Sheep is Picasso's most famous occupation sculpture. He produced over 50 sketches for this work, which represents a middle-aged man carrying a trussed sheep and offering it in sacrifice. The sacrificial aspect has clear overtones for the war. At a time when the youth of all nations was being sacrificed at the altar of war, and when Jews, Resistance fighters and other victims of National Socialist policy were being rounded up and deported to concentration camps, Picasso's focus on the sacrifice of the innocent carried a painful resonance. The sculpture was modelled in the spring of 1943, shortly after the Germans had surrendered to the Russians at Stalingrad, thus turning the tide of war towards an Allied victory. This may account for the more optimistic tenor of Picasso's work when compared with his *Death's Head* of two years earlier. Picasso's sculptural output during the occupation is all the more remarkable as many works were cast in bronze, despite the fact that the Germans were melting down public statues in Paris to build armaments during this period.

CREATED

Paris

MEDIUM

Bronze

SERIES/PERIOD/MOVEMENT

Second World War period

SIMILAR WORKS

The Calf-Bearer (Moscophorous), from the Acropolis in Athens, *c.* 560 BC

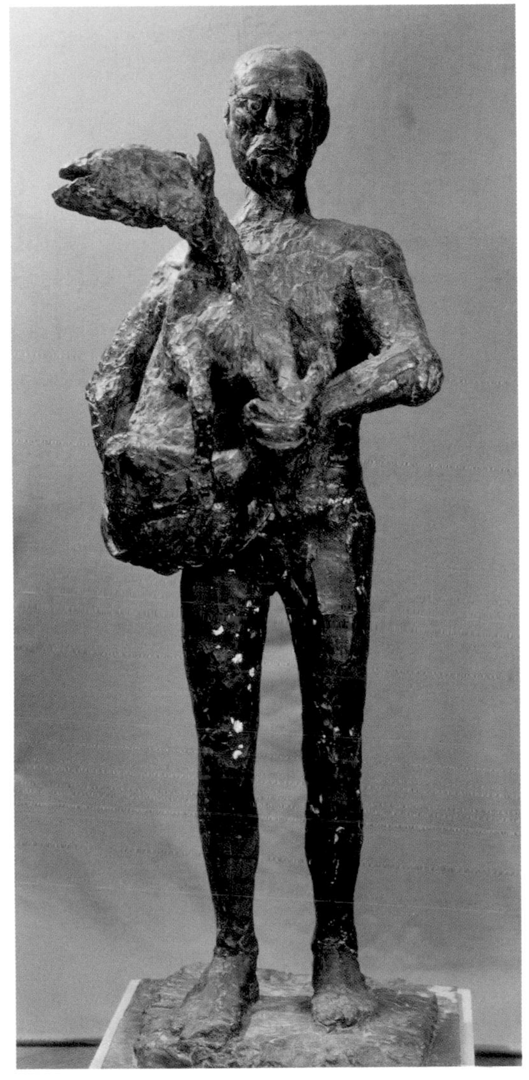

Still Life with Skull and Leeks, 1945

Still-life paintings featured prominently amongst Picasso's wartime works. In some ways, this is not surprising – confined to his studio for large periods of time, Picasso was limited in the motifs he could depict. Still lifes had also been a dominant aspect of early Cubism and Picasso now returned to this genre with a vengeance. However, far from producing works focusing predominantly on musical instruments and glasses of alcohol, Picasso's still lifes now directly addressed the straightened circumstances of occupied Paris. At a time of constant shortages, simply putting food on the table was a daily concern, and many of Picasso's wartime still lifes seem to accentuate this anxiety, with their emphasis on simple staples such as the meagre leeks and pitcher of water on a bare table in this work. The frequent presence of a skull also offered a clear reminder of death, giving Picasso's still lifes a symbolism that recalls seventeenth-century Dutch painting. Significantly, many of the still lifes Picasso produced shortly after the liberation, including this one, are executed in brighter, more optimistic tones than their occupation predecessors.

CREATED

Paris

MEDIUM

Oil on canvas

SERIES/PERIOD/MOVEMENT

Second World War period

SIMILAR WORKS

Vanitas Still Life by Pieter Claesz, 1630

Pitcher and Skull by Georges Braque, 1943

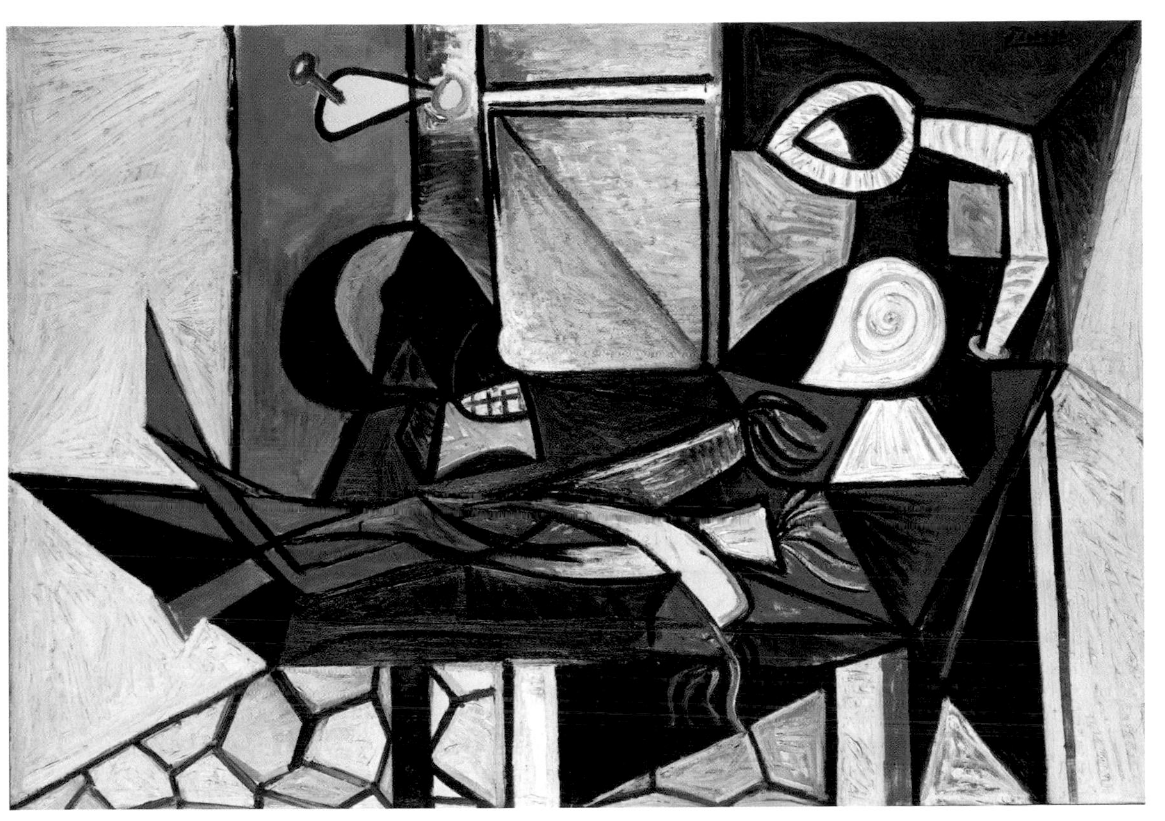

The Charnel House, 1945

Shortly after the liberation in 1944, a major exhibition was held in Paris, which was popularly referred to as the Salon of the Liberation. Picasso's wartime output featured heavily in this show. However, the artist courted significant controversy when, on the eve of the exhibition, he announced that he had joined the Communist Party. The following year, he set out to produce a major social painting condemning the atrocities of the war. The work, entitled *The Charnel House* is in many ways a direct descendent of *Guernica*. Like *Guernica*, *The Charnel House* is executed entirely in monochrome. It, too, represents the innocent victims of war – in this case a family. Picasso has represented a father lying upside-down on the right, his tied hands occupying the very centre of the image. The mother, seen lying horizontally across the middle of the work, is naked and blood runs from her neck, cascading down upon the small, dead child in the foreground. The domestic setting of the work, implied by the kitchen table in the upper left, serves further to emphasize the atrocity of this war crime.

CREATED

Paris

MEDIUM

Oil on canvas

SERIES/PERIOD/MOVEMENT

Second World War period

SIMILAR WORKS

Disasters of War series of etchings by Francisco de Goya, 1810–20

Guernica by Picasso, 1937

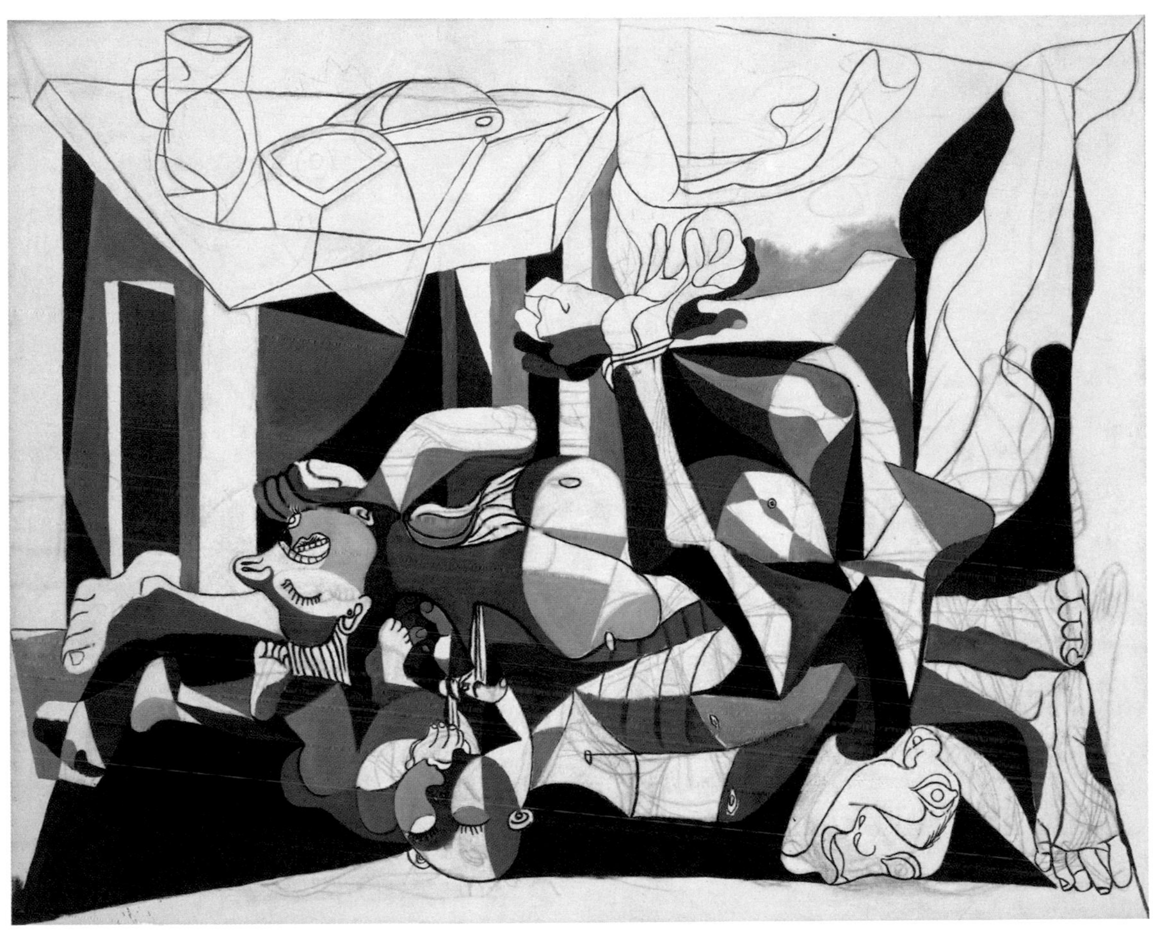

The Joy of Life, 1946

Remaining in Paris during the occupation had prevented Picasso from making his regular summer excursions to the south of France. Thus, in July 1945, he took a trip to Antibes, to which he returned the following spring and remained throughout the summer months. It was here that Picasso produced one of the most exuberant of his early post-war works, *The Joy of Life*. The painting literally oozes a newfound sense of liberty and exultation, in contrast to the confinement and drudgery of the occupation years. Recalling Henri Matisse's (1869–1954) earlier *Bonheur de Vivre* (1905–06), it revels in the warmth, bright light, blue skies and tranquillity of its Mediterranean setting. At the centre of the image, Picasso represents his new partner, Françoise Gilot, naked, her hair swirling in the air as she dances energetically, tambourine in hand. Surrounding her are mythological creatures and goats all joining in this ecstatic celebration. Notably Picasso here reintroduced the classical theme into his work, much as he had done in the wake of the First World War.

CREATED

Antibes

MEDIUM

Oil on canvas

SERIES/PERIOD/MOVEMENT

Second World War period

SIMILAR WORKS

A Dance to the Music of Time by Nicolas Poussin, *c.* 1640

Bonheur de Vivre by Henri Matisse, 1905–06

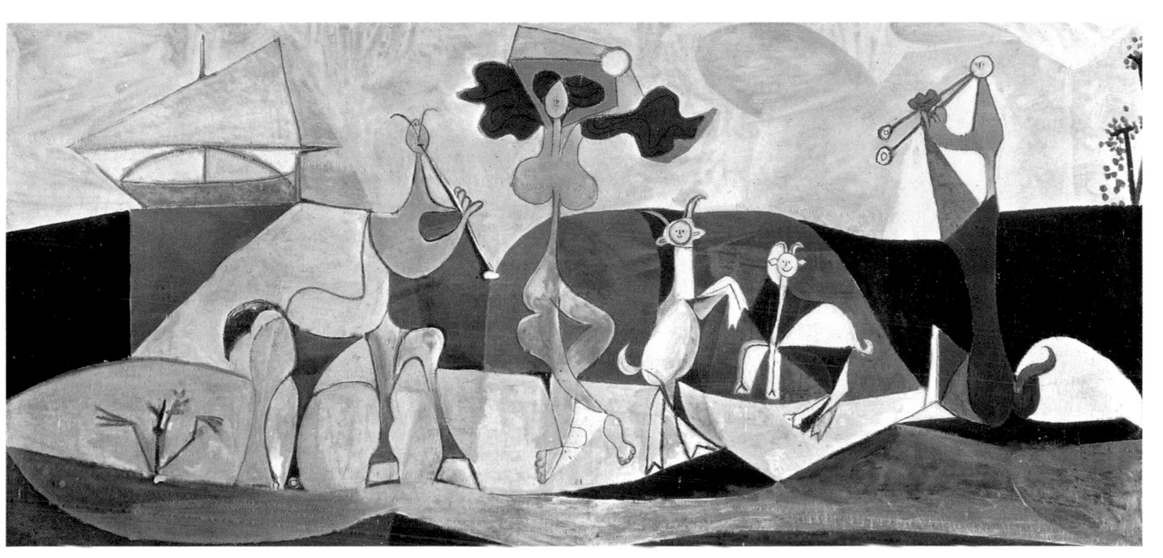

A Monument to the Spanish People who Died for France, 1947

At the end of the Second World War, one Fascist leader, Spain's General Franco, still remained in power. Picasso, whose support for the Spanish Republicans opposed to Franco had been aptly expressed in his painting *Guernica*, vowed not to return to his native Spain until democracy had been restored. In 1947, he re-articulated this solidarity by producing a painting as a monument to Spanish Republicanism. Many of the Spanish people who had died during the Second World War were Republican exiles who fought for the Resistance, or who had been deported to concentration camps. Picasso's painted monument follows the form of the many sculptural memorials that were being erected in towns and villages throughout France. It represents a funeral stele with a bust of a classical warrior adorned with an arrow and a bugle. The French tricolore is prominently displayed above the inscription 'To the Spanish people who died for France'. A skull and crossbones, and two plants frame the monument itself. Picasso's memorial dedicated to the Spanish people is highly unconventional, but nonetheless reveals his continuing political support for the Republican cause.

CREATED

Paris

MEDIUM

Oil on canvas

SERIES/PERIOD/MOVEMENT

Post-War Communist period

SIMILAR WORKS

The Charnel House by Picasso, 1945

Post-War sculptural monuments to the war dead erected throughout France

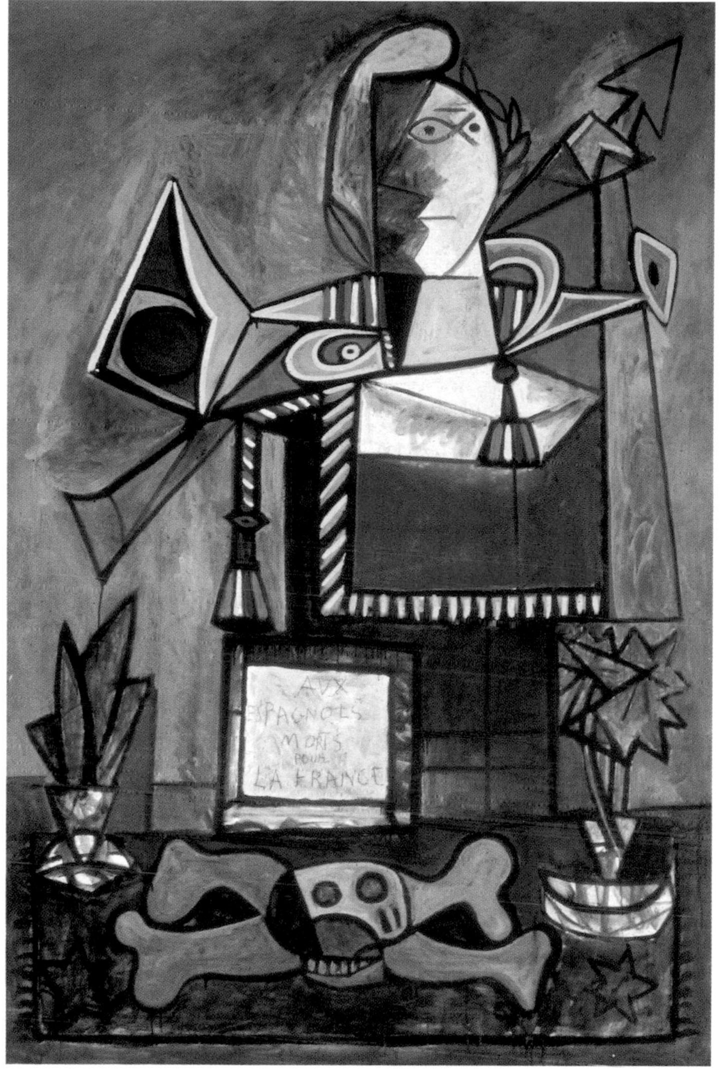
AUX
ESPAGNOLS
MORTS
POUR
LA FRANCE

Dove, 1949

Picasso's image of a dove, first produced in 1949, became one of the best-known icons of international peace when it was adopted as the symbol for the First World Peace Congress organized by the Communist Party. Ironically, the original lithograph represented a pigeon, not a dove. Nor was it intended to symbolize peace. However, when shown Picasso's lithograph, Louis Aragon (1897–1982), an influential member of the French Communist Party, instantly adopted this 'dove' as a symbol for the peace movement. The image adorned posters promoting the Congress and was widely reproduced throughout the world. Picasso, it seems, was more than happy for his pigeon to become a dove. The detailed, realistic nature of the work served the Communist peace movement well. Not only did the name of Picasso enhance its prestige, but the work also conformed to the more realistic approach to art supported by the Communist Party in the Soviet Union. Over the next few years Picasso produced countless more doves in a variety of styles, all of which confirmed his credentials as an advocate of international peace.

CREATED

Paris

MEDIUM

Lithograph on paper

SERIES/PERIOD/MOVEMENT

Post-War Communist period

SIMILAR WORKS

The Pigeon Loft by José Ruiz Blasco (Picasso's father), 1878

Child with a Dove by Picasso, 1901

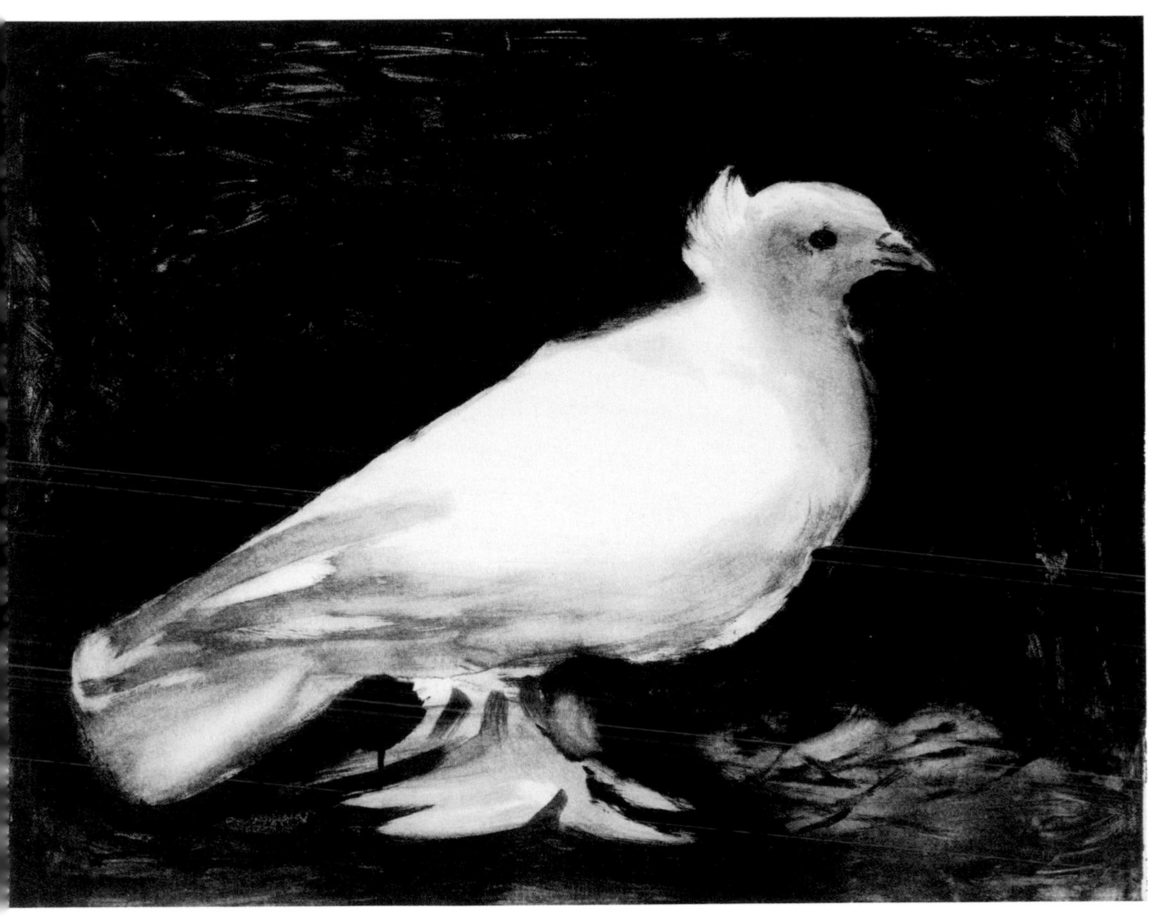

Massacre in Korea, 1951

In 1950, a dispute between North and South Korea escalated into full-scale conflict. The United States, fearing the spread of Communism, came to the assistance of the South Koreans, thus precipitating an international crisis and widespread fear that a new world war was imminent. As a supporter of the Communist Party, Picasso roundly condemned American involvement in Korea, and in 1951 produced the 'protest' painting *Massacre in Korea*. In line with the majority of Picasso's political paintings, the work used little specific detail, but rather addressed the general theme of the massacre of the innocents. Here, atrocities are enacted by a group of quasi-mechanical male figures, simultaneously futuristic and medievalizing, upon a group of defenceless women and children, whose physiognomies in no way suggest Korean identity. Despite this, the allusion to American military might being deployed to brutalize innocent people was clearly read by both supporters and critics of the work. Here, in both subject and composition, Picasso has made a clear reference to another famous scene of massacre, Francisco de Goya's (1746–1828) *Executions of the Third of May, 1808* (1814).

CREATED

Vallauris

MEDIUM

Oil on plywood

SERIES/PERIOD/MOVEMENT

Post-War Communist period

SIMILAR WORKS

Executions of the Third of May, 1808 by Francisco de Goya, 1814

The Execution of Emperor Maximilian by Edouard Manet, 1867–68

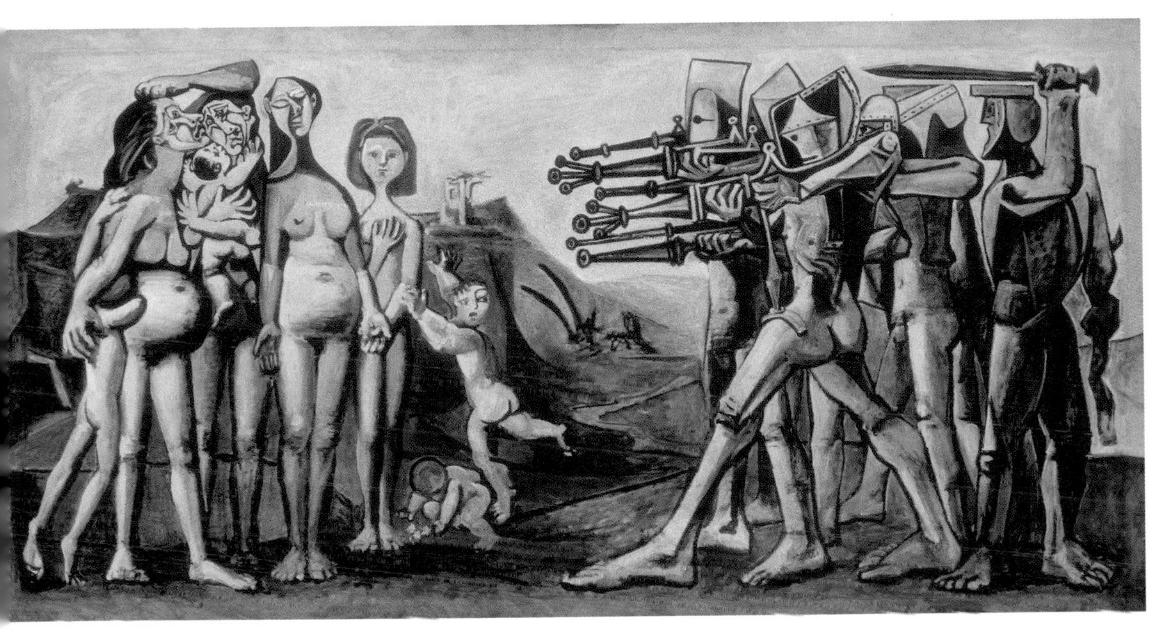

Portrait of Madame H. P., 1952

Picasso's support for Communism was at its strongest in the decade after the Second World War, although he remained a lifelong member of the Party. During this time many of Picasso's closest friends were also strong supporters of Communism, amongst whom were the art critic and writer Hélène Parmelin (1915–98) and her husband, the painter Edouard Pignon (1905–93). Both were active in Communist cultural circles, and regularly spent the summer months with Picasso in the south of France. Parmelin had expressly shown her distain for America's involvement in Korea in one of her novels. She also wrote two articles in praise of Picasso's *War* and *Peace* murals, and several books recounting the time she spent with Picasso. This portrait shows Parmelin seated on the floor, as if engrossed in one of the intense political conversations that often took place between Picasso and the writer. Her wild red hair cascades over her shoulders uncontrollably, which, together with her engaged but ungainly posture, suggests a spirited and passionate individual.

CREATED

Vallauris

MEDIUM

Oil on plywood

SERIES/PERIOD/MOVEMENT

Post-War Communist period

SIMILAR WORKS

The Women of Algiers by Eugène Delacroix, 1834

Zorah on the Terrace by Henri Matisse, 1912

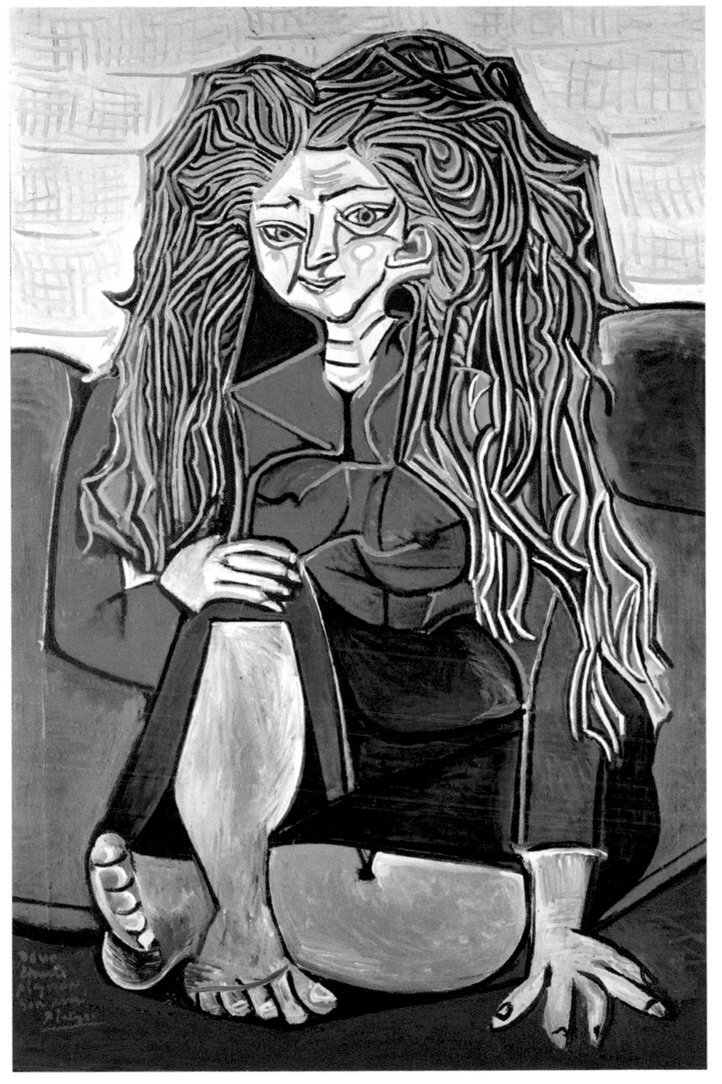

War and *Peace*, in Vallauris Chapel, 1952–54

Picasso's anti-war sentiments were widely expressed in several of his major projects, including the large-scale works he produced in Vallauris in the midst of the Korean War. Since 1947 Picasso had been spending his summers in this southern French town, and in 1950 he was commissioned to produce a major mural in a local deconsecrated chapel. Picasso may well have chosen to work on this project to rival his friend Matisse, who was at that time decorating a Dominican chapel in Vence. In contrast to Matisse's religious project, however, Picasso's chapel was to be a secular temple, dedicated to world peace. The two murals produced occupy both sides of a barrel-vaulted space, joining at the centre. On one side, representing War, a demonic charioteer and his entourage spread death and destruction through a dark and gloomy landscape, only to be halted by a steadfast peace warrior carrying a shield emblazoned with Picasso's peace dove. On the opposite wall, Peace is represented by an Arcadian scene of leisure, abundance and tranquillity in a paradise inhabited by nymphs and shepherds.

CREATED

Vallauris

MEDIUM

Oil on panel

SERIES/PERIOD/MOVEMENT

Post-War Communist period

SIMILAR WORKS

The Chapel of the Rosary at Vence by Henri Matisse, 1950

Decorations at the Church of Notre-Dame de Toute-Grâce at Assy by Marc Chagall, Fernand Léger, Henri Matisse, Georges Rouault and others, *c.* 1950

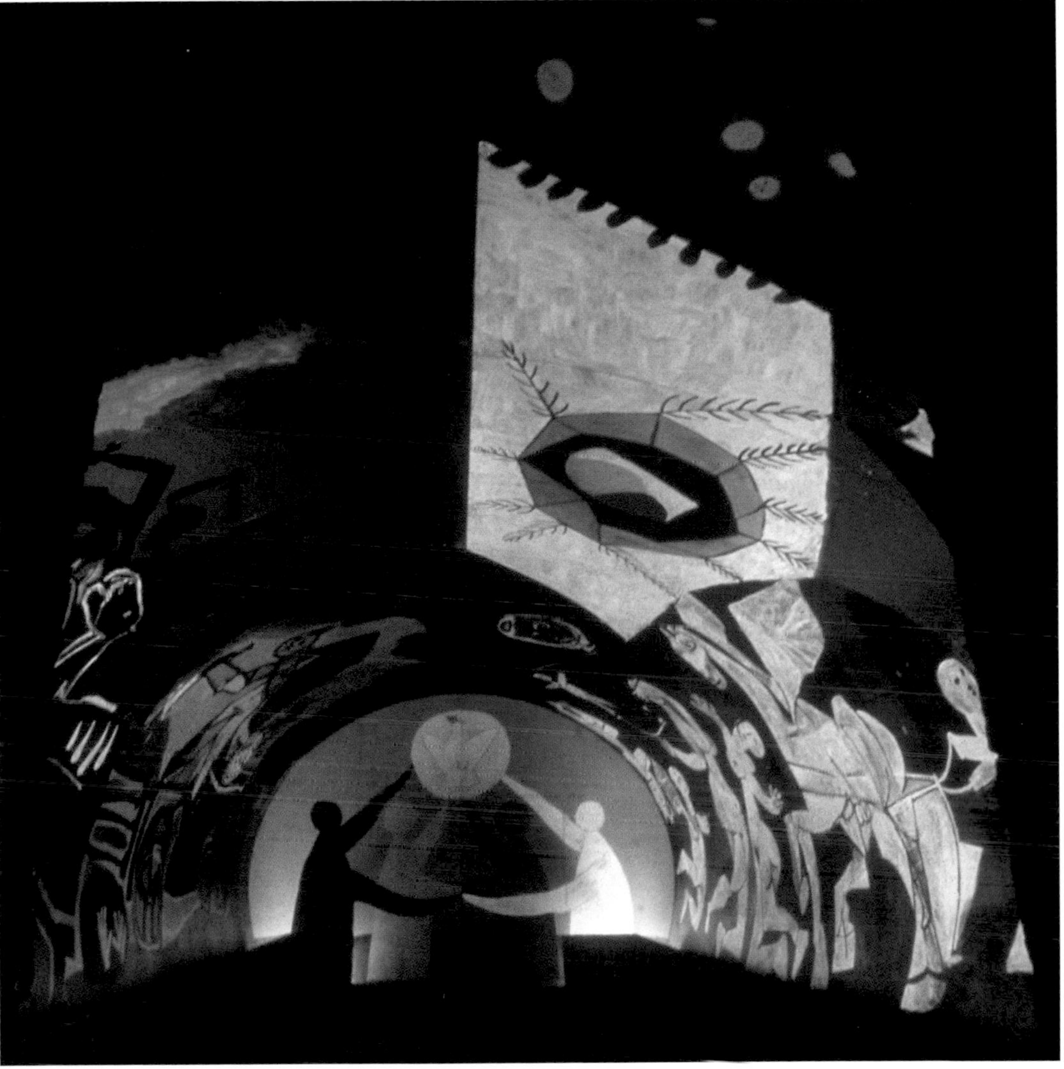

'The Four Corners of the World', from *War* and *Peace*, in Vallauris Chapel, 1952–54

Due to the awkward shape and condition of the walls of the chapel, Picasso's *War* and *Peace* murals were produced on fibreboard panels, installed into the chapel space. These panels were initially exhibited in Vallauris, and later in Rome and Milan, before being installed in the chapel in February 1954. However, the chapel wasn't finally opened to the public for another four years. Picasso had originally intended to install a large sculpture representing a peace dove at the far end of the vault. In 1958, however, this plan was abandoned and Picasso instead produced this semi-circular panel representing four figures raising a disk. The figures schematically symbolize what Picasso regarded as the four races of the world lifting aloft the Sun, upon which is inscribed the dove of peace. Thus Picasso was offering a universalizing symbol of international peace and co-operation to challenge the division of the world into the two Superpowers during the Cold War. Referring to the *War* and *Peace* murals, Picasso later stated: 'If peace wins in the world, the war I have painted will be a thing of the past.'

CREATED

Vallauris

MEDIUM

Oil on panel

SERIES/PERIOD/MOVEMENT

Post-War Communist period

SIMILAR WORKS

The Chapel of the Rosary at Vence by Henri Matisse, 1950

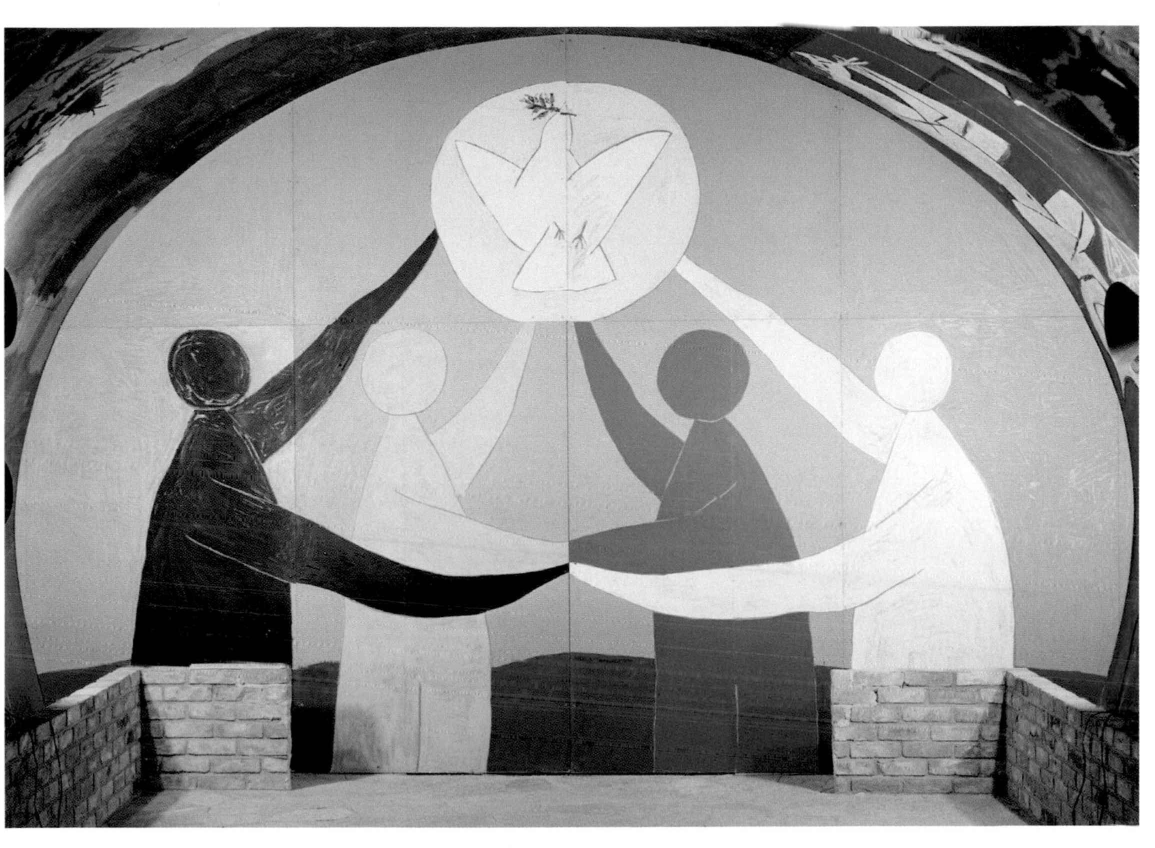

Vive la Paix, 1954

Throughout the early 1950s, Picasso produced countless representations of his 'peace dove'. In contrast to his earlier detailed lithograph, these doves were often reduced to simple outline drawings representing the bird in flight. The symbolism of the dove carried universal values. Since ancient times it had been associated with peace and sacrifice and, within the Christian tradition, signified the Holy Spirit. When depicted holding an olive branch in its beak – as in this image – it also symbolized hope for the future of humankind, epitomized in the Old Testament story of Noah and the flood. This work, entitled *Vive la Paix*, or 'Long Live Peace', was produced as a cover for the French journal *L'Humanité Dimanche* to celebrate the signing of a peace agreement bringing an end to war in Indochina. Here Picasso has represented a group, including a small animal in the foreground, dancing in celebration around a fire. The dove flying overhead signifies that peace, rather than any individual nation, is the victor. Notably, the simple but broad brushstrokes clearly derive from Chinese brush painting and calligraphy.

CREATED

Cannes

MEDIUM

India ink on paper

SERIES/PERIOD/MOVEMENT

Post-War Communist period

SIMILAR WORKS

Ceramic works produced at Vallauris by Picasso, *c.* 1947–57

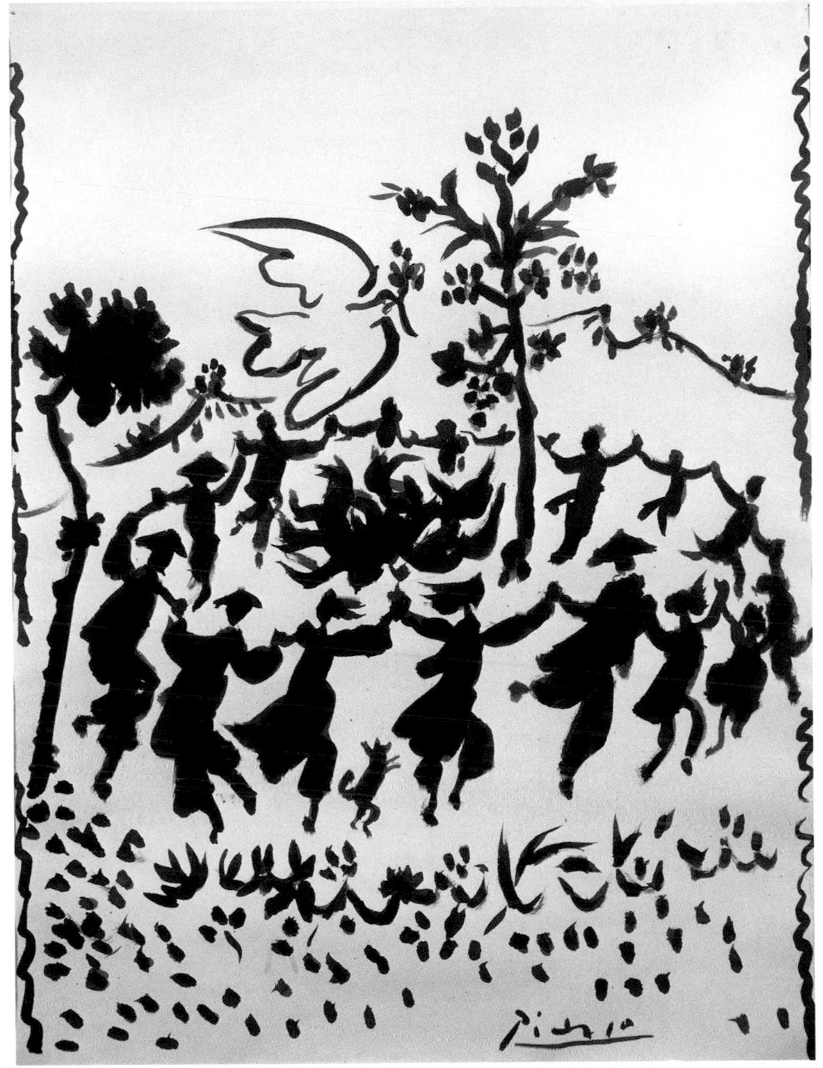

Illustration for *Toros y Toreros*, 1959

Throughout the postwar period, Picasso's work was significantly affected by his sense of the huge political and ideological struggle between Capitalism and Communism. As a supporter and member of the Communist Party he produced a number of lithographs for publication in the popular journals of the day. He also turned his hand more extensively to book illustration. In 1957 he produced a series of illustrations for a book entitled *La Tauromaquia* ('The Art of Bullfighting') by the Spaniard Pepe Ilio. The book was a celebration of bullfighting and Picasso's series of 26 aquatints showed the various stages of the bullfight, charting the toreador's struggle with, and final conquest of the bull. He followed this up in 1959 with another set of illustrations representing the bullfight for a book by Luis Miguel Dominguín, which was published two years later and entitled *Toros y Toreros* ('Bulls and Toreadors'). His use of bold, loosely brushed forms has reduced the image to two opposing masses, toreador and bull. Picasso's love of bullfighting was largely based on this sense of the enduring struggle between two forces, a metaphor that encapsulated the Cold War condition of world politics during the late 1950s.

CREATED

Mougins or Vauvenargues

MEDIUM

India ink on paper

SERIES/PERIOD/MOVEMENT

Post-War Communist period

SIMILAR WORKS

The Bullfight by Francisco de Goya, 1816

Bullfighting by Picasso, 1934

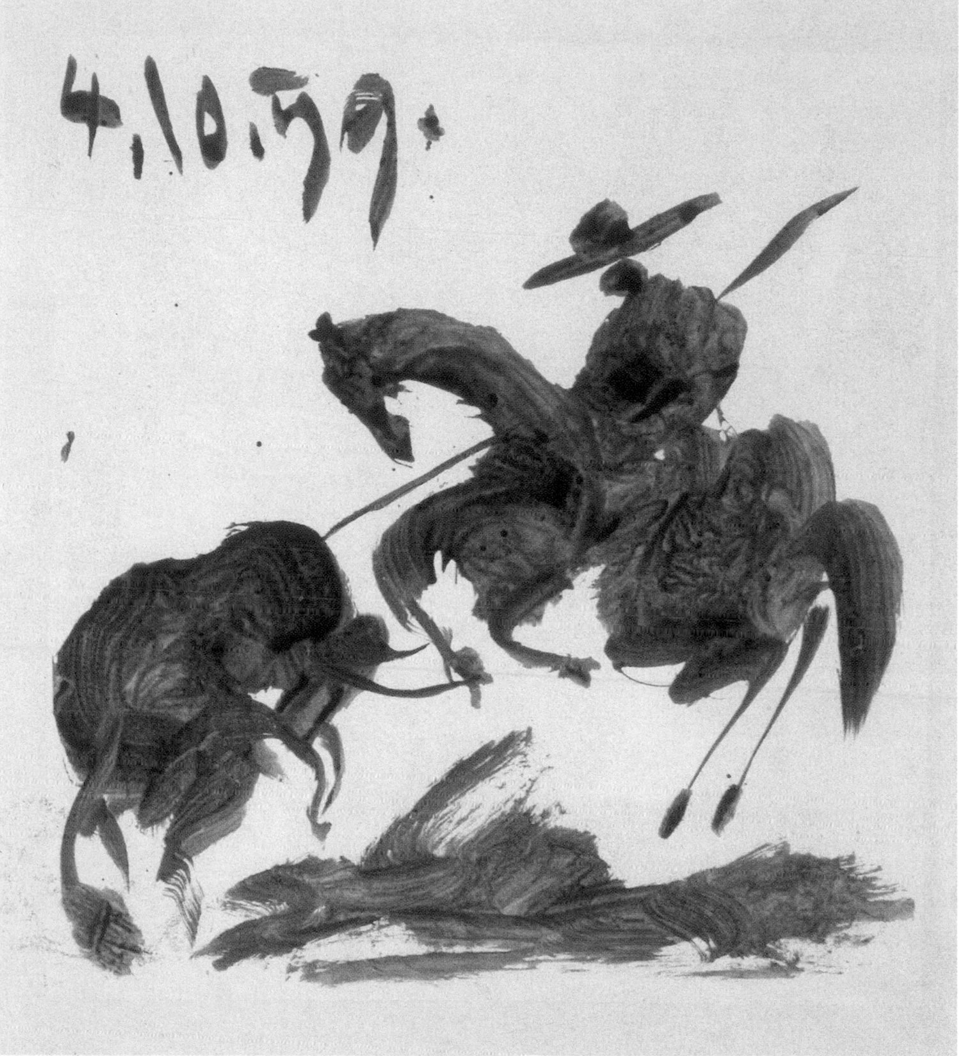
4.10.59.

Footballers, 1961

In the early 1960s Picasso produced a series of sculptures made from sheet metal. These works occupy an ambiguous status somewhere between painting and sculpture, recalling his Cubist sculptures of the 1910s. Originally Picasso used cardboard, which he cut out and folded, but sheet metal provided a sturdier material. The artist then used the flat surface of the cut-out metal as a ground for painting, thus producing polychromatic sculptures. This cut-out process recalls the late works of Matisse, bringing them into three dimensions. Picasso was probably also aware of the monumental sculptures of Alexander Calder (1898–1976), constructed from large sheets of steel, though Picasso's *Footballers* are on a more diminutive scale. Their bright, colourful outfits resemble bathing costumes more than football kits, although Picasso may well also have been recalling the 1908 painting of *Football Players* by Henri Rousseau (1844–1910). There is little evidence to suggest that Picasso had any affection for football; his sporting passions were usually reserved for bullfighting and boxing. However, the dominance of Spanish teams in the recently inaugurated European club competitions may not have been entirely overlooked.

CREATED

Mougins

MEDIUM

Painted sheet metal

SERIES/PERIOD/MOVEMENT

Late period

SIMILAR WORKS

Football Players by Henri Rousseau, 1908

Head of a Woman by Picasso, 1961

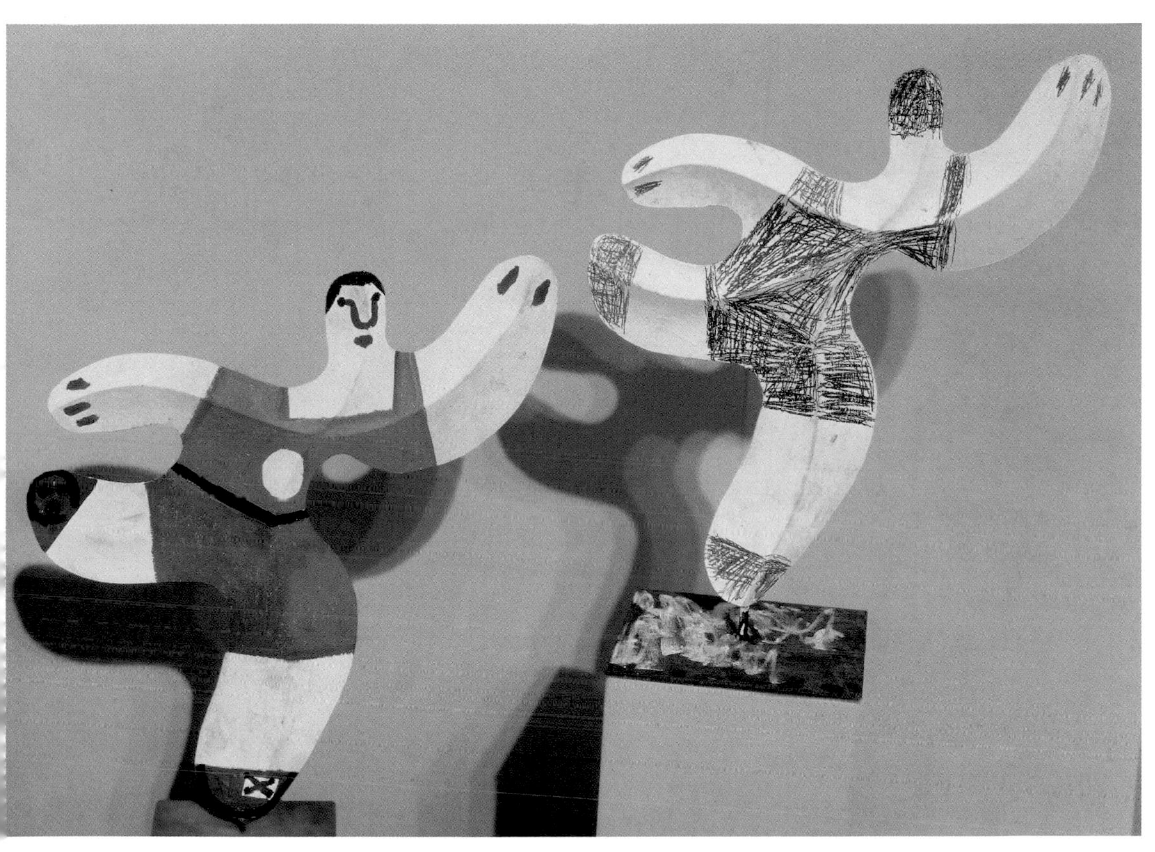

The Rape of the Sabines, 1962

Towards the end of 1962 Picasso turned his attention once more to the atrocities of war. *The Rape of the Sabines* draws upon two traditional sources – Jacques-Louis David's (1748–1825) painting of the same title (1794–99), and Poussin's *The Massacre of Innocents* (1630–31). Once again, Picasso reduced his palette to monochrome, as he had done earlier in both *Guernica* and *The Charnel House*, and presented a scene of violence, in which a naked woman attempts to flee in horror from a rider, sword in hand, bearing down upon her. Yet it is the horse that carries most threat. This aggressive stallion, its teeth bared menacingly and its genitalia explicitly highlighted, exudes sexual threat. The catalyst for this vision of horror was the Cuban Missile Crisis that erupted in November 1962, bringing the world as close as it has ever been to nuclear war. In Picasso's work, the minuscule rider seems physically incapable of controlling his mount much as – it must have seemed at the time – the march towards nuclear Armageddon seemed to be on an unstoppable course.

CREATED

Mougins

MEDIUM

Oil on canvas

SERIES/PERIOD/MOVEMENT

Late period

SIMILAR WORKS

The Rape of the Sabines by Jacques-Louis David, 1794–99

The Charnel House by Picasso, 1945

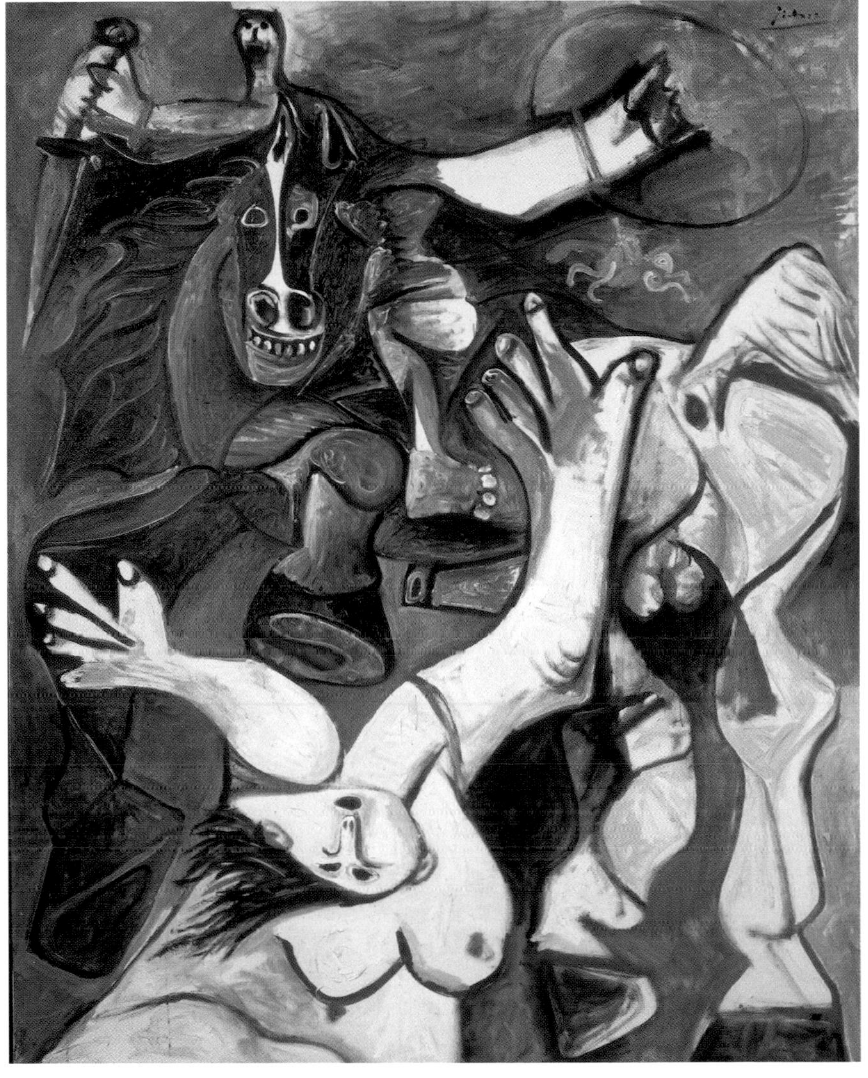

The Morning Concert, 1965

By the mid 1960s Picasso had largely withdrawn from his earlier political activism. Now in his mid-eighties, his paintings focused predominantly on private themes such as the painter and his model, or his series of works based on Old Master paintings. His output in no way diminished, though, and remains a remarkable testimony to his enduring strength. Throughout his life Picasso had never shied away from erotic subjects, representing the male and female nude in a highly explicit manner, and often representing scenes of sexual intercourse. During the last decade of his life, his paintings and etchings revisited this subject matter. Many of these works focus on recumbent female nudes, their bodies twisted and contorted to emphasize the fleshiness of breasts and to reveal genitalia. His *The Morning Concert* of 1965 represents a nude male standing before a female nude reclining upon cushions with her head thrown back as if in a dream. Here, the inclusion of the trumpet played by the male figure is an obvious phallic reference, adding an erotic frisson to the work.

CREATED

Mougins

MEDIUM

Oil on canvas

SERIES/PERIOD/MOVEMENT

Late period

SIMILAR WORKS

Odalisque with a Slave by Jean Auguste Dominique Ingres, 1840

Odalisque with Red Culottes by Henri Matisse, 1921

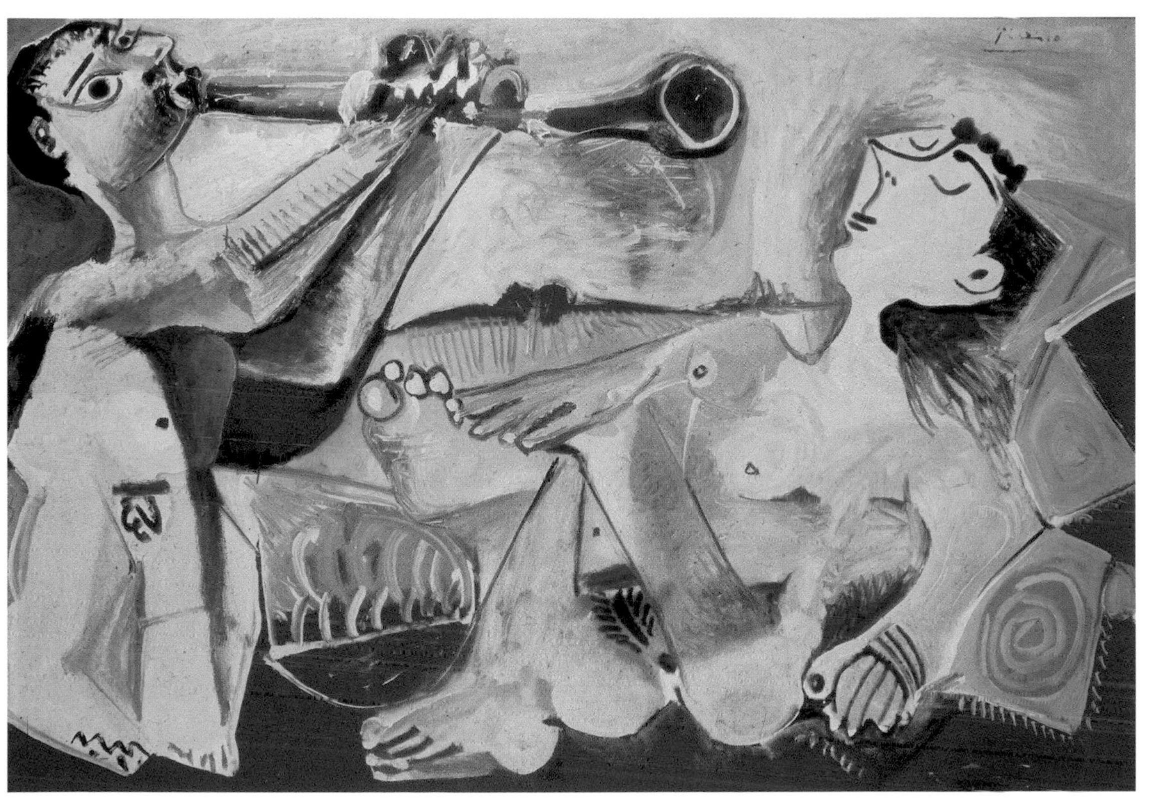

Suite 156, L10, 1970

Between January 1970 and June 1972 Picasso produced a series of 156 engravings. These were the last works in this medium that he was to produce. Many of the works paid homage to past artists who had inspired him during his career, including Rembrandt (1606–69) and Edgar Degas (1834–1917). Some focused upon brothel scenes, one even including the subject of La Celestine, the eponymous hero of a fifteenth-century Spanish novel. Sixty-six years earlier Picasso had produced a portrait of the one-eyed brothel-keeper Carlota Valdivia, who plied her trade near Picasso's Barcelona studio, in the guise of La Celestine. Such reminiscences were a key part of these late works. This astonishingly complex engraving represents a theatrical stage upon which many of the characters from Picasso's life are presented. The stage itself is surrounded by other characters derived from a lifetime of works, many floating above the stage in a dreamlike manner. It is as if Picasso has tried to sum up his whole artistic life in a single image.

CREATED

Mougins

MEDIUM

Etching on paper

SERIES/PERIOD/MOVEMENT

Late period

SIMILAR WORKS

Christ's Entry into Brussels (etching) by James Ensor, 1898

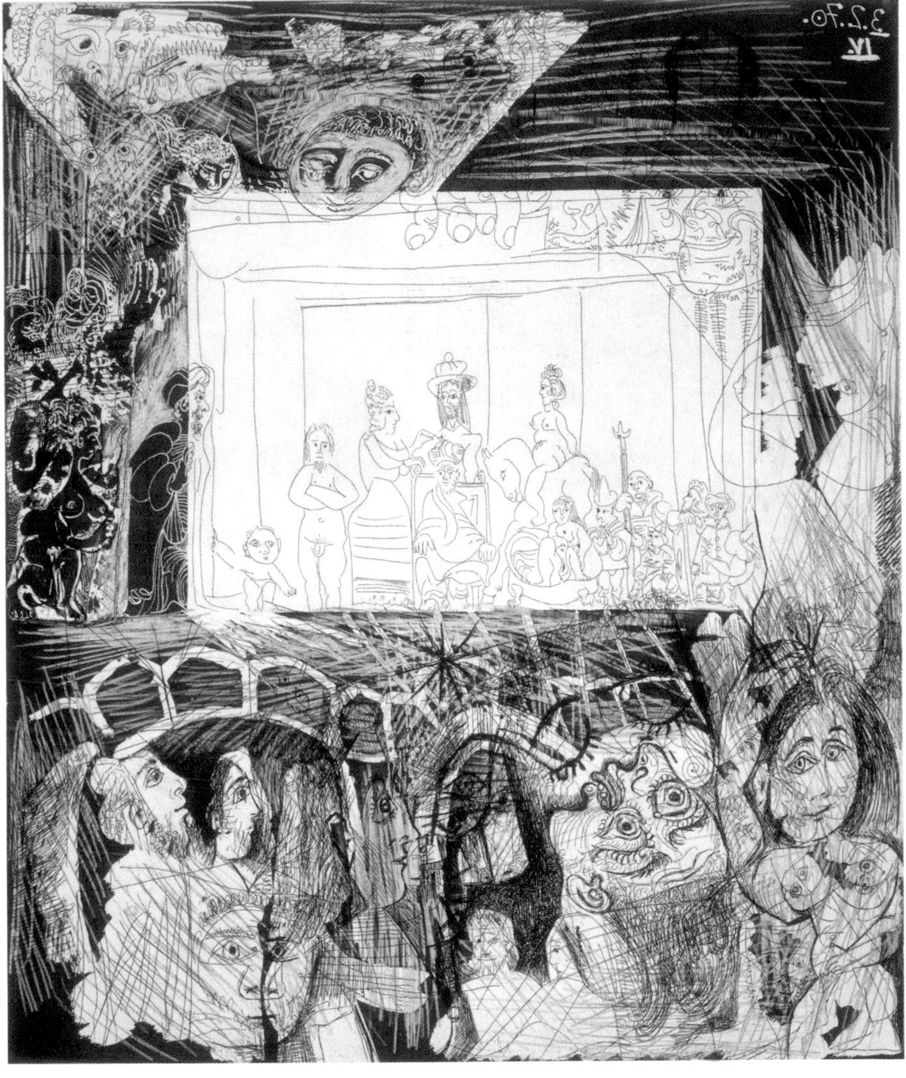

Picasso

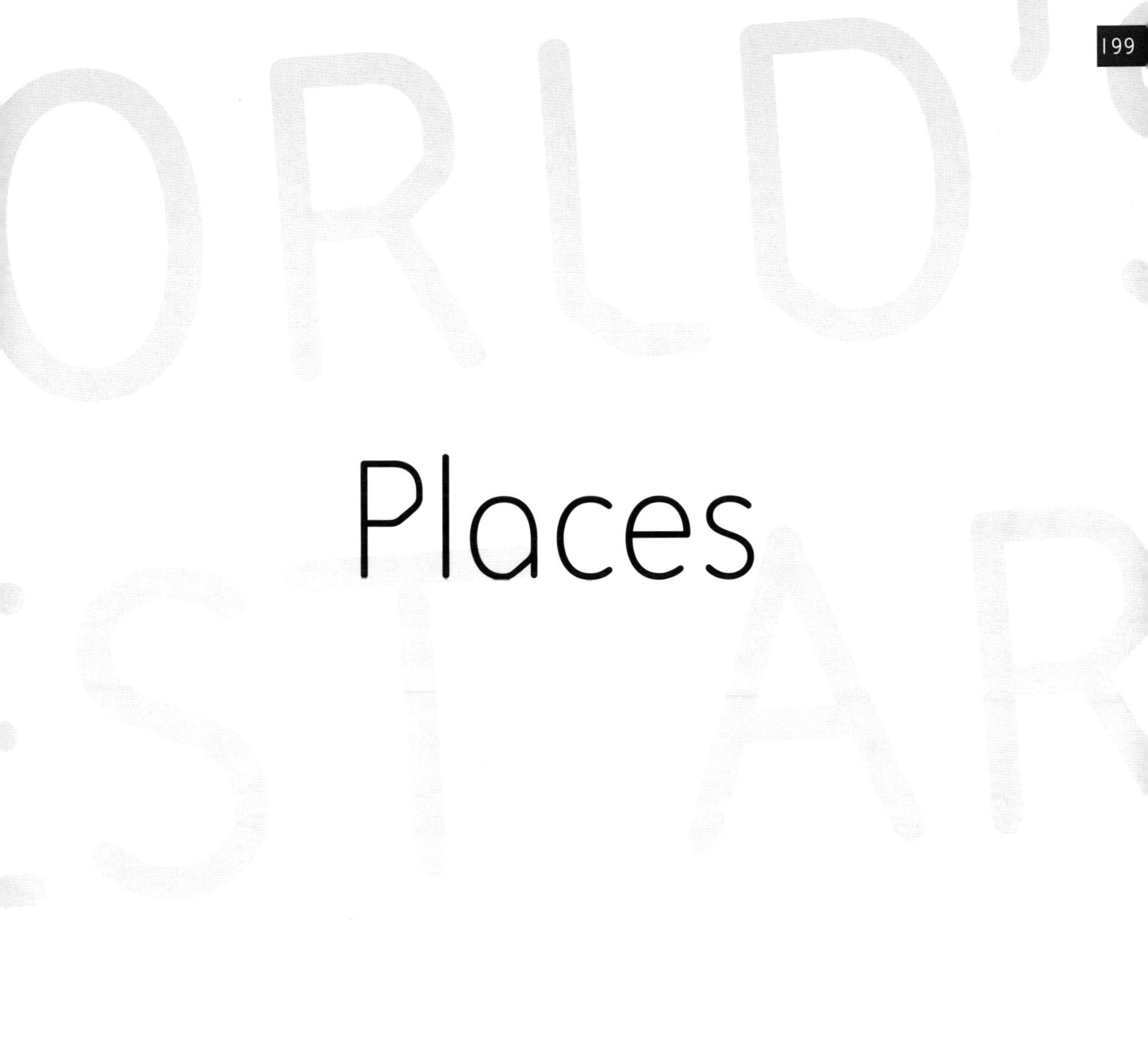

Places

Mountains of Málaga, 1897

Throughout his career, Picasso produced works in many genres, from history painting and portraits, to nudes and still lifes. He also produced an extensive range of landscapes, many painted in the numerous sites in which he lived and worked. Picasso's earliest landscape painting, a view of the port in his native Málaga, dates from around 1890 when he was just nine years old. Five years later he produced another series of views of the Spanish Mediterranean coast at Alicante and Valencia. These were executed on a summer vacation shortly before the Picasso family moved to Barcelona. In 1897, when Picasso produced this landscape, he was still just 16 years of age and about to leave his family to study in Madrid. The relatively small-scale oil sketch represents a quiet scene overlooking a barren hillside, with low-lying mountains in the distance, notably emphasizing the loneliness and isolation of this space beyond the city. This image recalls the many regional landscape paintings produced in France throughout the nineteenth century.

CREATED

Málaga

MEDIUM

Oil on canvas

SERIES/PERIOD/MOVEMENT

Early period

SIMILAR WORKS

Harvest by Charles-François Daubigny, 1851

The Angelus by Jean François Millet, 1857–59

Pablo Picasso *Born* 1881 Málaga, Spain

Died 1973

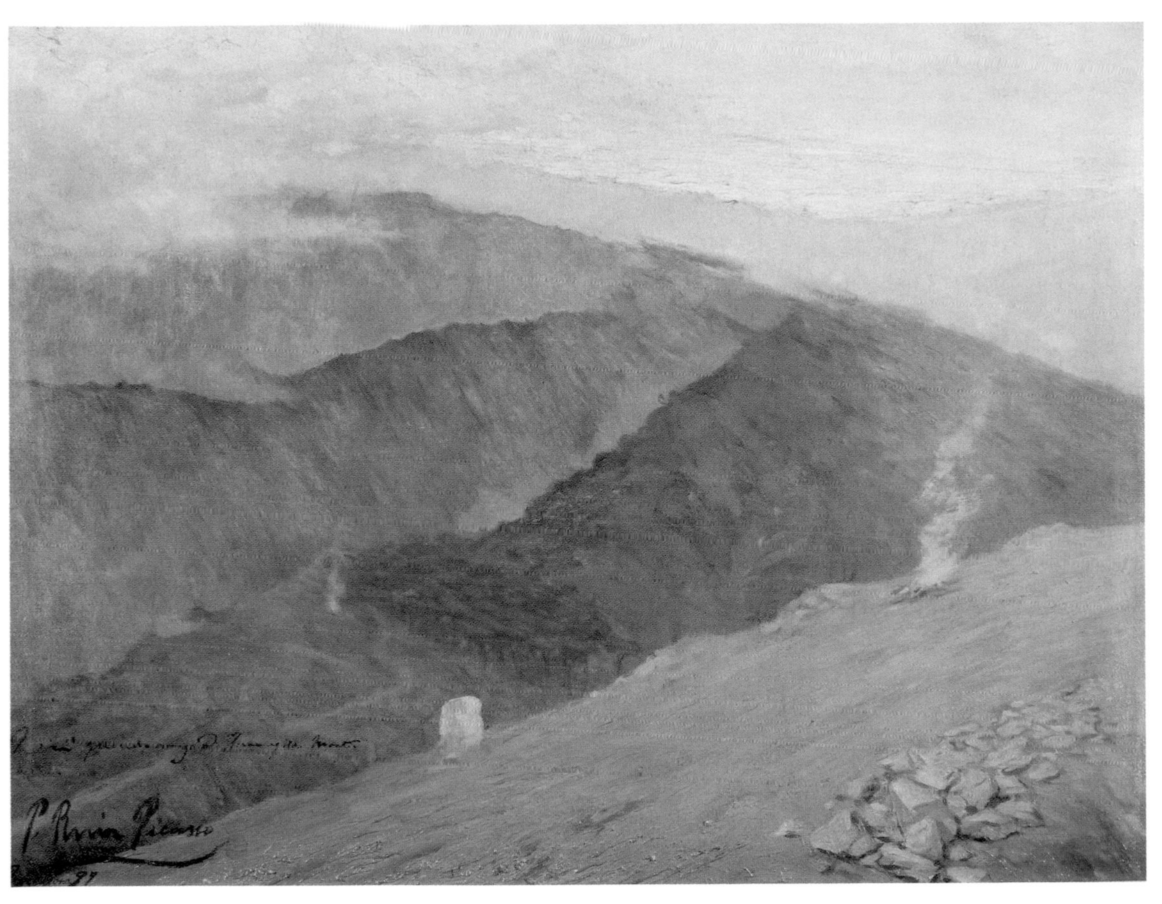

The Four Cats Café, 1900

In 1899, the young Picasso returned to Barcelona. At this time, the city was an exciting, cosmopolitan, urban centre that attracted a wide range of artists, writers and political radicals. It was the centre of the cultural movement known as Modernismo, a Catalan variation of Art Nouveau, exemplified by the weird and wonderful architecture of Antoni Gaudí (1852–1926). Picasso spent much of his time at El Quatre Gats, or The Four Cats, a tavern that opened in 1897 and was based upon Aristide Bruant's famous Parisian tavern Le Chat Noir. The Four Cats rapidly became a haunt for the artistic and the political radicals of Barcelona. For the young Picasso, The Four Cats was a place of great excitement, a space where he met many of the avant-garde artists of Spain, including Ramon Casas (1866–1932) and Santiago Rusiñol (1861–1931), and where he was introduced to the most recent artistic developments in Europe. Picasso's painting of a couple drinking at The Four Cats places the viewer down amongst the clientele, as if engaging in a conspiratorial conversation with the drinking couple.

CREATED

Barcelona

MEDIUM

Oil on canvas

SERIES/PERIOD/MOVEMENT

Early period

SIMILAR WORKS

In a Café (The Absinthe Drinker) by Edgar Degas, 1875–76

Interior of a Café by Edouard Manet, 1880

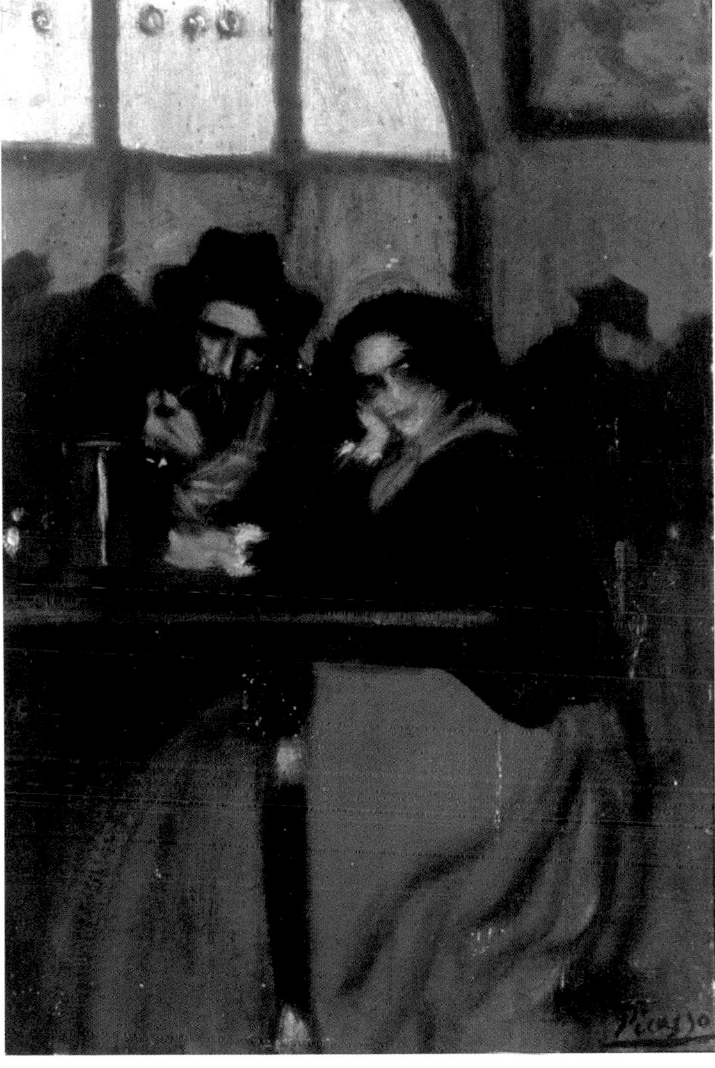
Picasso

Menu from The Four Cats, 1899–1900

'An inn for the disillusioned ... a corner full of warmth for those who long for home ... a place to cure the ills of our century, and a place for friendship and harmony....' This was how the painter Rusiñol described The Four Cats tavern. Part beer hall, part cabaret and part restaurant, The Four Cats catered for a wide spectrum of Barcelona's bohemian society, from the poverty-stricken artist to the rich art collector. Lectures and musical events were staged and, for a period of time, it even published its own journal, also under the title *Els Quatre Gats*. Picasso became a key member of the Four Cats family. In 1900 he produced a series of charcoal drawings, including many of the tavern's regulars, for an exhibition at the Sala Parés, a prestigious gallery in Barcelona. The proprietor of The Four Cats, Pere Romeu, also asked him to design menu cards and advertising flyers. This one reveals Picasso's awareness of the work of Henri de Toulouse-Lautrec (1864–1901), not least of all the advertising posters he produced for the Moulin Rouge and Bruant's Ambassadeurs.

CREATED

Barcelona

MEDIUM

Pencil on printed paper

SERIES/PERIOD/MOVEMENT

Early period

SIMILAR WORKS

Moulin Rouge (poster) by Henri de Toulouse-Lautrec, 1891

Ambassadeurs: Aristide Bruant (poster) by Henri de Toulouse-Lautrec, 1892

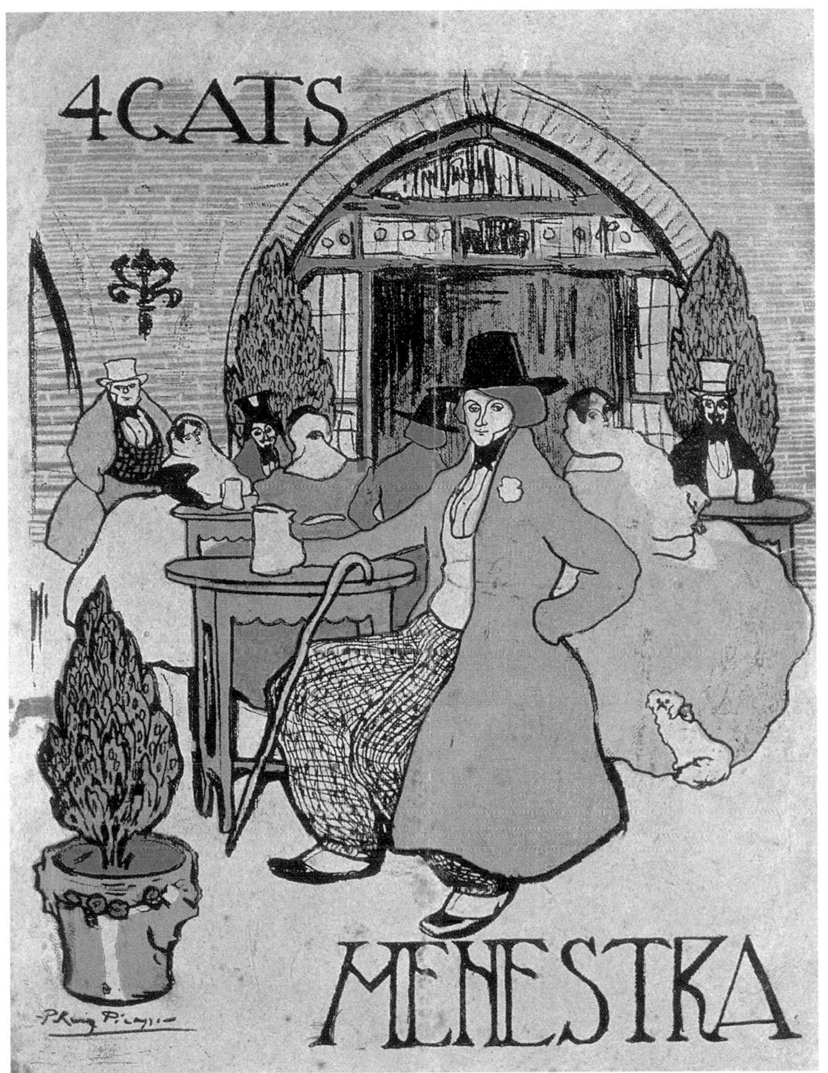
4CATS
MENESTRA
P. Ruiz Picasso

Le Moulin de la Galette, 1900

Picasso first visited Paris in 1900 and set up a studio in Montmartre. By this time Montmartre had developed a reputation as the bohemian centre of the city and was a mecca for artists. Situated on the hills to the north of the city, Montmartre's rural past could still be detected by the presence of its most famous windmill, the Moulin de la Galette. By the time Picasso first visited it, however, the Moulin de la Galette had long since ceased to function as a working windmill, having been transformed into a tavern and dance hall that had become a centre of Parisian nightlife. Picasso was not the first artist to paint the Moulin de la Galette – both Pierre-Auguste Renoir (1841–1919) and Toulouse-Lautrec had previously depicted this famous site. Indeed, Picasso was heavily influenced by Toulouse-Lautrec at this stage of his career. This work shows a busy night scene crowded with well-dressed men and women. The bright, lurid colours and garish lighting aptly highlight the gaiety and splendour of turn-of-the-century Paris, widely regarded as the playground of Europe.

CREATED

Paris

MEDIUM

Oil on canvas

SERIES/PERIOD/MOVEMENT

Early period

SIMILAR WORKS

Le Moulin de la Galette by Pierre Auguste Renoir, 1876

At the Moulin de la Galette by Henri de Toulouse-Lautrec, 1889

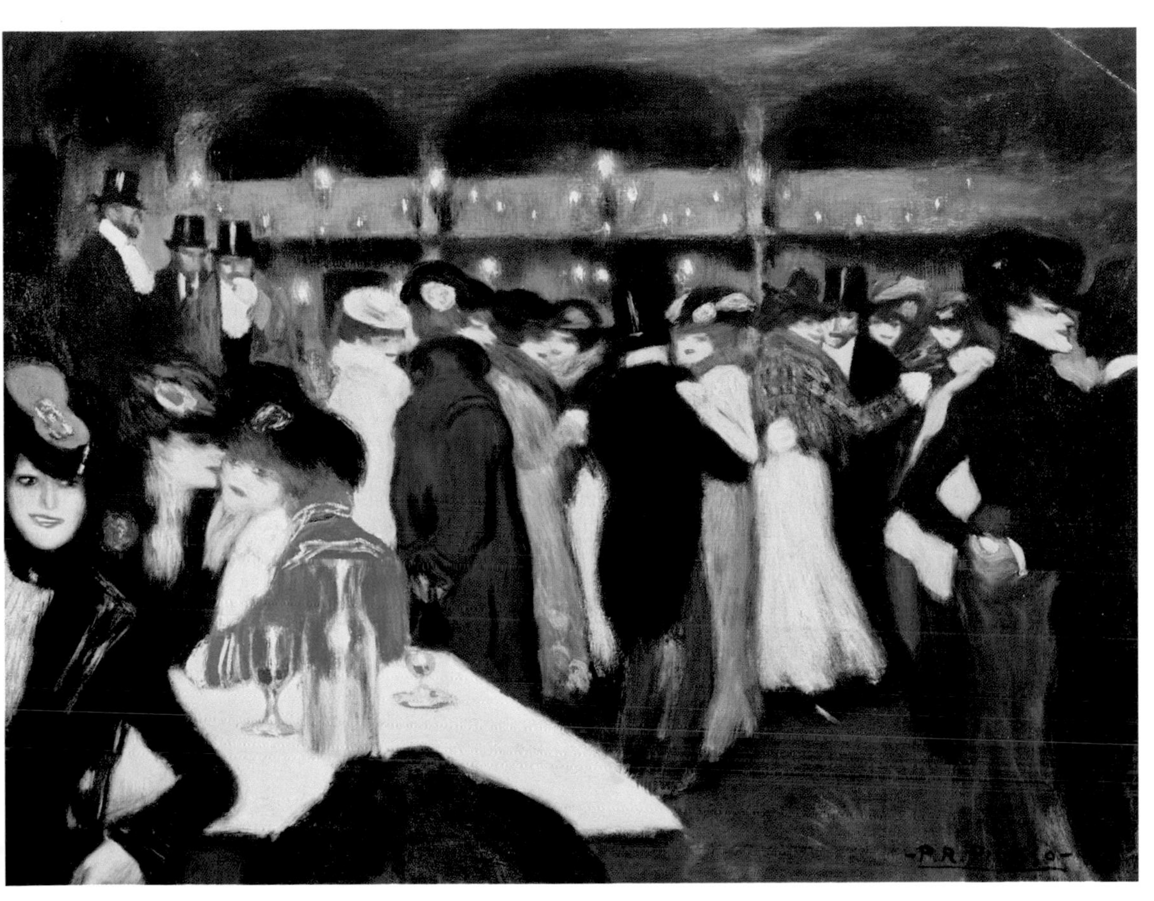

Public Garden, 1901

Picasso's first trip to Paris was an inspiration to the artist, and he hurried back there in the summer of 1901. The city by now had a long-established reputation as the centre of the art world and had attracted artists from all over the world for many years. Several of the major artistic innovations of the period had been associated with Paris and the city boasted a fantastic collection of public and private galleries. In addition, many dealers and collectors gravitated towards Paris, thus making it one of the key economic centres of the art world. Since the transformation of the city in the mid-nineteenth century, Paris had also become a city full of public parks, squares and boulevards, where Parisians regularly spent their leisure hours. Picasso's *Public Garden* shows such a space. However the exclusive emphasis on women and children suggests that this work, reminiscent of similar scenes by the French Nabi painter Edouard Vuillard (1868–1940), was painted during the working week, and the figures represented are working nannies, rather than mothers.

CREATED

Paris

MEDIUM

Oil on canvas

SERIES/PERIOD/MOVEMENT

Early period

SIMILAR WORKS

A Sunday Afternoon on the Island of La Grande-Jatte by Georges Seurat, 1884–86

Repast in a Garden by Edouard Vuillard, 1898

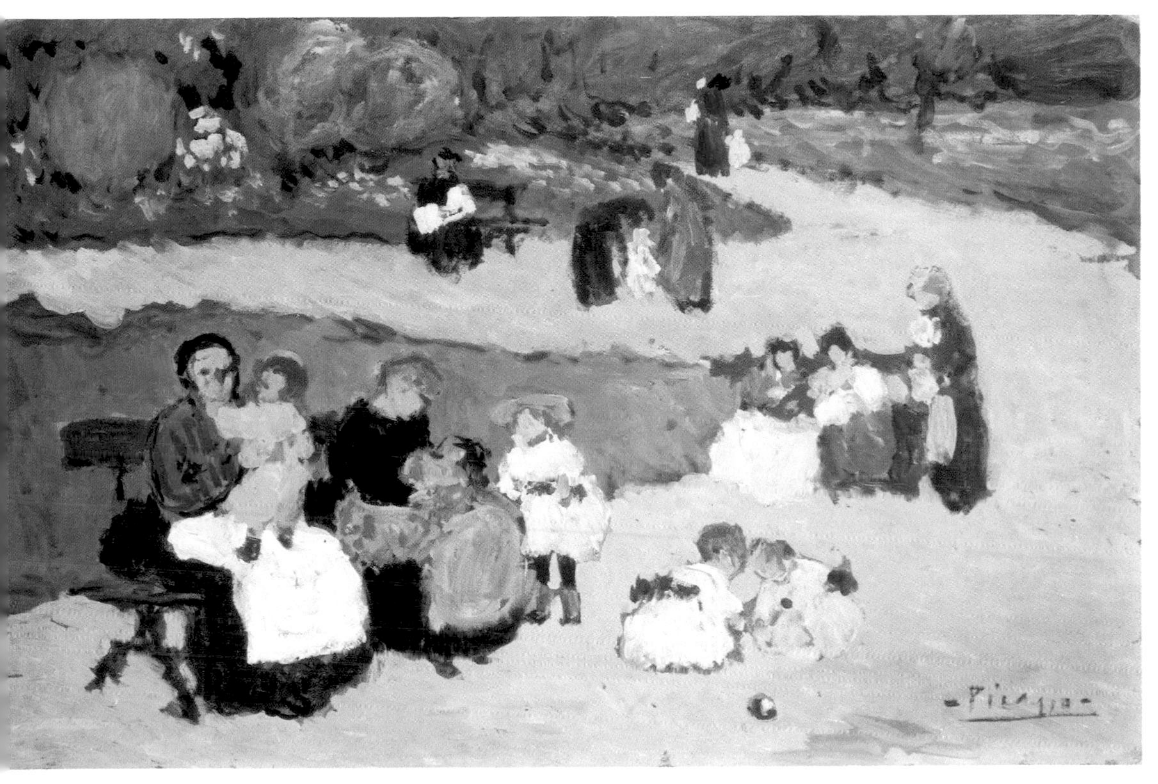
Picasso

Rooftops in Barcelona, 1903

By the spring of 1903 Picasso was once more back in Barcelona. Over the previous three years he had moved back and forth between Paris and Barcelona, the bohemian nature of both cities seeming to suit his personality well. By now, however, the mood of Barcelona was changing, and Picasso's circle of friends was beginning to break up. In July 1903 The Four Cats tavern – the renowned haunt of Barcelona's artistic and political radicals – closed its doors. Its existence had been brief, just six years, but coincided with the peak of the Modernista movement, and its closure heralded the decline of Barcelona's glorious turn-of-the-century cultural renaissance. Picasso's *Rooftops in Barcelona* seems to echo this sense of a passing moment. Here the artist has presented a view over a ramshackle conglomeration of buildings, the distant horizon obscured by the amorphous mass of undifferentiated architecture. Here, the absence of people is striking, and Picasso seems to be recording his increasing loneliness in the city. In many ways, this painting can be read as Picasso's final farewell to Barcelona.

CREATED

Barcelona

MEDIUM

Oil on canvas

SERIES/PERIOD/MOVEMENT

Blue period

SIMILAR WORKS

Houses at L'Estaque by Georges Braque, 1908

Houses on the Hill (Horta de Ebro) by Picasso, 1909

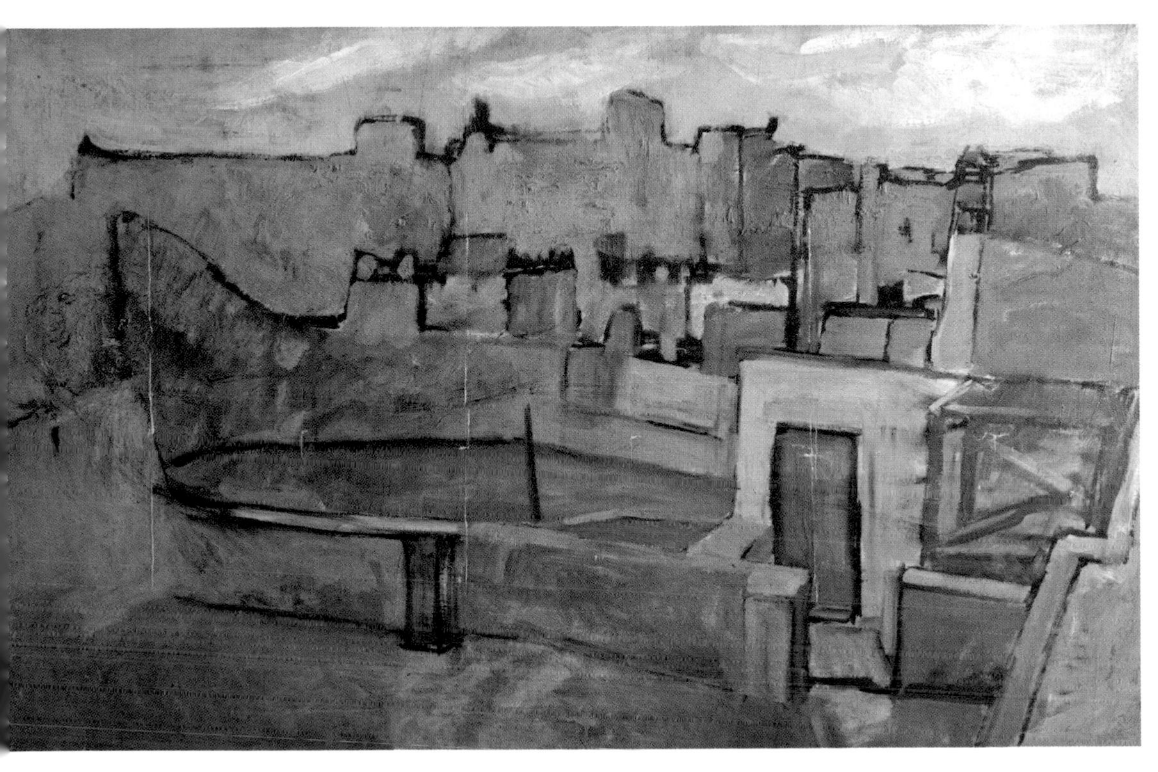

Gósol, 1906

The tiny village of Gósol rests in a valley in the Pyrenees, on the Spanish side of the border. In 1906, Picasso and his partner Fernande Olivier visited the village together. At this time, Gósol was a remote site and no roads passed through the village. Indeed, it was necessary for Picasso and Fernande to make the last part of their journey by mule. They stayed at the village's only inn, the Cal Tampanada, and took excursions into the mountains or visited the ruined medieval village that had been largely abandoned for centuries. Picasso produced a significant body of paintings during the period of over two months he spent in the mountains. Some, like this landscape, celebrate the remoteness of the village and highlight the way in which the buildings blend into the mountain landscape. The dark ochre shading that determines the walls of the buildings is barely distinguishable from the mass of rocks rising behind, showing nature and civilization co-existing in peace and harmony.

CREATED

Gósol

MEDIUM

Oil on canvas

SERIES/PERIOD/MOVEMENT

Proto-Cubist period

SIMILAR WORKS

Houses at L'Estaque by Paul Cézanne, 1879–82

Houses on the Hill (Horta de Ebro) by Picasso, 1909

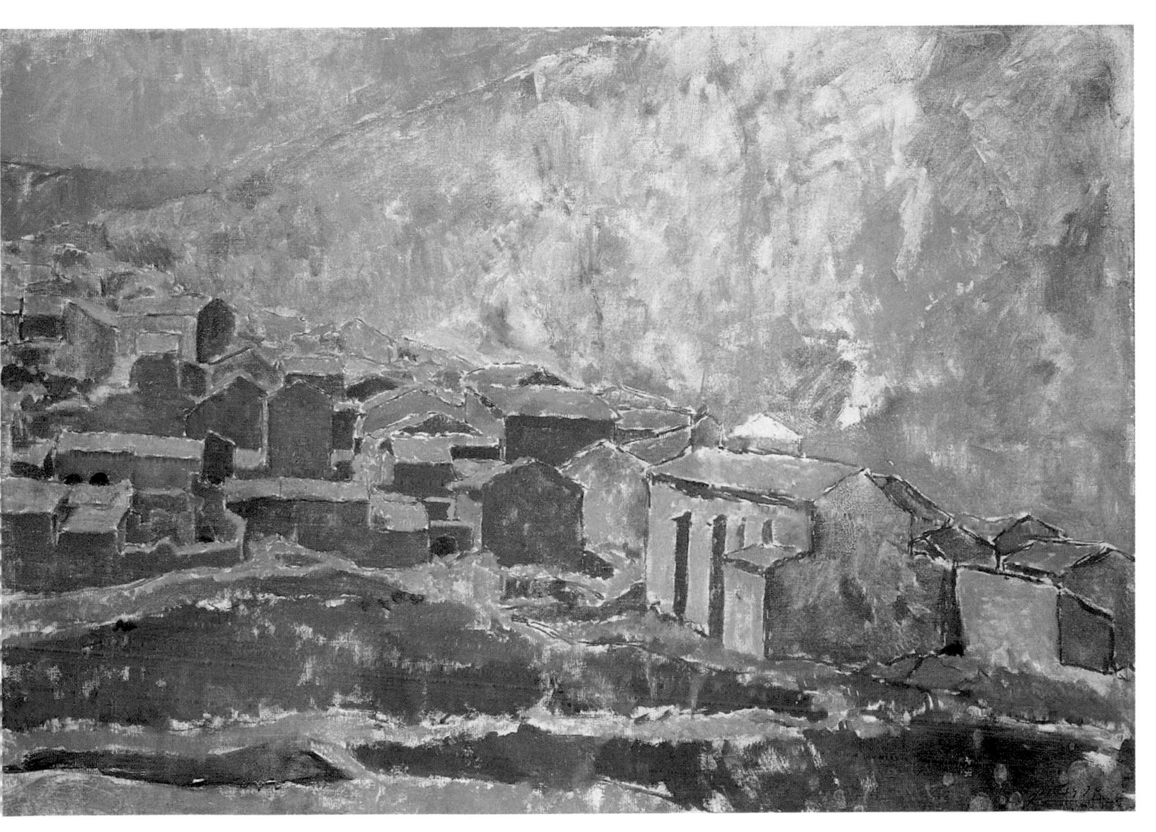

Landscape (La Rue-des-Bois), 1908

Many of Picasso's landscape paintings of this period were produced during his various summer trips out of Paris. In 1908, he took a trip with Fernande to a small French village called La Rue-des-Bois, 65 km (40 miles) north of Paris. The region is heavily forested and trees dominate the landscape. Picasso soon embraced this and produced a series of wooded landscape scenes that capture the mood of the place. However, the works also pay homage to the French painter Paul Cézanne (1839–1906). Since the death of Cézanne in 1906, Picasso had been striving to find a way to forge a dialogue with the older artist in his own works. 'Cézanne was my one and only master,' Picasso later claimed. This was certainly an exaggeration, not least of all as Picasso's works reveal a wide range of influences – from old masters and more contemporary artists. However, the landscapes produced by Picasso at La Rue-des-Bois certainly reveal a heavy debt to Cézanne, as can clearly be detected in the boldly Cézannesque forms and colours of *Landscape (La Rue-des-Bois)*.

CREATED

La Rue-des-Bois

MEDIUM

Oil on canvas

SERIES/PERIOD/MOVEMENT

Proto-Cubist period

SIMILAR WORKS

Pine Tree near Aix-en-Provence by Paul Cézanne, 1890s

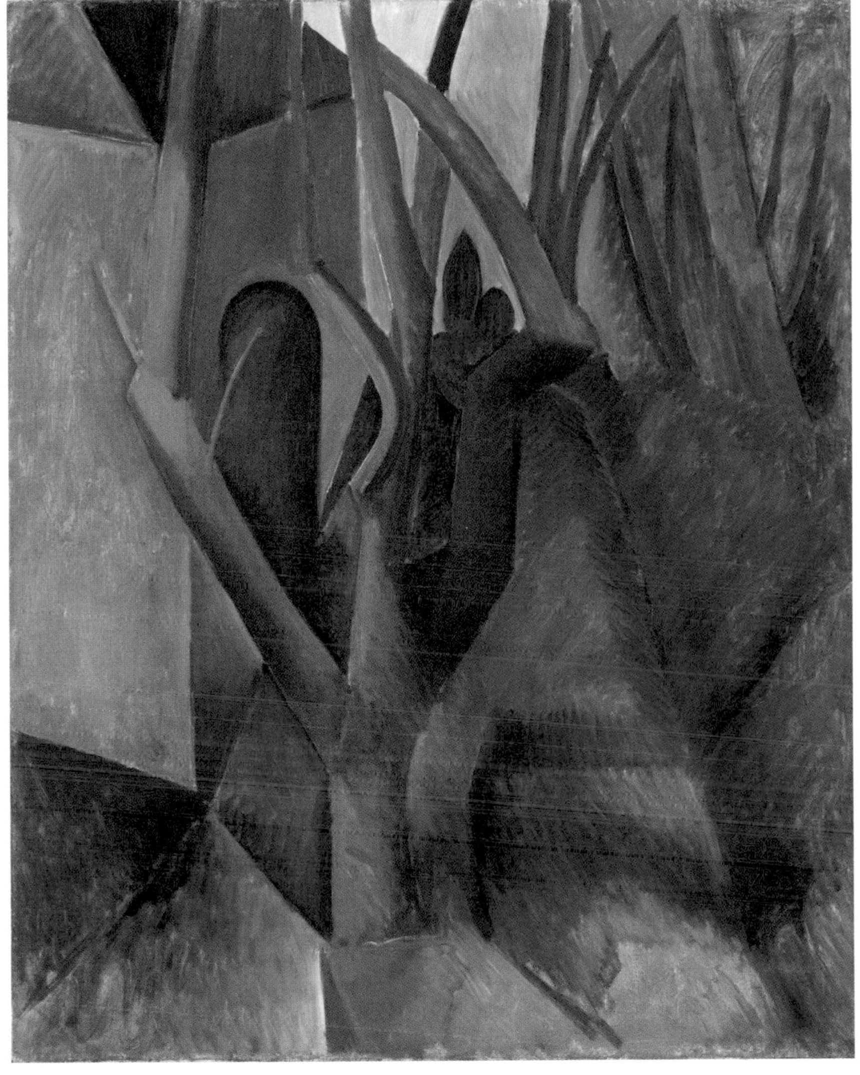

Small House in a Garden, 1908

Another of the landscapes Picasso produced at La Rue-des-Bois reinforces the link between Picasso and Cézanne. Here Picasso presents a humble scene, a small house fenced off from a pathway and framed by two trees. In the background a third tree appears silhouetted against a bluish-grey sky. It is the absence of detail and the solidity of the forms that relates most closely to Cézanne's work. The house itself has been reduced to three solid planes – end wall, side wall and roof, though the latter two areas blend into each other. There is no indication of door, window or chimney, and the colours used to depict this house match those used to describe the surrounding landscape. Also the use of bold, diagonal brushstrokes reduces the sense of spatial recession and the background sky seems every bit as solid as the foreground tree. Notably, while Picasso was producing his Cézannesque landscapes in northern France, Georges Braque (1882–1963) was producing similar works in the south at L'Estaque, in Cézanne's native Aix-en-Provence. Picasso and Braque exhibited these works together in Paris towards the end of 1908.

CREATED

La Rue-des-Bois

MEDIUM

Oil on canvas

SERIES/PERIOD/MOVEMENT

Proto-Cubist period

SIMILAR WORKS

The House of the Hanged Man by Paul Cézanne, 1873

Houses at L'Estaque by Georges Braque, 1908

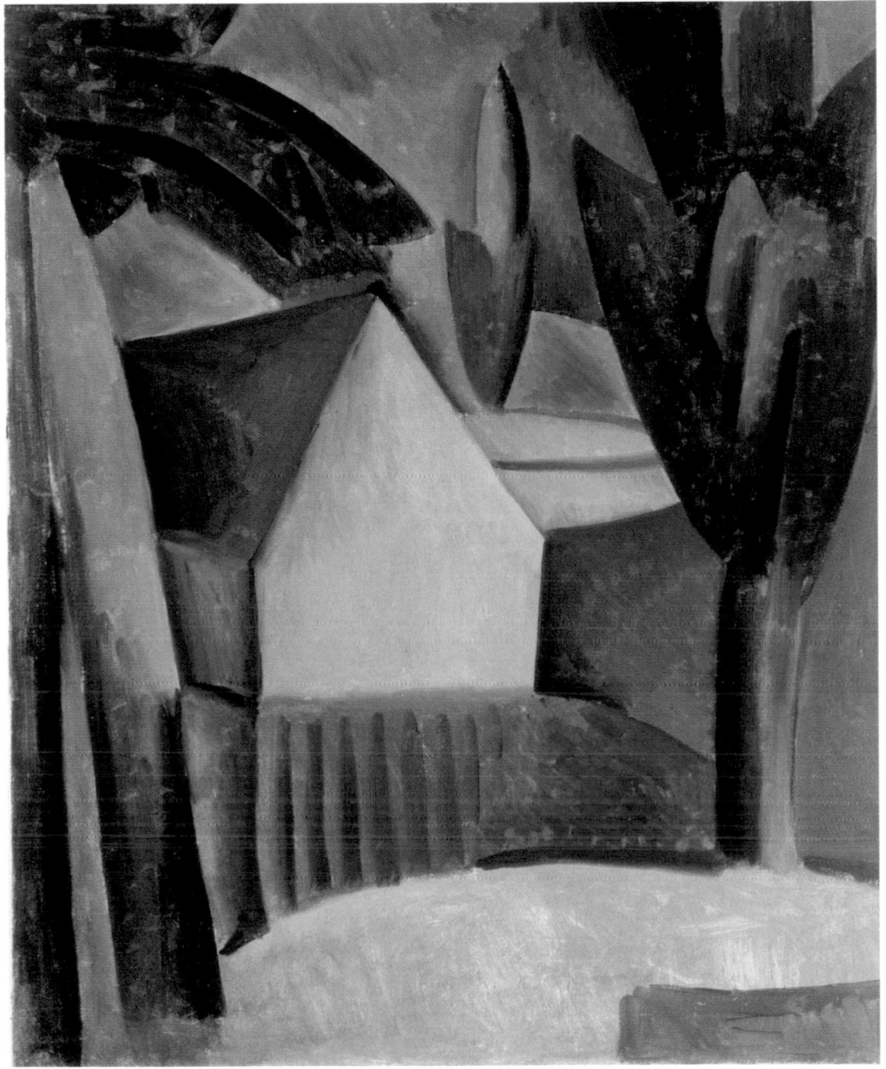

Factory at Horta de Ebro, 1909

When Picasso visited Horta de Ebro in the summer of 1909, it was his second visit to the village on the Aragon border, having earlier spent seven months there in 1898 with his friend Manuel Pallarès. Horta, like Gósol, was a quiet mountain village and here Picasso began a series of landscape views. These followed on from the paintings he had produced a year earlier at La Rue-des-Bois, as well as Braque's views of L'Estaque. One of the best known of these works, *Factory at Horta de Ebro*, again draws heavily from Cézanne both in colour and form. One of the most notable features, however, is the way in which Picasso has happily manipulated the topographical features of the landscape. The chimney that appears in the background is, in fact, nowhere evident in Horta. Rather it represents a chimney used for burning olive waste, situated away from the village. Similarly, Picasso has included palm trees in this work, though no such trees grew in or near the village. Picasso has freely introduced these motives to serve the compositional structure of the work.

CREATED

Horta de Ebro

MEDIUM

Oil on canvas

SERIES/PERIOD/MOVEMENT

Early Cubist period

SIMILAR WORKS

Factory near Pontoise by Camille Pissarro, 1873

Workshops at the Porta Romana by Umberto Boccioni, 1909

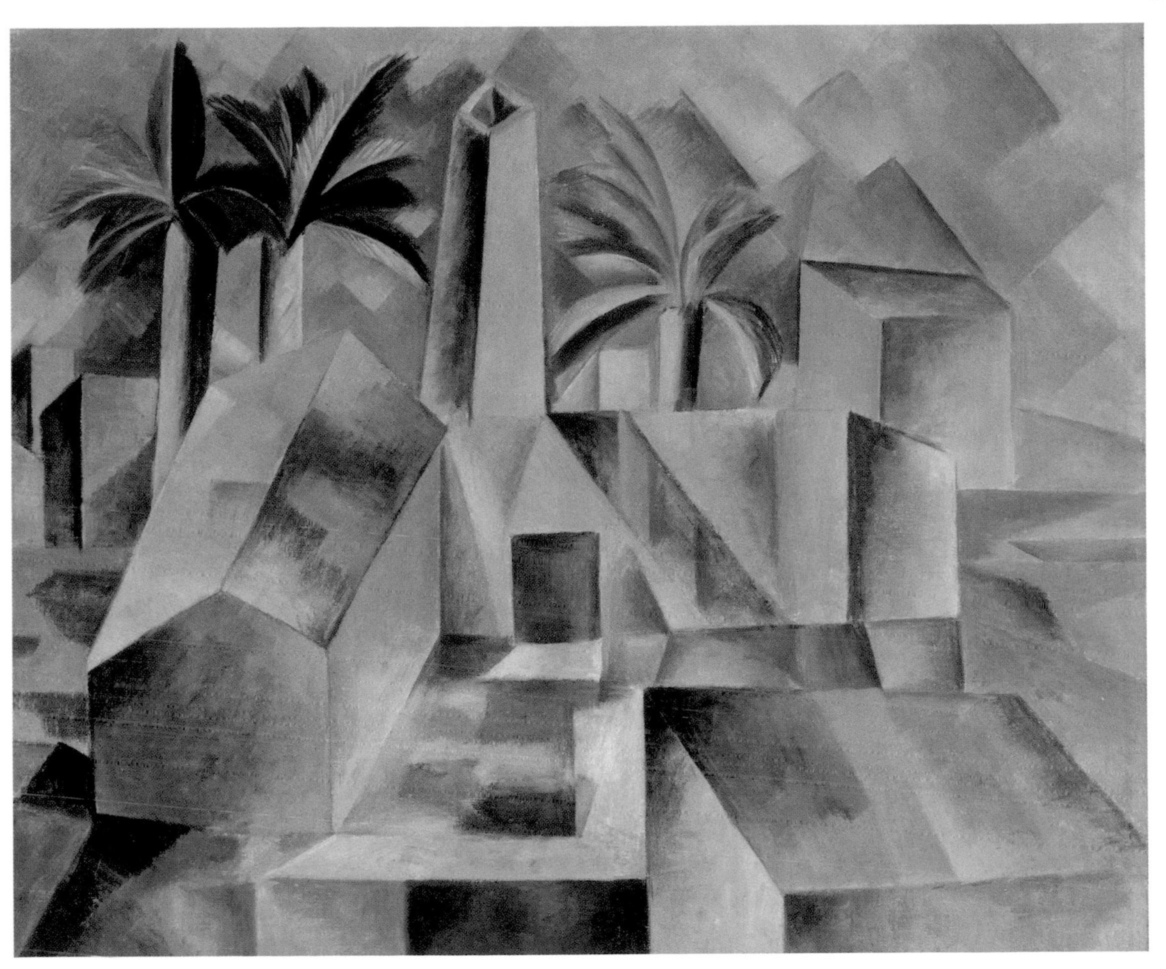

Bather, 1909

The experience of the Horta de Ebro landscapes was certainly to influence a number of works based on the bathers theme that Picasso produced throughout 1909. Some of these were produced at Horta, others back in Paris. What is interesting here is the way in which Picasso has taken liberties with the anatomy of the body, much as he did with the topography of the landscape at Horta. In this work, for example, Picasso has twisted and contorted the body so that we seem simultaneously to see separate parts of the bather from different angles. Thus both the left and right shoulder can be seen, despite the twist of the body, and both back and side views are offered to the viewer. Moreover, the body itself is difficult to distinguish from the background, its forms painted in the same grey and ochre tones, and its outline at times blending into the background space. Here the surface of the body is treated like the Horta landscape, its various components freely reordered and rearranged at the artist's whim.

CREATED

Paris

MEDIUM

Oil on canvas

SERIES/PERIOD/MOVEMENT

Early Cubist period

SIMILAR WORKS

The Valpinçon Bather by Jean Auguste Dominique Ingres, 1808

Large Nude by Georges Braque, 1908

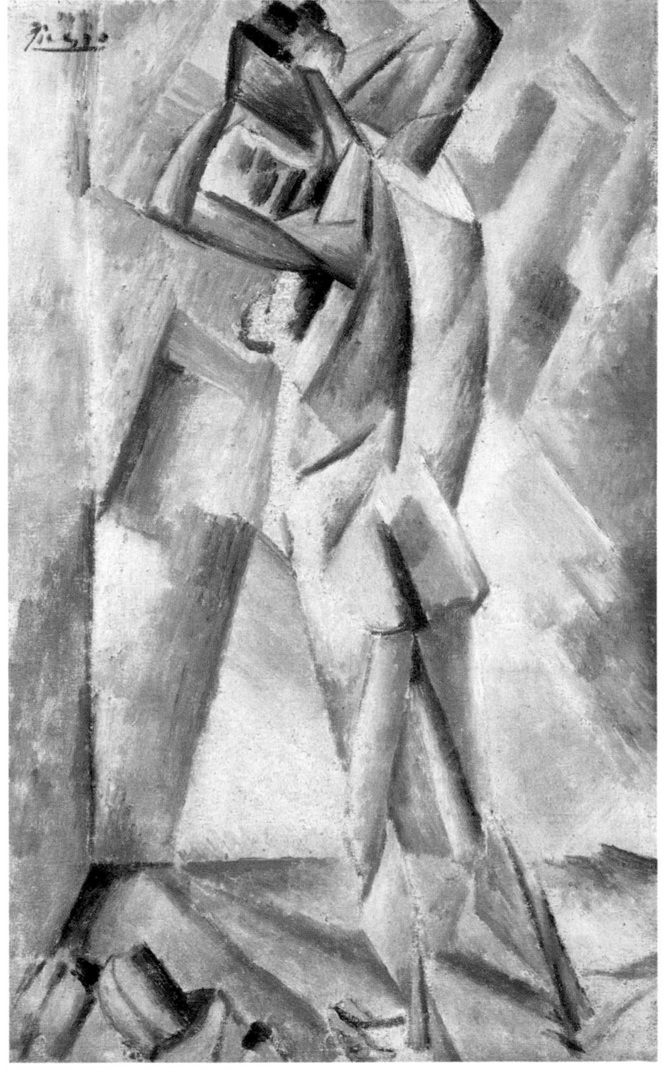

El Paseo de Colon, 1917

Picasso spent much of the First World War in Paris. In 1917, however, he accompanied Sergei Diaghilev's (1872–1929) Ballets Russes on a European tour. As well as visiting Rome, Naples and Pompeii, the tour took Picasso back to his native Spain, making stops at Madrid and Barcelona. Back in Barcelona, he painted this image representing the port district of the city of his youth. El Paseo de Colon is situated at one end of Las Ramblas, the long street that cuts a swathe through the centre of Barcelona. At the south end is a large monument dedicated to Christopher Columbus. Erected as part of the Barcelona Universal Exhibition of 1888, the monument consists of a large column surmounted by a statue showing the famous explorer looking out to sea and pointing towards the New World. Picasso's image, painted from his hotel room overlooking the site, places the column at the centre of the canvas, while the statue of Columbus is silhouetted against a blood-red sun. A large Spanish flag hanging from the balcony, and echoing these sunset colours, adds a nostalgic nationalism to the scene.

CREATED

Barcelona

MEDIUM

Oil on canvas

SERIES/PERIOD/MOVEMENT

Cubist period

SIMILAR WORKS

Open Window, Collioure by Henri Matisse, 1905

The Open Window by Juan Gris, 1921

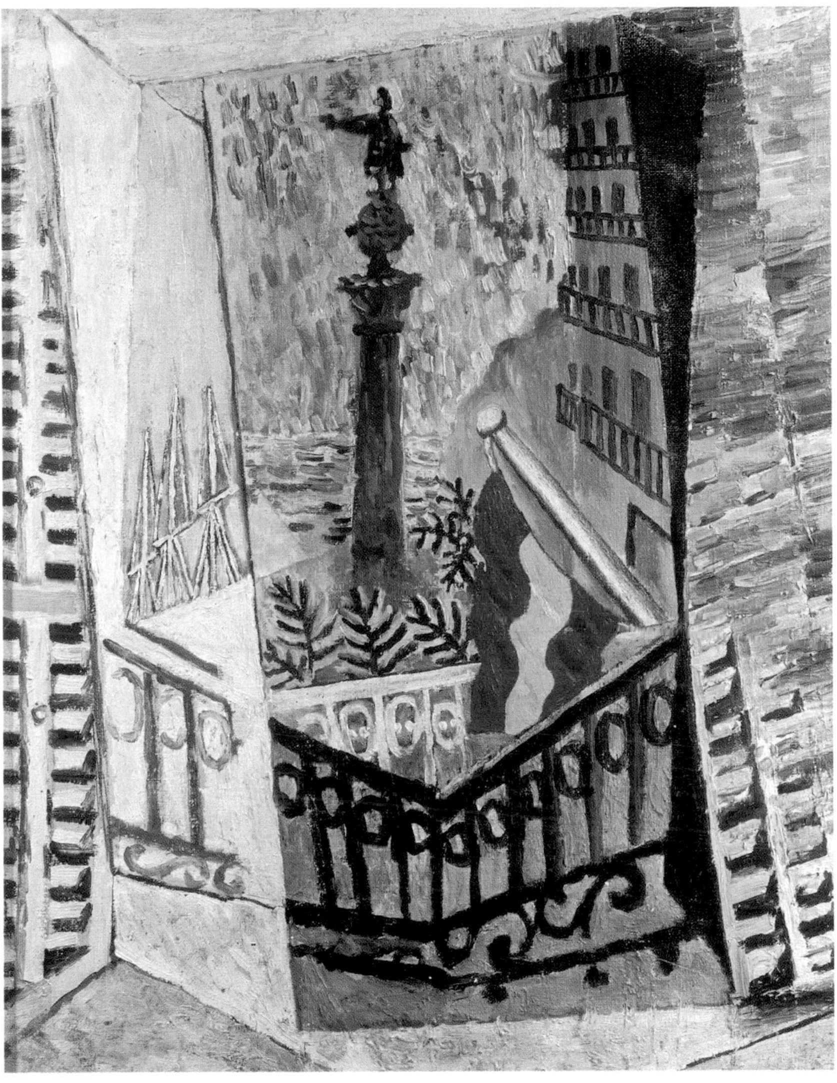

Sketch for the Stage Curtain for *Tricorne* by Manuel de Falla, 1919

A sense of nostalgia for his native Spain pervaded much of Picasso's theatre work in the period just after the First World War. Since his marriage to the Russian ballet dancer Olga Khokhlova in 1918, Picasso's work for the Ballets Russes had significantly increased, and in the summer of 1919 he travelled to London to work on stage and costume designs for a new performance, *Tricorne* ('The Three-Cornered Hat'). Picasso was delighted to participate in this romantic celebration of eighteenth-century Spanish life, based on a novel by Pedro Alarcón (1833–1891) and featuring the music of Manuel de Falla (1876–1946). His stage curtain, seen here in an oil sketch produced for Diaghilev, features an array of Spanish characters, all in traditional costume. The scene is set at a bullfight, at the moment when the dead bull is being removed from the ring. Picasso has situated the spectator very much as an audience member, overlooking the scene from an arcaded balcony. Here Picasso was drawing upon his extensive experiences attending bullfights back in his native Spain.

CREATED

London

MEDIUM

Oil on canvas

SERIES/PERIOD/MOVEMENT

Neoclassical period

SIMILAR WORKS

Set Design for the Ballets Russes Production of *Le Coq d'Or* by Natalya Goncharova, 1914

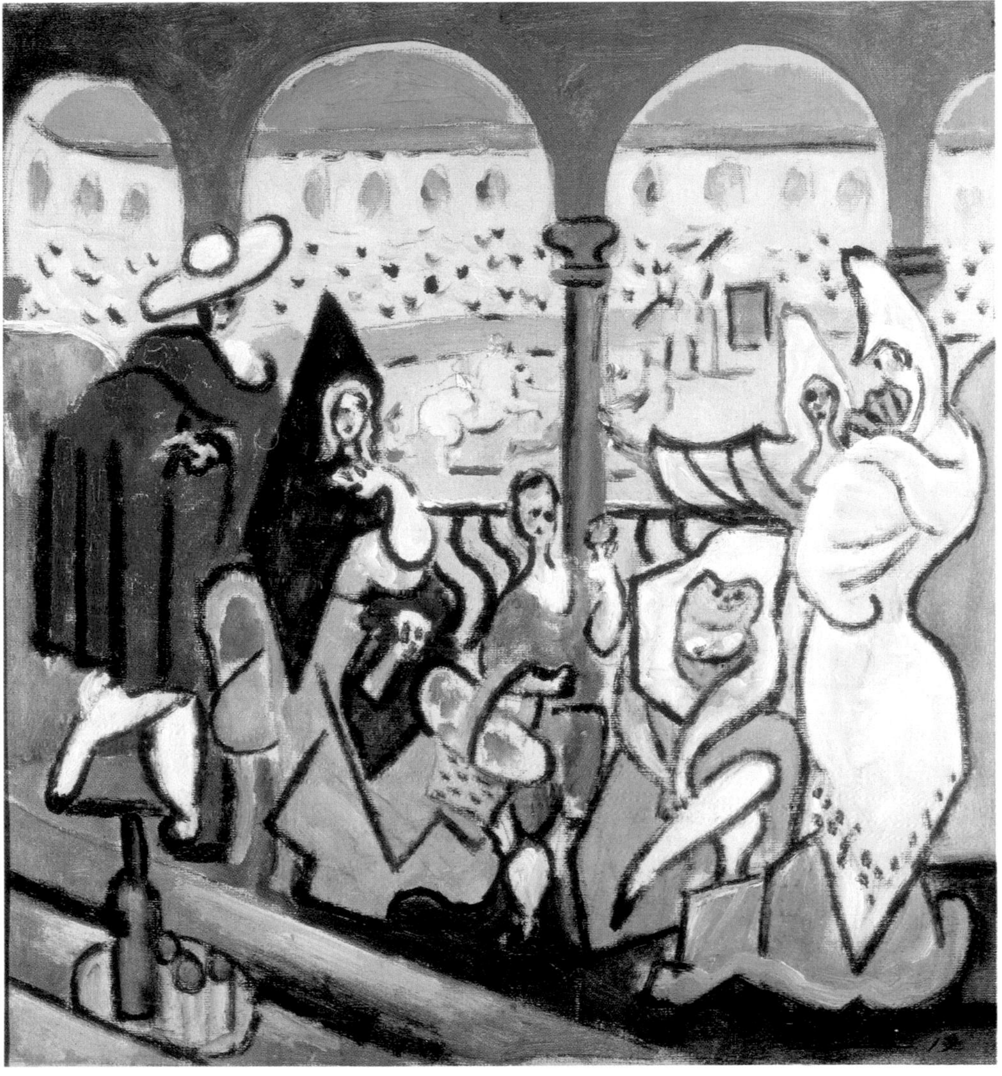

Nude Lying Down Beside the Sea, 1922

In the years immediately after the First World War, Picasso spent many of his summers on the French Riviera, together with his wife Olga and their young son Paulo. In 1922, however, the Picasso family headed north to the Brittany coast, staying at the fashionable resort of Dinard, renowned for its luxury hotels and fine, sandy beaches. Situated along the coast from Mont-St-Michel and overlooking St Malo, Dinard was originally a small fishing village. It was developed as a tourist resort in the mid-nineteenth century and soon established a reputation as an international resort regularly frequented by both American and British tourists. Expensive villas lined the coast and the resort exuded wealth and leisure. It was here that Picasso produced many of his Neoclassical paintings representing monumental male and female figures in beach settings. He also produced *Nude Lying Down Beside the Sea*, a timeless, Arcadian image of leisurely indulgence, that amply captures the sensual pleasures and holiday mood that pervaded much of Picasso's life at this time.

CREATED

Dinard

MEDIUM

Oil on canvas

SERIES/PERIOD/MOVEMENT

Neoclassical period

SIMILAR WORKS

The Birth of Venus by Alexandre Cabanel, 1863

Blue Nude, Memory of Biskra by Henri Matisse, 1907

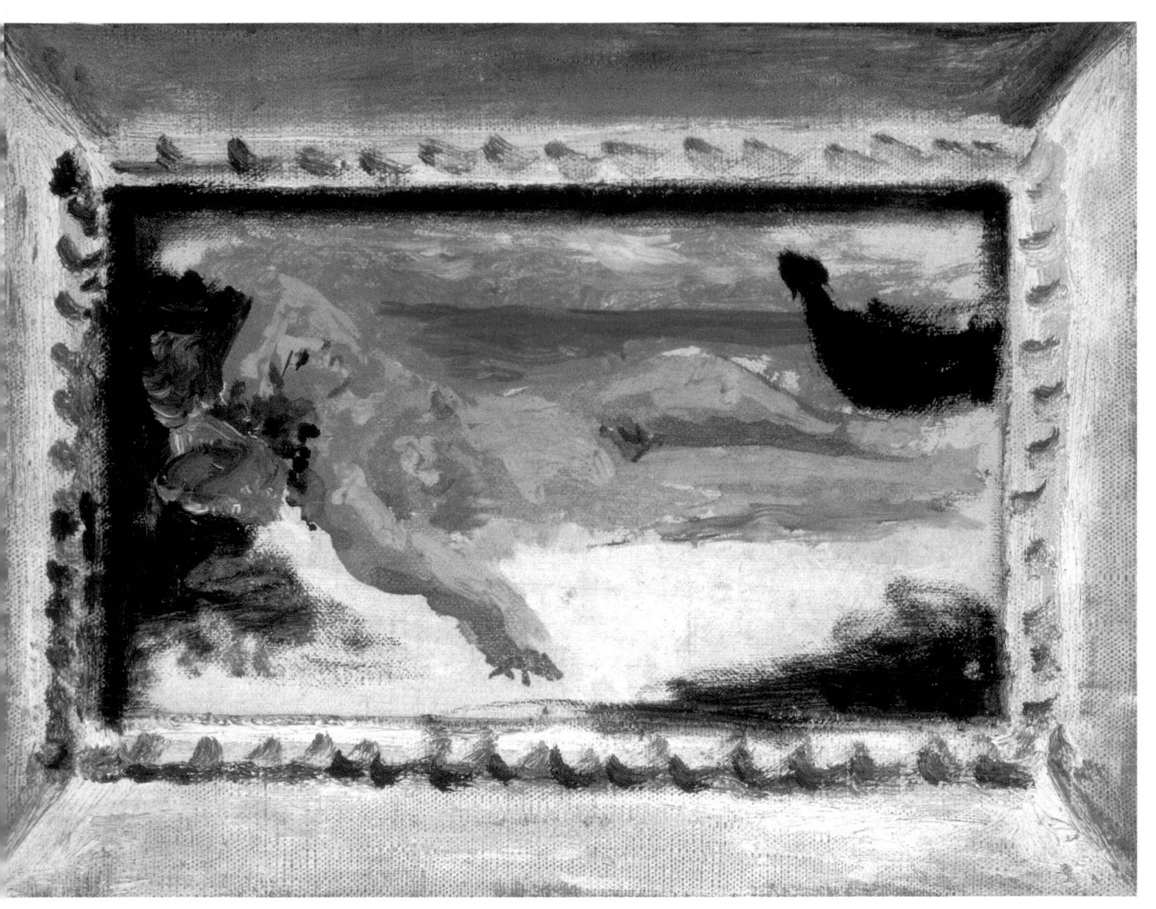

Two Figures, 1922

The paintings Picasso produced while in Dinard were clearly inspired by the leisurely nature of this seaside resort, yet Picasso's beach scenes notably avoided all reference to the modern world. Instead, the works recall a mythical world of classical order and harmony where all is at peace. The figures are monumental in form and thus reminiscent of classical statues. They are massive and earthbound, yet they seem to exist in a world that is neither past, present or future, but is beyond the confines of time. The static nature of the figures adds a sense of order and stability to the scene. Moreover, Picasso's simple treatment of space – the background restricted largely to three bands of colour to represent sky, sea and land – adds a further sense of compositional stability to the work. These classically inspired paintings typified much of Picasso's post-First World War work, as well as conforming to a wider return to classical values that permeated much cultural activity throughout France, and indeed Europe, in the 1920s.

CREATED

Dinard

MEDIUM

Oil on canvas

SERIES/PERIOD/MOVEMENT

Neoclassical period

SIMILAR WORKS

Young Girls by the Seashore by Pierre Puvis de Chavannes, 1879

The Mediterranean by Aristide Maillol, 1905

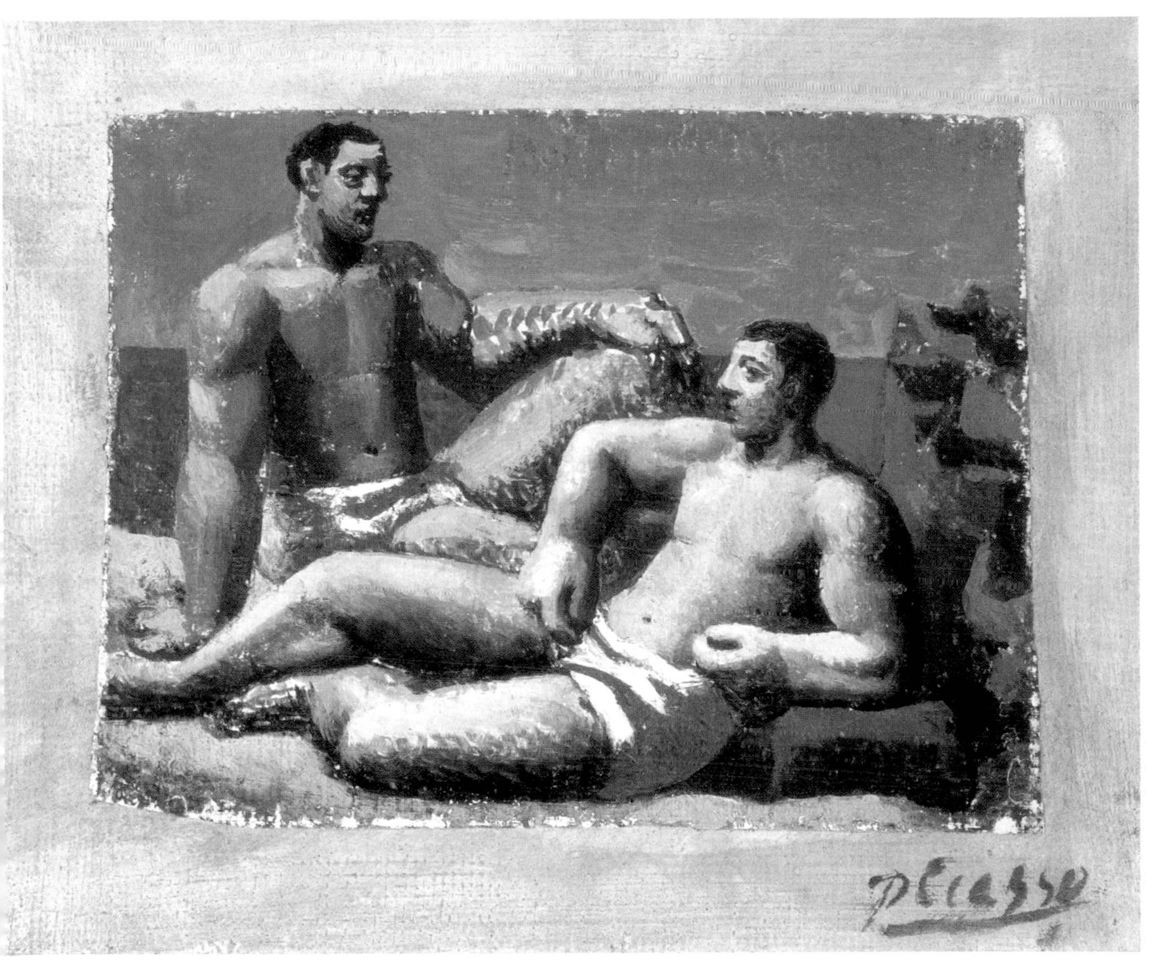
Picasso

Two Women Running on the Beach (The Race), 1922

One striking feature of the Neoclassical paintings Picasso produced at Dinard in 1922, is that they seem barely distinguishable from the works he had produced earlier on the Mediterranean coast. Indeed, many of the Dinard works seem bathed in the warmth of a Mediterranean sun. However, his small-scale gouache *Two Women Running on the Beach* captures a different mood – one more reminiscent of the bracing climate and atmosphere of the northern coast. Here two women are depicted running energetically across the sand, their arms stretched wide and their hair streaming behind them. Devoid of all inhibitions, they exude a joyous energy in stark contrast to the stability and passivity of works such as *Two Figures*. Even the perfectly blue sky, so typical a feature of Picasso's other Neoclassical beach scenes, is here interrupted by wispy clouds, while the perfect horizontal of the line demarcating sea and shore is broken by the sand, seemingly thrown up by the energetic action of the runners. Two years later this image was significantly enlarged and redeployed to form the stage curtain for the Ballets Russes performance of *Le Train Bleu*.

CREATED

Dinard

MEDIUM

Gouache on plywood

SERIES/PERIOD/MOVEMENT

Neoclassical period

SIMILAR WORKS

Football Players by Henri Rousseau, 1908

Three Women by Fernand Léger, 1921

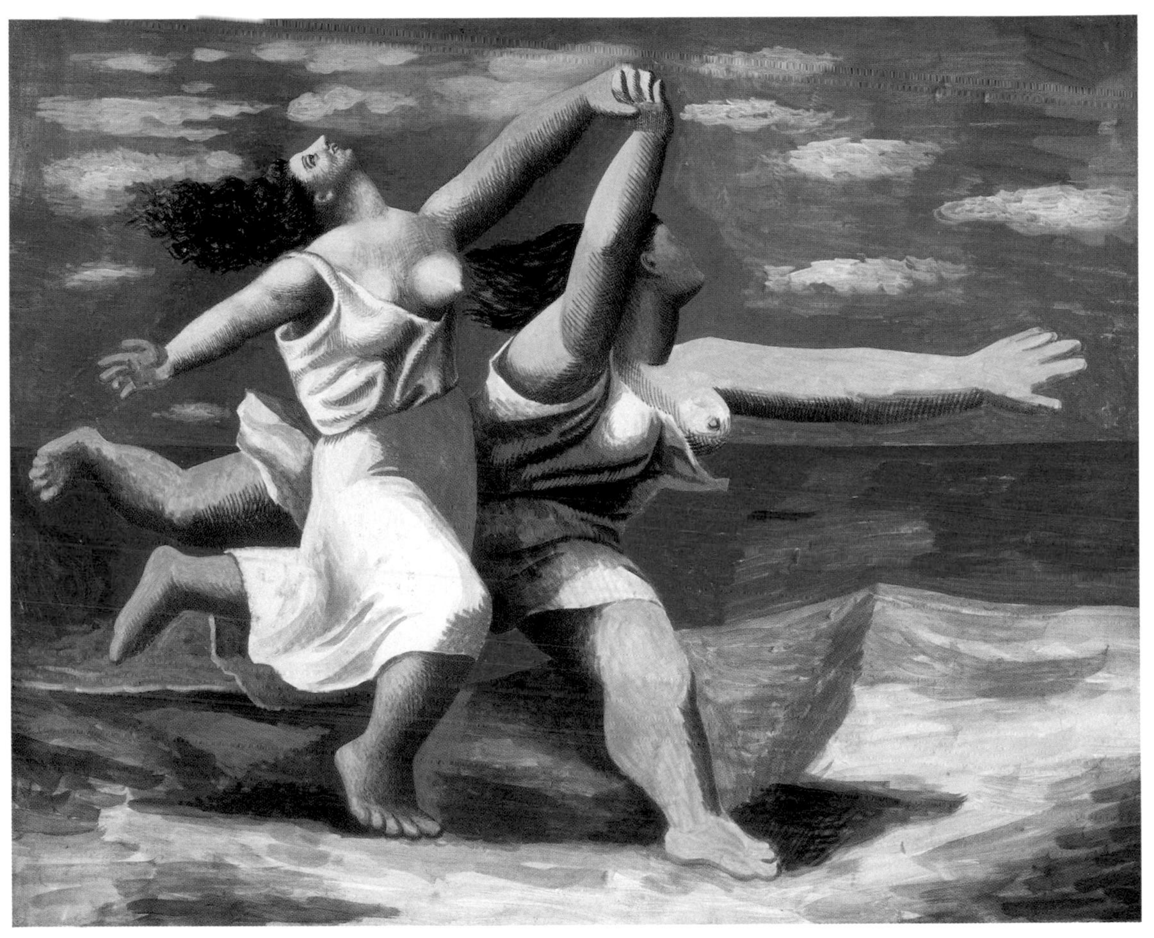

Juan-les-Pins, 1924

In 1920 Picasso travelled south, staying at the small coastal town of Juan-les-Pins. Over the next decade he was to spend many of his summers in this French Riviera resort. Named after the numerous pine trees, which run down to the edge of the sea, Juan-les-Pins had become a popular holiday resort by the 1920s, attracting wealthy American tourists including the novelist F. Scott Fitzgerald, and the Hollywood stars Douglas Fairbanks and Rudolf Valentino. The French singer Mistinguet and Picasso himself were amongst the rich and famous Europeans who added glamour and prestige to this summer playground of the jet set. Picasso produced many paintings representing the landscape surrounding Juan-les-Pins. In this small sketch he has introduced several motifs to characterize the region. These include a castellated tower, probably influenced by a number of such towers throughout the region, including one at the Chateau Grimaldi at nearby Antibes. Throughout the composition Picasso has included several of the pine trees that dominate the local countryside, characterized by their tall, dark trunks and densely canopied foliage.

CREATED

Juan-les-Pins

MEDIUM

Oil on canvas

SERIES/PERIOD/MOVEMENT

Neoclassical period

SIMILAR WORKS

Theatre Curtain for *Parade* by Picasso, *c.* 1917

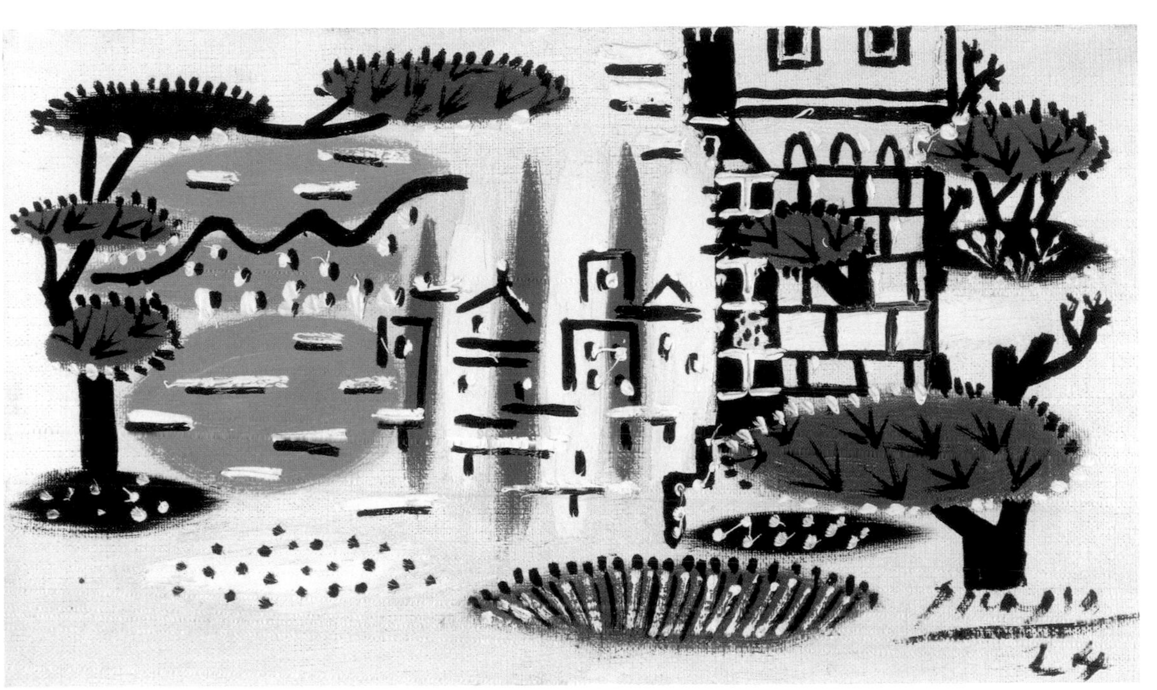

Landscape at Juan-les-Pins, 1924

Picasso's views of Juan-les-Pins are often very childlike in their appearance. Here the artist has focused once again upon the castellated tower, a typical feature of the local architecture. However, Picasso seems less interested in presenting an accurate rendering of the local topography. Instead he sets his fantasy castle against a romantic backdrop of sea, sky and distant hills. The various components are put together with large blocks of unmodulated colour, and the whole gives the impression of an illustration for a book of fairy-tales, or a stage curtain for a theatrical production. Indeed, this was the period when Picasso was working extensively in theatre design. In 1924, for example, he produced a stage curtain and costume designs for a production entitled *Mercure*, which also featured music by Erik Satie (1866–1925) and choreography by Léonide Massine (1895–1975). Picasso's extensive experience in theatre design certainly inspired this approach to landscape painting.

CREATED

Juan-les-Pins

MEDIUM

Oil on canvas

SERIES/PERIOD/MOVEMENT

Neoclassical period

SIMILAR WORKS

The Beach at Juan-Les-Pins by Claude Monet, 1888

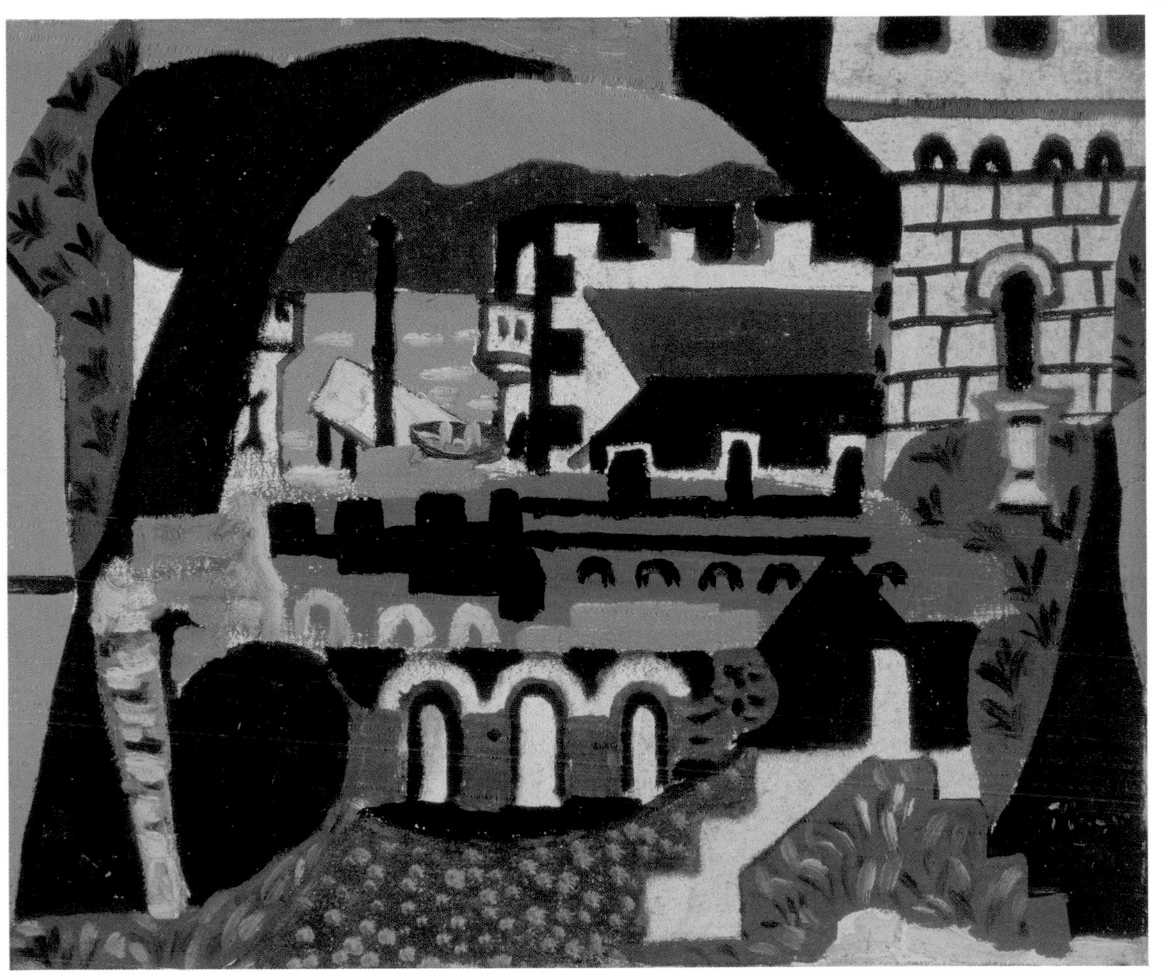

The House at Juan-les-Pins, 1931

Here Picasso has represented a view of the Villa Chêne-Roc in Juan-les-Pins, the elegant home in which he spent many summers during the 1920s and 1930s. The villa stands before a distant view of the bay at night, beneath a dark but starry sky. The distant glow of lights, lining the bay, suggests the continuing activity in the town after the sun has set. Juan-les-Pins was famous for its nightly entertainments. During the 1920s, both French and American entrepreneurs built up the town, establishing summer casinos, cabarets and nightclubs to cater for the ever-growing tourist trade. The arrival of American tourists also introduced a new form of music to the resort – jazz. From early New Orleans style to the smooth melodies of Cole Porter, jazz, with its syncopated rhythms and regular beat, rapidly became the soundtrack to the luxurious and decadent lifestyle of 1920s Juan-les-Pins. To this day the resort is intimately linked with the musical form and is regarded by many as the jazz capital of Europe. While jazz provided the soundtrack to Juan-les-Pins in the interwar years, Picasso gave the resort visual form.

CREATED

Juan-les-Pins

MEDIUM

Oil on canvas

SERIES/PERIOD/MOVEMENT

Surrealist period

SIMILAR WORKS

The Beach at Juan-Les-Pins by Claude Monet, 1888

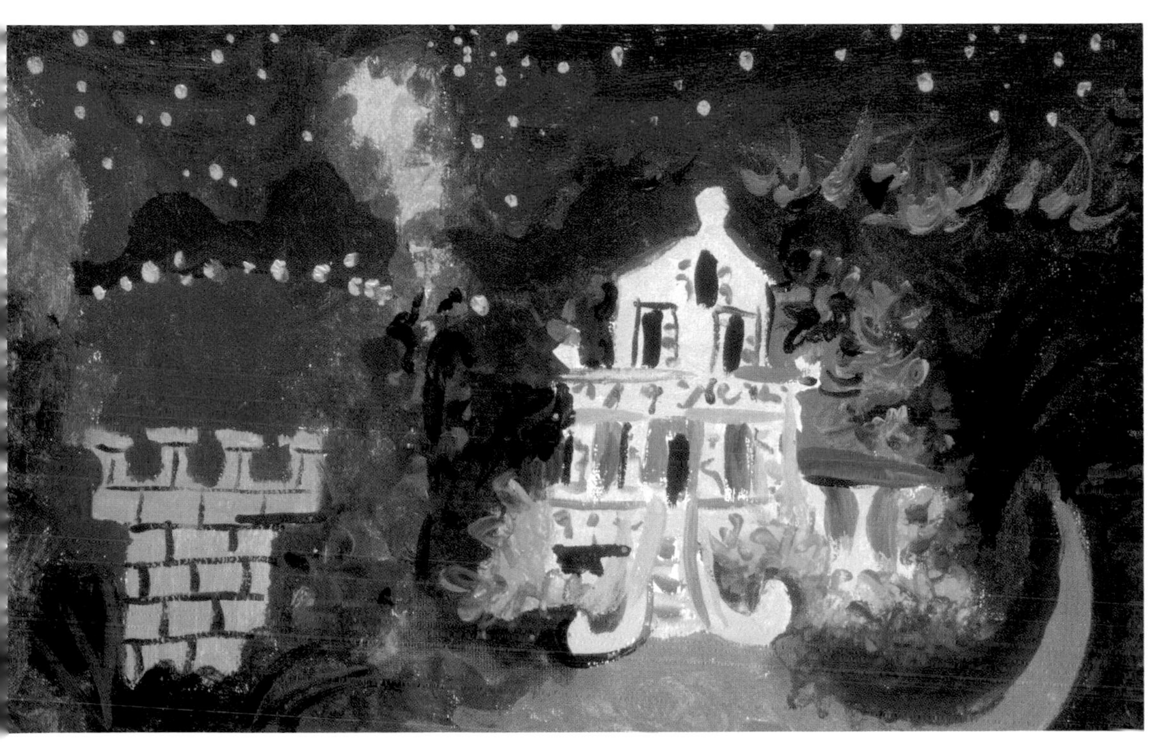

Woman Lying on the Beach, 1932

Throughout the interwar years, Picasso produced countless images of bathers. In *Woman Lying on the Beach* he has emphasized the complete abandon of sleeping in the sun. Here, the arms of the sleeping figure fall casually above the head, while the right leg is represented as if suspended, despite being positioned flat on the sand. Picasso has also twisted the body around so that the viewer is simultaneously shown all sides. Even the brightly coloured swimming costume is simultaneously opaque and transparent. The colours deployed here seem striking. The bottom half of the swimming costume, with its red and yellow bands, recalls the colours of the Spanish national flag, while the blue and white of the upper half suggests part of the French tricolore. Notably, the point at which these two halves touch the skyline coincides precisely with a split in the horizon line which, on the right, dips to join the lower line of the bathing costume. Here Picasso seems to be making a reference to his own split identity, both Spanish and French, whilst mapping this on to the body of his model.

CREATED

Boisgeloup

MEDIUM

Oil on canvas

SERIES/PERIOD/MOVEMENT

Surrealist period

SIMILAR WORKS

Blue Nude, Memory of Biskra by Henri Matisse, 1907

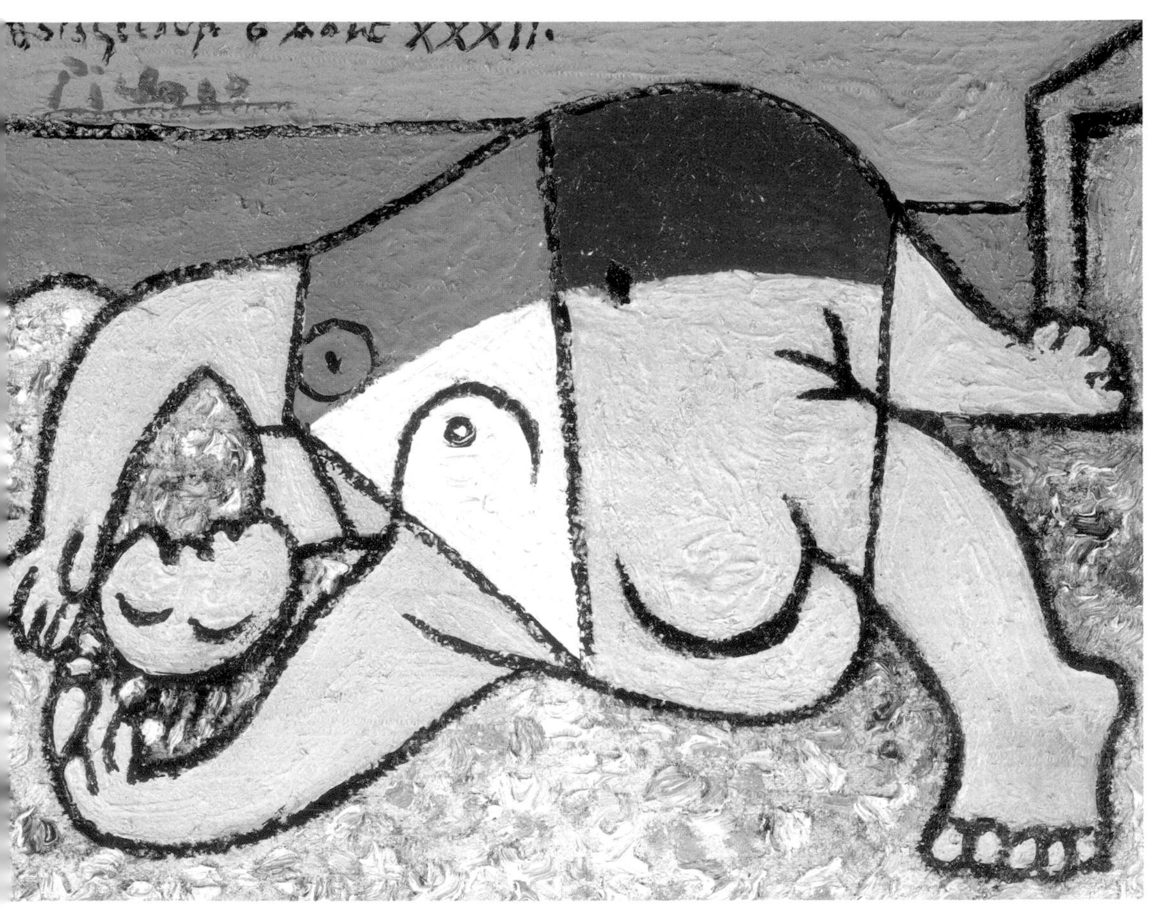

Night Fishing at Antibes, 1939

One night, while strolling around the harbour at Antibes, Picasso was intrigued to watch the local fishermen at work. In the darkness they shone lights from the sides of their boats to attract fish to the surface. Once in sight, the prey was speared by the fishermen. In response to this Picasso produced a nocturnal scene showing two fishermen adopting this strategy. On the right, two women look on from the dock. *Night Fishing at Antibes* is quite distinct from many of Picasso's views of the French Riviera and has been interpreted as revealing his anxieties about the impending war and the inevitable violence and destruction that would be wrought upon humanity. The theme of mortality is certainly explored, as it is not only the fish that are lured to their deaths by the fishermen's lanterns. Triangular-shaped moths also flutter around the artificial light, before being consumed by its heat. In the wake of Picasso's emphasis on the destruction of Guernica, *Night Fishing at Antibes* offers a prescient vision of the destruction shortly to engulf Europe.

CREATED

Antibes

MEDIUM

Oil on canvas

SERIES/PERIOD/MOVEMENT

Surrealist period

SIMILAR WORKS

Landscape with Crab Catchers by Moonlight by Nicolaes Berchem, 1645

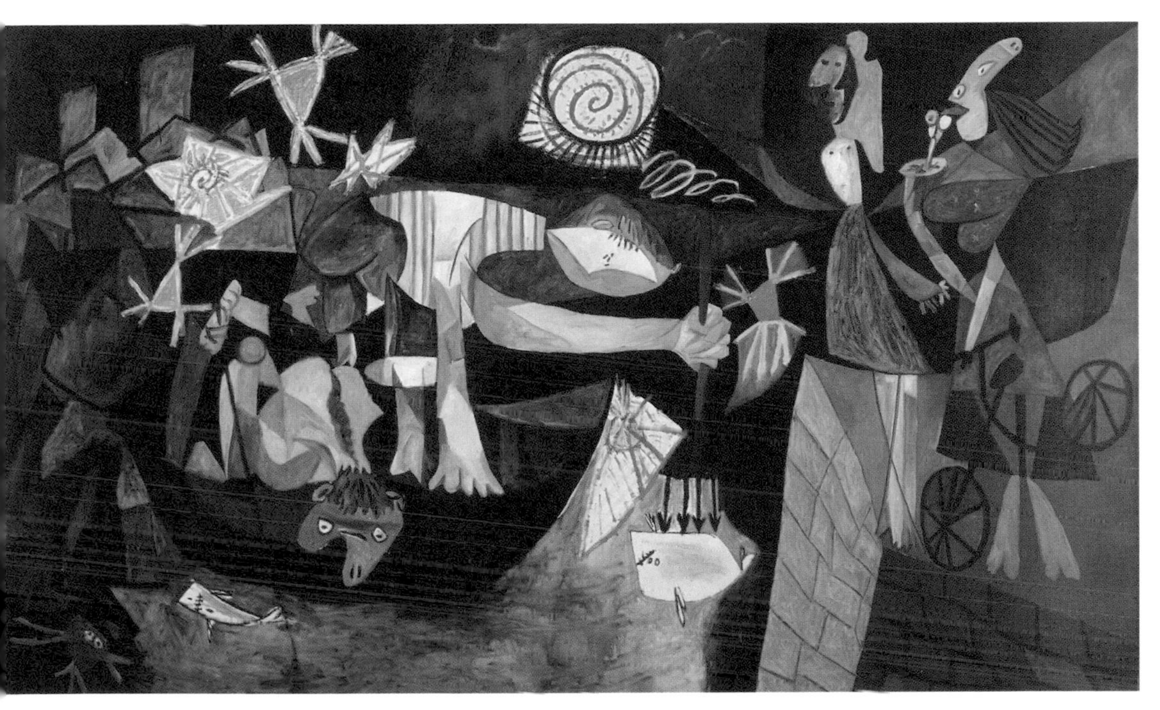

The Bull, 1949–50

Both during and after the Second World War Picasso produced a number of sculptures representing animals. These included his *Bull's Head* (1943) and *Monkey and her Baby* (1951) as well as sculptures of a crane and a goat. During the same period he made a number of ceramic birds executed in the pottery at Vallauris. Around 1949 he also produced this small-scale sculpture of a bull. For Picasso, the bull had always symbolized his native Spain, the country from which he was now effectively in exile. Throughout this year, nostalgia for the country of his birth seems to have pervaded much of Picasso's work and inspired him to produce this sculpture. It was also at this time that he turned his attention to producing a set of variations on one of Spain's most famous works of art, Diego Velazquez's (1599–1660) *Las Meninas* (1656). Over the next few years Picasso would produce dozens more images of bulls and bullfighting, during a period that has been described as his metaphorical 'return to Spain'.

CREATED

Vallauris

MEDIUM

Bronze

SERIES/PERIOD/MOVEMENT

Late period

SIMILAR WORKS

The Bullfight by Francisco de Goya, 1816

Monkey and her Baby by Picasso, 1951

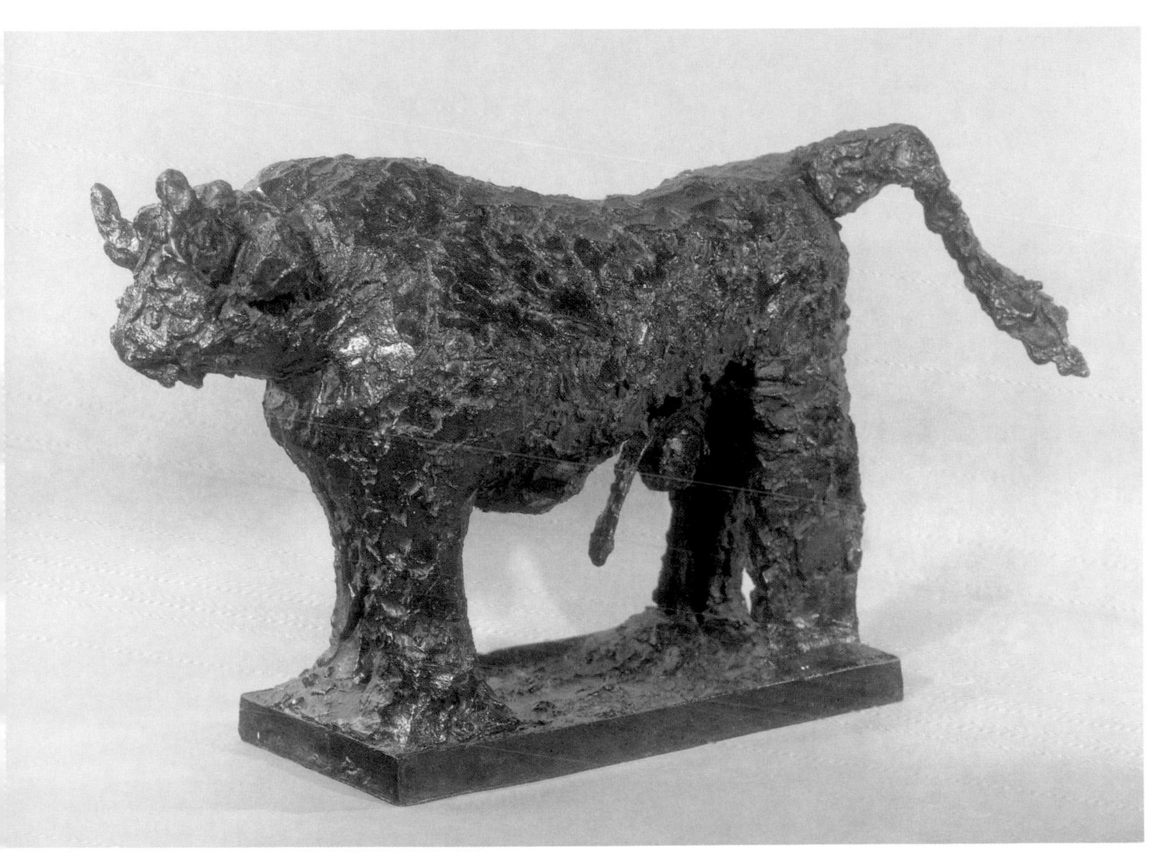

Notre-Dame de Paris, 1954

In the decade following the end of the Second World War Picasso divided his time between summers at the coast and winters in Paris. Although many of the works he produced during the summer months focused on outdoor subjects, his Parisian works were largely confined to the studio. In the autumn of 1954, however, he produced this view of the cathedral of Notre-Dame. The viewpoint seems to have been taken from a building overlooking the cathedral, and includes the banks of the river Seine, the cathedral itself and the Eiffel Tower in the background. At the time Picasso was living in his studio on the rue des Grands-Augustins, just a few minutes walk from Notre-Dame. This had been the famous studio in which he had painted *Guernica* and where he spent a great deal of his time during the German occupation of Paris. Following the liberation, the studio rapidly acquired a reputation as one of the key tourist sights of Paris, and Picasso was regularly inundated by scores of American GIs, press reporters and photographers.

CREATED

Paris

MEDIUM

Oil on canvas

SERIES/PERIOD/MOVEMENT

Post-War-Communist period

SIMILAR WORKS

Rouen Cathedral by Claude Monet, 1894

Notre-Dame in the Late Afternoon by Henri Matisse, 1902

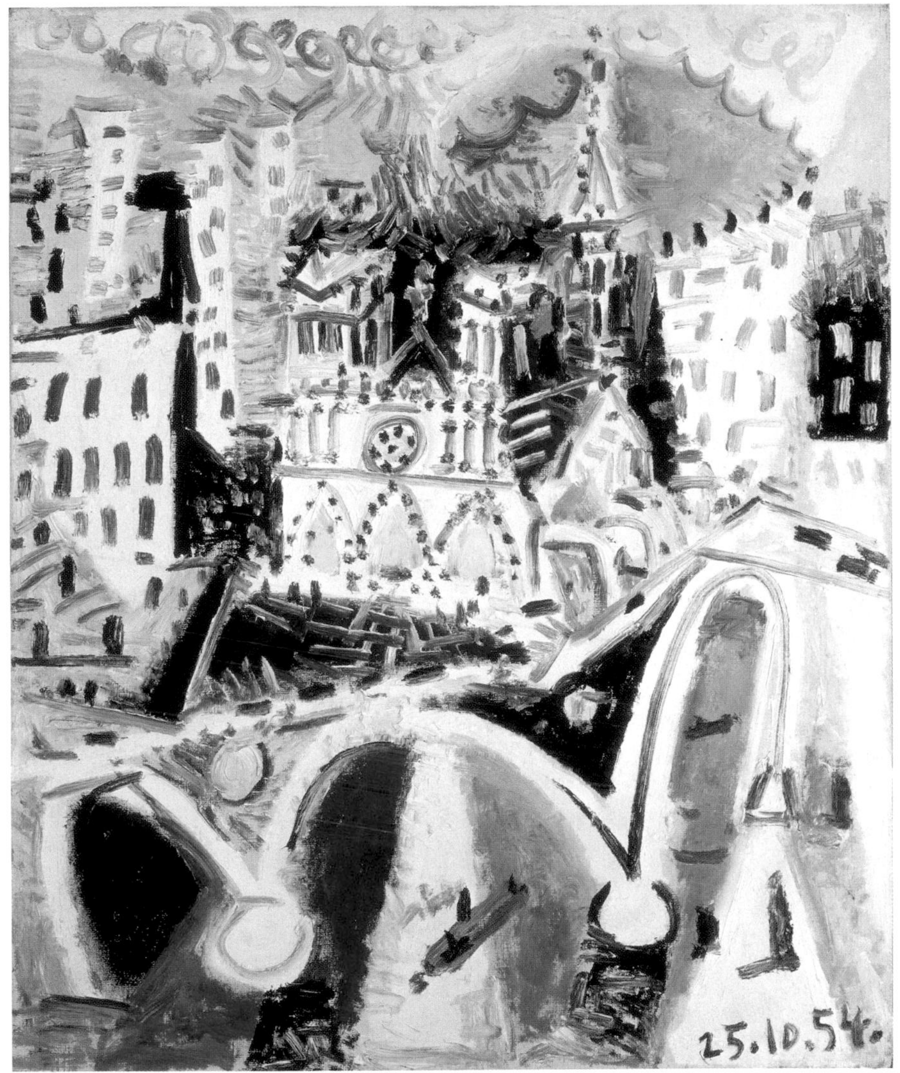
25.10.54.

The Studio, 1955

Throughout his life Picasso had owned many houses and lived in many different places. In 1955, however, he purchased a villa called 'La Californie', situated on a hill overlooking Cannes. 'La Californie' was the largest and grandest of all the properties Picasso had owned, with enormous high-ceilinged rooms on the ground floor that opened up on to an elaborate garden. In his new studio space Picasso surrounded himself with the many objects and art works that he had acquired and produced throughout his life. Here, he also worked on a series of paintings that he referred to as 'interior landscapes' – views of the studio that operated almost as self-portraits. In this work Picasso looks across the studio space and out through the baroque windows into the garden. A palm tree in the distance reminds us of the warm, tropical climate and contrasts with the cooler interior space. In the lower right Picasso has included a sculptor's turntable surmounted with a bust. The inclusion of this object metaphorically suggests the presence of the artist, alongside the various tools of his trade scattered throughout the studio space.

CREATED

Cannes

MEDIUM

Oil on canvas

SERIES/PERIOD/MOVEMENT

Late period

SIMILAR WORKS

The Red Studio by Henri Matisse, 1911

Studio II by Georges Braque, 1949

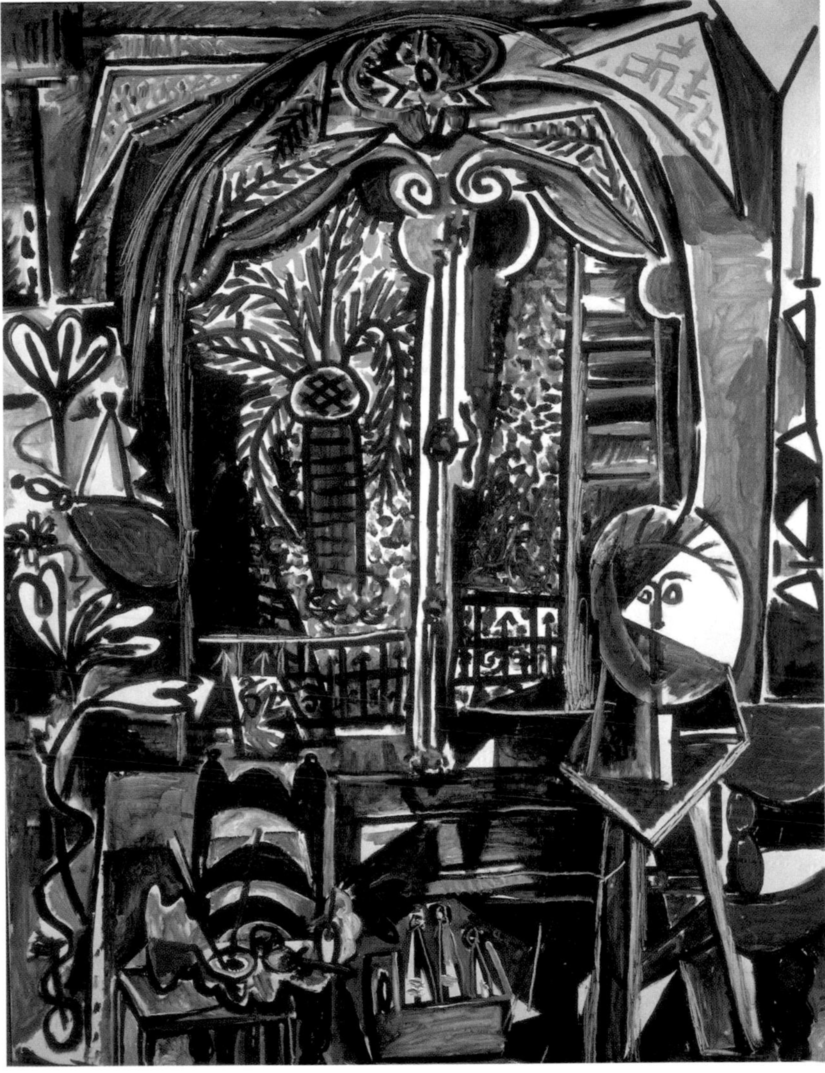

The Pigeons, Cannes, 1957

Many of Picasso's works produced during the later 1950s show views through a window or out over a balcony. Some of these may have been inspired by the actual layout of the studio at 'La Californie'. However, these balcony views also recalled the work of Henri Matisse (1869–1954), who had been both a friend and a rival to Picasso for over half a century. The death of Matisse in 1954 had a profound effect upon Picasso. Indeed the balcony views can be read as a homage to the older artist. At the same time, the emphasis here upon pigeons recalls Picasso's father, the great painter of pigeons, as well as the recent success of Picasso's dove lithographs produced for the Communist Party. Here the view out through a window overlooking the bay at Cannes shows peaceful blue waters and a small island, or outcrop, gently breaking the stillness of the sea. Picasso has brought together the private world of the interior with the public world of the exterior, linking both in an image of reverie and nostalgia.

CREATED

Cannes

MEDIUM

Oil on canvas

SERIES/PERIOD/MOVEMENT

Late period

SIMILAR WORKS

Open Window, Collioure by Henri Matisse, 1905

Bird Returning to its Nest by Georges Braque, 1955

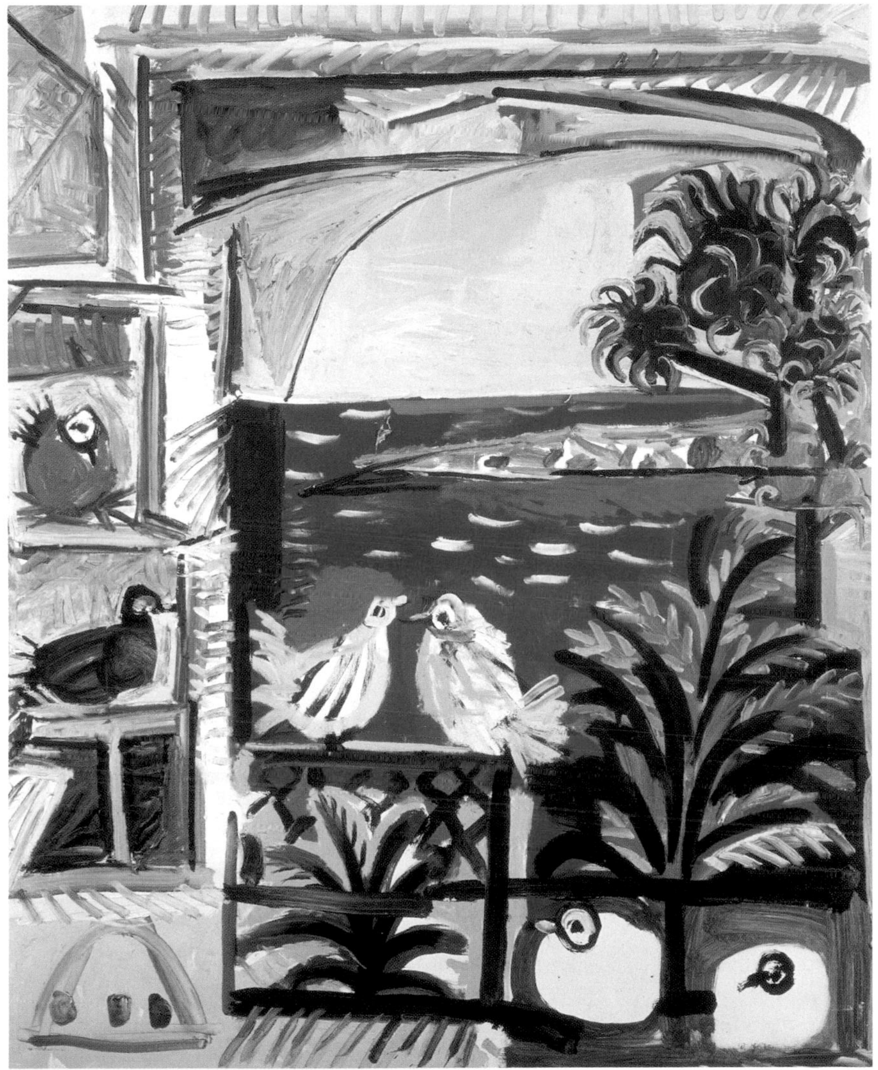

'La Californie' at Night, 1958

Amongst the many 'interior landscapes' produced at 'La Californie' is this one, representing the large studio overlooking the garden. As in many of these studio paintings, Picasso has highlighted the view through the studio window into the garden, with its striking palm trees. However, the dark blue of the sky indicates that this is a nocturnal scene. Moreover, Picasso has blocked the passage into the garden by placing large and heavy furniture between the spectator and the window. The cooler blue exterior also contrasts notably with the warmer browns, reds and yellows of the interior space. Of all the studio paintings, this one seems the most enclosed, as if Picasso has withdrawn into his own private space away from the outside world. This may have been inspired in part by the increasing development of Cannes and the encroachment of new buildings. Notably, just three months after completing this painting, Picasso bought a new home at Vauvenargues, in a much quieter region of Provence – a place that reminded him more of his native Spain.

CREATED

Cannes

MEDIUM

Oil on canvas

SERIES/PERIOD/MOVEMENT

Late period

SIMILAR WORKS

The Red Studio by Henri Matisse, 1911

Studio II by Georges Braque, 1949

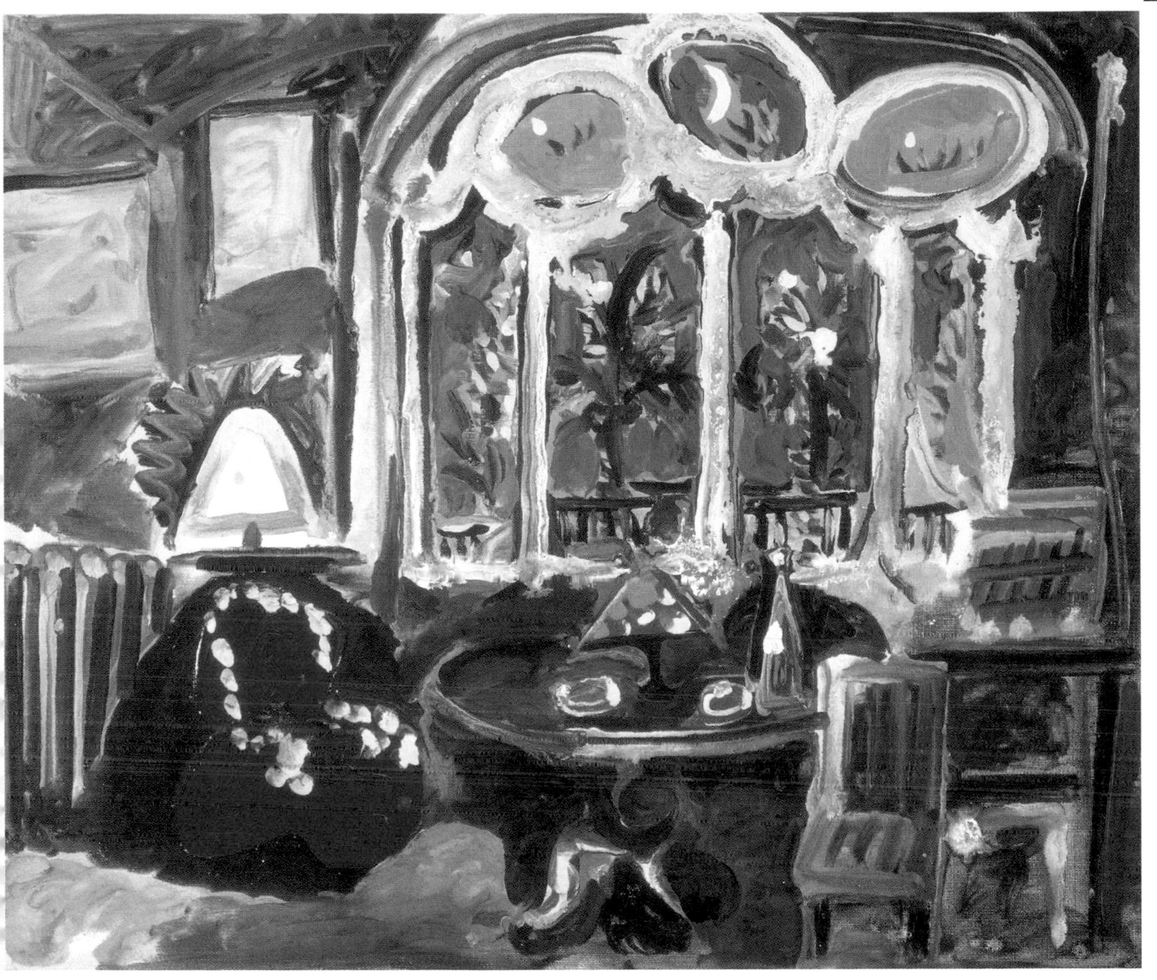

The Bay at Cannes, 1958

At the beginning of the nineteenth century, Cannes was still a small fishing village, barely distinguishable from many others along the Mediterranean coast. By the early twentieth century it had gradually grown into a thriving international tourist resort, attracting the rich and famous, who regularly moored their yachts in the bay to come ashore and taste the numerous pleasures of the now significantly expanded town. Since 1946 it had also been the venue for an international film festival, drawing the rich and famous of the world to the resort. Picasso's painting of *The Bay at Cannes* encapsulates the then-growing prestige of Cannes as a bustling tourist centre and the change that this inevitably precipitated. Here the palm trees encircling the quiet bay are gradually becoming dwarfed by a series of high-rise buildings, luxury hotels that encroach upon the waterfront. The bay, too, is populated with yachts, while more boats line the shore. Here nature itself is pushed to the very margins of the composition, seen only on the distant horizon restricted to the very top of the canvas.

CREATED

Cannes

MEDIUM

Oil on canvas

SERIES/PERIOD/MOVEMENT

Late period

SIMILAR WORKS

Antibes seen from the Notre-Dame Plateau by Claude Monet, 1888

Fishing Port, Collioure by André Derain, 1905

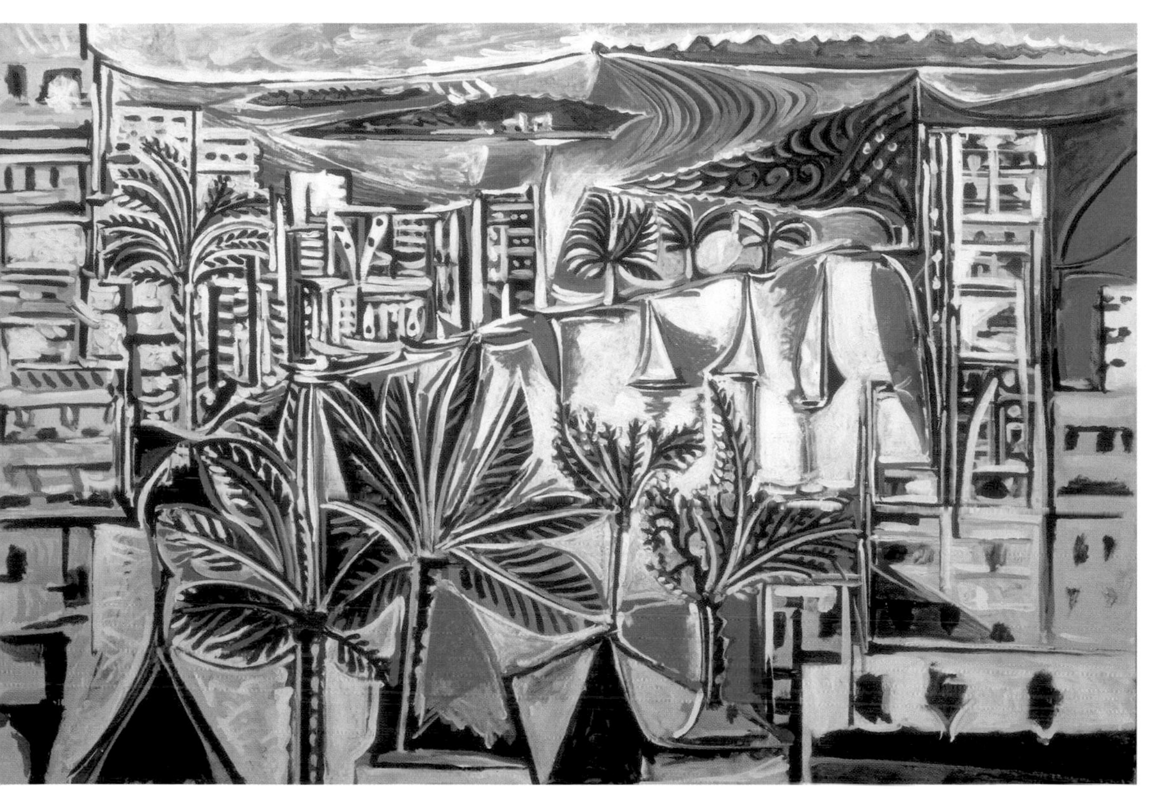

Landscape, 1967

'You have to turn in order to paint the landscape with your eyes. To see a thing you have to see all of it.... It would be nice to paint only detail. But in order to understand it and transform it into an image, it is necessary to paint the entire vista.' This is one of the few observations Picasso is known to have made regarding landscape painting. It is not entirely clear where this landscape scene was created, although Picasso was living at his villa, Notre-Dame-de-Vie at Mougins, at the time of its production. The abundantly green hillsides with their carefully ordered trees, the winding pathways and roads, and the small, red-roofed houses on the right certainly resemble the landscape around Mougins. What is most striking here, however, is how Picasso has tilted the entire landscape upwards, towards the surface of the canvas, as if this is the most straightforward way to include the abundance of topographic detail, 'the entire vista' that could not otherwise be seen from a single viewpoint.

CREATED

Mougins

MEDIUM

Oil on plywood

SERIES/PERIOD/MOVEMENT

Late period

SIMILAR WORKS

Houses in Provence by Paul Cézanne, *c.* 1880

Fishing Port, Collioure by André Derain, 1905

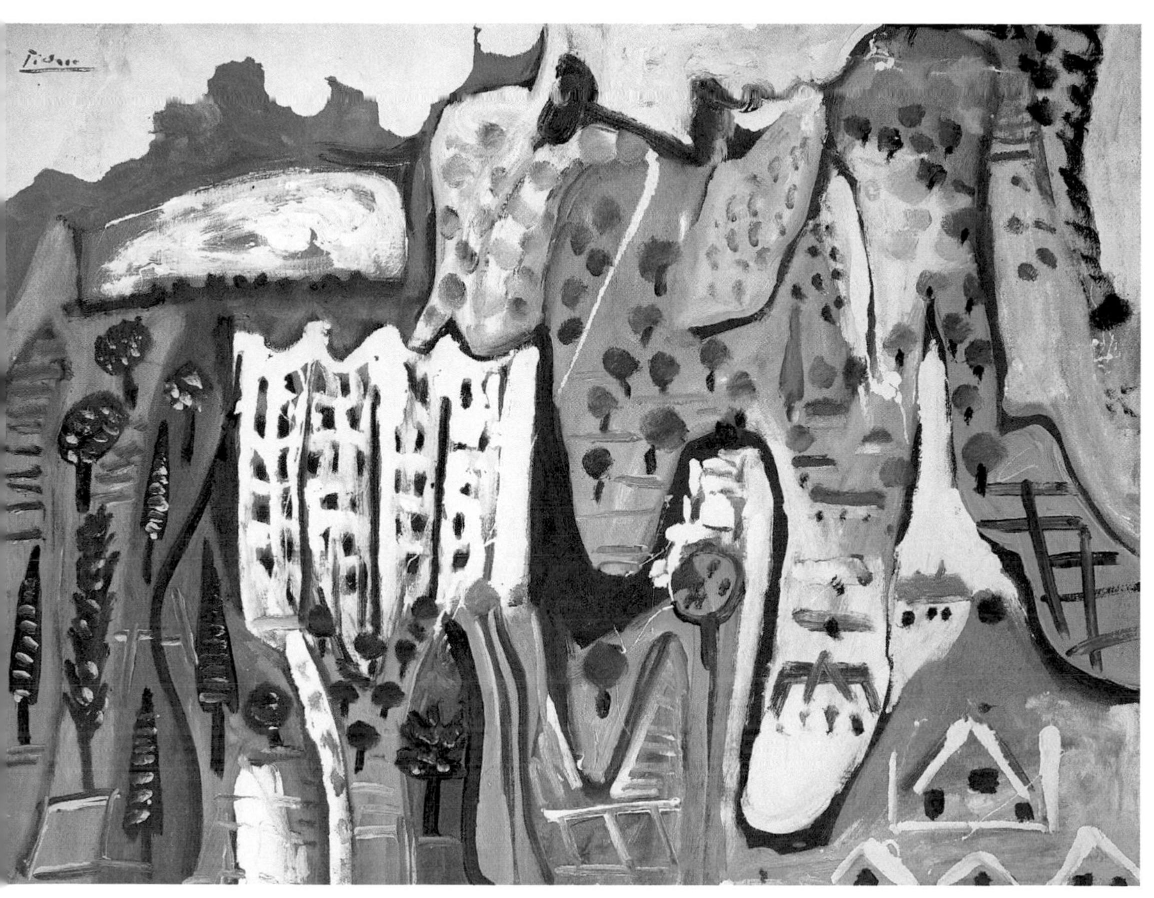

Head, 1967

Although Picasso spent most of his life living and working in France, his work has attracted considerable attention throughout the world. From early in his career, Picasso's works had been sought by American collectors such as Gertrude Stein and, with the formation of the Museum of Modern Art in New York in the late 1920s, his works increasingly drew the attention of wider American audiences. The artist's reputation was further enhanced in the wake of the Liberation of Paris, when dozens of American press reporters and photographers visited his studio to interview the artist. It was thus fitting that, in the mid 1960s, he was commissioned to produce a monumental sculpture to be erected in Chicago. The work, based on his series of cut-out heads of women, stands 50 feet tall, and is made from Cor-Ten steel. Its colossal scale and rust-coloured patina recalls the trend for monumental Minimalist sculptures, installed throughout American cities during the 1960s. The presence of this huge-scale monument is fitting tribute to the popularity of Picasso's work far beyond the shores of Europe.

CREATED

Mougins

MEDIUM

Cor-Ten steel

SERIES/PERIOD/MOVEMENT

Late period

SIMILAR WORKS

Model for Constructed Head No. 3 by Naum Gabo, 1917

Early One Morning by Anthony Caro, 1962

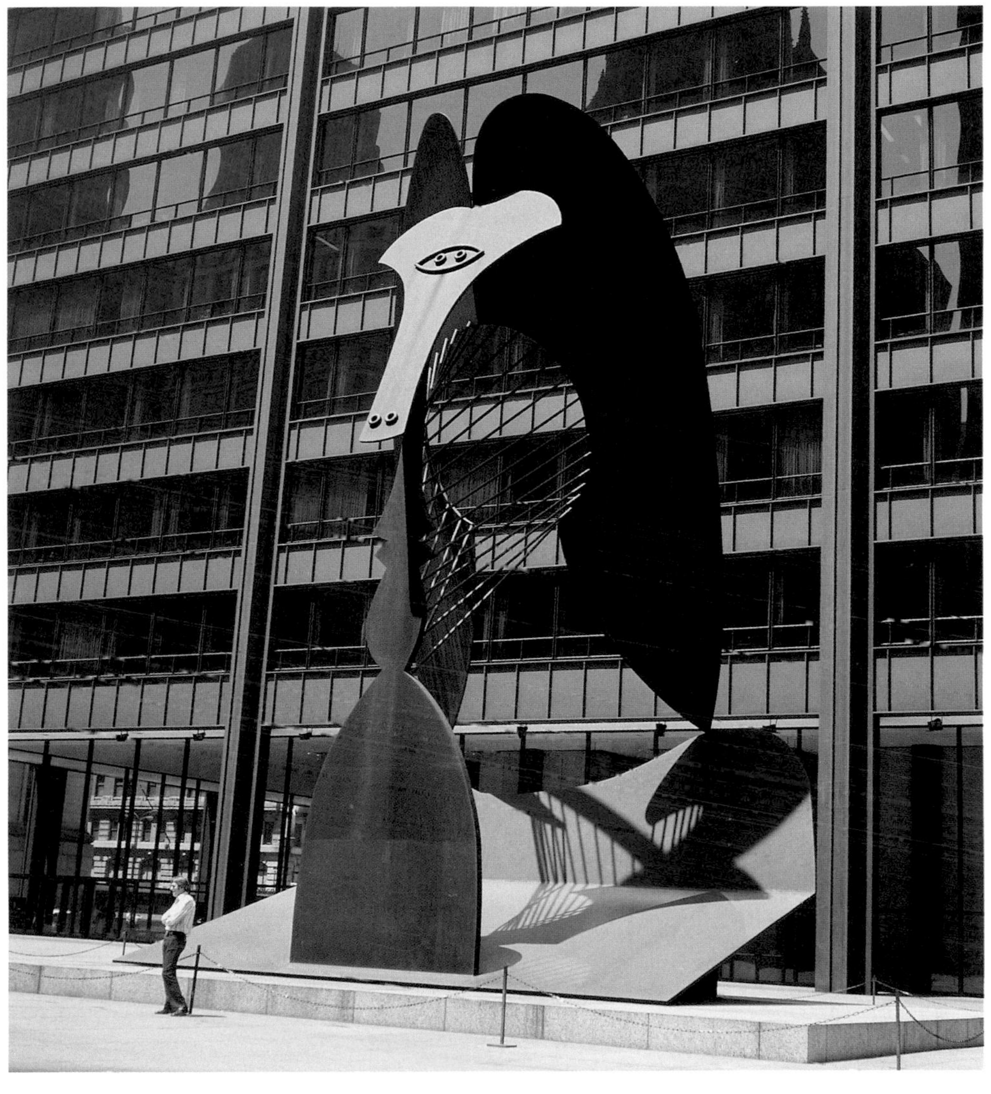

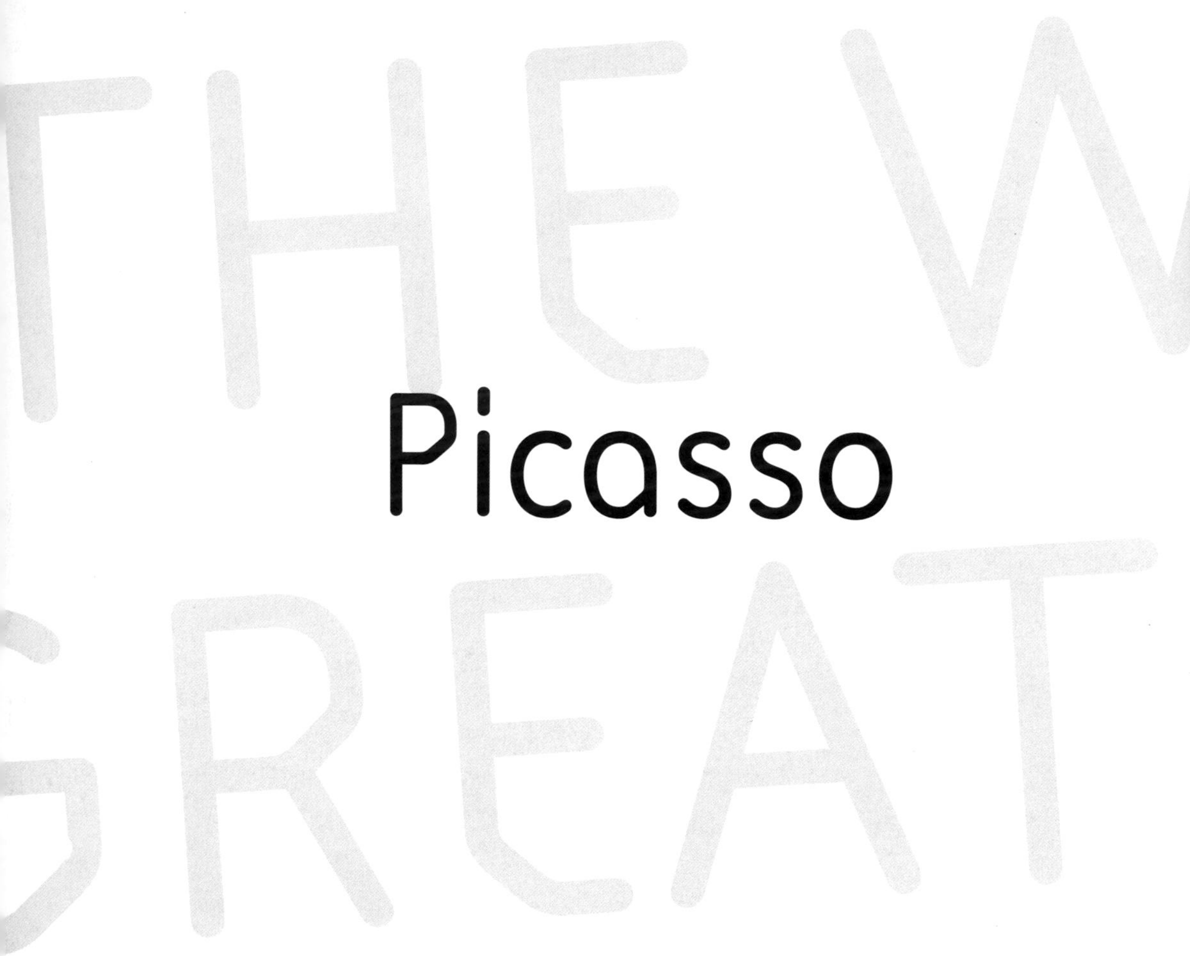

Picasso

Influences

Angel Fernandez de Soto, 1900

Undoubtedly the first influence on Picasso's art was the work of his father, José Ruiz Blasco, a painter and art teacher who nurtured his son's talents from an early age. However, by his early teens Picasso was already rejecting this academic style and was experimenting with styles derived from contemporary avant-garde practitioners. Picasso's first successful works were a series of drawings and pastels representing the bohemian circle of friends he had joined as a young man in Barcelona. In 1900, these drawings formed the core of his first major exhibition in the city. Picasso's major influences at this time were an older Spanish artist, Ramon Casas (1866–1932), and the Spanish Old Masters El Greco (1541–1614) and Francisco de Goya (1746–1828), whose works he had seen in the Prado. He was also aware of the work of Henri de Toulouse-Lautrec (1864–1901), whose influence can be detected in this portrait of Picasso's close friend Angel Fernandez de Soto. Here the swiftly executed pastel marks and the mood of melancholic contemplation recall Toulouse-Lautrec's many pastel sketches of the late-nineteenth century.

CREATED

Barcelona

MEDIUM

Charcoal and crayon on paper

SERIES/PERIOD/MOVEMENT

Early period

SIMILAR WORKS

Self-Portrait by Ramon Casas, 1899

The Hangover, Portrait of Suzanne Valadon by Henri de Toulouse-Lautrec, 1889

Pablo Picasso *Born* 1881 Málaga, Spain

Died 1973

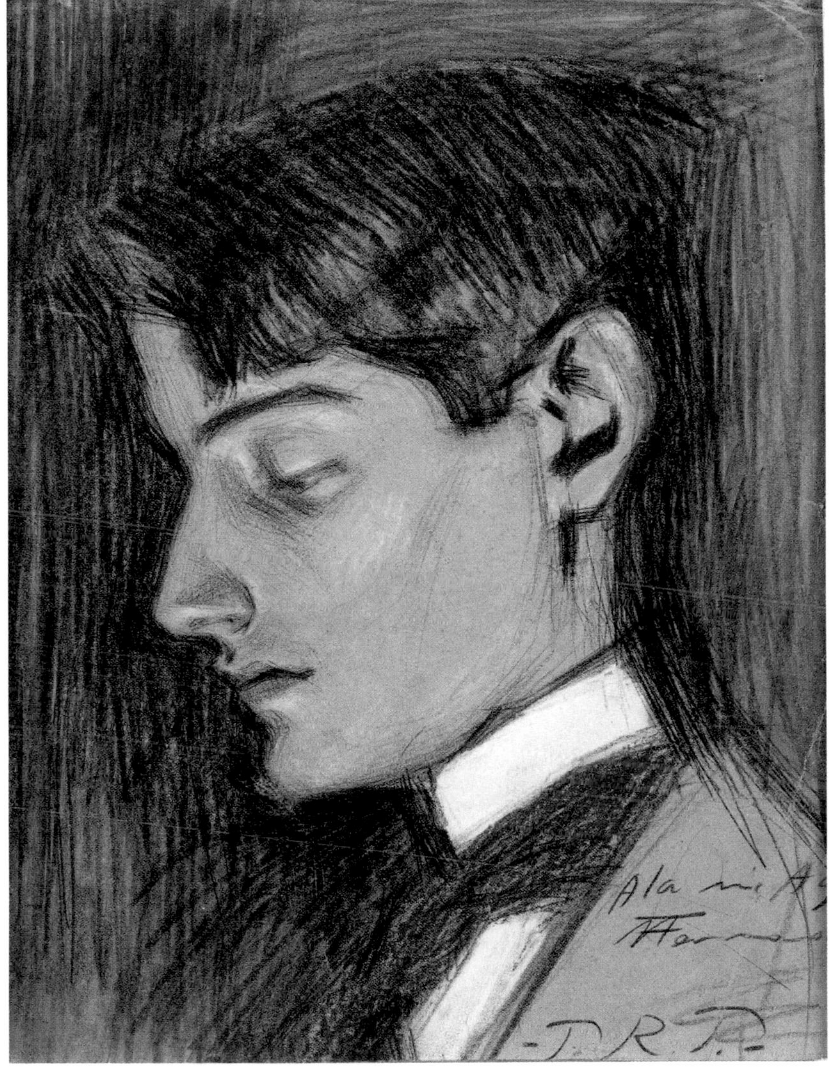

Woman with a Hat, 1901

From his earliest days, Picasso developed a broad knowledge of the history of art and was familiar with a wide range of different historical styles. As an art teacher, Picasso's father had introduced the young Pablo to the works of the Old Masters and, whenever possible took him to art galleries and museums. Picasso was just 13 years old when his father took him to the Prado in Madrid for the first time. During this relatively brief visit Picasso made two sketches after Diego Velazquez (1599–1660). Picasso's first-hand knowledge of Old-Master painting was significantly increased during his studies in Madrid and Barcelona, and later by his regular visits to the Louvre in Paris. He was never to forget the lessons of the Old Masters and their work remained a constant source of inspiration for him throughout his career. As this work shows, however, Picasso was also interested in more contemporary French painters, and he here employs the loose brush strokes and heightened colour palette of Vincent van Gogh (1853–90), whose works were widely discussed in the bohemian circles of both Barcelona and Paris.

CREATED

Paris

MEDIUM

Oil on cardboard

SERIES/PERIOD/MOVEMENT

Early period

SIMILAR WORKS

At the Milliners by Edgar Degas, 1883

Woman with a Hat by Henri Matisse, 1905

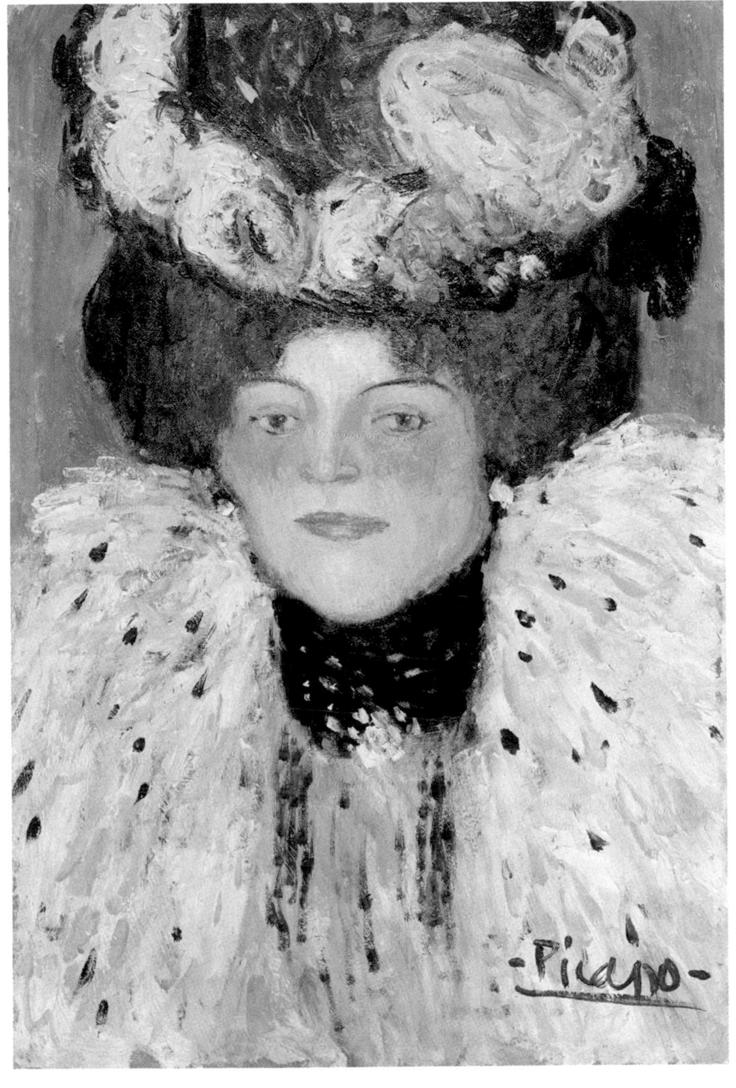
-Picasso-

Waiting (Margot), 1901

At the start of his career Picasso, like most young artists, was in search of a style of his own. His earliest exhibited works had been executed in an academic style reminiscent of many of the salon painters of the mid- to late-nineteenth century. After his first trip to Paris in 1900, however, Picasso experimented with a number of new painterly vocabularies derived from some of the key artists of the day. Picasso was particularly interested in the representation of social outcasts, and for this he looked to the work of van Gogh, Paul Gauguin (1848–1903) and Toulouse-Lautrec. He also admired the stylistic innovations of these painters, whose use of heightened colours and frequently exaggerated forms adopted a more expressive, individualistic approach to painting, largely derived from late nineteenth-century French Symbolism. In *Waiting (Margot)*, Picasso draws upon the work of a number of contemporary artists. In addition to the three mentioned above, he is also showing an awareness of the claustrophobic spaces and loose handling of the Nabi painters, including Edouard Vuillard (1868–1940) and Pierre Bonnard (1867–1947).

CREATED

Barcelona or Paris

MEDIUM

Oil on cardboard

SERIES/PERIOD/MOVEMENT

Early period

SIMILAR WORKS

At the Café by Paul Gauguin, 1888

Dancer from the 'Rat Mort' by Maurice Vlaminck, 1906

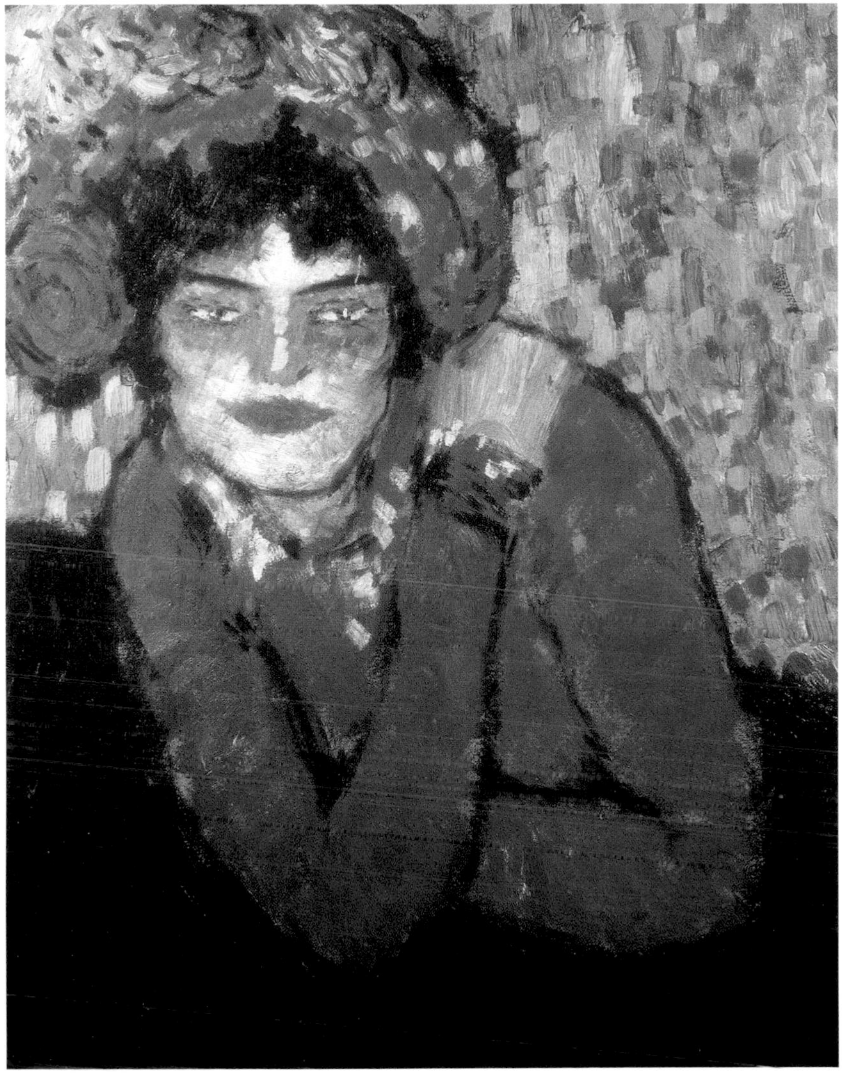

Woman with a Cigarette, 1901

Picasso's numerous scenes of women in cafés, often represented alone, drinking or smoking, record his experiences of life in Montmartre in the early twentieth century. At the same time, they develop a subject much explored by many painters associated with the Impressionists. Amongst these, Edgar Degas (1834–1917) was best known for his numerous portrayals of women in cafés, thus capturing a changing aspect of social behaviour brought about largely by the transformation of Paris in the mid-nineteenth century under Napoleon III. However, Picasso's *Woman with a Cigarette* also draws on other sources stylistically. In particular, the elongated form of the body, with its excessively long limbs and hands, recalls the work of El Greco. The spirituality and mysticism that inspired El Greco resulted in the representation of ethereal bodies, almost devoid of physical substance. Such a means of representation provided Picasso with the perfect vocabulary with which to represent his social outcasts, their languid postures and emaciated physiques symbolic of the harshness of modern urban poverty.

CREATED

Paris

MEDIUM

Oil on canvas

SERIES/PERIOD/MOVEMENT

Early period

SIMILAR WORKS

Plum Brandy by Edouard Manet, 1877

The Woman of Arles by Vincent van Gogh, 1888

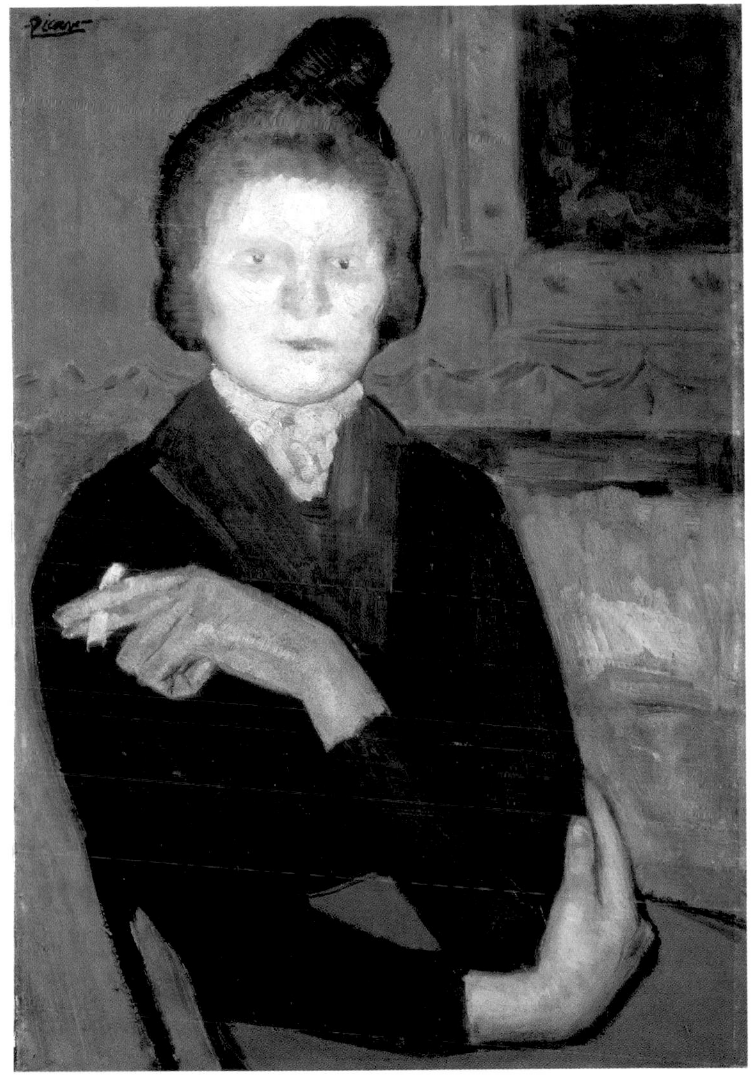

Bust of a Nude, 1907

In addition to his broad awareness of both Old Master and contemporary European art, Picasso was, famously, to be influenced by African masks. Since the late-nineteenth century, many avant-garde European artists had been expressing a fascination with non-western culture. The French Colonial occupation of parts of the African continent had facilitated access to a body of artefacts previously largely unfamiliar to western eyes, while the development of ethnography and anthropology as academic disciplines meant that many of these new objects were collected, classified and displayed in museums such as the Museum of Ethnography in Paris. The precise dating of Picasso's first trip to this museum is the subject of much controversy. What does seem clear, however, is that Picasso's first encounter with African masks had a significant impact upon his work. *Bust of a Nude*, for example, reveals the artist's familiarity with the elongated nose and concave face typical of many examples of masks from the African continent. Picasso freely developed these forms within his own works, particularly throughout 1907 and 1908.

CREATED

Paris

MEDIUM

Oil on canvas

SERIES/PERIOD/MOVEMENT

Early Cubist period

SIMILAR WORKS

African Masks on display at the Trocadero in Paris

Self-Portrait by Picasso, 1906

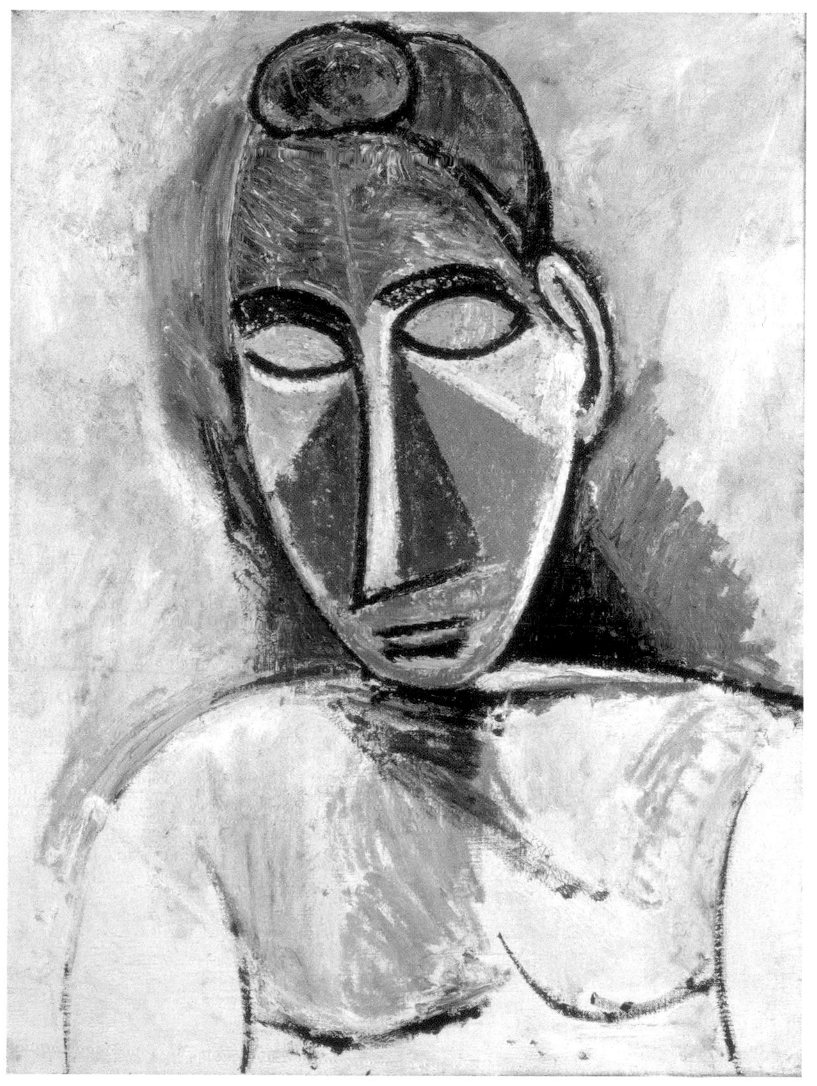

The Peasants' Repast, 1917

The intense nationalism fostered by the First World War resulted in many artists turning back to the French artistic heritage. In essence this meant the classically inspired works of the eighteenth and early nineteenth centuries. Another popular model for contemporary French painters, however, was the work of the eighteenth-century Le Nain brothers Louis (*c.* 1593–1648) and Antoine (*c.* 1588–1648). *The Peasant's Repast*, by Louis Le Nain, was a highly respected painting that occupied a prestigious position in the Louvre. It had also inspired the mid-nineteenth century French realist painters Jean François Millet (1814–75) and Gustave Courbet (1819–77). In 1917 Picasso produced his own version of the work based – albeit loosely – on the famous original. Picasso has retained many of Le Nain's compositional features, especially in the positioning of the main characters. However, some figures are entirely absent and Picasso has even changed the horizontal format of the original to the vertical. More importantly, Picasso has replaced Le Nain's muted browns with a chromatic explosion of colours, all executed in a pointillist style. Here Picasso has simultaneously quoted from the past, yet has not abandoned modern developments in painting.

CREATED

Montrouge

MEDIUM

Oil on canvas

SERIES/PERIOD/MOVEMENT

Neoclassical period

SIMILAR WORKS

The Peasants' Repast by Louis Le Nain, 1642

After Dinner at Ornans by Gustave Courbet, 1848–49

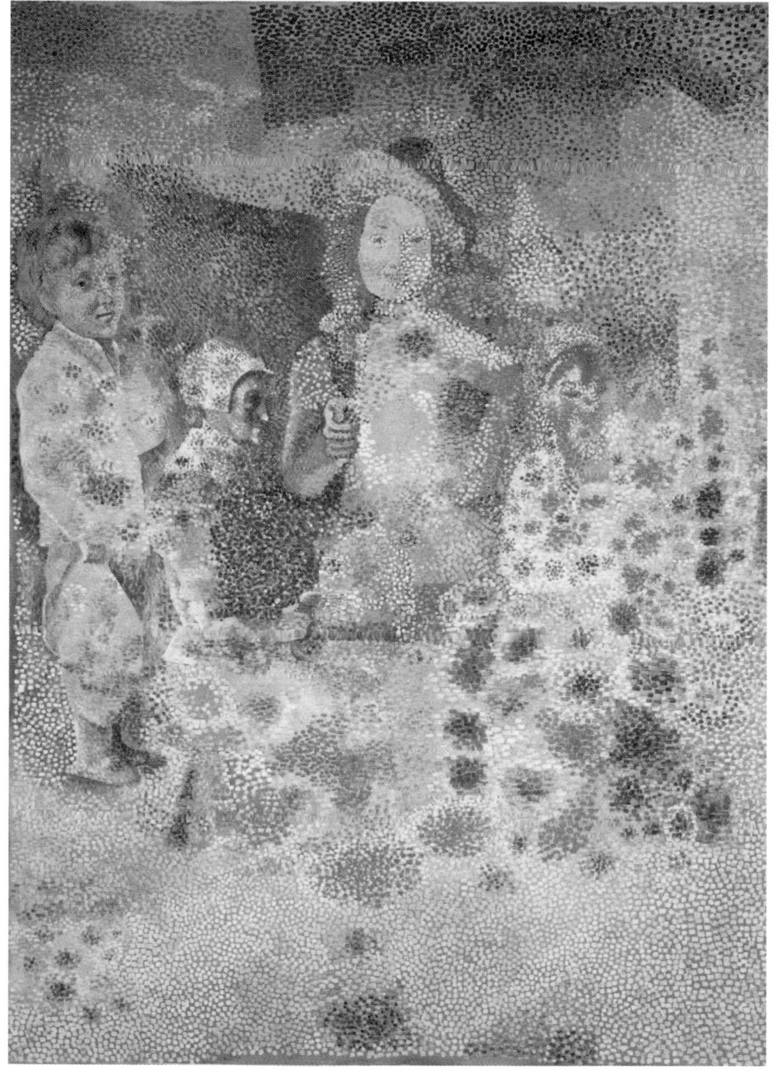

The Bathers, 1918

Picasso produced his small painting entitled *The Bathers* whilst on his honeymoon in Biarritz in the summer of 1918. Although very much a contemporary scene, exemplified by the fashionable bathing costumes, *The Bathers* recalls the traditional Arcadian paintings of the nineteenth-century academic painter Pierre Puvis de Chavannes (1824–98). In particular, the postures adopted by these modern bathers conform closely to one of Puvis's most famous works, entitled *Young Girls by the Seashore* (1879). In both works, one figure is standing with her arms above her head arranging her hair. A second is seated with her back to the spectator, also recalling the work of Jean Auguste Dominique Ingres (1780–1867), and a third lies sleeping on the ground. The body types represented, however, depart from the Puvis model. The childlike distortion of forms and the peculiar relationship of scale in the body parts also recall the work of another artist in whom Picasso had previously shown a great interest, the so-called 'naïve' painter Henri Rousseau (1844–1910). In particular the blue-and-white striped bathing costume of the standing bather seems to be a direct quotation from Rousseau's *Football Players* of 1908.

CREATED

Biarritz

MEDIUM

Oil on canvas

SERIES/PERIOD/MOVEMENT

Neoclassical period

SIMILAR WORKS

Young Girls by the Seashore by Pierre Puvis de Chavannes, 1879

Football Players by Henri Rousseau, 1908

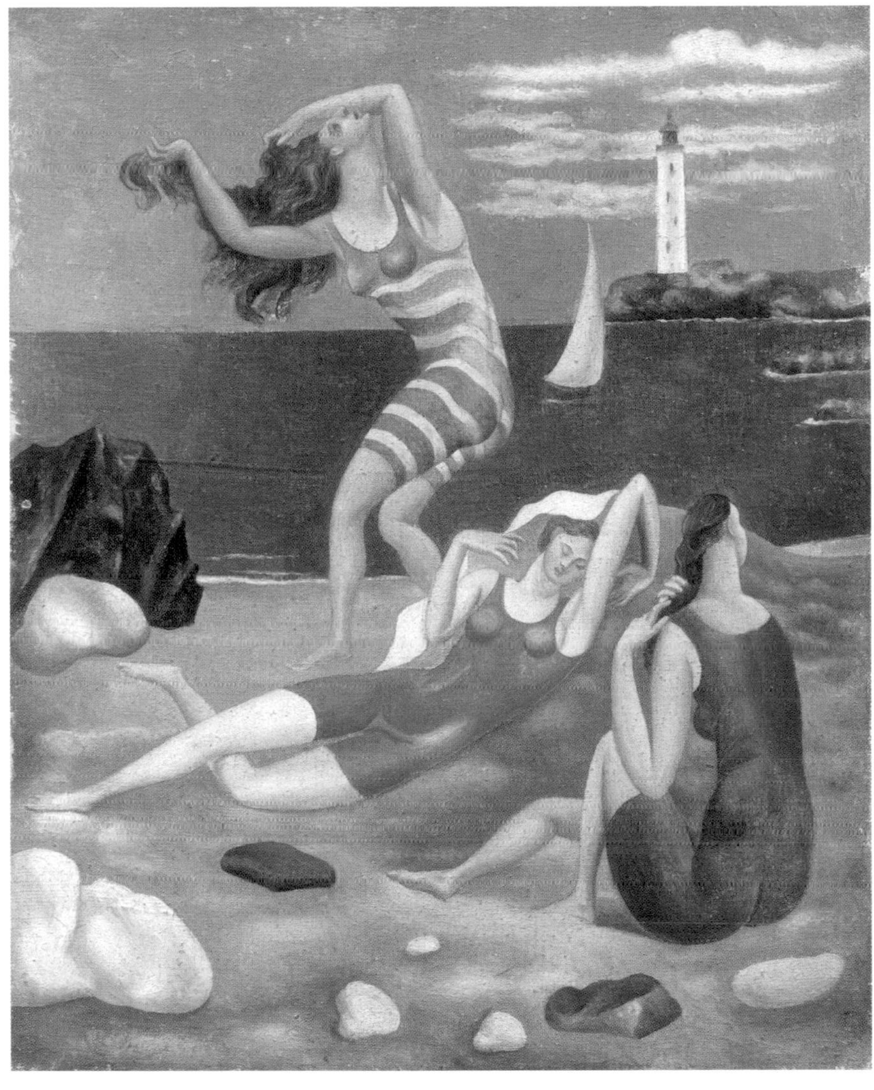

His Son, Paulo, 1921

Picasso's technical skill as a draughtsman, and not least of all his ability to draw the human form, was established from a very early age. During the First World War Picasso moved away from his recent Cubist work to return to figurative art, producing a series of portraits of his friends, drawn in pencil and charcoal. The source for Picasso's return to figurative drawing is usually attributed to the work of Ingres, and it is certainly the case that many of Picasso's Neoclassical works quote directly from the French master. This charcoal and chalk drawing is a study for the painting of 1921 entitled *Mother and Child*. The subject was certainly inspired by the recent birth of Picasso's first son, Paulo. However, consideration should also be given to the mood of renewed optimism that permeated post-First World War France. Indeed, the idea of a metaphorical rebirth was widely promoted. In this drawing we also see Picasso's interest in the monumental forms of classical antiquity, the bulky form of the small child seeming to be almost hewn out of stone.

CREATED

Paris

MEDIUM

Charcoal and sanguine on paper

SERIES/PERIOD/MOVEMENT

Neoclassical period

SIMILAR WORKS

Child with Doll by Henri Rousseau, 1904–05

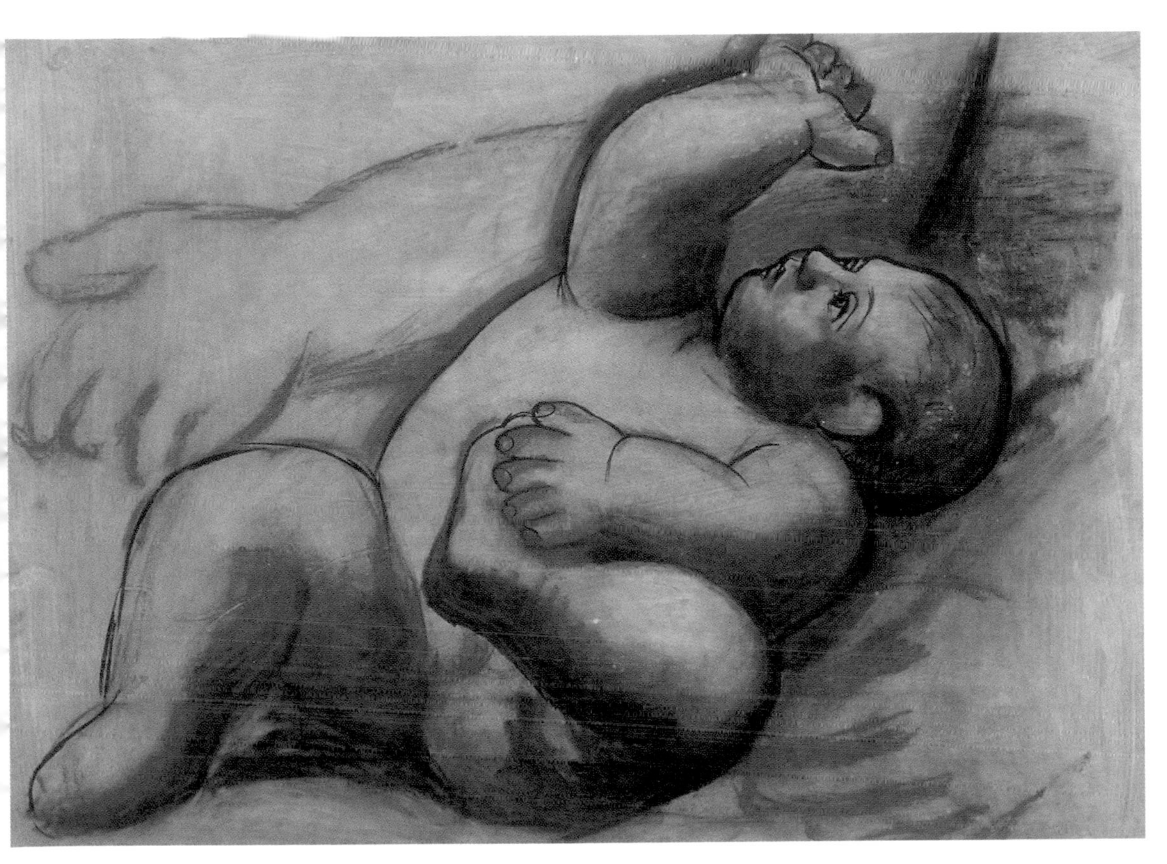

The Pipes of Pan, 1923

The Pipes of Pan might well be considered the apogee of Picasso's Neoclassical period. Executed in the summer of 1923 in Antibes, the work exudes Mediterranean light and warmth. At the same time it makes a clear reference to an antique past. The two figures, one playing pan-pipes, the other standing contemplatively as if listening to the music of his companion, are incredibly static and resemble ancient Greek statues. The boy on the left, in particular, with his antique head and columnar body, broken only by the slightly raised right leg, recalls the Kouros figures – amongst the earliest figurative statues of the ancient Greeks, in which Picasso had expressed a great interest. *The Pipes of Pan* also recalls the work of Puvis de Chavannes, especially his *Shepherd's Song* (1891). Puvis's Symbolist works often incorporated classically inspired subjects and were executed in muted, dry tones similar to those deployed here by Picasso. Another possible source of influence is Paul Cézanne's (1839–1906) series of late bather paintings, and particularly his images of male bathers, works with which Picasso would probably have been familiar.

CREATED

Cap d'Antibes

MEDIUM

Oil on canvas

SERIES/PERIOD/MOVEMENT

Neoclassical period

SIMILAR WORKS

Kouros figure from Ancient Greece, *c.* 575–570 BC

Young Girls by the Seashore by Pierre Puvis de Chavannes, 1879

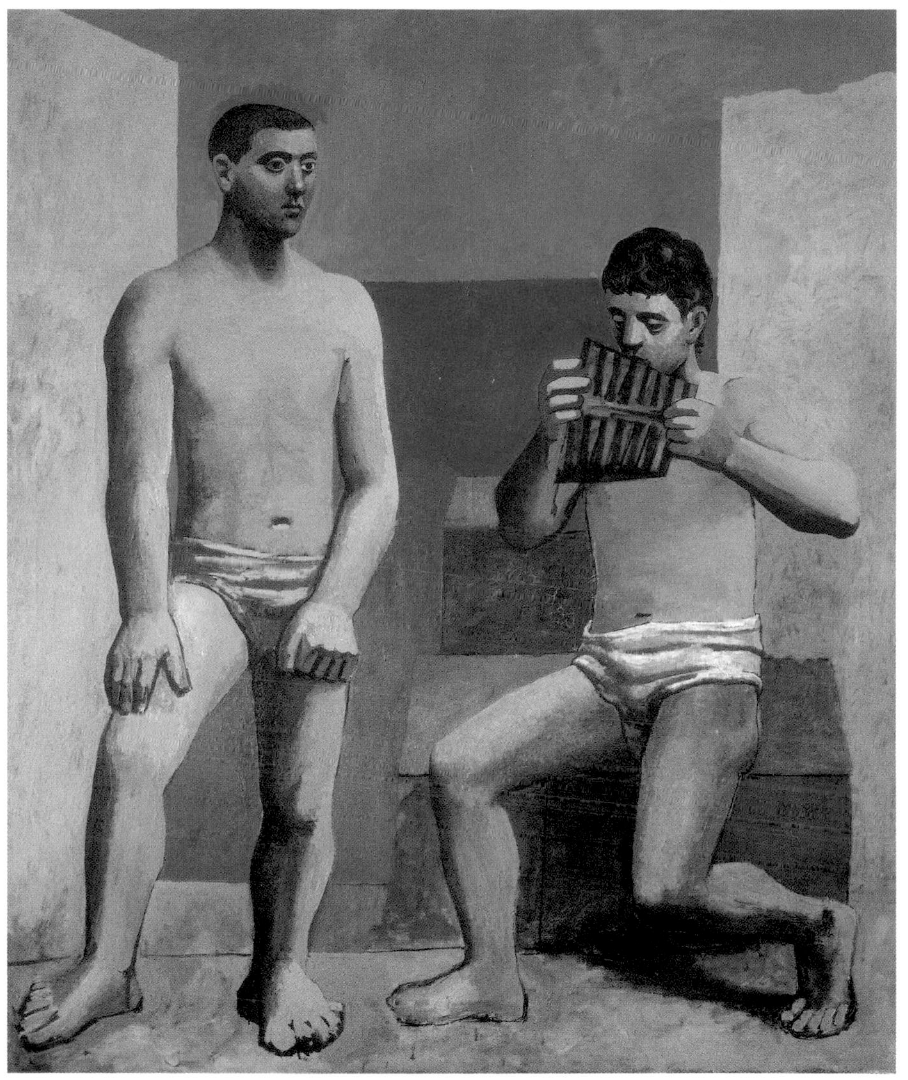

Woman with a Guitar, 1924–25

Throughout the period from 1918–25 Picasso continued to work in two styles simultaneously, one derived from the antique forms of the classical epoch, the other from his Cubist experiments of the pre-First World War era. However, even in the Cubist works, Picasso made explicit reference to past French painting. His *Woman with a Guitar*, for example, can be linked to another nineteenth-century French painter very much in vogue in the early post-First World War period, Jean Baptiste Camille Corot (1796–1875). Significantly, Corot's painting of *c.* 1860, entitled *Girl with a Mandolin*, had previously inspired a Cubist re-rendering of the subject by Picasso's Spanish compatriot Juan Gris (1887–1927). In his *Woman with a Mandolin* (1916), Gris quoted directly from Corot, representing his figure in an identical costume to Corot's original. Picasso has avoided using such a direct quotation in this work. However, his emphasis on the seated female form – this time represented nude, with an undefined stringed instrument on her lap – bears many similarities to both Corot's work and Gris' copy after it.

CREATED

Paris or Juan-les-Pins

MEDIUM

Oil on canvas

SERIES/PERIOD/MOVEMENT

Neoclassical period

SIMILAR WORKS

Girl with a Mandolin by Jean Baptiste Camille Corot, *c.* 1680

Woman with a Mandolin by Juan Gris, 1916

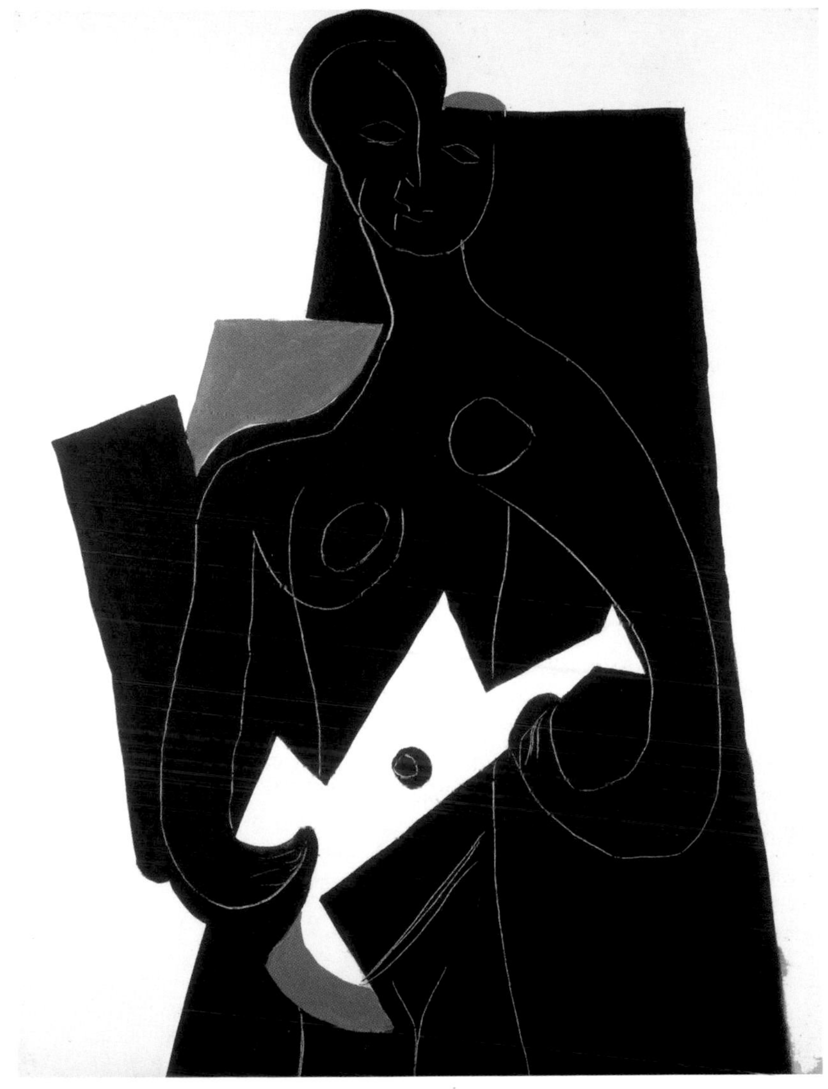

Woman in a Red Armchair, 1932

During the mid 1920s Picasso's representations of the female form began to take on a more aggressively distorted and contorted form. This might be partially explained by a change in the artist's personal circumstances. Certainly the first signs of tension in Picasso's marriage to Olga Khokhlova began to emerge at this time. However, consideration should also be given to other factors, not least of all Picasso's knowledge of the emerging Surrealist movement, with its emphasis on metamorphosis. Though embraced by the Surrealists, Picasso remained very much on the fringe of the movement, only occasionally exhibiting with them and maintaining an identity independent of the main group. However, the impact of Surrealism on his work is highly evident. *Woman in a Red Armchair* reveals a significant shift in Picasso's work from his Neoclassicism. Monumental antique forms have here given way to abstract biomorphic forms reminiscent of Stone Age carvings. More importantly, these forms metamorphose to suggest the appearance of a woman, constructed from various components, while two red obelisks in the background imply the armchair upon which this strange creature is seated.

CREATED

Boisgeloup

MEDIUM

Oil, conté, crayon and chalk on canvas

SERIES/PERIOD/MOVEMENT

Surrealist period

SIMILAR WORKS

Human Concretion by Jean (Hans) Arp, 1937

Recumbent Figure by Henry Moore, 1938

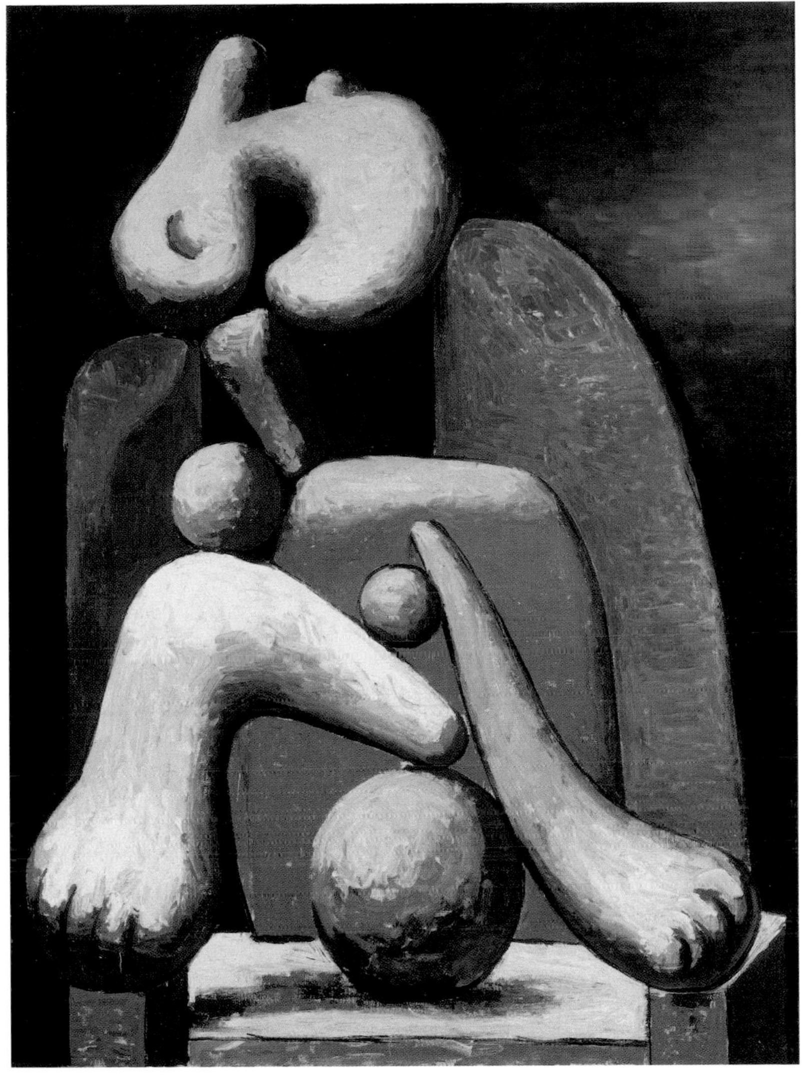

On the Beach (Bathing), 1937

On the Beach (Bathing) also draws upon aspects of Surrealism. Here we are once more confronted with two female forms constructed from an assemblage of peculiar biomorphic forms. The figures appear to be at the edge of the sea, and one lowers a small toy boat into the water. Another, similar form rises above the horizon, as if watching the activity of the foreground figures. However, as this figure is represented as approximately the same scale as the foreground figures, its presence on the horizon implies that it is a gigantic and threatening being. The work is full of narrative incongruities. Why are two grown women playing with a boat? Who – or what – is the form on the horizon, and what is its relationship to the two foreground women? This destabilizing sense of threat and uncertainty recalls similar strategies deployed in the Surrealist paintings of René Magritte (1898–1967) such as his *Threatened Assassin* of 1926. The anthropomorphic forms also recall the earlier sculptural work of Jean (Hans) Arp (1887–1966), and resemble the early sculptures of Henry Moore (1898–1986).

CREATED

Le-Tremblay-sur-Maulde

MEDIUM

Oil on canvas

SERIES/PERIOD/MOVEMENT

Surrealist period

SIMILAR WORKS

Threatened Assassin by René Magritte, 1926

Recumbent Figure by Henry Moore, 1938

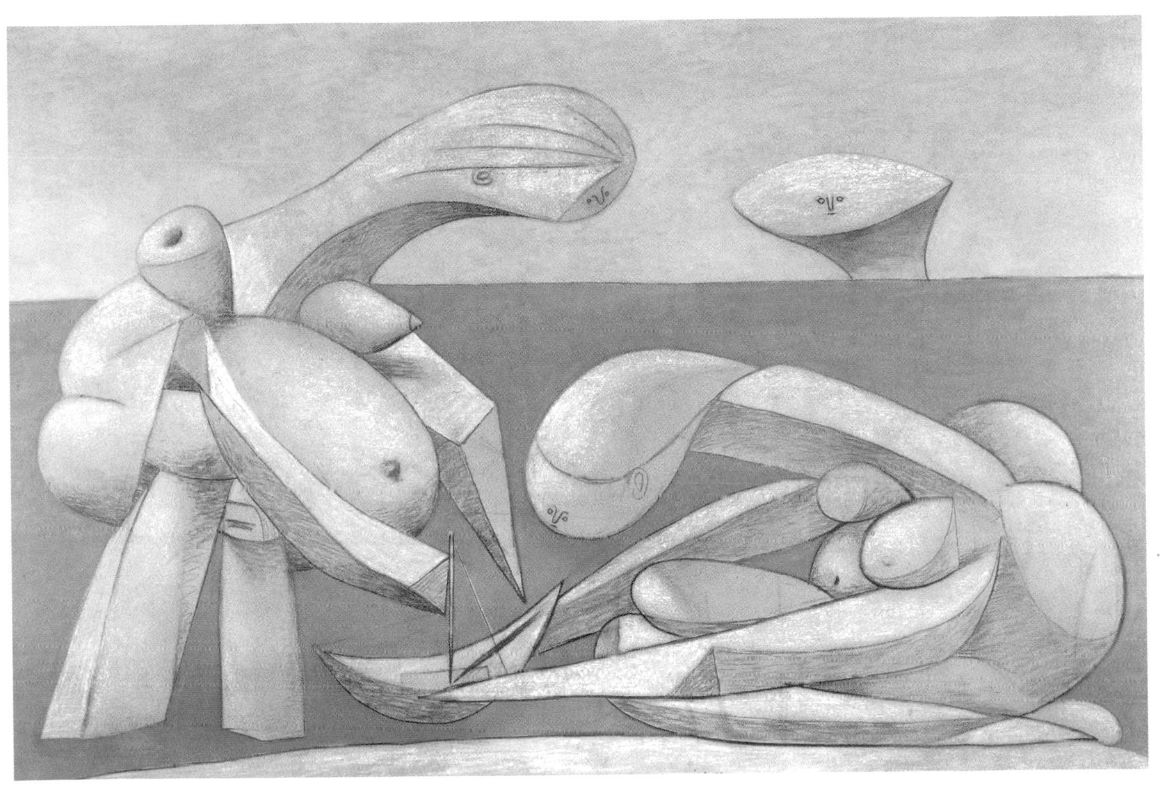

Portrait of a Painter, after El Greco, 1950

In the post-war period, now into his late sixties, Picasso began to take stock of his life's work. In 1947 he donated 10 paintings to the Musée Nationale d'Art Moderne in Paris and, as a result of this, got to see his work displayed, for the first time, alongside masterpieces from the Louvre. From this point onwards, Picasso increasingly produced pieces based explicitly on the work of Old Masters. In 1950 he created several such variations, including works based on Lucas Cranach (1472–1553) and Courbet. He also produced this portrait after El Greco's portrait of his son, also a painter. El Greco's work had left its mark on Picasso since his earliest days, and had influenced many of the paintings he had produced in Paris at the turn of the century. Picasso had even turned to El Greco as a source of inspiration for his early breakthrough work, *Les Demoiselles d'Avignon* of 1907. In his variation on El Greco's *Portrait of an Artist*, Picasso has adopted the warm browns and ochres of the other artist's style to represent a typical Golden Age Spanish gentleman. The Cubist-inspired forms, however, are very much of the twentieth century.

CREATED

Vallauris

MEDIUM

Oil on plywood

SERIES/PERIOD/MOVEMENT

Post-War Communist period

SIMILAR WORKS

Portrait of the Artist's Son, Jorge Manuel Theotokopoulos by El Greco, *c.* 1603

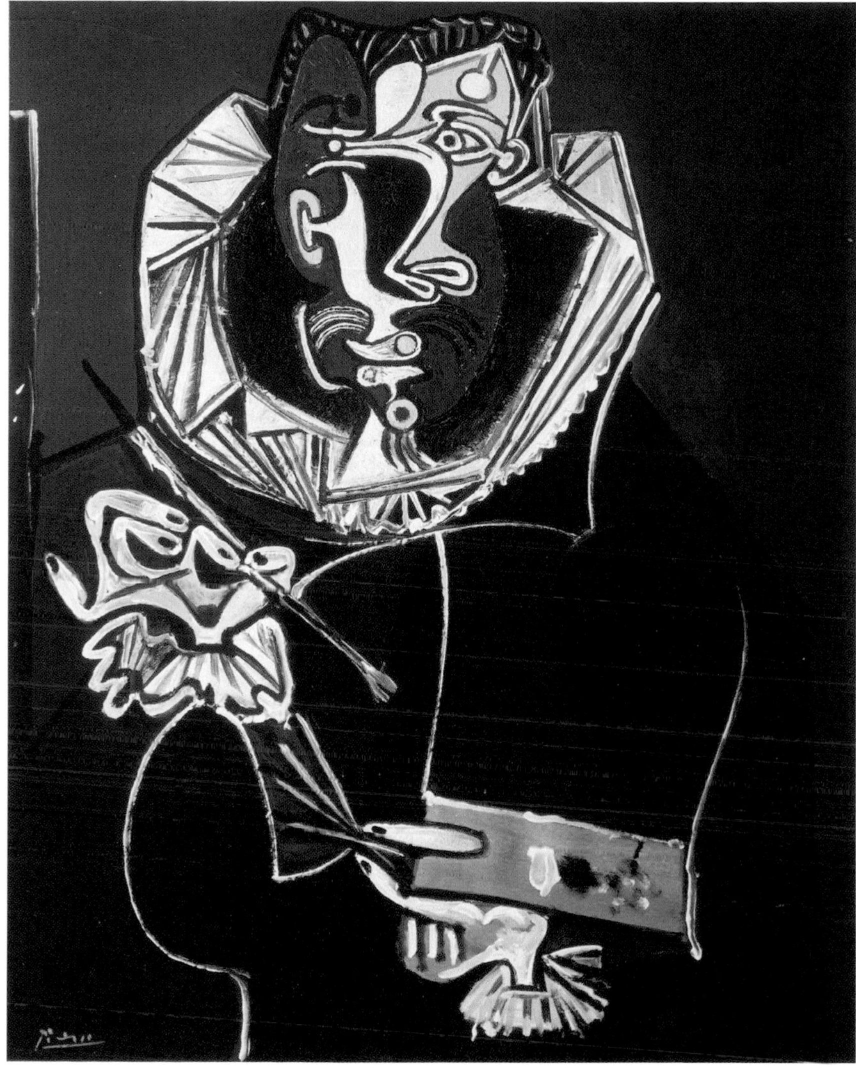

Monkey and her Baby, 1951

The inspiration for Picasso's *Monkey and her Baby* initially came from two toy cars owned by Picasso's young son, Claude. The cars, when placed chassis to chassis, resembled a monkey's head and from this starting point Picasso built up the rest of the animal. Two small balls were inserted for the eyes, and jug handles to indicate ears. The body was formed from a ceramic pot, while the tail was made from a bent metal door handle. Once assembled, Picasso had the model cast in bronze. Although highly original in conception, the work does recall the small bronze animal statuettes that were widely collected in the nineteenth century. At the same time the construction of a figure from identifiable – and seemingly unrelated – parts also has a precedent in the work of the sixteenth-century painter Guiseppe Arcimboldo (1527–1593). Arcimboldo's paintings of heads, constructed from fruit, shellfish and other products of nature, had been much admired by the Surrealists, for whom the metamorphosis of ordinary objects into living beings recalled the peculiar condition of the unconscious and of dreams.

CREATED

Vallauris

MEDIUM

Bronze

SERIES/PERIOD/MOVEMENT

Post-War Communist period

SIMILAR WORKS

Flora by Guiseppe Arcimboldo, 1591

Gorilla Taking a Woman Away by Emmanuel Frémiet, 1887

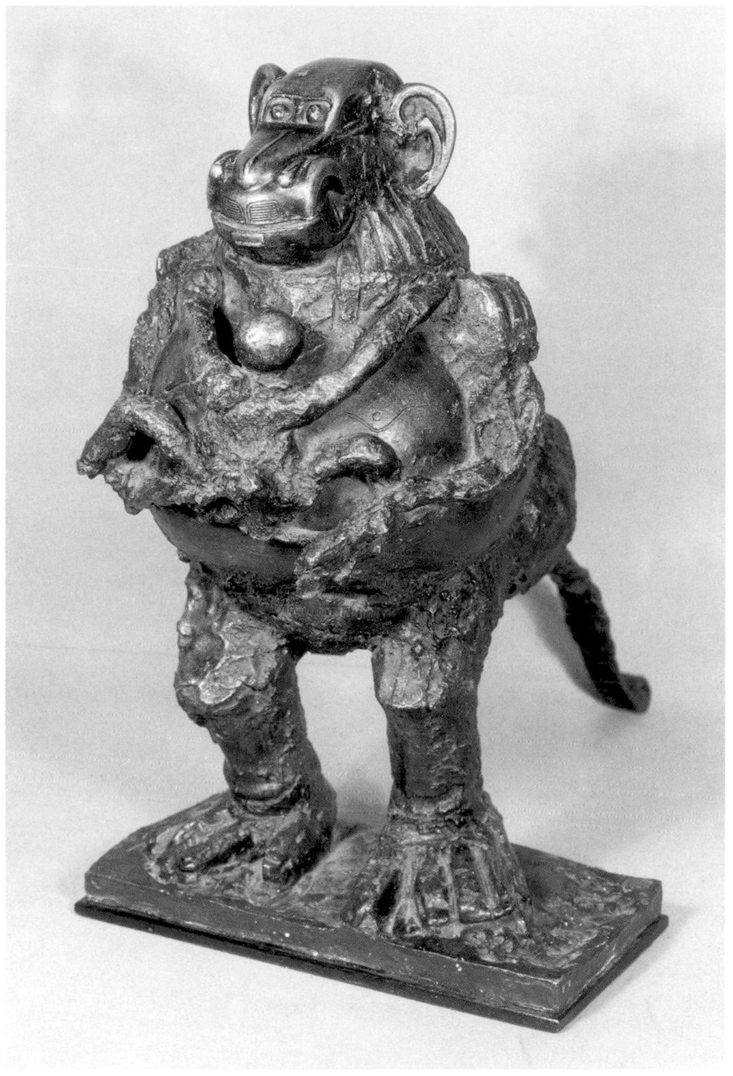

The Women of Algiers, after Delacroix, 1954

Between 1954 and 1963 Picasso produced several series of variations on Old Master paintings including reworkings of Edouard Manet's (1832–83) *Déjeuner sur l'herbe* (1863), Velazquez's *Las Meninas* (1656) and Jacques-Louis David's (1748–1825) *Rape of the Sabines* (1794–99). The first of these series, however, examined Eugene Delacroix's (1798–1863) *Women of Algiers* (1834). Picasso produced 15 oils based on this work in a frenzied period of activity in the winter of 1954-55. Picasso had first made a sketch version of the work as early as 1940 and throughout the decade regularly visited the Louvre specifically to look at Delacroix's canvas. However, like so many of Picasso's variations, the works, including this oil sketch, were only loosely based upon the original. Here Picasso has again distorted the forms of the women seated in the foreground, twisting their bodies into impossible contortions so that front and back views are simultaneously presented to the viewer. The emphasis on the odalisque is also closely related to Picasso's admiration for Henri Matisse (1869–1954), who specialized in the representation of women in such exotic costumes. Matisse's recent death inspired Picasso to engage with this subject.

CREATED

Paris

MEDIUM

Oil on canvas

SERIES/PERIOD/MOVEMENT

Late period

SIMILAR WORKS

The Women of Algiers by Eugène Delacroix, 1834

Odalisques by Henri Matisse, 1928

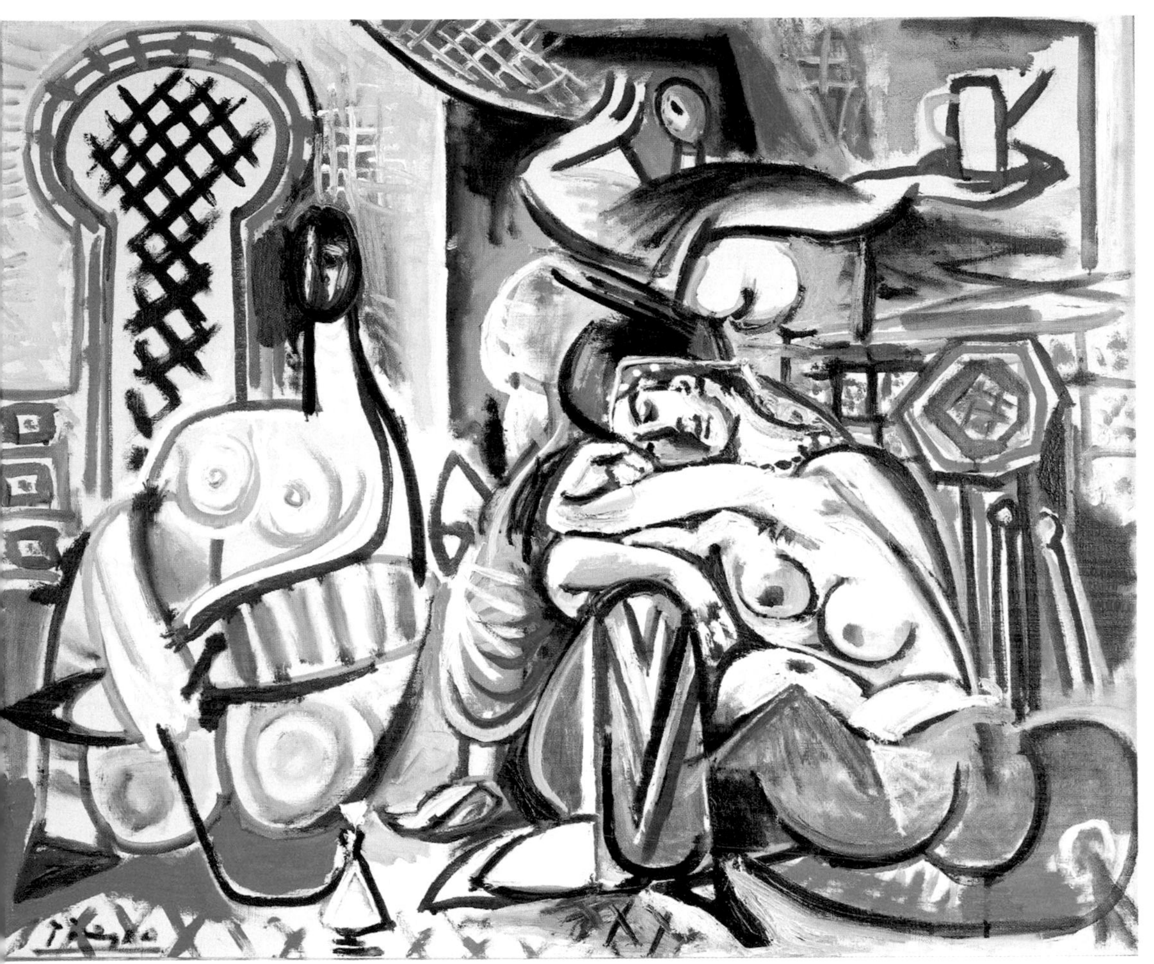

The Studio at 'La Californie', 1956

Shortly after moving into 'La Californie', near Cannes, Picasso produced a series of paintings representing the interior of his new studio. Amongst these, *The Studio at 'La Californie'* is most revealing of Picasso's ability to introduce a wide range of references from other artists' work into his own. The subject matter itself, as well as Picasso's emphasis on the decorative tracery of the studio architecture and the inclusion of a Moroccan brazier in the lower left, instantly recalls Matisse's studio scenes and his interests in North African motifs. The colour scheme, with its blacks, greys, browns and greens, also forms a direct link between Picasso's work and the most recent studio interiors of his artistic colleague from his Cubist days, Georges Braque (1882–1963). Other past artists are also invoked. Thus, the placement of a blank canvas at the very centre of the studio is a reference to one of Courbet's most famous works, *The Artist's Studio* (1855), whilst the organization of the space, composition and colour scheme are reminiscent of Velazquez's *Las Meninas* (1656).

CREATED

Cannes

MEDIUM

Oil on canvas

SERIES/PERIOD/MOVEMENT

Late period

SIMILAR WORKS

The Artist's Studio by Gustave Courbet, 1855

Studio II by Georges Braque, 1949

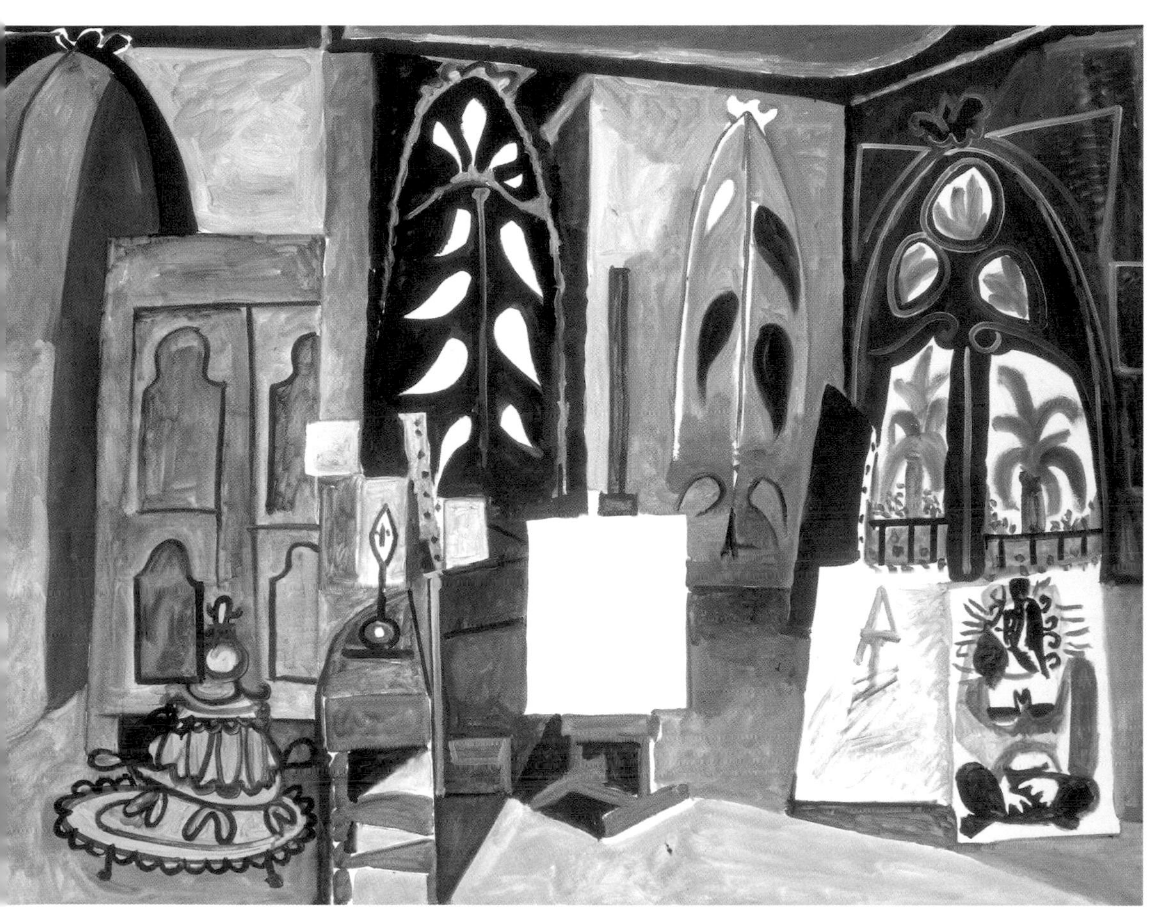

Lying Nude with Head of a Man in Profile, 1965

During the mid 1960s, two themes dominated Picasso's work: firstly, the painter and his model, and secondly the reclining nude. This work brings the two themes together. The majority of the canvas focuses on a female nude, lying recumbent on a couch. The woman is represented with her arms raised and her body tilted at an angle to allow the spectator an uninterrupted view of the naked torso. This instantly recalls the famous *Naked Maja* painted by Goya in 1797–98. In the original, a great emphasis is placed upon the gaze of the model out towards the viewer. In contrast here, the model gazes modestly downwards. However, the inclusion of a bearded figure, seen in profile on the far left, refocuses our attention on the issue of the gaze. Notably, this figure carries none of the attributes associated with the artist, such as brushes or a palette. However, both the beard and the strict profile are characteristics that Picasso regularly used in his representations of the painter and his model. Thus, by reference to Goya, Picasso conflates both past and present, both spectatorship and artistic creation.

CREATED

Mougins

MEDIUM

Oil on canvas

SERIES/PERIOD/MOVEMENT

Late period

SIMILAR WORKS

The Rokeby Venus by Diego Velazquez, *c.* 1644–48

The Naked Maja by Francisco de Goya, 1800

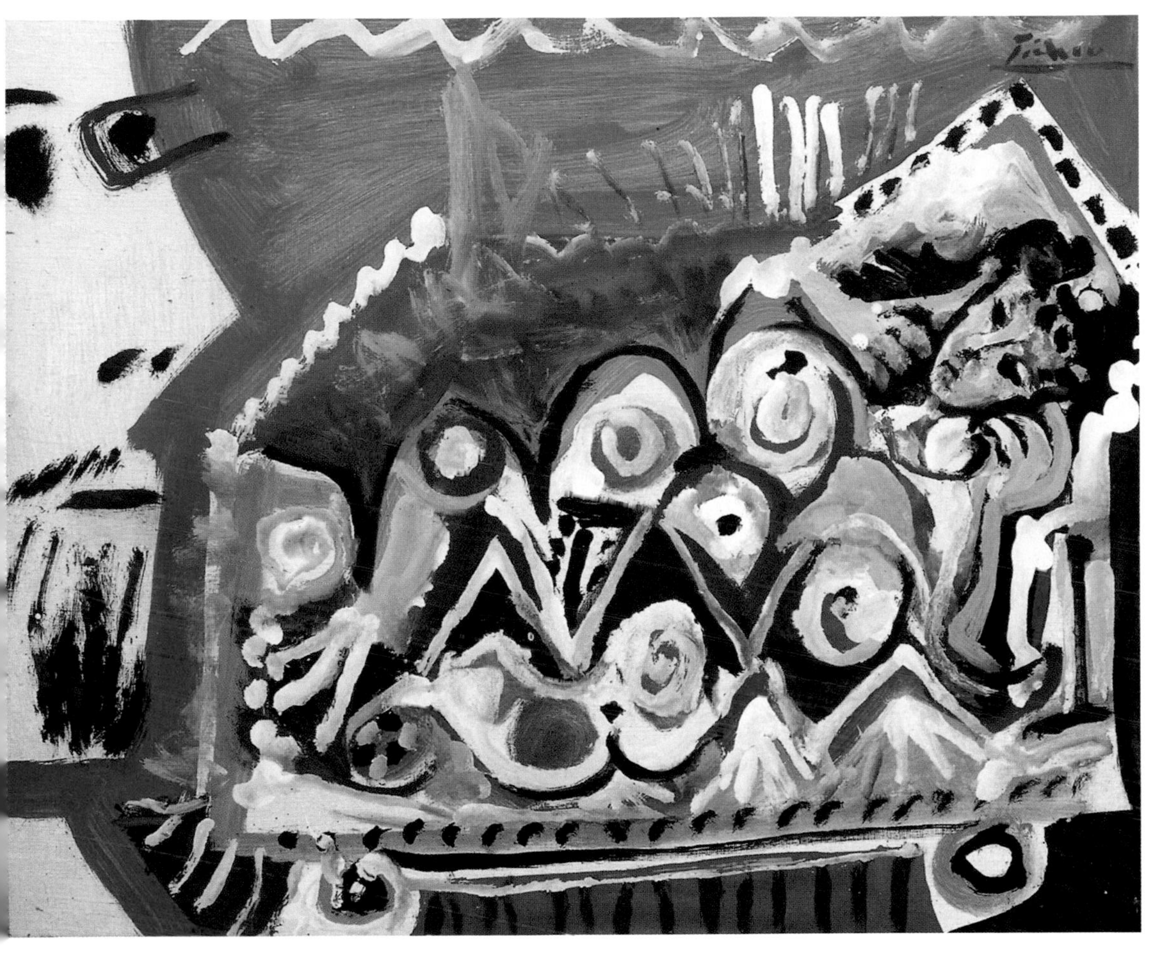

After Velazquez, c. 1960s

Towards the end of the 1960s, now approaching his ninetieth year, Picasso introduced a new character into his work – the musketeer. These figures are identifiable by their long-flowing locks, carefully shaped moustaches and ruff collars, encapsulating the charm and elegance of Golden Age romantic heroes. Picasso drew on a multitude of sources for these works, including both Dutch and Spanish Old Masters. In particular he looked to Rembrandt (1606–69) and Velazquez, both artists whom Picasso had admired throughout his life and who were renowned for producing some of their best works in their old age. Here Picasso has represented a seventeenth-century Spanish gentleman in a composition typical of the portraiture of both Rembrandt and Velazquez. The imaginary sitter is seen frontally and proudly displays his finest silks and satins to the world. However, Picasso's unique style is once more displayed through the use of simple, bold and abbreviated brushstrokes to capture the essence of this romantic figure.

CREATED

Mougins

MEDIUM

Oil on canvas

SERIES/PERIOD/MOVEMENT

Late period

SIMILAR WORKS

Self-Portrait as a Young Man by Rembrandt, 1634

Self-Portrait by Diego Velazquez, *c.* 1640

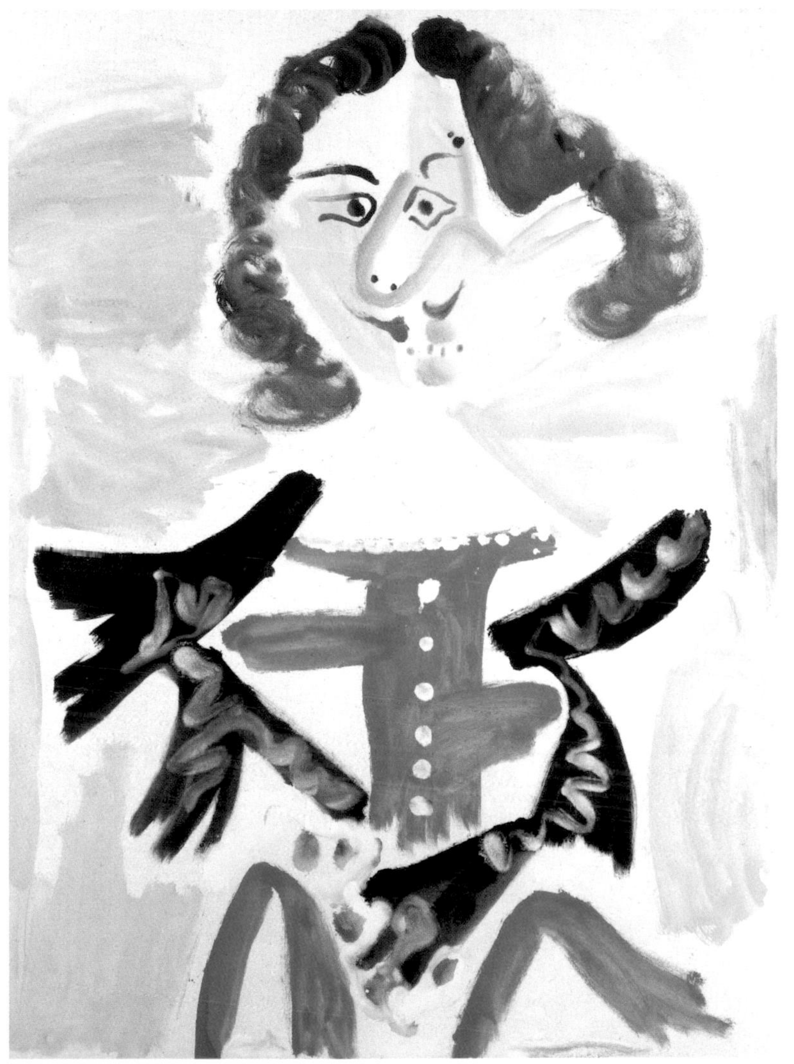

Picasso

Styles & Techniques

Two Women at a Bar, 1902

Picasso's 'blue period' is usually dated 1901–04. During this period he produced a series of works focusing upon the poor and dispossessed – all executed to convey a sense of melancholy and loss. Picasso's decision to execute these works in dominant tones of blue itself recognized the importance of colour within Symbolist art and literature. Following the Symbolist tenet not to 'subjectify the objective', but to 'objectify the subjective', Picasso's work rejected Impressionism and sought to use colour and form not to represent the physical world, but to allude to abstract emotional conditions. *Two Women at a Bar* provides a key example of this. Whilst the subject – two prostitutes in a Parisian café – is not untypical of many late nineteenth-century painters, the way the work is painted certainly is. Here Picasso combines cold, sombre blues with soft, melted body forms to convey a sense of the despair and melancholy of the scene depicted. Thus the use of colour and form makes a significant contribution to the viewer's interpretation of the subject matter.

CREATED

Barcelona

MEDIUM

Oil on canvas

SERIES/PERIOD/MOVEMENT

Blue period

SIMILAR WORKS

The Waitress by Edouard Manet, 1879

Vahine no te miti by Paul Gauguin, 1892

Pablo Picasso *Born* 1881 Málaga, Spain

Died 1973

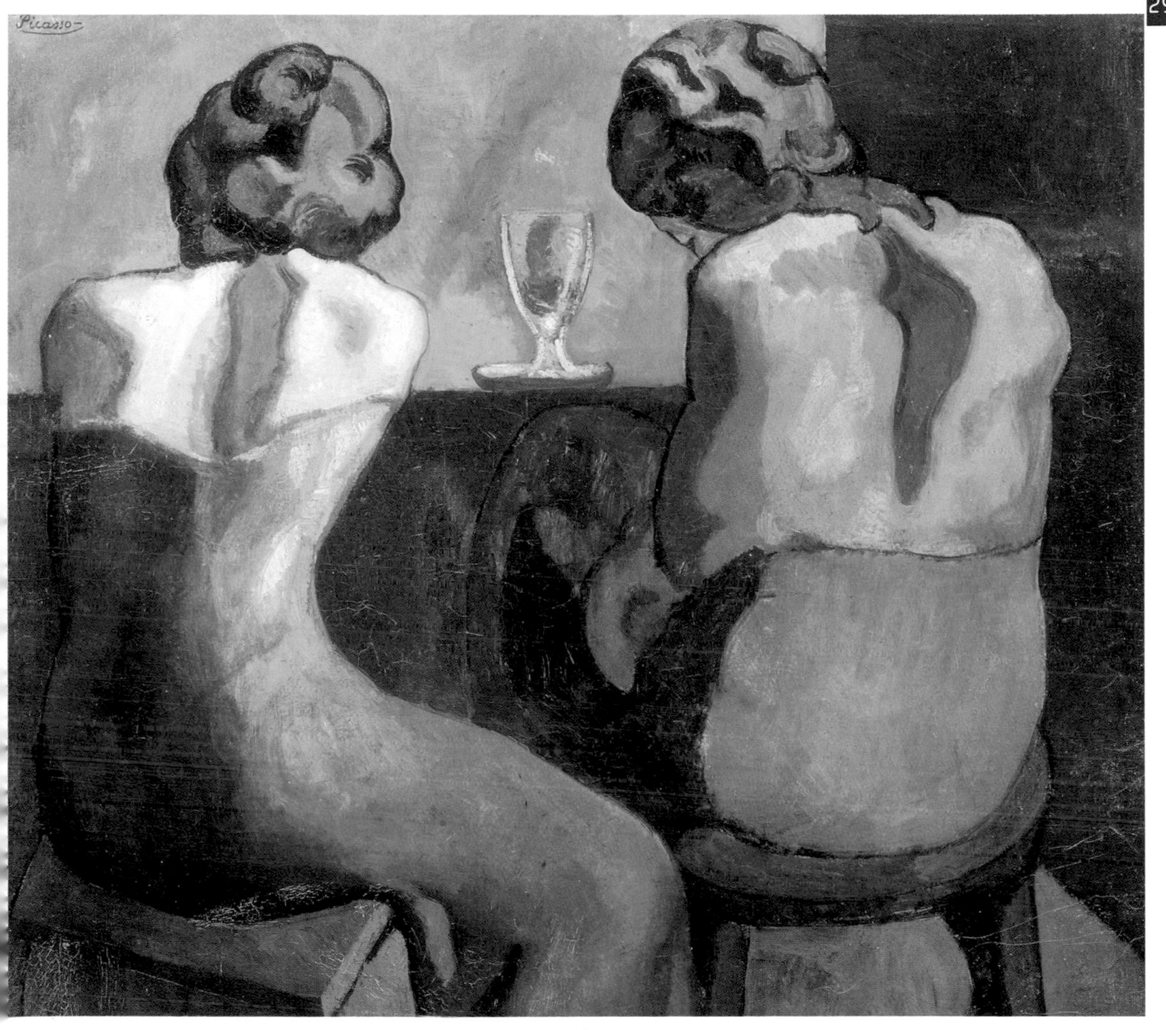
Picasso

Nude from the Back, 1902

This work from Picasso's 'blue period' bears all the hallmarks of the artist's extensive training in representing the human figure. The seated model, crouched with her back to the viewer, recalls poses frequently adopted in life classes, a factor further emphasized by the high viewpoint, looking down upon the figure. The absence of any background detail and seemingly hastily executed wash of colour also recalls the numerous studies that were part and parcel of art training at the turn of the century. However, this back view was also widely adopted by Paul Gauguin (1848–1903) in many of the paintings he executed in Tahiti. Here this posture serves to exclude the spectator from the scene, defining him or her as an outsider, situated beyond the margins of Gauguin's remote and exotic world. Picasso's adoption of a back view operates similarly to convey a sense of isolation and exclusion. The hunched, foetal position suggests introspection and self-protection, while the overall blue tonality casts a sombre mood over the work.

CREATED

Barcelona

MEDIUM

Oil on canvas

SERIES/PERIOD/MOVEMENT

Blue period

SIMILAR WORKS

The Valpinçon Bather by Jean Auguste Dominique Ingres, 1808

After the Bath (Woman Drying Herself) by Edgar Degas, 1895

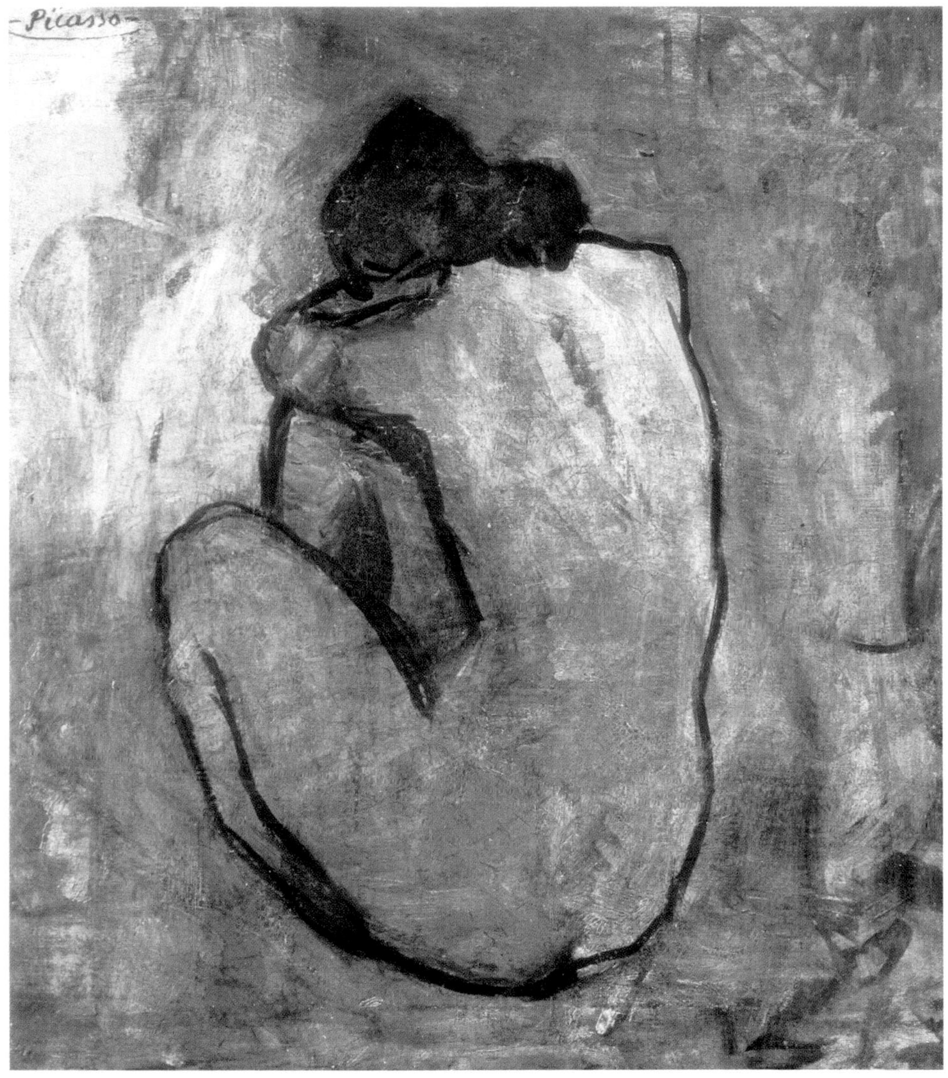
Picasso

Woman with a Crow, 1904

Woman with a Crow was produced towards the end of Picasso's 'blue period'. Here the blue tonality that had recently dominated Picasso's work is largely restricted to the rich, blue background that gives this work an eerie, nocturnal mood. The figure itself is represented in more naturalistic colours, though only loosely sketched in. The subject exudes mystery. A young woman kisses and gently caresses a crow – possibly a literary reference to the mysteries of Edgar Allan Poe (1809–49) – in a gesture of such tenderness that we sense a mood of loss or reverie. Here Picasso used gouache and pastel on paper, applying thin washes of pale colour over the more linear treatment of the hair, face and hand of the woman. This gives the figure a ghost-like ethereality, as if she might simply evaporate. In the bottom half of the work, the figure seems to dematerialize, her body becoming one with the foreground space. The severe attenuation of the fingers and the profile of the hunched and bony shoulders also imply a frail physique and thus the overall mood of fragility is reinforced.

CREATED

Paris

MEDIUM

Pastel and gouache on paper

SERIES/PERIOD/MOVEMENT

Blue period

SIMILAR WORKS

Beatrice by Odilon Redon, 1885

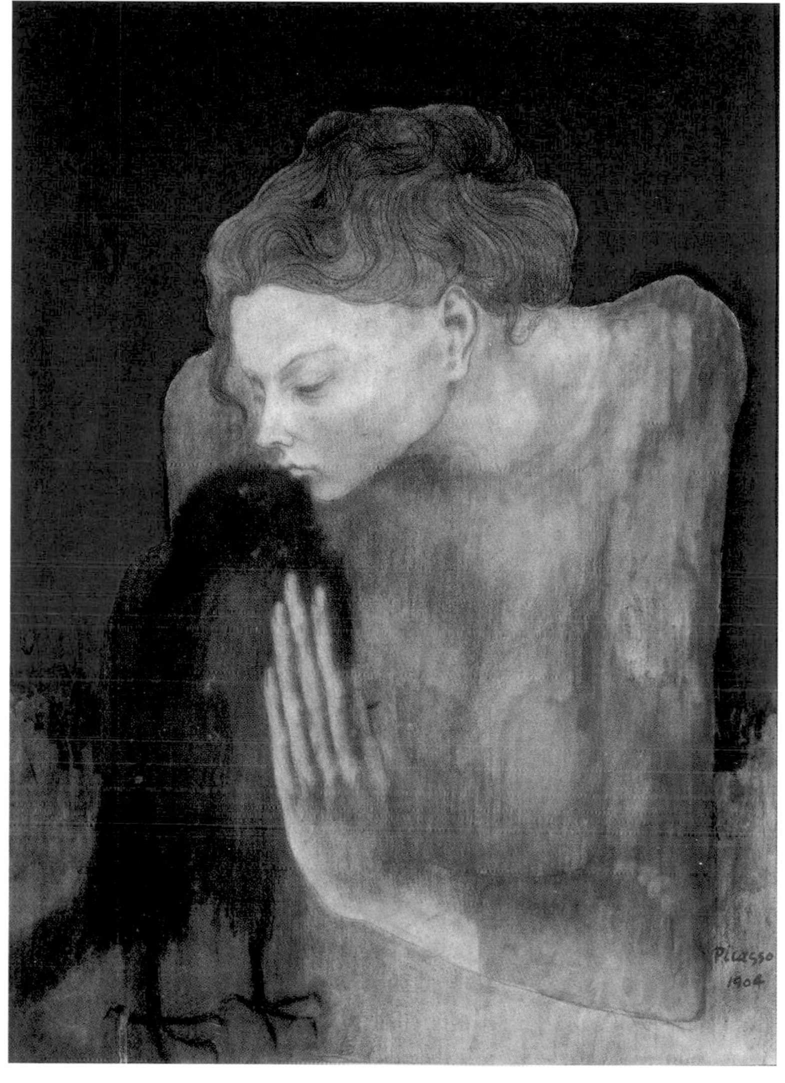
Picasso
1904

Seated Nude, 1905

Seated Nude was produced a couple of months after Picasso completed *Woman with a Crow*. Like the former, it seems to stand at the margins between his 'blue period' and his 'rose period'. The work is largely unfinished, although it has been signed in the lower right. Picasso has mostly completed the background, again a solid bluish-green tone, to form a starkly contrasting backdrop to the frail form of the naked female model. Picasso has also given detail to both face and right hand, but has left the remainder of the body only lightly sketched in. The pinkish-ochre ground upon which Picasso has painted the work shines through the figure, even where the body has been built up with subsequent layers of oil paint. This certainly suggests the brighter palette that Picasso soon adopted for his 'rose-period' works. The model for this work was probably a woman known only as Madeleine, with whom Picasso had an affair in 1904. Her frail, emaciated, and somewhat androgynous appearance seems to have inspired Picasso's melancholic paintings of this period, in many of which she appears.

CREATED

Paris

MEDIUM

Oil on cardboard on board

SERIES/PERIOD/MOVEMENT

Between Blue and Rose periods

SIMILAR WORKS

Ophelia by Odilon Redon, 1900–05

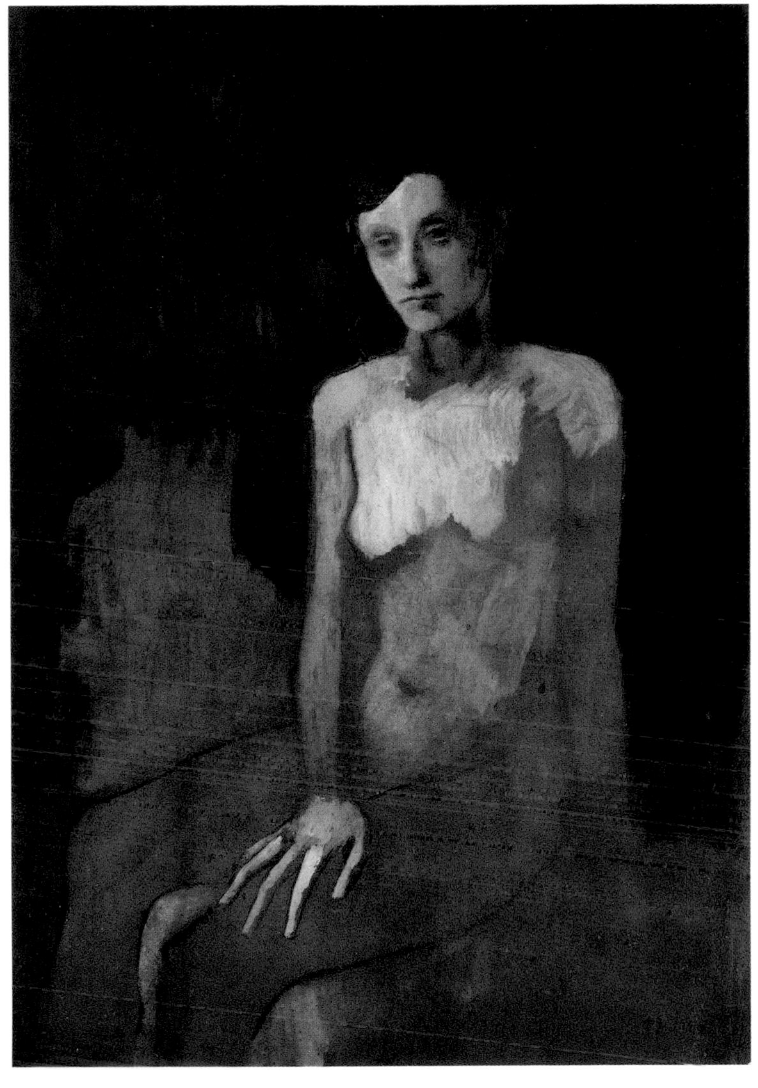

Girl and Boy with a Goat, 1905

Around 1905, Picasso abandoned the sombre blue that had dominated his recent work. He also moved away from his emphasis on tragic, poverty-stricken figures, replacing these with performers based on his regular attendance at the Médrano Circus in Montmartre. Soon even these still-melancholic figures made way for classically inspired male and female nudes, set against plain backgrounds and painted in a range of warm pink tones. *Girl and Boy with a Goat* epitomizes this 'rose-period' style. Here the central female figure stands before a curtain, adjusting her hair. To the right is a young boy bearing an amphora on his head, and to the left a goat. The work makes clear reference to the classical subject matter typical of artists such as Nicolas Poussin (1594–1665) and Jean Auguste Dominique Ingres (1780–1867), yet these figures occupy an ambiguous interior space. In both colour and form there is also a similarity to Greek vase painting. However, despite the explicit classical references, the bodies represented are strangely attenuated and non-naturalistic, revealing, once again, Picasso's visual inventiveness and willingness simultaneously to embrace and reinvent the art of the past.

CREATED

Gosól

MEDIUM

Oil on canvas

SERIES/PERIOD/MOVEMENT

Rose period

SIMILAR WORKS

The Source by Jean Auguste Dominique Ingres, 1856

The Harem by Picasso, 1906

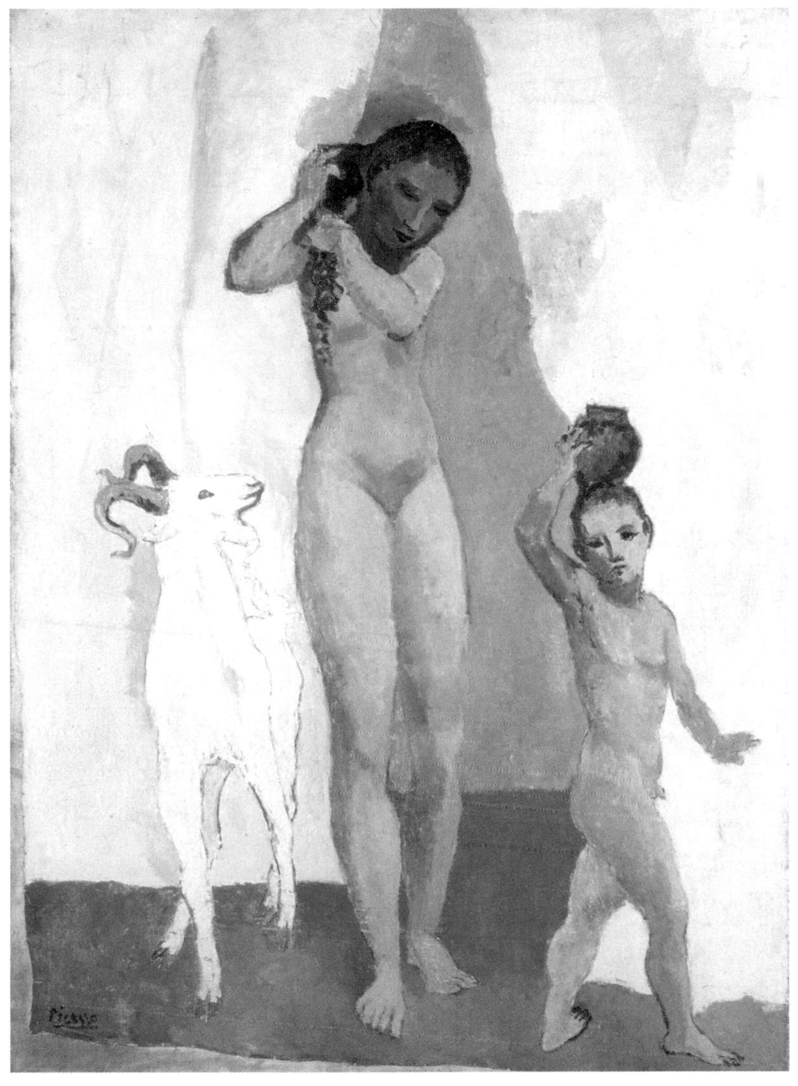

Two Nudes, 1906

Picasso's *Two Nudes* precipitated a radical shift in his artistic practices. Though executed in the warm, pinkish tones of his 'rose period', the figures are now characterized by their sheer volume and weight, a striking contrast to the frail, emaciated and ethereal bodies of his earlier works. Where the previous figures seemed to float, these more sculptural figures stand foursquare. Picasso has added a sense of three-dimensionality to these figures. Yet the viewer also gains a sense of seeing them simultaneously from several viewpoints. For example, the torso of the right-hand figure is notably twisted and extended width-wise, so that we see both back and side views. The single breast, in particular – oddly positioned in the centre of the torso – undermines any sense of a single point of view. The facial features of the left-hand figure also seem significantly depersonalized, derived as they are from the Iberian sculpted busts that Picasso had seen in the Louvre. Much of this solidity to the forms of his figures came from Picasso's increasing awareness of the work of Paul Cézanne (1839–1906), and particularly the older artist's late bather series.

CREATED

Paris

MEDIUM

Oil on canvas

SERIES/PERIOD/MOVEMENT

Rose period

SIMILAR WORKS

Three Bathers by Paul Cézanne, *c.* 1881–82

Two Women Running on the Beach (The Race) by Picasso, 1922

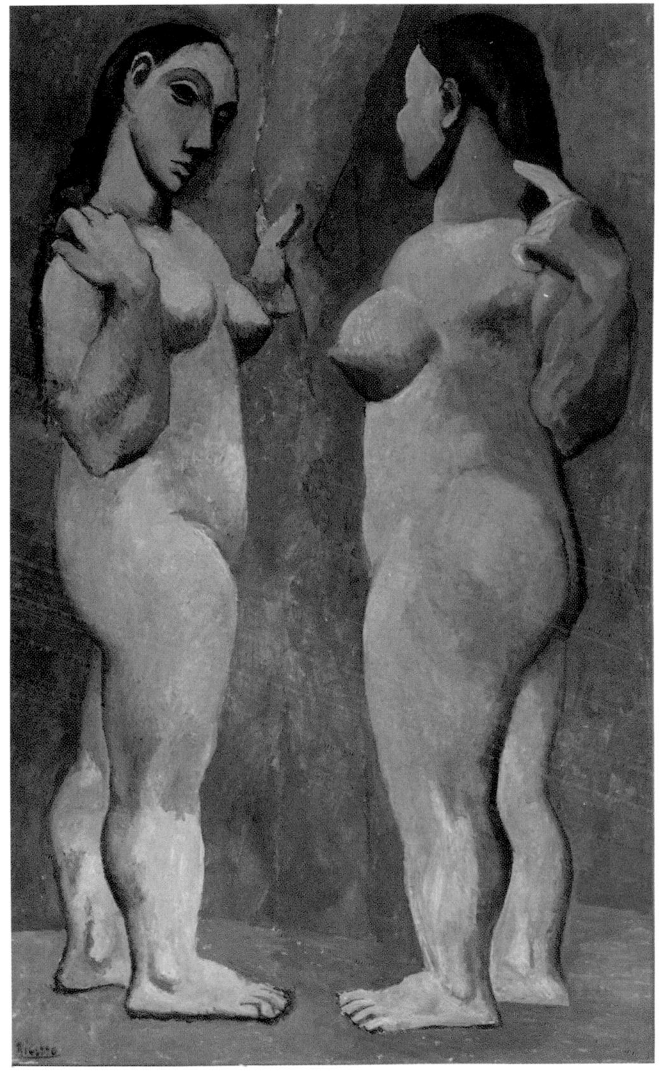

Head of a Woman, 1907

By 1907 Picasso had abandoned the academic conventions for representing the human body that he had been taught as a student. His most recent works, such as the *Two Nudes* and *Portrait of Gertrude Stein*, adopted monumental, sculptural forms, largely inspired by his discovery of Iberian sculpture. Now he encountered yet another source that would give him pause – the cultural artefacts of the African continent. *Head of a Woman* seems to stand at the margin between these two major influences. The painting is non-naturalistic, with the artist employing stylistic simplification to such an extent that the gender of the sitter seems difficult to determine (though such gender ambiguity is a typical feature of Picasso's work at this time). Here the large, lozenge-shaped eyes and elongated nose derive from Iberian sculpture. Similarly, the oddly shaped ear recalls the scroll-like ears of these busts. Yet the flat, oval form of the head itself is remarkably similar to the African masks that Picasso could have seen in the Museum of Ethnography in Paris, or indeed in the studios of fellow artists and the flea markets of Paris.

CREATED

Paris

MEDIUM

Oil on canvas

SERIES/PERIOD/MOVEMENT

Proto-Cubist period

SIMILAR WORKS

African Masks on display at the Trocadero in Paris

Les Demoiselles d'Avignon by Picasso, 1907

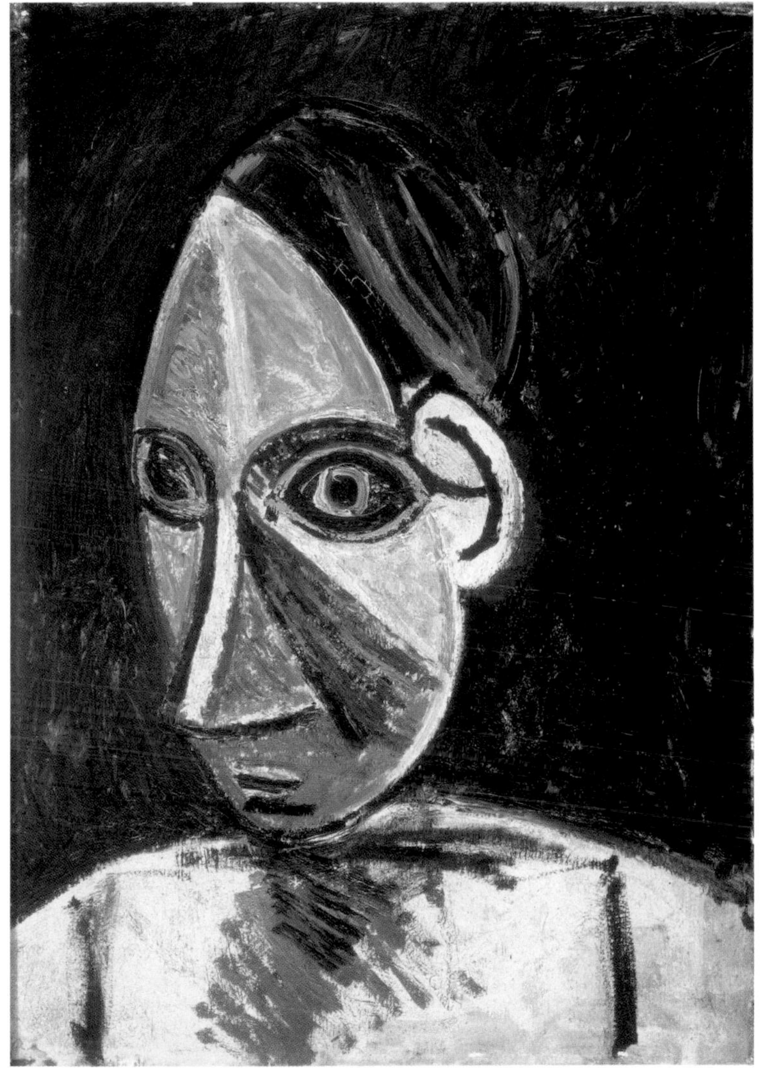

Dance with Veils (Nude with Drapery), 1907

Picasso's experiments in formulating new ways of representing the human body were enhanced in 1907 by the introduction of a new technique into his paintings – the use of hatch marks. These are most evident in his *Nude with Drapery*, where close parallel lines are deployed to suggest volume and shading. These lines, often referred to as striations, appear throughout the work, to model both the female body and the space it inhabits. The deliberately inconsistent use of such shading, however, serves to undermine our sense of a real, three-dimensional body in real space. Instead, the form seems to be constructed from a series of intersecting geometrical planes, which in turn echo the similar geometrical planes that make up the surrounding space, making the contours of the female nude difficult to discern. This hatching technique is most commonly deployed in drawing and printmaking, where linear execution and the absence of colour make it a useful means to imply depth. Here, however, Picasso employs it in an oil painting as a means to investigate different possibilities for the representation of the body in space.

CREATED

Paris

MEDIUM

Oil on canvas

SERIES/PERIOD/MOVEMENT

Proto-Cubist period

SIMILAR WORKS

Les Demoiselles d'Avignon by Picasso, 1907

Large Nude by Georges Braque, 1908

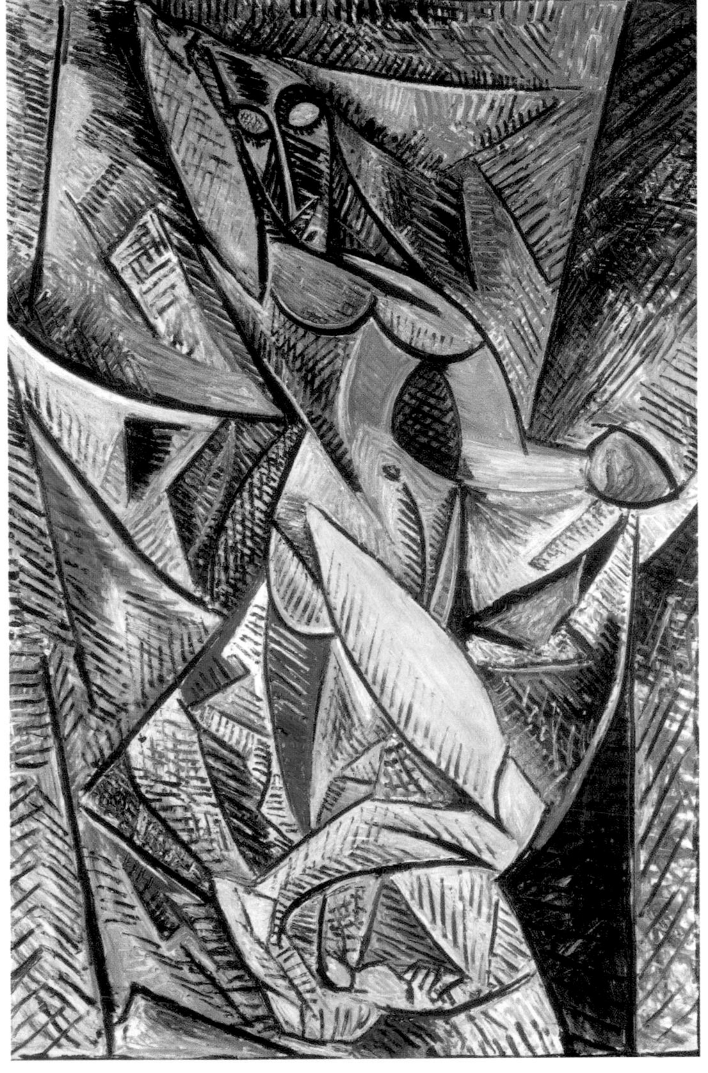

Carafe and Three Bowls, 1908

In 1908 Picasso produced a series of small still lifes. These were probably inspired by Cézanne's spatially complex still lifes, some of which Picasso had seen the previous year. *Carafe and Three Bowls* represents a modest assortment of still-life objects arranged, apparently randomly, on a small table. However, Picasso's principal concern seems to be the representation of space itself. Rather than being placed horizontally and next to each other, these objects notably overlap in depth, each placed behind the next object in sequence. This should create a sense of significant depth. However, Picasso compresses the space by tilting the table surface towards the spectator. The foreground bowl also refutes spatial logic, as its base is represented as if seen straight on, parallel to the picture plane, while its elliptical upper surface suggests a high viewpoint. The lighting is inconsistent, with shadows falling in two different directions, and the background space looks as solid as the foreground objects. This overall effect of spatial compression and inconsistency would be further deployed in Picasso's Cubist still-life paintings.

CREATED

Paris

MEDIUM

Oil on canvas

SERIES/PERIOD/MOVEMENT

Early Cubist period

SIMILAR WORKS

The Silver Goblet by Jean-Baptiste-Siméon Chardin, *c.* 1720s

Still Life with Bowl and Milk Jug by Paul Cézanne, 1877

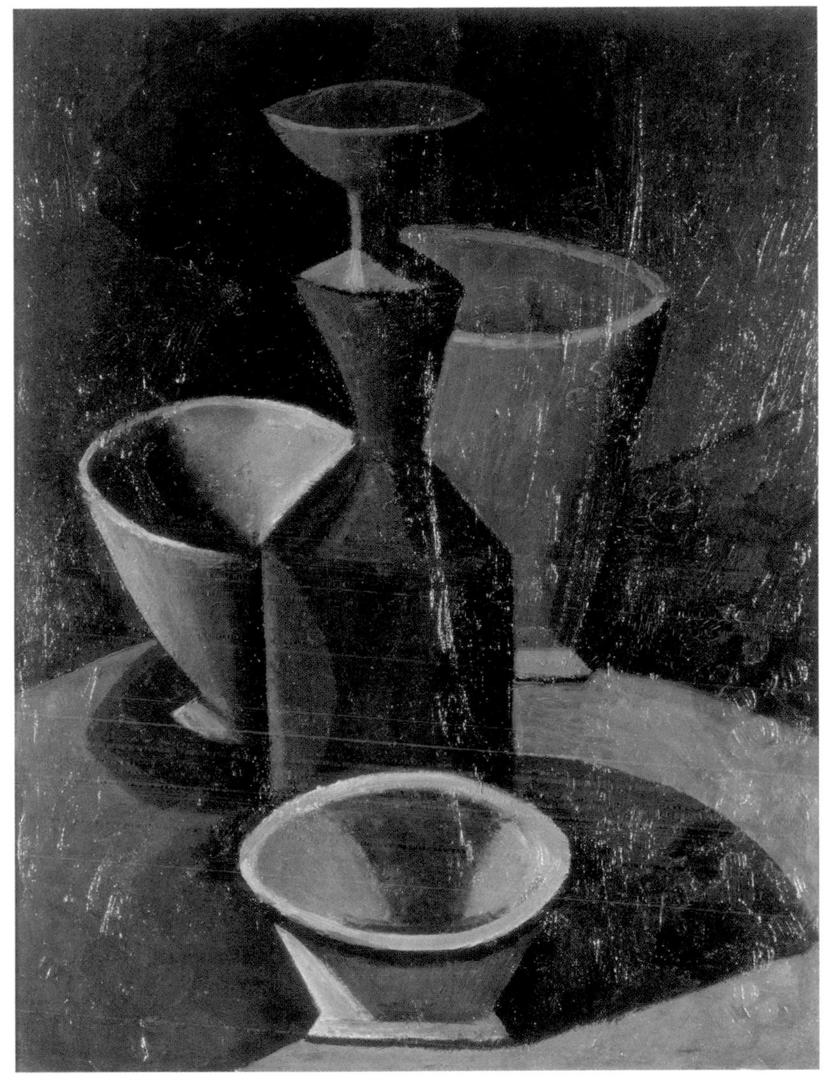

Head of a Woman, Fernande, 1909

During the summer of 1909 Picasso produced a series of paintings representing the head and shoulders of his mistress, Fernande Olivier. Like many of his recent figurative paintings, these were highly sculptural in form and integrated the geometrical planes that were now defining early Cubism. Back in Montmartre that autumn, Picasso produced a small sculpture based upon these paintings. In some ways, Picasso's *Head of a Woman* conforms to conventional sculpture. It was originally modelled in clay and forms a solid mass, its bust format recalling countless other such sculpted portraits. The handling, however, is radically different to other sculptures of the time. The head is executed as a series of flat planes, as if the viewer is looking at the muscles beneath the exterior surface of the body. To emphasize this, Picasso cast the clay original in plaster and carved the surface with a knife. The work was later cast in bronze. Picasso's *Head of a Woman*, with its jagged forms and sharply defined geometrical planar surface, constitutes the first fully developed Cubist sculpture.

CREATED

Paris

MEDIUM

Bronze

SERIES/PERIOD/MOVEMENT

Early Cubist period

SIMILAR WORKS

Ecce Puer (Behold the Child) by Medardo Rosso, 1906

Antigrazioso (The Mother) by Umberto Boccioni, 1912

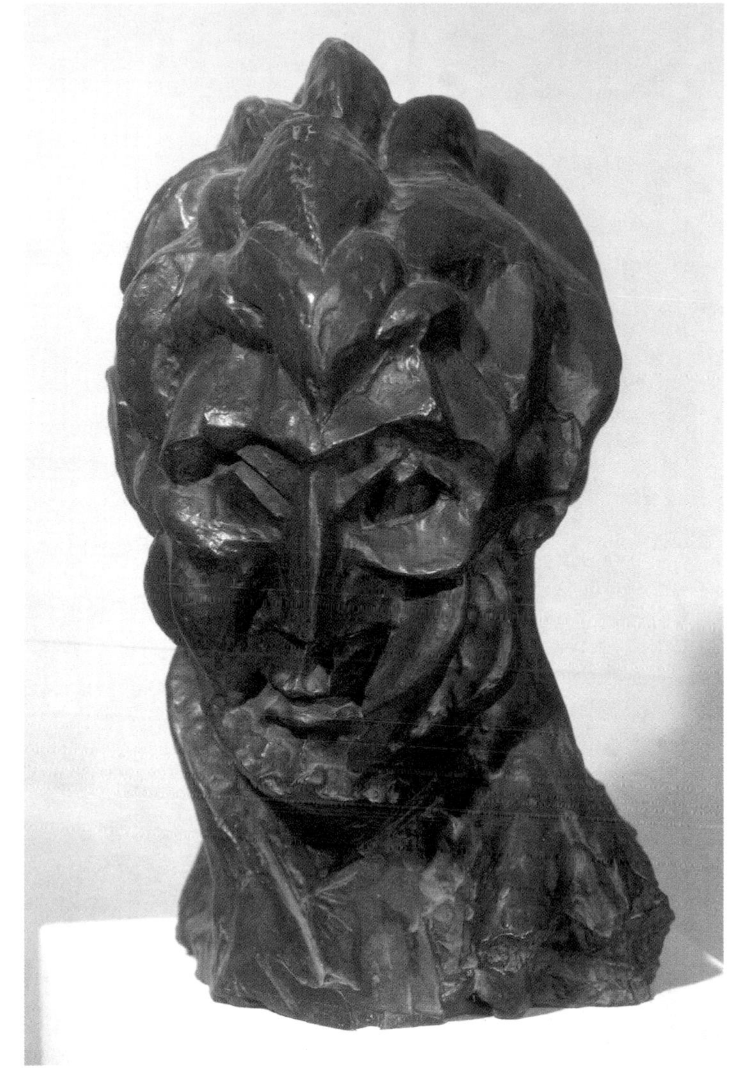

Still Life on a Piano, 1911

The years 1909–12 were characterized by Picasso's so-called 'analytical' Cubism. During this period Picasso, working closely with Georges Braque (1882–1963), produced a series of still-life paintings, executed predominantly in muted ochre tones. These incorporated barely discernible fragments of modern life – wineglasses, bottles of alcohol and musical instruments – the paraphernalia of Montmartre café culture. *Still Life on a Piano* conforms to this model and here it is possible to identify a few of these features. On the left, just below the letter 'T', Picasso has included a wine glass in outline. Just above, and slightly to the right, is a tubular form that signifies the neck of a bottle. References to musical instruments can be found throughout the work, from the black and white piano keys in the middle foreground, to the body of a violin centre-right, identifiable by the inclusion of the instrument's f-holes. The inclusion of the word 'CORT' is also striking here. It probably has a double meaning, referring to the pianist Alfred Cortet and to the Spanish word corto, meaning 'short' or 'cut-off'.

CREATED

Paris, Céret

MEDIUM

Oil on canvas

SERIES/PERIOD/MOVEMENT

Cubist period

SIMILAR WORKS

The Portuguese by Georges Braque, 1911

Clarinet and Bottle of Rum on a Mantelpiece by Georges Braque, 1911

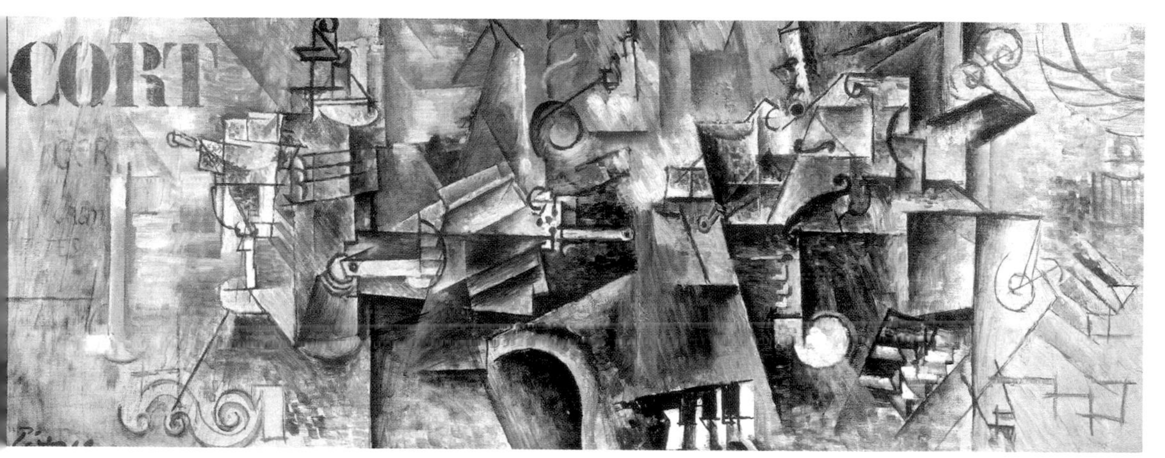
CORT

Still Life with Chair Caning, 1912

Picasso's *Still Life with Chair Caning* is widely regarded as the first example of Cubist *collage*. In many respects, the work conforms to Picasso's recent Cubist still-life paintings. Here, once again, the artist has shown fragments related to everyday life in the cafés he frequented. A glass can be detected in the upper half of the work and a knife and slices of lemon to the right. The three letters 'JOU' signify the newspaper *Le Journal*, another common attribute of café life, although it can literally be translated as 'game'. Here the potential double meaning is itself a 'game', devised to prevent the spectator from making a definitive interpretation. The technical innovation in this work, however, was the inclusion of a piece of printed oilcloth with a cane-work design, pasted to the lower-left of the canvas. The hyper-reality of this printed material contrasts with the non-naturalistic depiction of the still life, just as its mechanical production distinguishes it from the uniqueness of Picasso's painted brushstrokes. The rope that surrounds this oval work adds another dimension to the encroachment of everyday objects into Picasso's work.

CREATED

Paris

MEDIUM

Oil, oilcloth and pasted paper on canvas, framed with rope

SERIES/PERIOD/MOVEMENT

Cubist period

SIMILAR WORKS

Violin and Pipe (le Quotidien) by Georges Braque, 1913

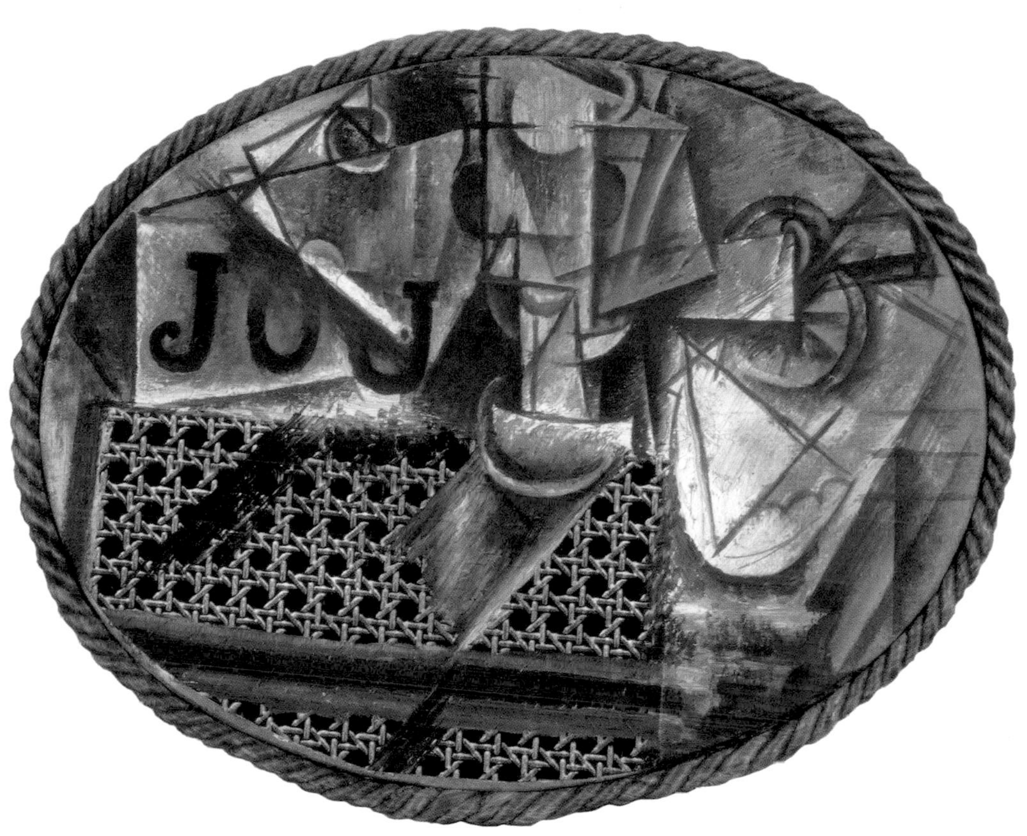
JOU

Guitar, 1912–13

In the winter of 1912, Picasso produced one of the key icons of Cubist sculpture, entitled simply *Guitar*. The first version of this work was made from cardboard and string. However, it was so fragile that Picasso later reconstructed the work using sheet metal and wire. The artist may have been inspired to make his guitar after watching a local Montmartre guitar-maker at work. Equally he may have been recalling the countless guitarists who provided musical entertainment in the cafés and taverns he regularly frequented, or highlighting an association between the instrument and his native Spain. One way or the other, guitars played a dominant role in Picasso's work throughout 1912–13. One of the most striking features of Picasso's *Guitar* sculpture, however, is the way it redefines spatial relationships. The body of the guitar, usually a flat plane, is opened up, while the sound-hole has been transformed from a recessed space to a projected one. It has also been suggested that this projected sound-hole may have been inspired by the cylindrical eye-sockets found on an African Grebo mask owned by Picasso at the time.

CREATED

Paris

MEDIUM

Sheet metal

SERIES/PERIOD/MOVEMENT

Cubist period

SIMILAR WORKS

African Masks on display at the Trocadero in Paris

Corner Counter Relief by Vladimir Tatlin, 1914–15

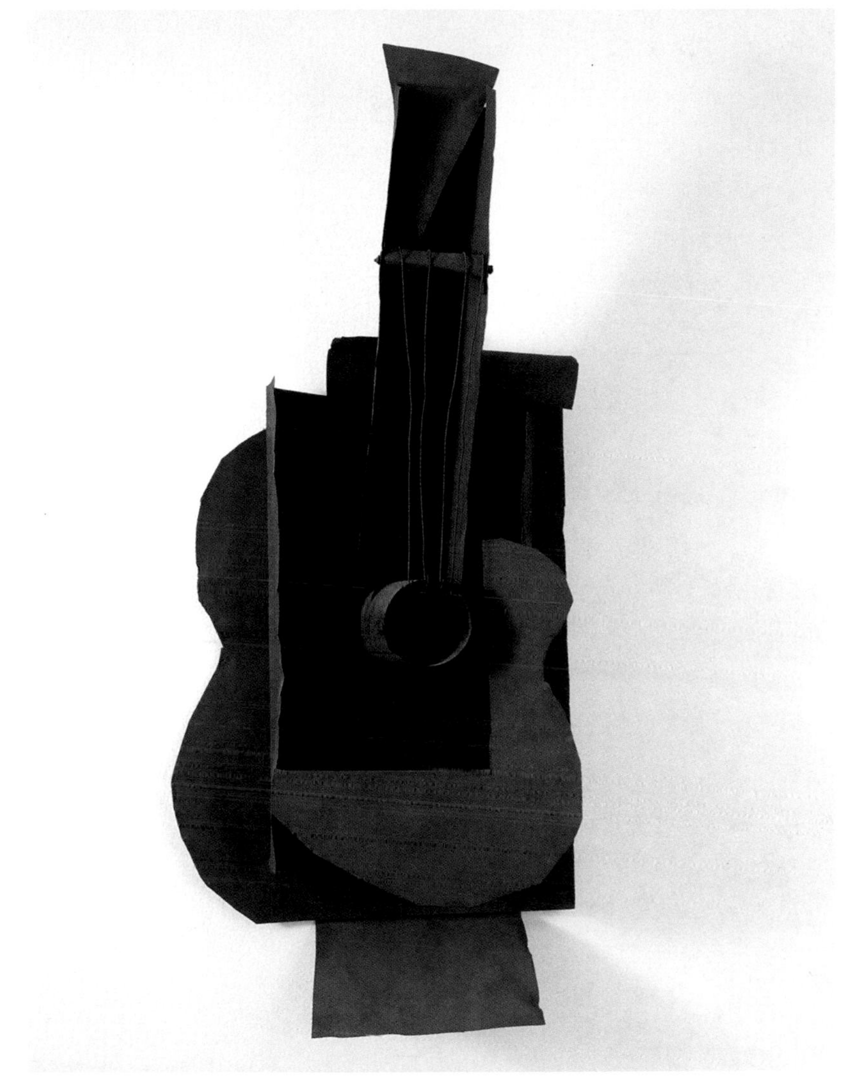

Guitar, 1913

From 1912 onwards Picasso's works were increasingly reduced to fragmentary signs, constructed from everyday materials and difficult to decipher. This phase is often referred to as 'synthetic' Cubism. *Guitar* is a key example of this practice. The work is constructed from fragments of newspaper, decorated damask wallpaper and pieces of coloured paper. These fragments are placed to suggest the form of a guitar. The white form at the centre, with its curved body and sound-hole here echoes a similarly curved form to its right, this time constructed from the decorative wallpaper. The dress-like material seems simultaneously to be suggesting the curvaceousness of the female form. In this context, the sound-hole can be read as a lewd reference to female anatomy. The fragment of newsprint comes from the Spanish journal *El Diluvio*, and notably includes references to gynaecological ointments and treatment for venereal and eye diseases. Is Picasso here alluding to the dangers of prostitution, so bound up with the cabaret culture of Montmartre? Such a reading would be entirely consistent with the abundance of references to this issue throughout Picasso's pre-1914 works.

CREATED

Céret

MEDIUM

Cut paper, charcoal, India ink and chalk on paper

SERIES/PERIOD/MOVEMENT

Cubist period

SIMILAR WORKS

Bottle, Cup and Newspaper by Picasso, 1912

Violin and Pipe (le Quotidien) by Georges Braque, 1913

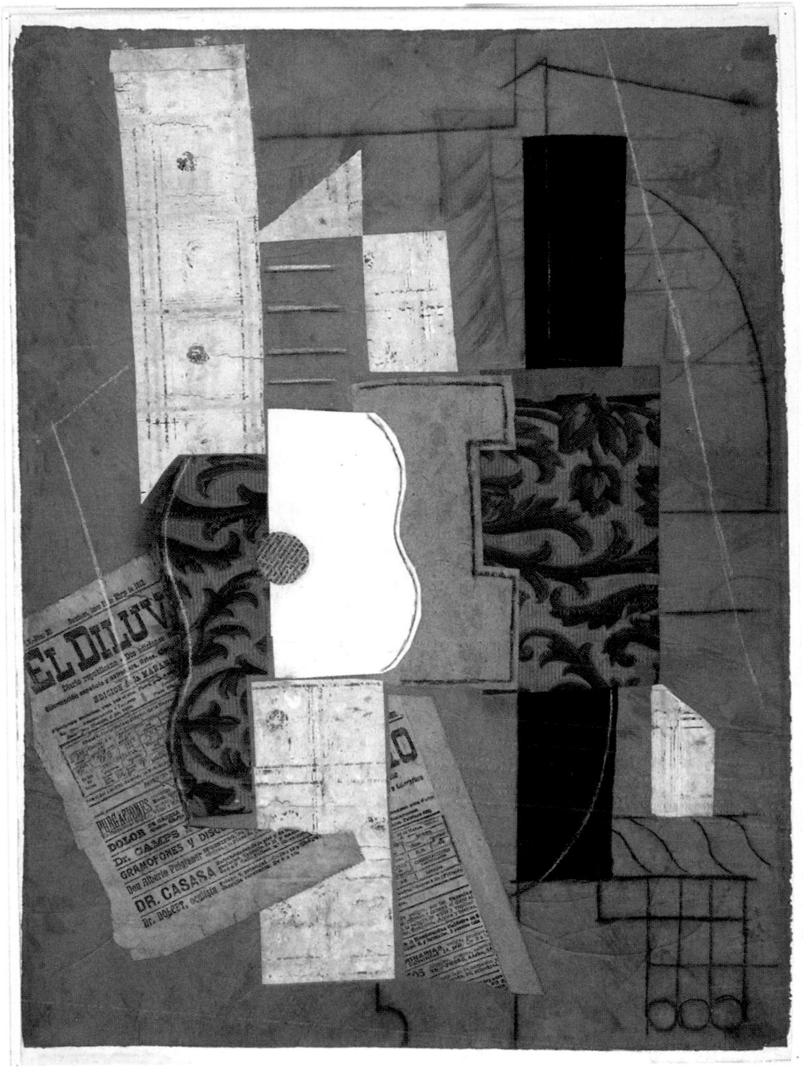
EL DILUV
DOLOR
GRAMOFONES Y DISC
DR. CASASA

Glass of Absinthe, 1914

In his sculpture *Glass of Absinthe* Picasso brought together the traditional practices of bronze casting, painting and the incorporation of everyday materials, into one key work. As with his *Guitar* of two years earlier, Picasso again chose an unusual subject for a sculpture. Traditionally, the medium had emphasized the human figure, but here Picasso effectively produced a three-dimensional still life. To produce this work, Picasso first made a model in wax and then had it cast in bronze. However, he also used a real absinthe spoon – a flat spoon designed with holes in it to allow the drink to be poured over a sugar cube and into the glass below. Picasso also distorted the form of the glass so that it appears to spiral out of control, as if seen simultaneously from several different angles. He then painted the surface with bright, coloured dots to further the sense of spatial disorientation. All this serves to emphasize the intoxicating effects of the strong, alcoholic drink, much consumed by Picasso and many of his Bohemian circle in the cafés of Montmartre.

CREATED

Paris

MEDIUM

Painted bronze and absinthe spoon

SERIES/PERIOD/MOVEMENT

Cubist period

SIMILAR WORKS

Development of a Bottle in Space by Umberto Boccioni, 1913

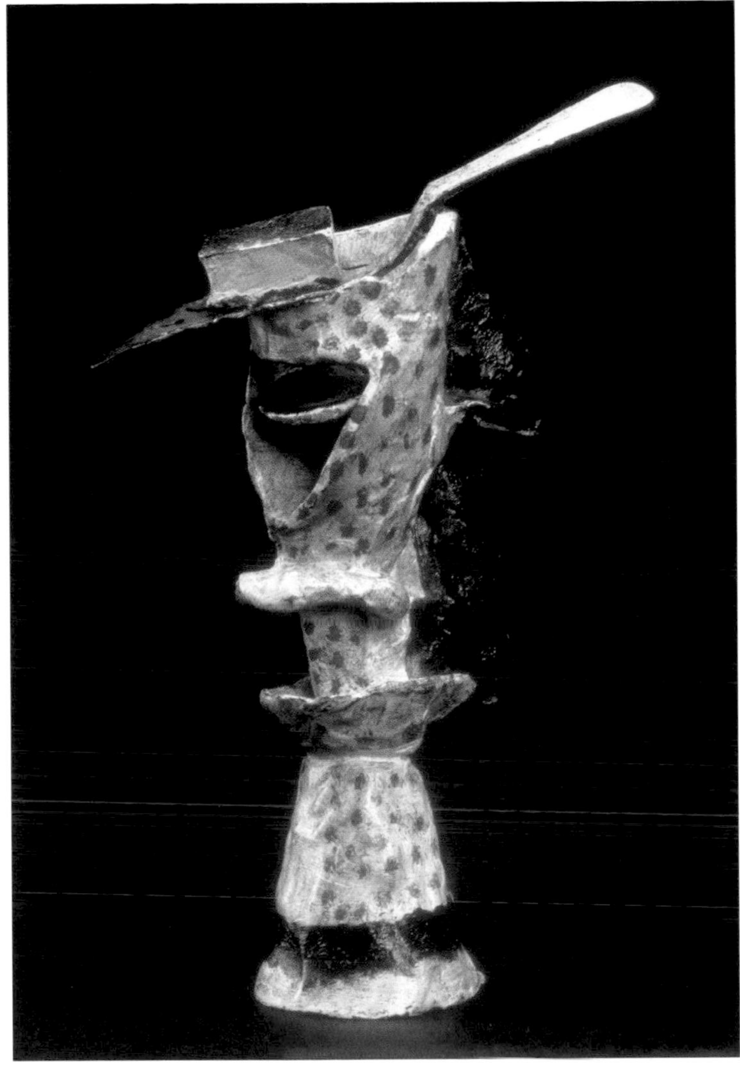

Composition with Cut Pear, 1914

Composition with Cut Pear presents a simple still-life scene, rendered in a combination of pencil drawing, gouache and wallpaper collage. The main structure of a table is outlined in pencil, while a brown rectangle seems to represent a tablecloth with a notable fold along its horizontal. However, the tablecloth does not align with the table upon which it notionally lies. A textured background with a leaf motif seems to suggest decorative wallpaper, yet simultaneously overlaps with the table. The presence of a piece of cut fruit sitting on the table further confuses a simple reading, as the leaf motif might therefore relate directly to this. Colour is added by the presence of a loosely drawn bottle on a yellow piece of paper stuck to the surface of the canvas, whilst Neo-Impressionist-style dots have been added to suggest areas of shading. This reduction of the forms represented to barely identifiable signs, combined with the use of heightened colour, is a typical characteristic of Picasso's so-called 'synthetic' Cubist phase.

CREATED

Paris

MEDIUM

Gouache, pencil and wallpaper on cardboard

SERIES/PERIOD/MOVEMENT

Cubist period

SIMILAR WORKS

Apples, Peaches, Pears and Grapes by Paul Cézanne, *c.* 1879–80

Fruit Dish and Glass by Georges Braque, 1912

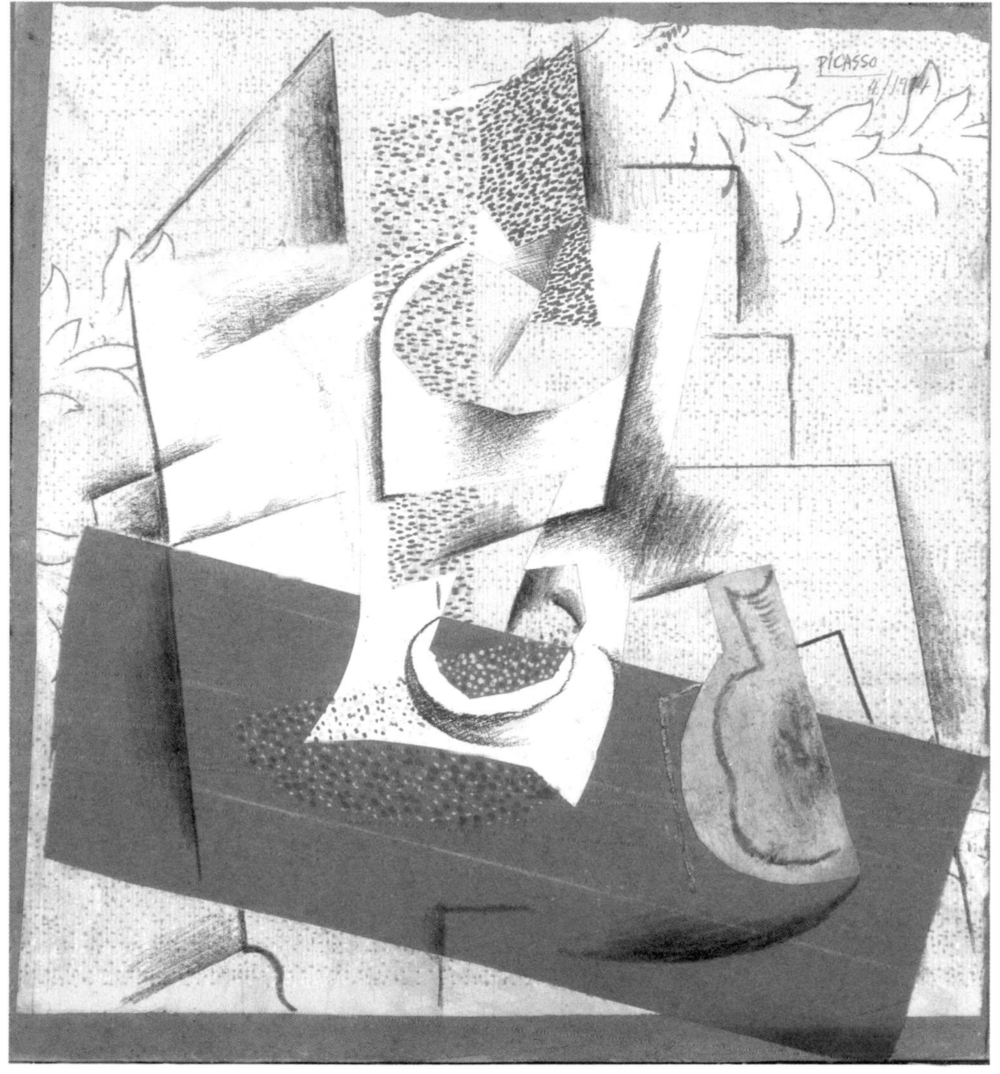
PICASSO

Violin, 1915

In 1915, Picasso's work began to make the transition from 'synthetic' Cubism to the Neoclassicism that characterized his post-war work. Amongst his Cubist works produced at this time is *Violin*. The work is made from cut and folded sheet metal, and clearly recalls his constructed *Guitar* of a few years earlier. Unlike the earlier work, however, Picasso painted this in a range of bright colours. This, combined with the difficult-to-read forms, makes the work barely identifiable as a violin. Its scale – a metre in height – also distinguishes it significantly from the musical instrument it represents. As with many of Picasso's constructed sculptures, solid and void are treated as interchangeable. Thus the key identifiable feature of the violin, the symmetrically positioned f-holes, are here represented as solid, projecting from the empty space that represents the body of the instrument. *Violin*, in its exuberant forms and colours, marked a key turning point in Picasso's technique. Over the next few years he would abandon the use of everyday, cheap materials and revert predominantly to the medium of oil on canvas.

CREATED

Paris

MEDIUM

Painted metal with iron wire

SERIES/PERIOD/MOVEMENT

Cubist period

SIMILAR WORKS

Guitar by Picasso, 1912

Violin and Pipe (le Quotidien) by Georges Braque, 1913

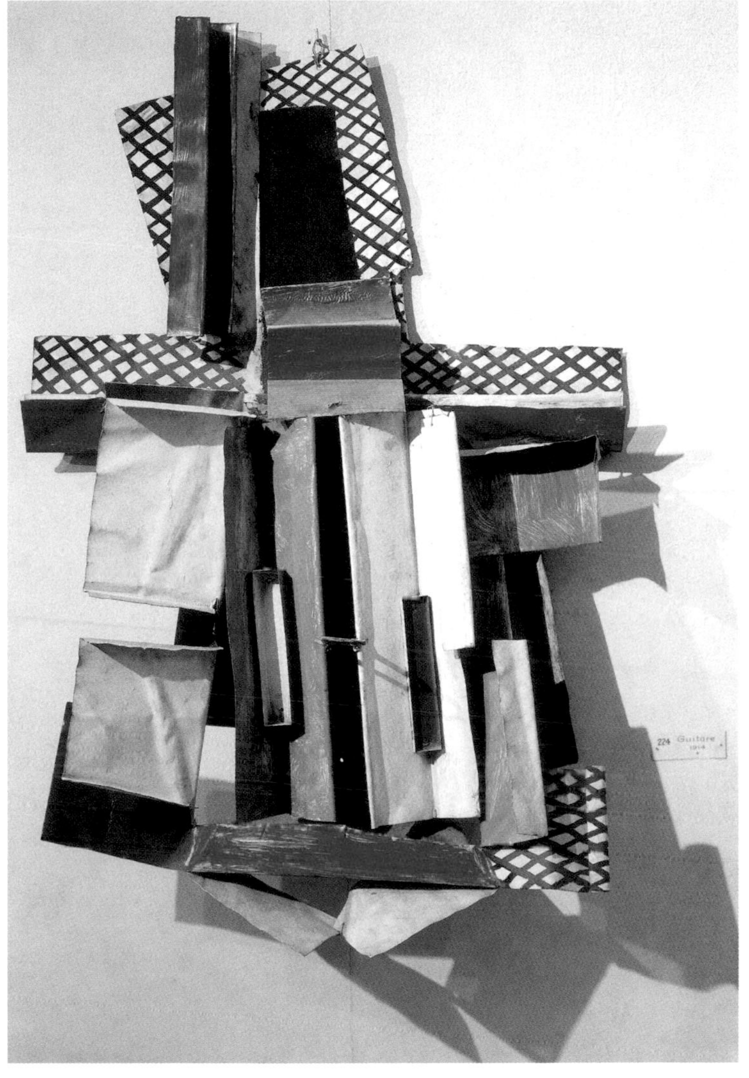
224 Guitare
1914

Scenes from the Ballet *La Boutique Fantastique*, 1919

In 1919 Picasso travelled to London to work on a series of set and costume designs for the Ballets Russes production of *Tricorne* ('The Three-Cornered Hat'). While in London he also produced a number of pen-and-ink drawings representing dancers rehearsing for the other major ballet of the season, *La Boutique Fantastique* ('The Fantastic Toyshop'). Here Picasso has combined several studies of the movement of the dancers on one sheet of paper. The couple dancing is Leonide Massine (1895–1975) and Lydia Lopokova (1892–1981), rehearsing the famous Can-Can dance central to *La Boutique Fantastique*. He has also included a more detailed study of Lopokova adopting a position on one leg, as well as several marginal sketches highlighting the gestures made by the dancer's hand. Picasso reveals the easy fluency with which his draughtsmanship can capture the grace and elegance of the performers, while simultaneously recalling the numerous sketches of ballet dancers made by the nineteenth-century French artist Edgar Degas (1834–1917). The sketch is inscribed with a dedication to Massine, the Russian choreographer and dancer who worked on both *Tricorne* and *La Boutique Fantastique*.

CREATED

London

MEDIUM

Pen on paper

SERIES/PERIOD/MOVEMENT

Neoclassical period

SIMILAR WORKS

Dancer Seen from Behind and *Three Studies of Feet* by Edgar Degas, *c.* 1878

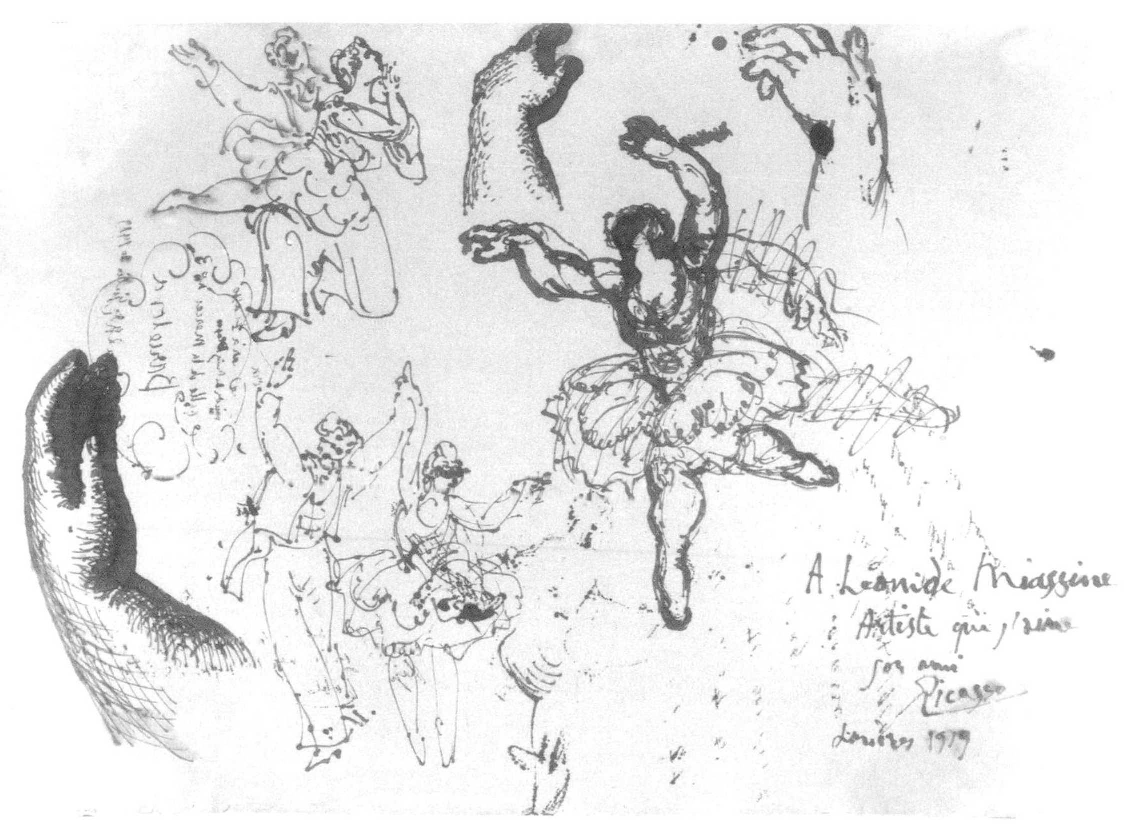
A Léonide Miassine
Artiste qui j'aime
son ami
Picasso
Londres 1919

Set Design for the Ballet *Pulcinella*, 1920

Picasso's work for the Ballets Russes resulted in numerous sketches, which he would then present to Sergei Diaghilev (1872–1929) for approval. In this sketch for *Pulcinella*, Picasso used a limited colour-scheme of white and gold, highlighted by the plush red of the curtains, all executed in watercolour. The intention was to have a stage backdrop that also included scenes from the audience. Thus the nocturnal view of Mount Vesuvius in Naples, seen at the back, is framed by a representation of the interior of a theatre, complete with members of the audience seated in boxes below an ornately decorated ceiling. The action would effectively take place in front of an inner stage, making a feature of the artificiality of the performance. Sadly Diaghilev did not like Picasso's design and rejected it in favour of a more Cubist-inspired scene focusing solely upon the view of Mount Vesuvius. However, the sketch remains to remind us of Picasso's initial conception.

CREATED

Paris

MEDIUM

Gouache, India ink and pencil

SERIES/PERIOD/MOVEMENT

Neoclassical period

SIMILAR WORKS

Stage set for the Ballets Russes performance of *Sheherazade* by Leon Bakst, 1909

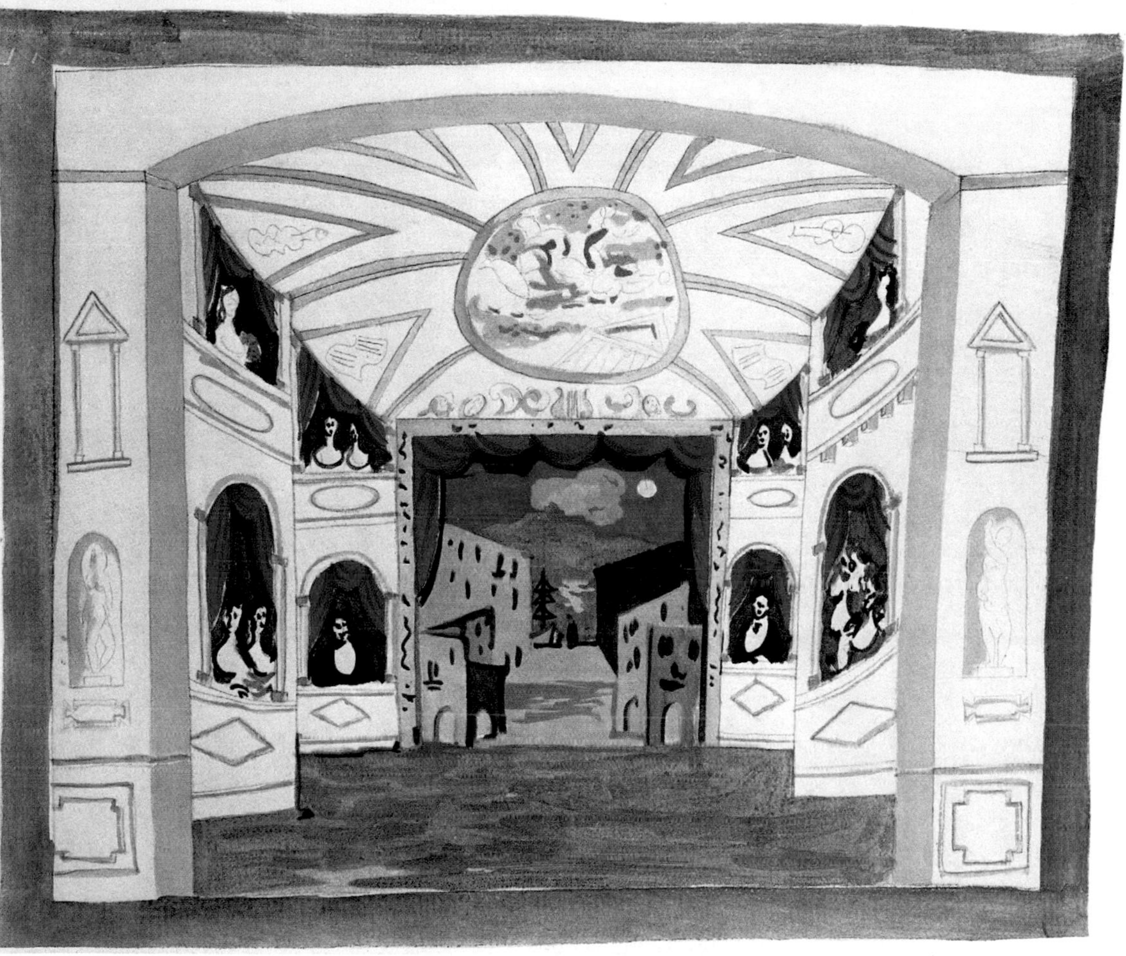

Mother and Child, 1921

In 1921, Picasso painted the large-scale *Mother and Child*, possibly in response to the recent birth of his son Paulo. However, the work is also typical of Picasso's post-First World War Neoclassical style of painting. Here the artist gives his figures monumental form, the sheer weightiness recalling the sculpturally inspired figures in his *Two Nudes* of 1906. In contrast to the chromatic explosion of his pre-war Cubist works, Picasso has here returned to a relatively muted palette of pale blues and whites, which accentuate the warm flesh tones of the figures. Compositionally, all is reduced to verticals and horizontals. The background consists simply of three bands of colour to suggest sky, sea and foreground, a factor echoed in the strictly geometrical forms of the mother. Even the right thigh, which should otherwise run at a 45-degree angle, is made horizontal to reinforce the sense of careful balance and order in the composition. However, Picasso introduces one element to disrupt this rigid order. The small child, wriggling restlessly in his mother's lap, introduces a sense of movement into this otherwise static image.

CREATED

Fontainebleau

MEDIUM

Oil on canvas

SERIES/PERIOD/MOVEMENT

Neoclassical period

SIMILAR WORKS

Young Girls by the Seashore by Pierre Puvis de Chavannes, 1879

The Mediterranean by Aristide Maillol, 1905

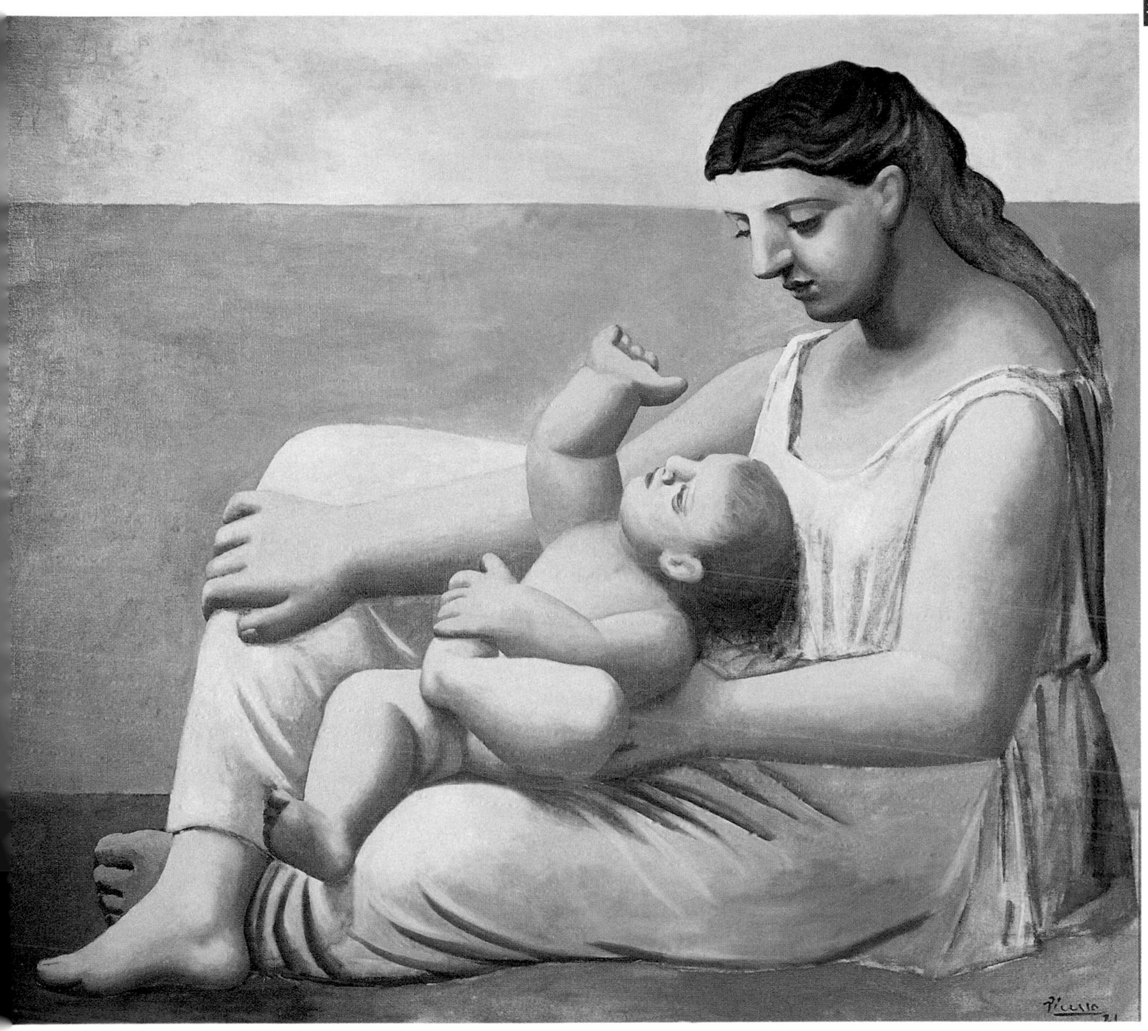

The Studio, 1927–28

The Studio, of 1927–28, gives an indication of how Picasso attempted to reconcile two disparate approaches to painting – his pre-war Cubism and post-war Neoclassicism. The work explores the subject of the artist and his model, a common theme in Picasso's work at this time. Here both figures are reduced to highly abbreviated forms: the body of the artist, seen on the left, consists of a framework of geometrical lines surmounted by a grey oval form for the head, with three eyes inscribed on a white floating form, while the model, on the right, is similarly reduced to a white form, recalling a bust mounted on a sculptor's table. Despite this non-naturalistic depiction, the work notably adopts a rigid compositional order and harmony. The strict geometry of the yellow canvas, before which the artist stands, the frames on the back wall and the red tablecloth with its transparent fruit bowl, are all flatly painted in a colour-scheme reduced to four colours – red, yellow, grey and black. This more ordered approach to Cubism also recalls the works of the Purists, Charles-Edouard Jeanneret (1887–1965), better known as Le Corbusier, and Amedée Ozenfant (1886–1966).

CREATED

Paris

MEDIUM

Oil on canvas

SERIES/PERIOD/MOVEMENT

Surrealist period

SIMILAR WORKS

Self-Portrait with Model by Ernst Ludwig Kirchner, 1910/26

Composition with Red, Blue and Yellow by Piet Mondrian, 1930

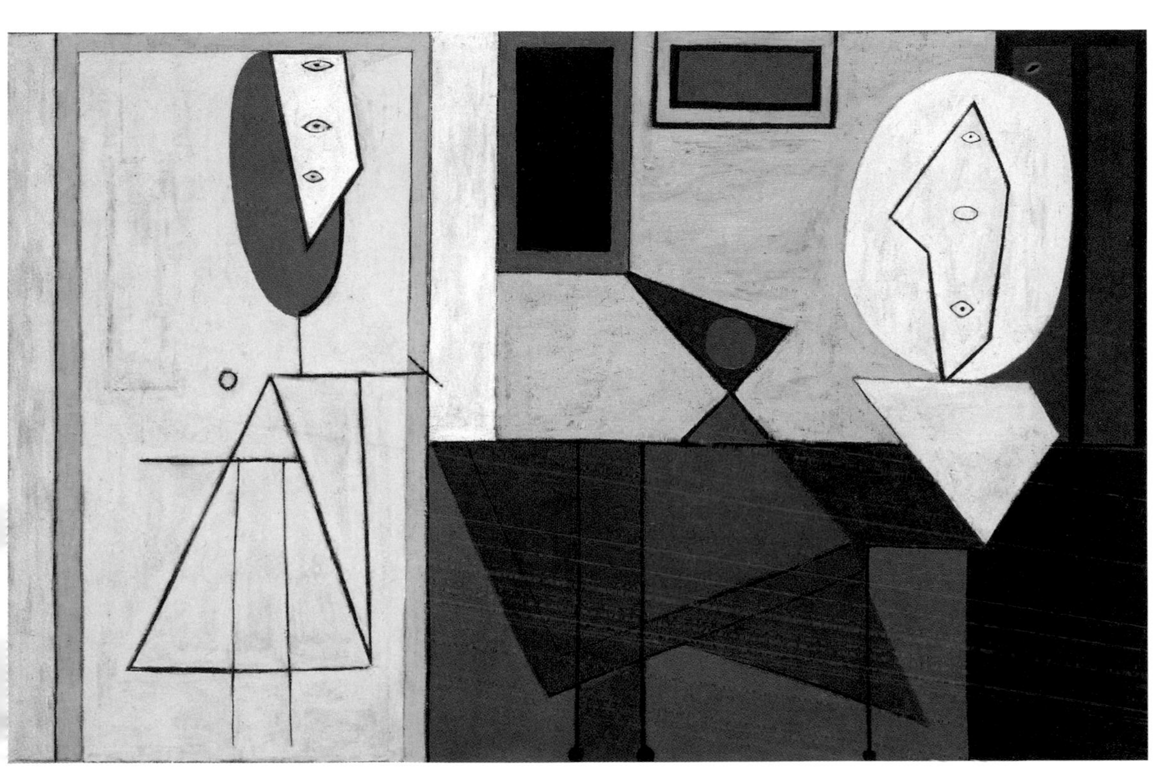

Project for a Monument to Guillaume Apollinaire, 1928

In 1928 Picasso turned his hand once more to sculpture. That summer he had produced a series of simple drawings consisting of dots connected by lines. These recalled similar works he had produced four years earlier. However, with the help of the sculptor Julio González (1876–1942), he turned these into three-dimensional sculptures constructed from wire rods. Though seemingly abstract, the works are figurative; the small round disk at the top of the scaffolding is pierced with three holes indicating two eyes and a mouth. This small-scale model represents a woman on a swing. Here the oval form represents the woman's torso and the curved forms at the front, the rope of the swing. Picasso submitted this, and other similar models, as a proposed monument to his close friend, the poet Guillaume Apollinaire (1880–1918), who had died 10 years earlier. Sadly the proposal was rejected, but this did not stop Picasso from constructing a full-scale version of this model.

CREATED

Paris

MEDIUM

Iron, wire and sheet metal

SERIES/PERIOD/MOVEMENT

Surrealist period

SIMILAR WORKS

Harlequin by Julio González, 1929

The Chariot by Alberto Giacometti, 1950

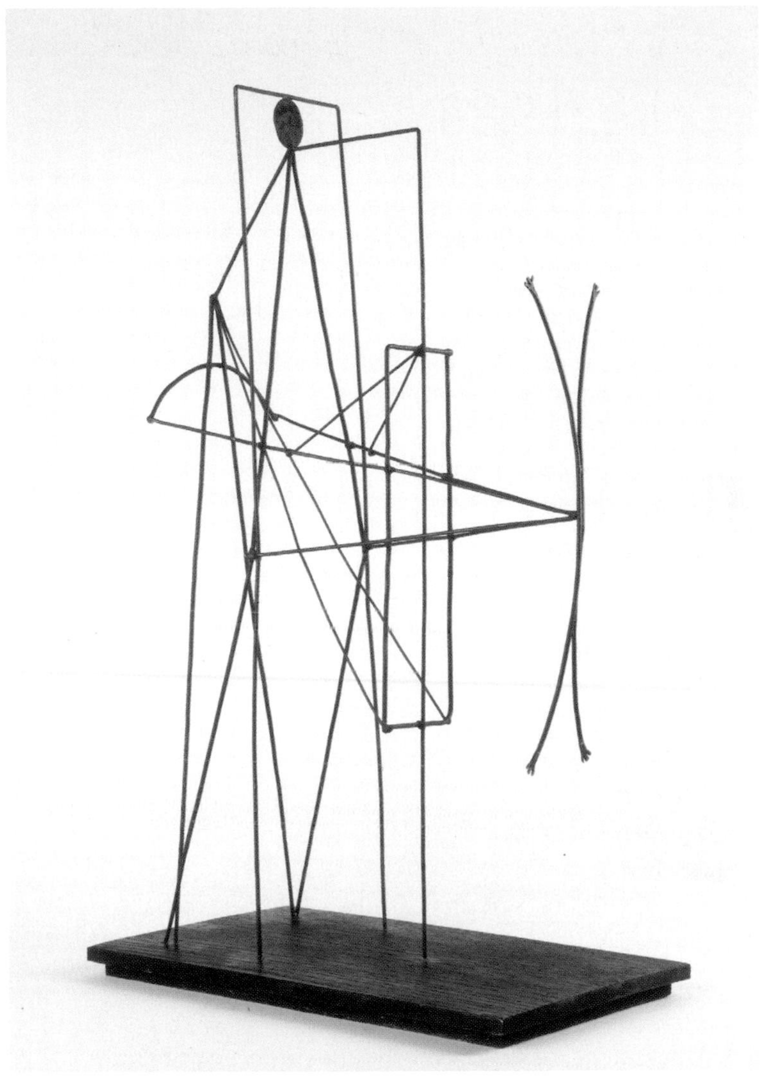

Still Life with Pitcher and Bowl of Fruit, 1931

Much of Picasso's time in the late 1920s had been taken up with his newfound enthusiasm for sculpture. He did not neglect painting, however, and during the winter of 1931 he produced a series of still lifes, including this large-scale work. *Still Life with Pitcher and Bowl of Fruit* once again reveals the ease with which Picasso could introduce new pictorial means into his works. A simple arrangement of everyday objects on a table is given monumental form by the adoption of the broad curving lines that form the contours of the objects depicted. There is no attempt to model in three-dimensions, and the decorative patterns, on both jug and tablecloth, are painted absolutely flat so as to resemble collage elements crudely cut out and stuck on the canvas. However, this is a deliberate ploy to highlight the flatness of the picture plane. This flatness, combined with the bright luminosity of the colours, and the thick black contours, recalls medieval stained glass and gives the impression of light flooding in. Thus Picasso's humble, everyday objects are imbued with religious connotations, recalling liturgical objects on a church altar.

CREATED

Paris

MEDIUM

Oil on canvas

SERIES/PERIOD/MOVEMENT

Surrealist period

SIMILAR WORKS

Still Life by Amédée Ozenfant, 1920–21

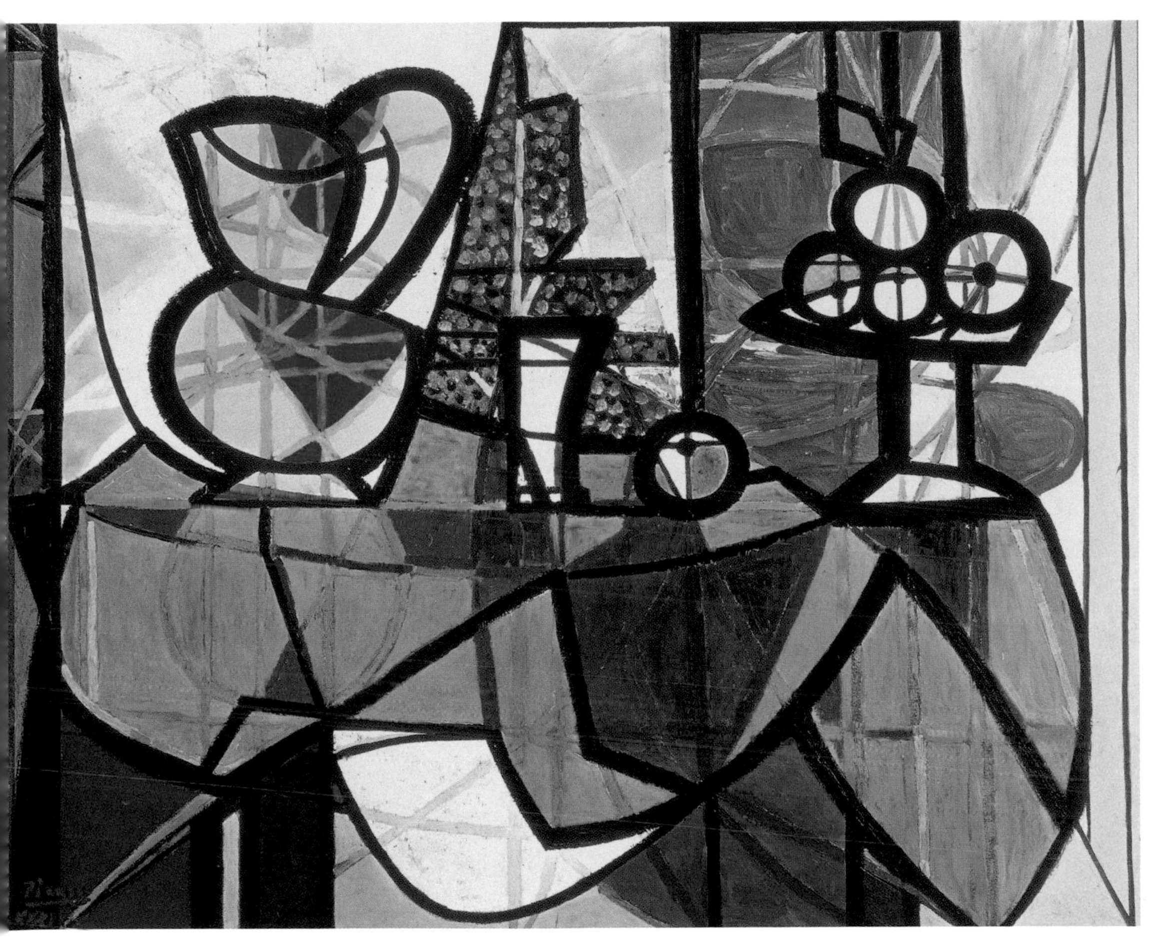

Reading, 1932

Picasso's affair with Marie-Thérèse Walter, which had begun in the late 1920s, resulted in a remarkable series of portraits of the younger woman. Their relationship was an intensely private affair and was conducted largely behind the back of his wife Olga Khokhlova, even after Picasso had acquired an apartment for his mistress near to his studio. Many of the portraits of Marie-Thérèse suggest this privacy and are notably set in comfortable, domestic interiors. In *Reading*, Picasso has placed his mistress in a decoratively upholstered armchair positioned in the corner of the room. Although she has a book on her lap she is not reading, but sits as if waiting or just acknowledging the presence of another person. Picasso has used wide, sweeping curves to express the sensuality of Marie-Thérèse's youthful body. The head is divided into a profile caressed by golden-blonde hair, but extended to a full-face view on the left. Picasso has also emphasized the rounded breasts of the sitter, as if exposed to the spectator's gaze through her clothing. Although Marie-Thérèse is seated alone, the inclusion of a frame in the left background implies the presence of the artist.

CREATED

Boisgeloup

MEDIUM

Oil on canvas

SERIES/PERIOD/MOVEMENT

Surrealist period

SIMILAR WORKS

Portrait of Olga in an Armchair by Picasso, 1917

Woman Reading at a Dressing Table by Henri Matisse, 1919

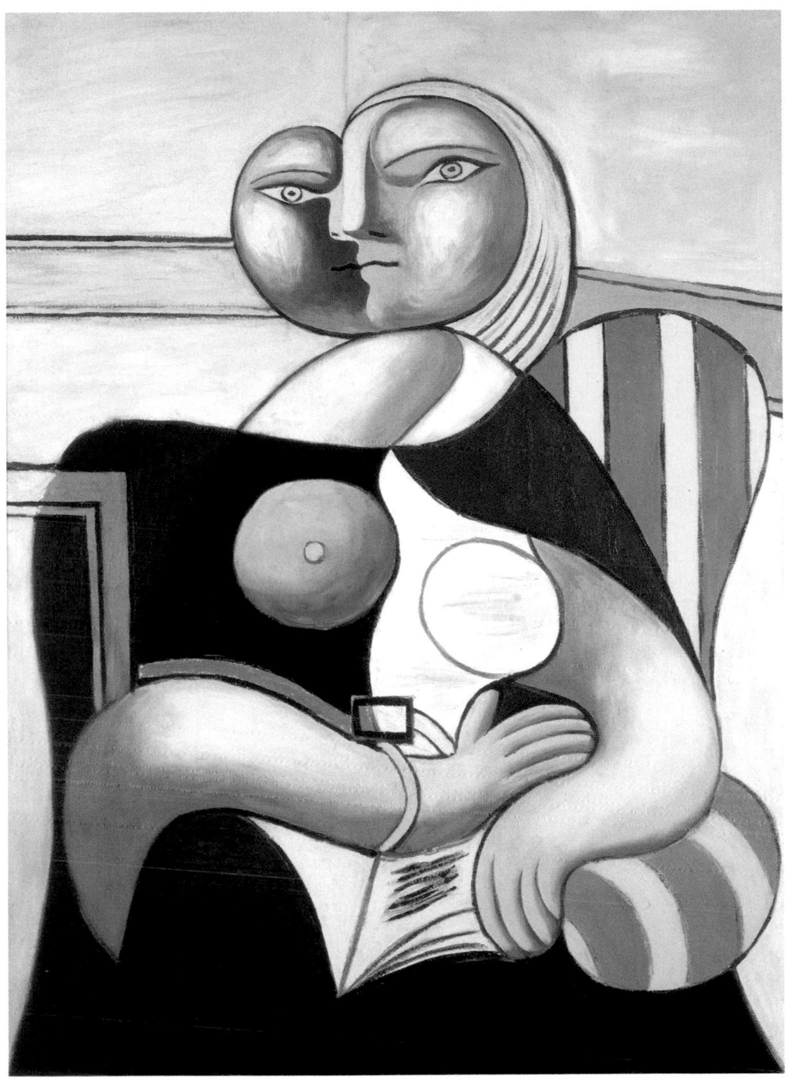

The Dream, 1932

Marie-Thérèse appears once more in *The Dream*, painted just a fortnight after *Reading*. Once again seated in an armchair, this time she is represented asleep, her head thrown back on to her shoulder and her hands resting in her lap. The soft, pastel shades and swollen, rounded forms of the sitter, contoured by bold, gestural outlines executed in a range of blues, yellows, reds and blacks, exude a mood of sensuality. These forms are set off against the bright red, heavily upholstered armchair in which she sleeps, adding a sense of comfort and containment. The head, once more, is separated into two halves, the lower part seen in profile, whilst the upper, somewhat phallic, pink form suggests a simultaneous full-face view. The sensual nature of the work is further emphasized by the exposure of the shoulders and left breast, a consequence of the dress slipping down from the shoulders. The domestic setting, with its dark, heavily patterned wallpaper, furthers the sense of comfort, luxury and security. Here it is as if the viewer is gazing surreptitiously upon an intensely private moment.

CREATED

Boisgeloup

MEDIUM

Oil on canvas

SERIES/PERIOD/MOVEMENT

Surrealist period

SIMILAR WORKS

Mana'o Tupapa'u (The Spectre Watches over Her) by Paul Gauguin, 1892

Still Life with Sleeping Woman by Henri Matisse, 1940

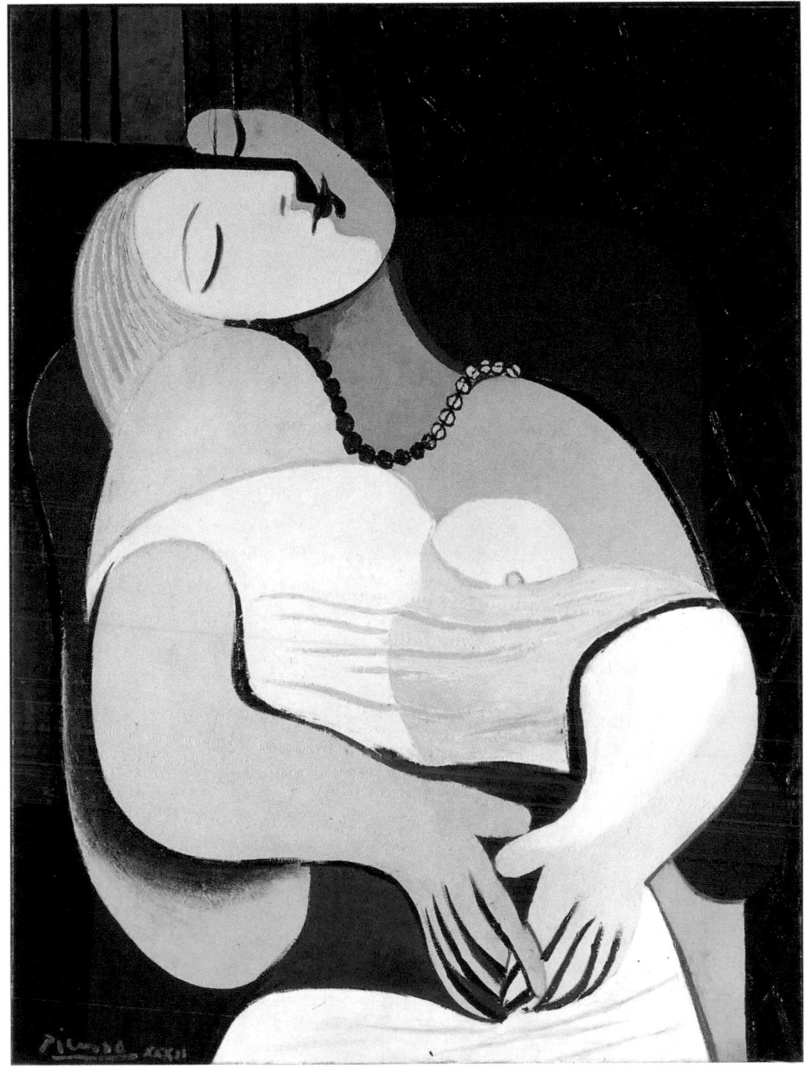

Asleep, 1932

Among the numerous portraits of Marie-Thérèse produced in 1932 is this small-scale oil sketch entitled *Asleep*. Picasso has again emphasized a sense of privacy and comfort as he represents his mistress lying back and resting her head in her hands. The composition uses a great economy of forms, seen most evidently in the simple, graceful curve of black paint that indicates the closed eye. This simple line is echoed throughout the work, signifying the line of the shoulder, the fall of the hair and the interlocked fingers. These lines contain the gentle whites and purples used to suggest the smooth, soft texture of Marie-Thérèse's face and hands. A few colour accents modulate this surface: bright red to emphasize the lips and a slight blush on the cheek, and yellow to suggest the blonde hair, which curls around the sitter's wrist to give the appearance of a gold bracelet. Once again the reds and greens that frame the sleeping figure suggest a secure and richly decorated interior setting.

CREATED

Boisgeloup

MEDIUM

Oil on canvas

SERIES/PERIOD/MOVEMENT

Surrealist period

SIMILAR WORKS

The Dream by Picasso, 1932

Still Life with Sleeping Woman by Henri Matisse, 1940

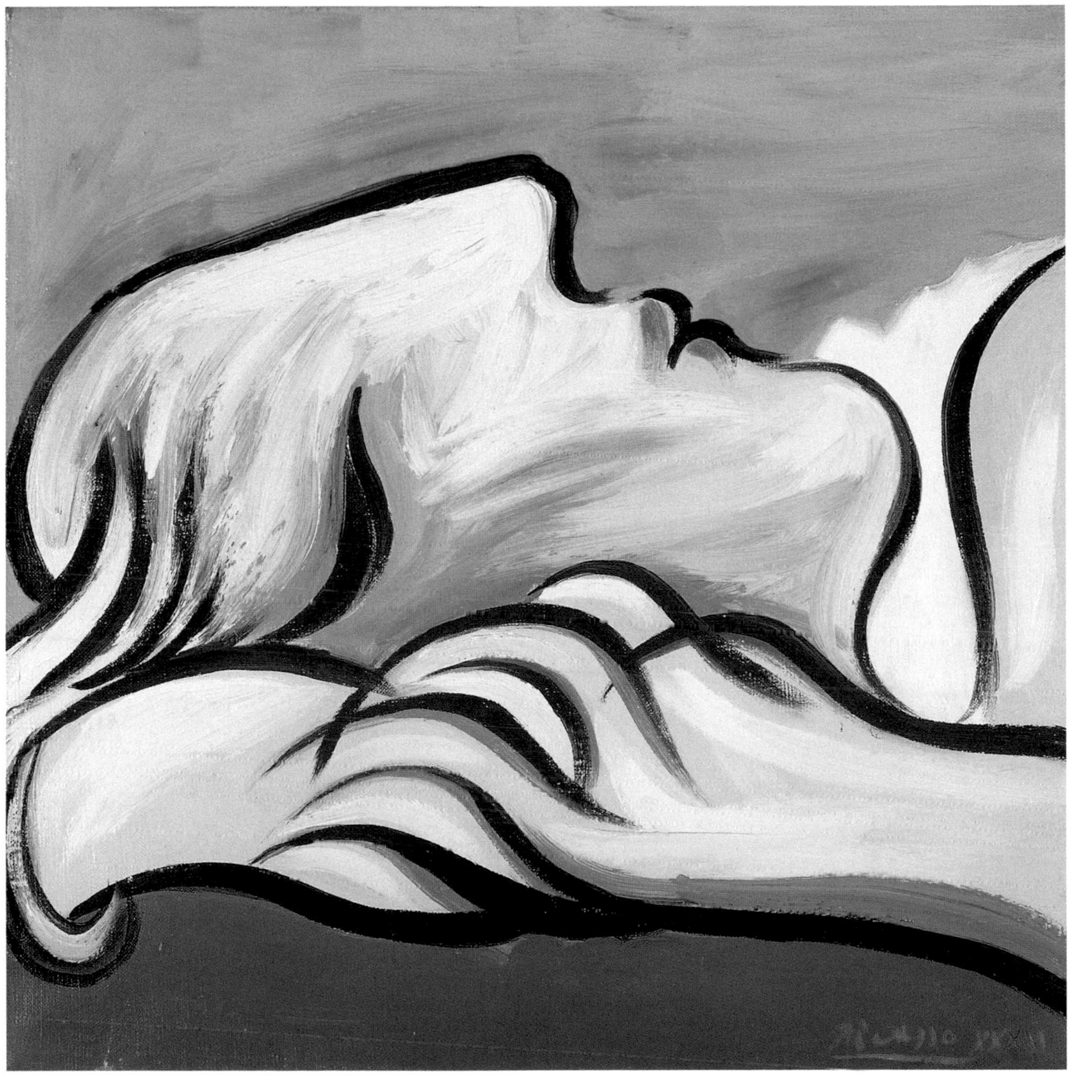

Minotauromachie, 1935

Between 1930 and 1937 Picasso was very active in printmaking, producing well over 100 etchings and engravings. The most famous of these works was entitled *Minotauromachie*. In this work Picasso has exploited the dramatic lighting effects produced by the etching process, so that the left-hand figures are highlighted in white, against a black background, while the right-hand figures are delineated black against white. This strangely inexplicable scene is inhabited by a host of mysterious characters, including a blind minotaur on the right, being led by a young girl carrying a candle; a dead female matador lying on the body of a disembowelled horse; two young women watching the scene from a high window; and a Christ-like figure climbing a ladder. There is no simple explanation that ties these characters into an easily legible narrative. Rather, Picasso has developed his own personal symbolism to express a sense of tension and anguish. Some of these characters had appeared in Picasso's recent etchings. Others, such as the dying horse and the candle-carrying girl, would reappear with dramatic effect in his famous *Guernica*.

CREATED

Paris

MEDIUM

Etching and grattoir

SERIES/PERIOD/MOVEMENT

Surrealist period

SIMILAR WORKS

Disasters of War series of etchings by Francisco de Goya, 1810–20

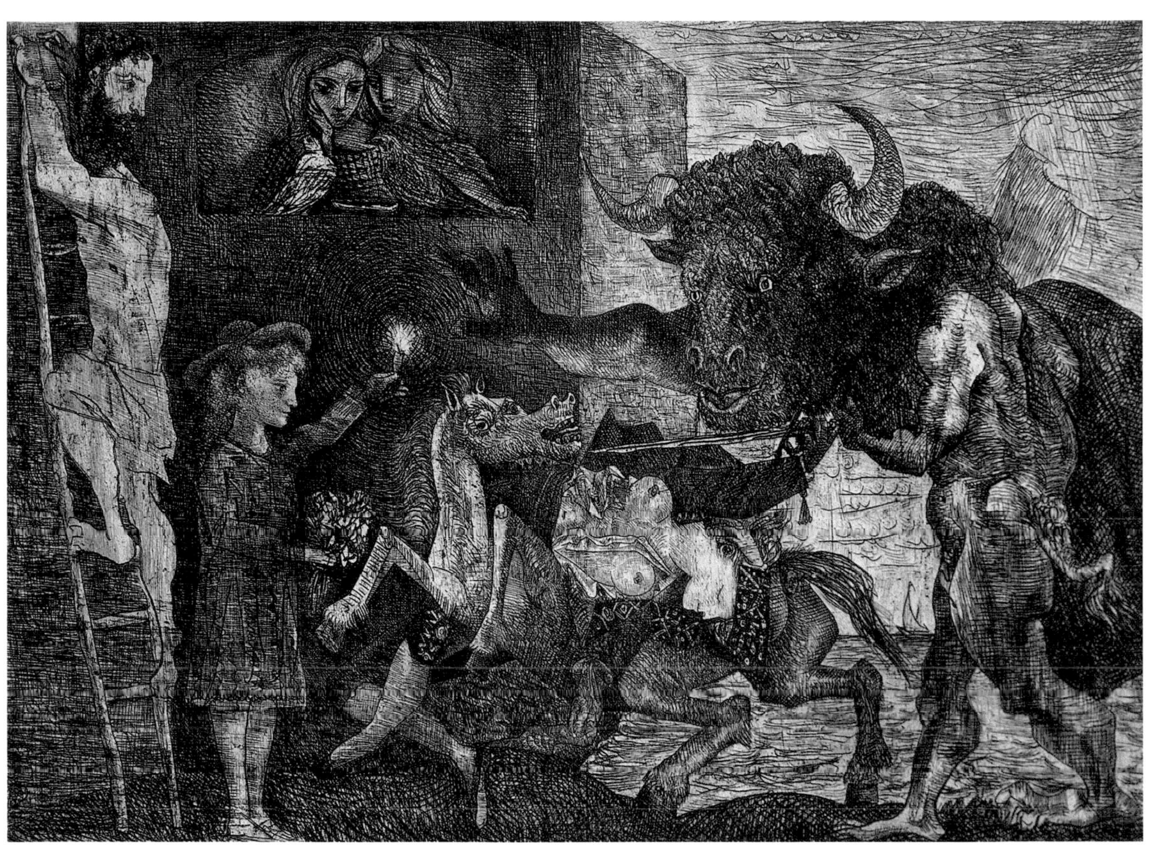

Preparatory Drawing for *Guernica*, 1937

Picasso was first approached to produce a mural for the Paris International Exhibition in January 1937. He did not begin work on the project, however, until the beginning of May, a few days after the bombing of the Basque town of Guernica by Fascist forces. Keen to produce a work of major importance, Picasso returned to the artistic procedures and techniques he had learned as a student. Thus he began by sketching out a series of ideas in pencil on paper. One of the earliest of these drawings represents the central motif of the finished work, the dying horse. With just a few sketchy lines Picasso has indicated the collapsing body of the horse, barely sustaining its weight on its front leg. Here we can also see how Picasso experimented with different positions for the legs – some stretched out, others tucked underneath the body. Picasso's conception of the animal's head seems clearest. Here he has emphasized the muscles of the neck and jaw as this dying animal, reminiscent of the gored horses included in his many recent bullfighting scenes, raises its head in its final death cry.

CREATED

Paris

MEDIUM

Pencil on paper

SERIES/PERIOD/MOVEMENT

Surrealist period

SIMILAR WORKS

The Bullfight by Francisco de Goya, 1816

Bullfighting by Picasso, 1934

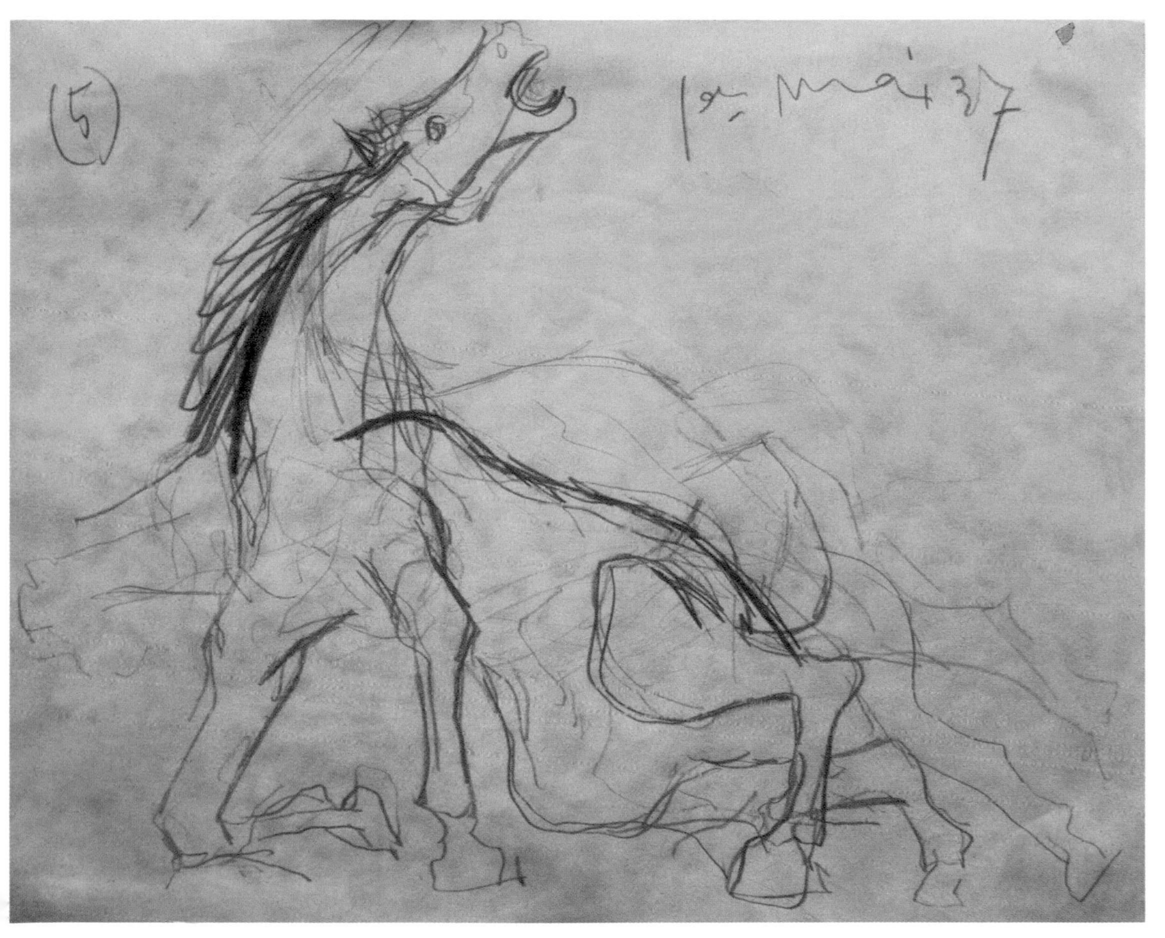
(5)
1er mai 37

Horse's Head, Study for *Guernica*, 1937

Picasso continued the process of sketching out his original ideas for *Guernica* over the next few days. Following on from his earlier preparatory drawing, he turned his attention to the horse's head and, in particular, its dying scream. In contrast to the more naturalistic handling in the previous sketch, Picasso now began to reshape the head dramatically. Although the strong jaw and open mouth remained, he now placed eyes, ears and nostrils all on one side of the animal's face. From these sketches he produced the large-scale oil sketch illustrated here. The straight line of the head has given way to more rounded forms, suggestive of a dramatic throw of the head upwards. Picasso has also included the animal's teeth and tongue, the latter reduced to a sharp spear-like form that echoes the spear penetrating the horse's side in the final image. The oil sketch is produced in a range of whites and greys over a black ground. Here Picasso has established the monochrome tonality that is such a striking feature of the finished work.

CREATED

Paris

MEDIUM

Oil on canvas

SERIES/PERIOD/MOVEMENT

Surrealist period

SIMILAR WORKS

The Bullfight by Francisco de Goya, 1816

Bullfighting by Picasso, 1934

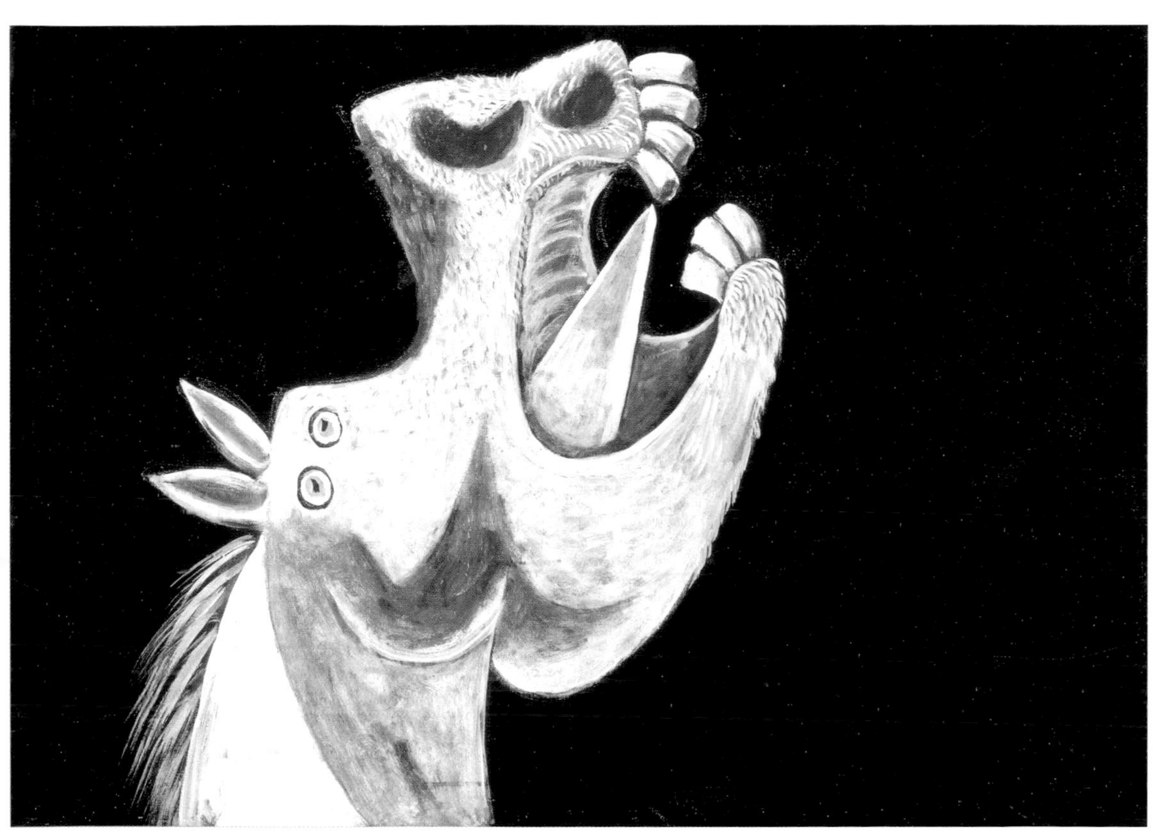

Weeping Woman, 1937

Shortly after the completion of *Guernica*, Picasso produced several works representing weeping women. The best known of these is *Weeping Woman* of October 1937. Here Picasso has used Cubist distortion and heightened, dissonant colour to great emotional effect. The work shows a highly anguished woman raising a handkerchief to her tear-strewn face. The jagged forms of the handkerchief, however, become one with the woman's face and right hand, while the tear that falls from her right eye doubles up as a finger nail. Picasso has also highlighted the woman's elaborate make-up, including her heavily mascaraed eyes. This only serves to emphasize shock and anguish, as well as highlighting the strangely winged shapes reflected in the pupils. These suggest birds of prey, or possibly even the aircraft that had launched the first full-scale saturation bombing of civilians in Guernica. *Weeping Woman* was based on the figure of Dora Maar, a Yugoslavian photographer whom Picasso had met the previous year. Here it is interesting to note the sharper, more angular forms deployed by Picasso, in contrast to the softer rounded forms reserved for representations of Marie-Thérèse.

CREATED

Paris

MEDIUM

Oil on canvas

SERIES/PERIOD/MOVEMENT

Surrealist period

SIMILAR WORKS

The Scream by Edvard Munch, 1893

Guernica by Picasso, 1937

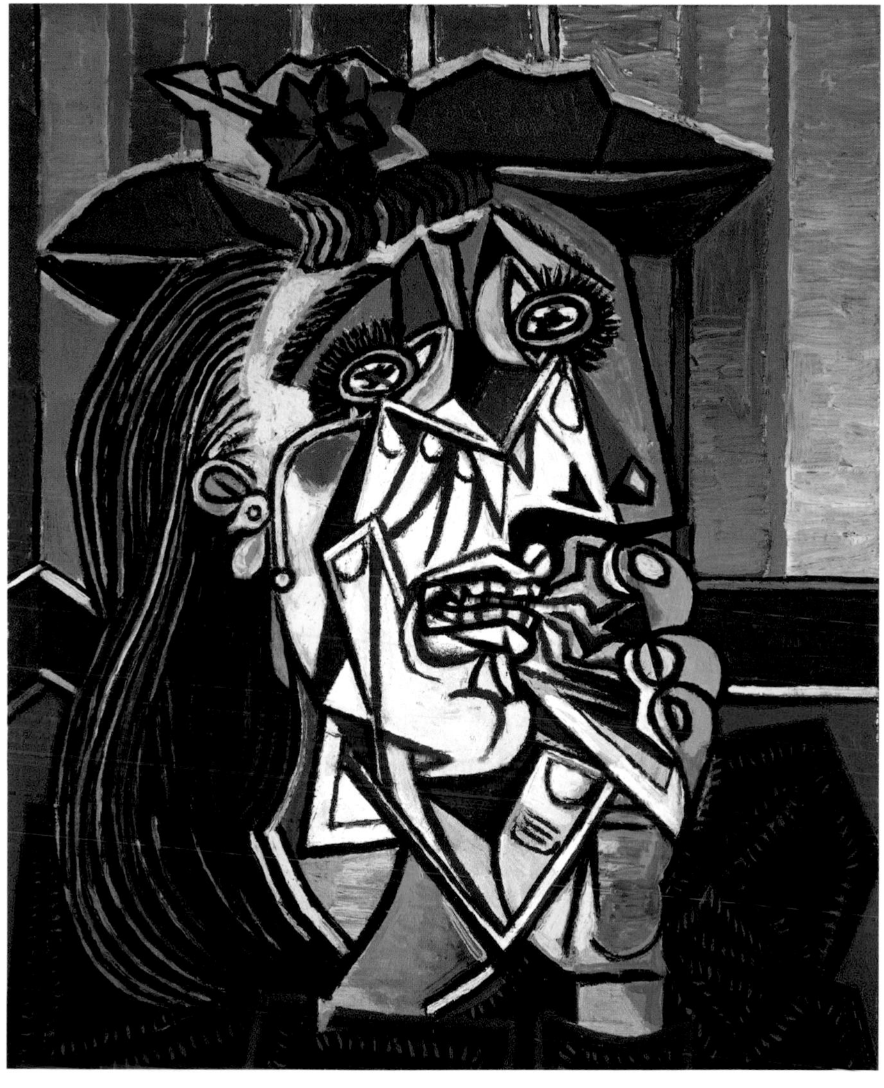

Bull's Head, 1943

Picasso was largely confined to his studio during much of the wartime occupation of Paris. However, he continued to produce countless drawings, paintings and even sculptures. One of the most intriguing of these works is *Bull's Head*. Picasso had been introducing everyday objects into his works from the time of his earliest Cubist *collages*. Here, however, he combined two simple elements to produce an evocatively metamorphosed creature. As Picasso later explained: 'One day I found an old bicycle saddle in a heap of scrap metal, and right next to it there was a rusty old handlebar.... All I had to do was weld the two pieces together.' Shortly afterwards, Picasso had the sculpture cast in bronze. Despite the evident playful nature of this simple exercise, Picasso's *Bull's Head* is much more than a simple exercise in illusion. For Picasso, trapped in occupied Paris, the bull's head operated as a resonant symbol of his Spanish roots and his newfound nationalism in the wake of the Spanish Civil War. It also recalled the abundance of bicycles used in Paris in a time when fuel shortages were part of everyday life.

CREATED

Paris

MEDIUM

Bronze

SERIES/PERIOD/MOVEMENT

Second World War period

SIMILAR WORKS

Lobster Telephone by Salvador Dali, 1938

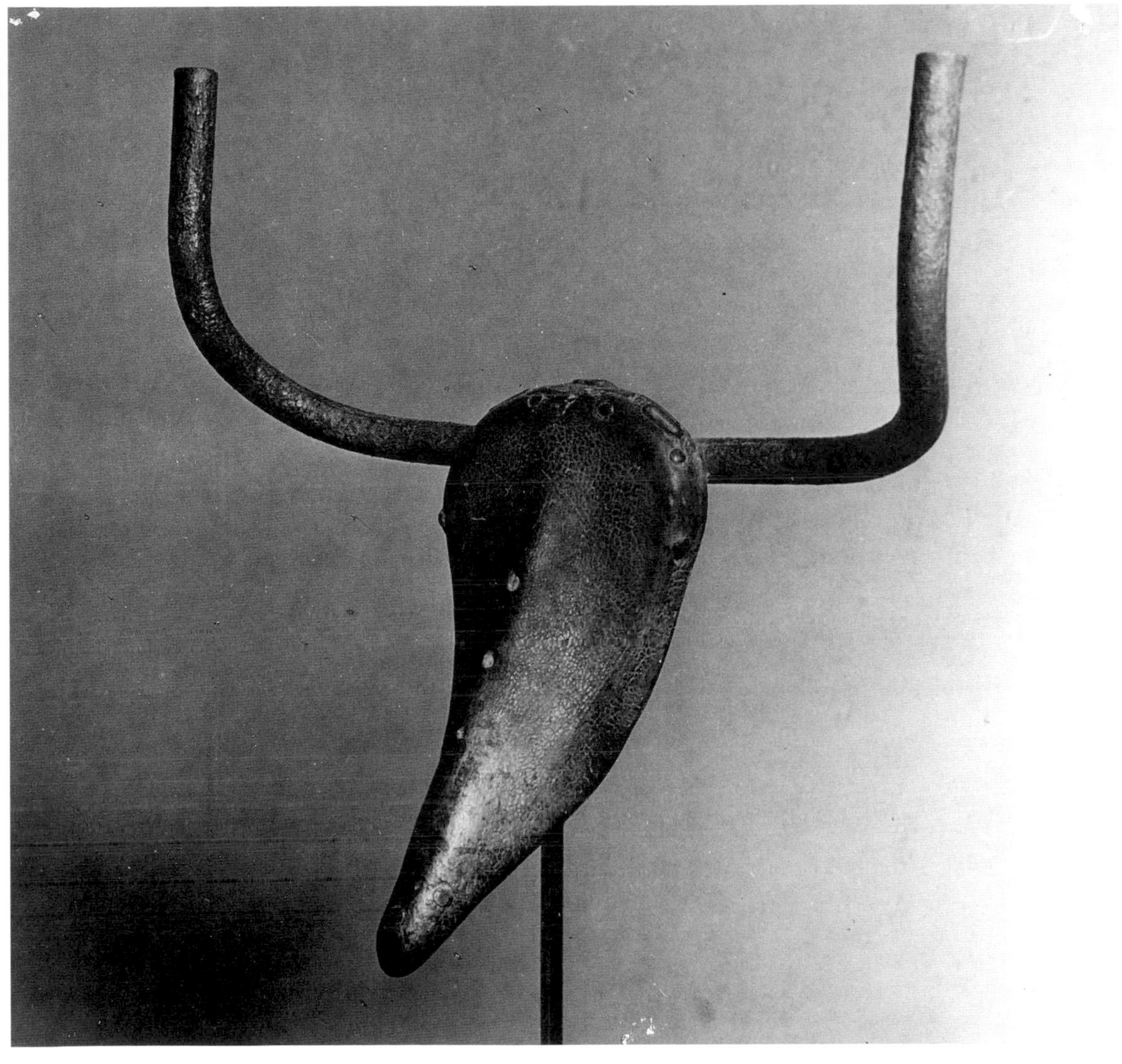

Condor and *Owl*, 1949

From 1946 onwards the small town of Vallauris, in the south of France, famous for its local potteries, became a centre of fevered activity for Picasso. Inspired by the local artisans, and recognizing the ancient traditions of the craft, Picasso began to work extensively on a series of ceramics. At first, he simply decorated existing pieces of pottery. Soon, however, he developed a range of new techniques to exploit this medium, shaping his own clay forms to produce a diverse range of vases, pots and pitchers. He also worked on a series of sculptural forms, whose bodies resembled the traditional clay vessels of Vallauris, yet, with the addition of a few painted marks, metamorphosed into identifiable animals. Both *Condor* and *Owl* provide examples of this work. In *Condor*, Picasso has constructed the bird-like form from a simple base, supporting a terracotta, amphora-shaped body. The neck of the vessel is twisted upwards to form the head. Simple black marks have been added to form the wings of the creature, the colour scheme thus recalling the red and black attic vases of Ancient Greece.

CREATED

Vallauris

MEDIUM

Ceramic

SERIES/PERIOD/MOVEMENT

Post-War Communist period

SIMILAR WORKS

Woman-Pitcher by Picasso, 1951

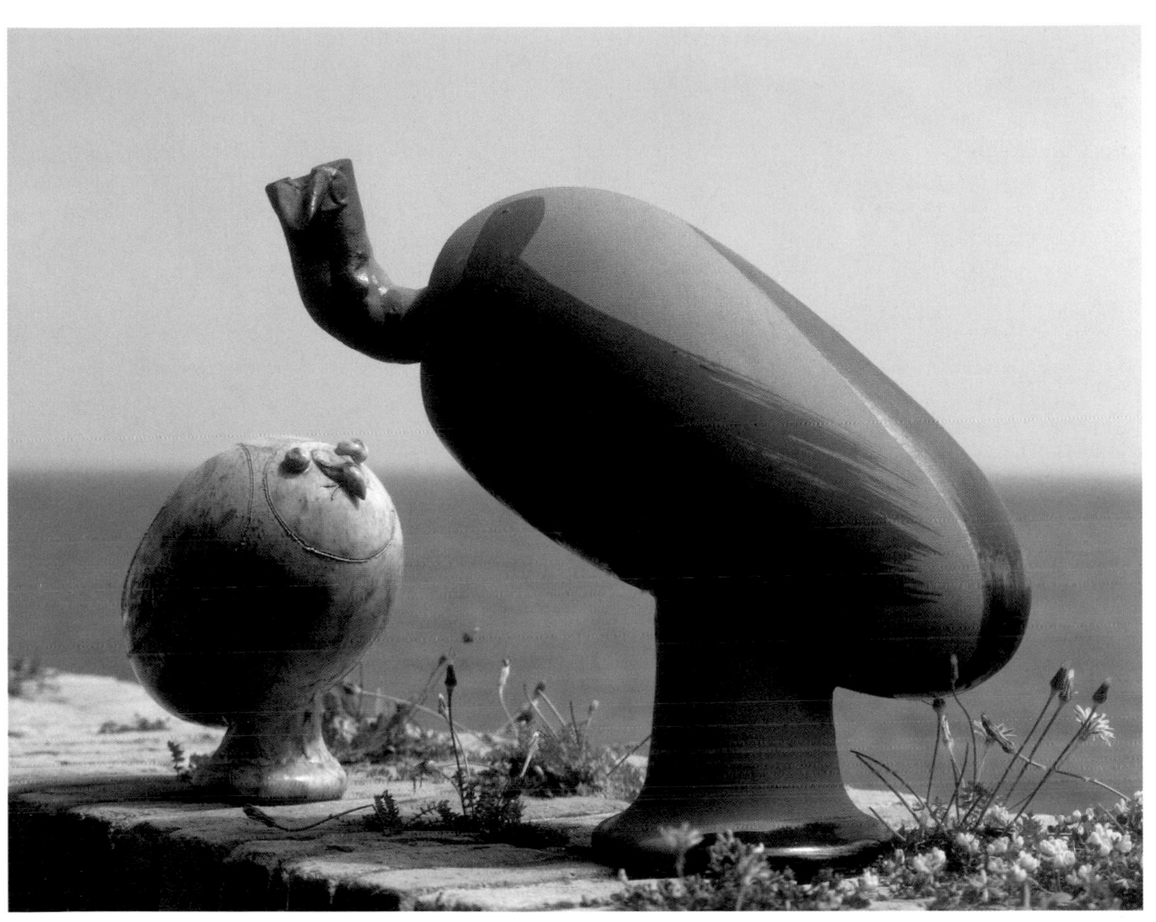

Portrait of Françoise Gilot with Paloma and Claude, 1951

Picasso's portrait of his live-in lover, Françoise Gilot, and their two children was produced in early 1951, when the couple were spending the winter in Paris. The work is executed in pen and ink with wash in blacks and greys. The monochrome appearance of the piece reveals Picasso's skill in using tone to render light and shade and to model forms in space. Here the two children, Paloma and Claude, pose for the artist, the latter standing beside his tricycle as if impatient to get out into the open air and ride. In the background his mother lies restlessly with her head in her hand. Here the medium is expressly used to emphasize the dark, ponderous forms of this winter interior setting and the mood of confinement it brings. This is a dramatic contrast to the Mediterranean light and colour that frequently flooded Picasso's work at this time. It was also a dark time politically, with the Korean War still raging. Indeed, just two months earlier Picasso had completed his damning critique of the conflict, the painting entitled *Massacre in Korea*.

CREATED

Paris

MEDIUM

Pen and ink on paper

SERIES/PERIOD/MOVEMENT

Post-War Communist period

SIMILAR WORKS

The Family of the Artist by Pierre Auguste Renoir, 1896

Claude drawing Françoise and Paloma by Picasso, 1954

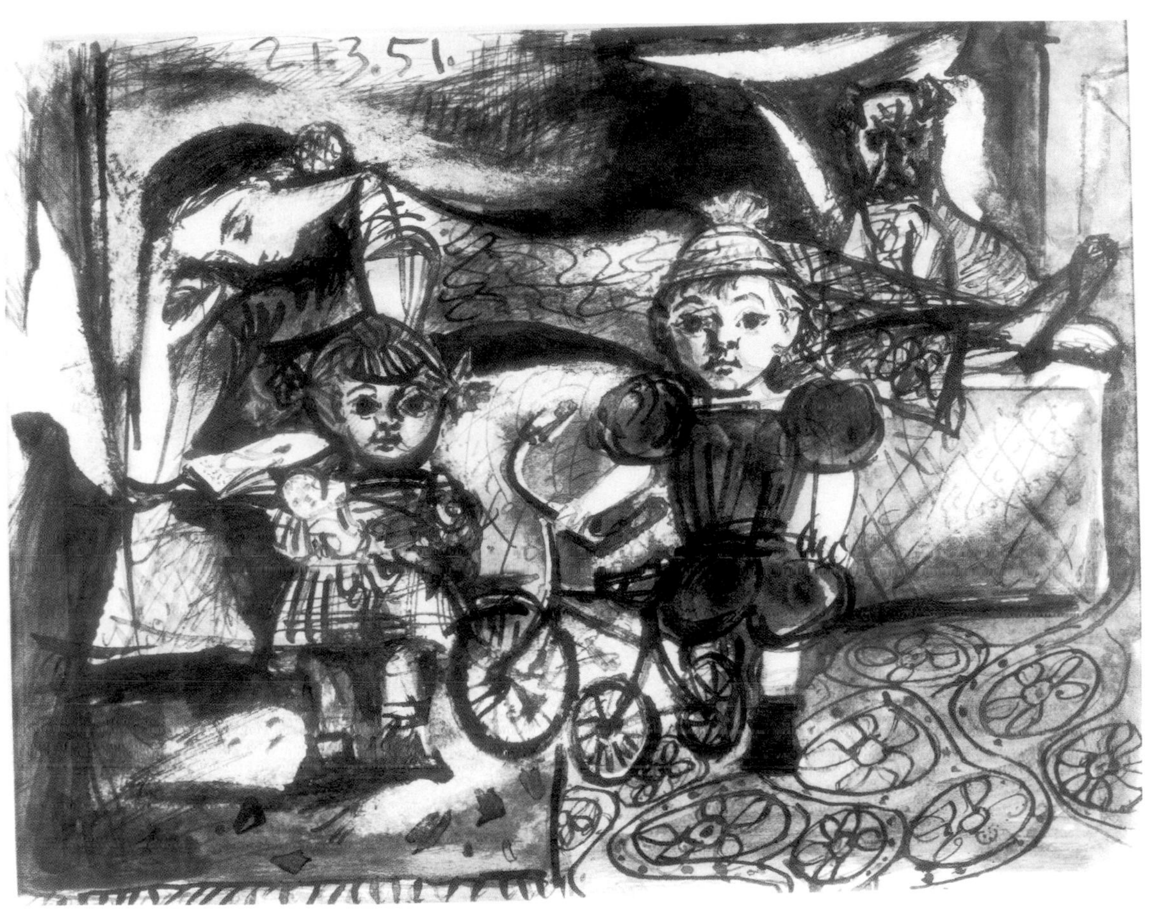
2.1.3.51.

Don Quixote, 1955

Picasso's close affiliation with the Communist Party was a major factor in many of the artistic projects that he undertook in the post-war period. In some cases this resulted in politically motivated subject matter, as in *Massacre in Korea*; in others it directed Picasso towards making his work more accessible to the masses. His extensive work in book and journal illustration provided a key example of this. This simple drawing of Don Quixote and Sancho Panza was reproduced in the Communist journal *Les Lettres Français* to celebrate the 350th anniversary of the publication of Miguel de Cervantes's (1547–1616) famous novel. At Vallauris, Picasso had developed a new technique for painting on pots. Here, thick brushes were used with fluid paint to form images from rapidly executed, almost calligraphic, marks. Here the simplicity of mark-making was paramount. Picasso also deployed this technique in a number of gouache and watercolour drawings, including this one, many of which were reproduced as lithographs. Picasso may well also have been recalling similar images of Don Quixote produced by Honoré Daumier (1808–79) in the 1860s.

CREATED

Cannes

MEDIUM

Pen and ink on paper

SERIES/PERIOD/MOVEMENT

Post-War Communist period

SIMILAR WORKS

Don Quixote and Sancho Panza by Honoré Daumier, *c.* 1850

Illustrations for *Don Quixote* by Gustave Doré, 1862

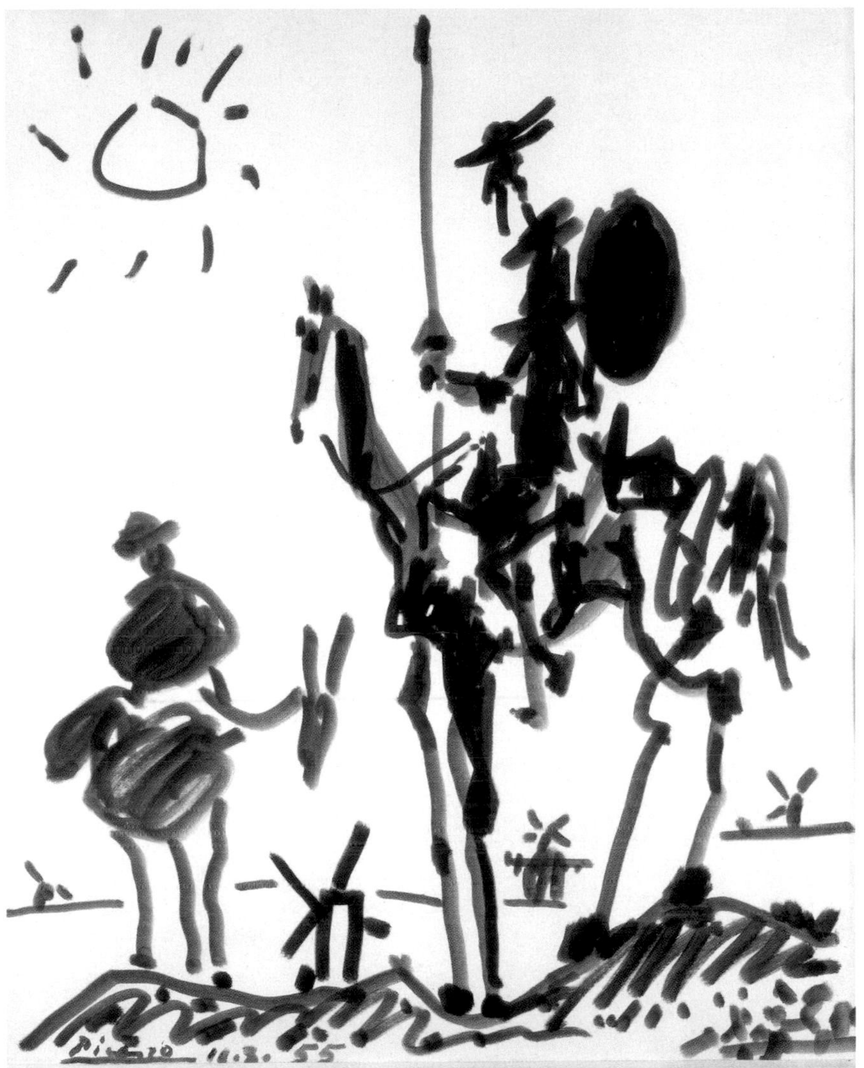

The Bathers, 1956

Throughout his career, Picasso's work provided a constant dialogue between painting and sculptural techniques. This came to the fore once more in an ensemble of works produced in 1956. Here Picasso returned to the theme of bathers on the beach to produce six flat sculptures assembled from various pieces of wood. Much of this material consisted of found objects: broom-handles, table legs, picture frames and other scrap material. Like many of Picasso's sculptures, these wooden originals were then cast in bronze. This was Picasso's first sculpted group and was intended to decorate a fountain. Yet despite its status as a sculptural ensemble, each work is predominantly flat and designed to be seen from the front. The bodies themselves are inscribed with lightly carved marks to represent the anatomical details of the torsos and legs, and the shallow projection of the forms is in low relief. In this way, *The Bathers* hovers somewhere between the two-dimensionality of drawing and the three-dimensionality of sculpture. This technique also anticipated Picasso's other strange amalgamation of painting and sculpture, the painted sheet metal sculptures of the early 1960s.

CREATED

Cannes

MEDIUM

Bronze

SERIES/PERIOD/MOVEMENT

Post-War Communist period

SIMILAR WORKS

Early One Morning by Anthony Caro, 1962

Teodelapio by Alexander Calder, 1962

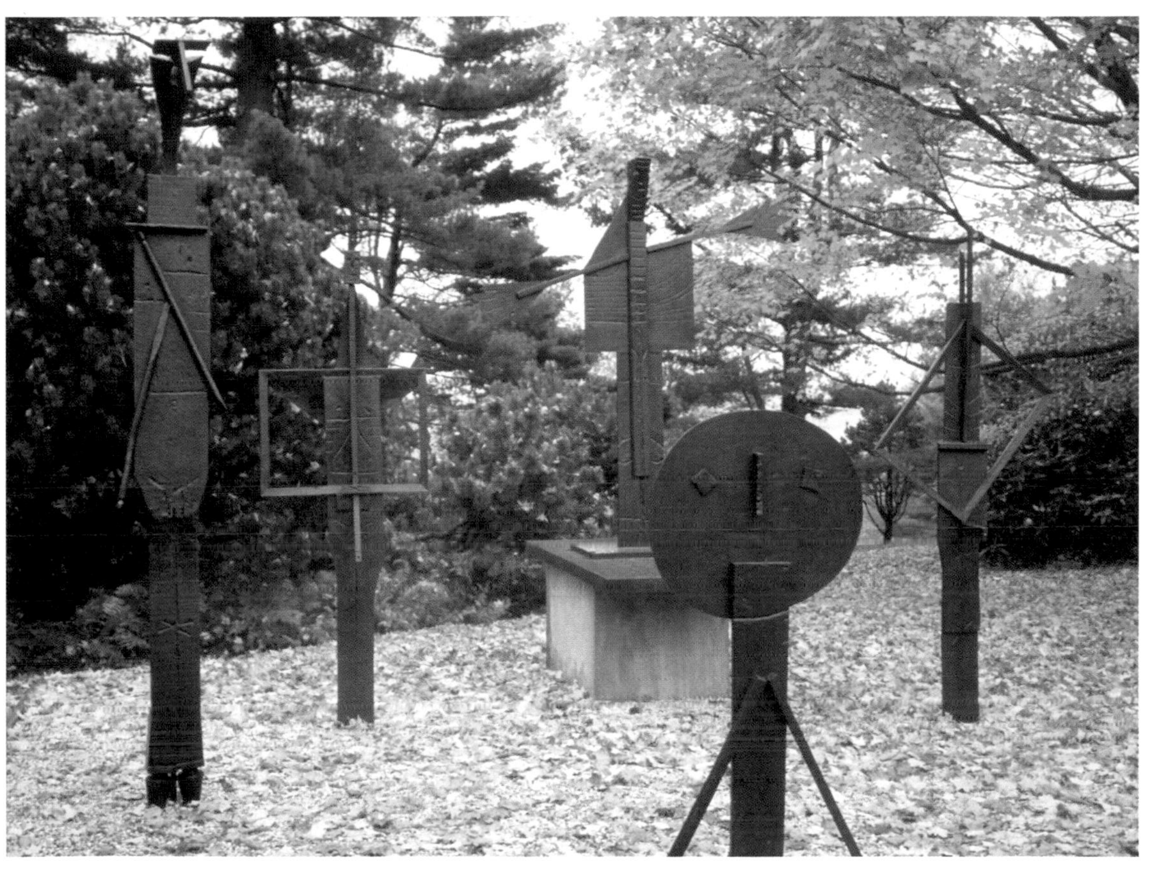

Las Meninas, 1957

Picasso's fascination for the work of the Old Masters was thoroughly explored during the late 1950s and early 1960s, when he produced countless works based on paintings hanging in the Louvre. In 1957, he also produced a large number of paintings drawing on one of the most famous works in the Prado – Diego Velazquez's (1599–1660) *Las Meninas* (1656). This highly colouristic version incorporates most of the characters seen in the original. In the lower-centre, the Infanta is seen wearing a bright green and yellow dress, surrounded by her entourage of servants and staff. To the left, with a yellow cross on his chest, is Velazquez himself, standing in front of the large canvas. To the right of the painter's head, a small, green-framed mirror reflects two tiny white dots – all that remain of the king and queen in Velazquez's original work. The dazzlingly coloured space and characters, recalling childrens' drawings or playing cards, adds a sense of exuberance, joy and freedom to the work and is in stark contrast to the sombre tonality and gravity of the original.

CREATED

Cannes

MEDIUM

Oil on canvas

SERIES/PERIOD/MOVEMENT

Late period

SIMILAR WORKS

Las Meninas by Diego Velazquez, 1656

Untitled, Montrouge by Bram van Velde, 1953

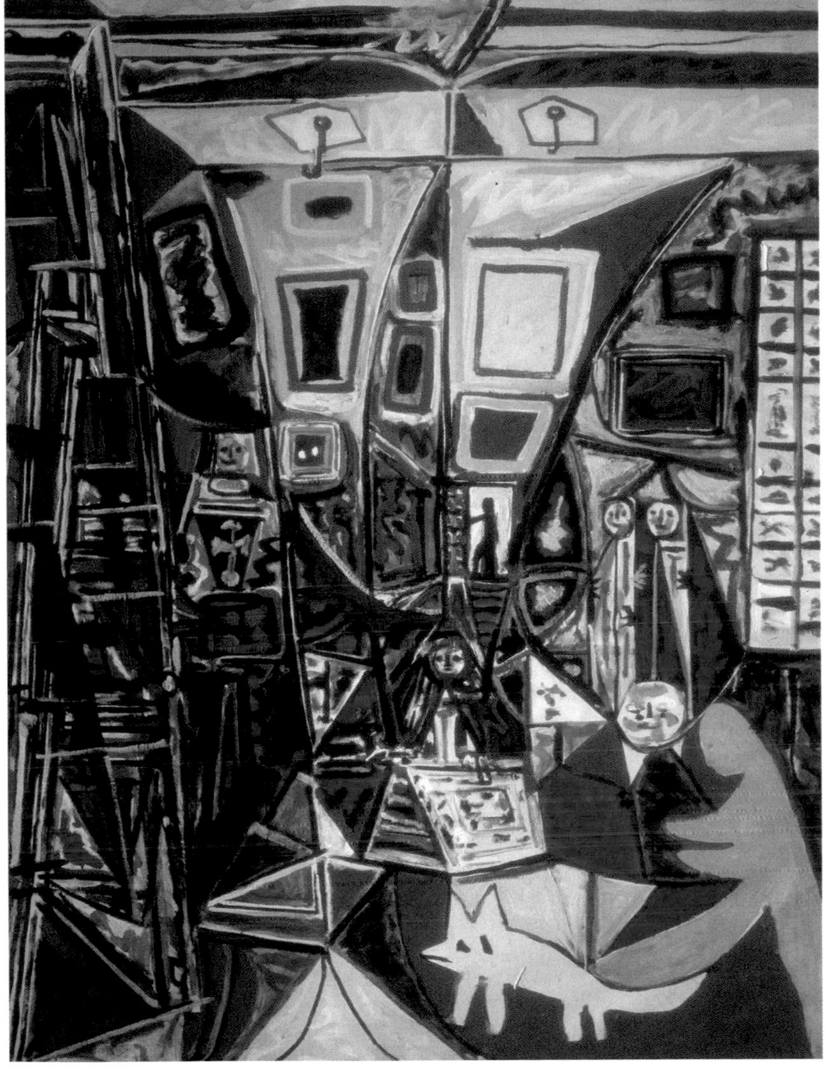

Head of a Woman, 1961

Picasso's experiments in making flat sculptures were followed up in the early 1960s with a series of works in an entirely new medium and technique. At first Picasso produced small models using folded paper and cardboard, thus recalling his use of these materials in his early Cubist sculptures. To make the models sturdier, however, Picasso introduced sheet metal. He then painted the surface of the metal as if it was a canvas, thus producing an amalgam of painting and sculpture. In this example, Picasso has treated line and colour as independent. Black lines define the features of the sitter, outlining the hair, eyes, nose, mouth, and the shape of the neck and shoulders. However, these lines fail to contain the non-naturalistic colours that have been randomly applied to model the face. Thus, Picasso adds drawing to his conflation of painting and sculpture. The bold, red line running down the centre of the face also makes a reference to Henri Matisse's (1869–1954) famous portrait *Mme Matisse (The Green Line)*, executed over half a century earlier and well known for the bold green line of paint Matisse used to dissect the face of his sitter.

CREATED

Mougins, Cannes or Vauvenargues

MEDIUM

Painted sheet metal

SERIES/PERIOD/MOVEMENT

Late period

SIMILAR WORKS

Mme Matisse (The Green Line) by Henri Matisse, 1905

Model for Constructed Head No. 3 by Naum Gabo, 1917

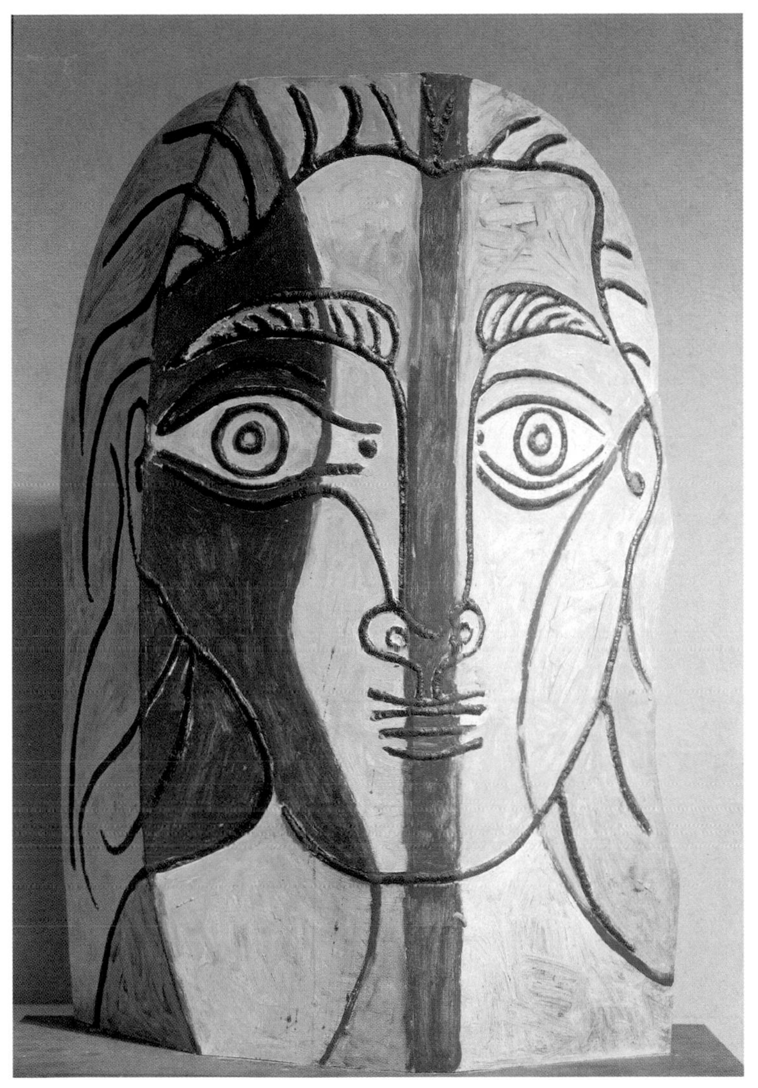

Woman with Outstretched Arms, 1961

In addition to the busts executed using sheet metal, Picasso also produced full figures. Here the sturdiness of the metal allowed him to extend the limbs outwards and to work on a larger scale. This example, entitled *Woman with Outstretched Arms*, is life-sized, standing at nearly 180 cm (71 in). Once again, the surface of the metal has been painted, here using simple black-and-white tones to distinguish the figure from the background, which itself becomes a part of the sculpture. Picasso also allowed the patterned surface of this industrial material to show through. The bulky, organic white forms of this figure, when set against the sweeping black forms of the surrounding space, bears more than a passing resemblance to the unique architectural forms of Le Corbusier's (1887–1965) *Chapel at Ronchamp*, completed just a few years earlier. The figure was later recast in concrete and scaled up to a height of 6 metres (20 ft). This new, monumental version of the work was produced for Picasso's friend and former art dealer Daniel-Henry Kahnweiler and installed in his garden.

CREATED

Cannes

MEDIUM

Painted sheet metal

SERIES/PERIOD/MOVEMENT

Late period

SIMILAR WORKS

Le Dejeuner sur l'Herbe (after Manet) by Picasso, 1962

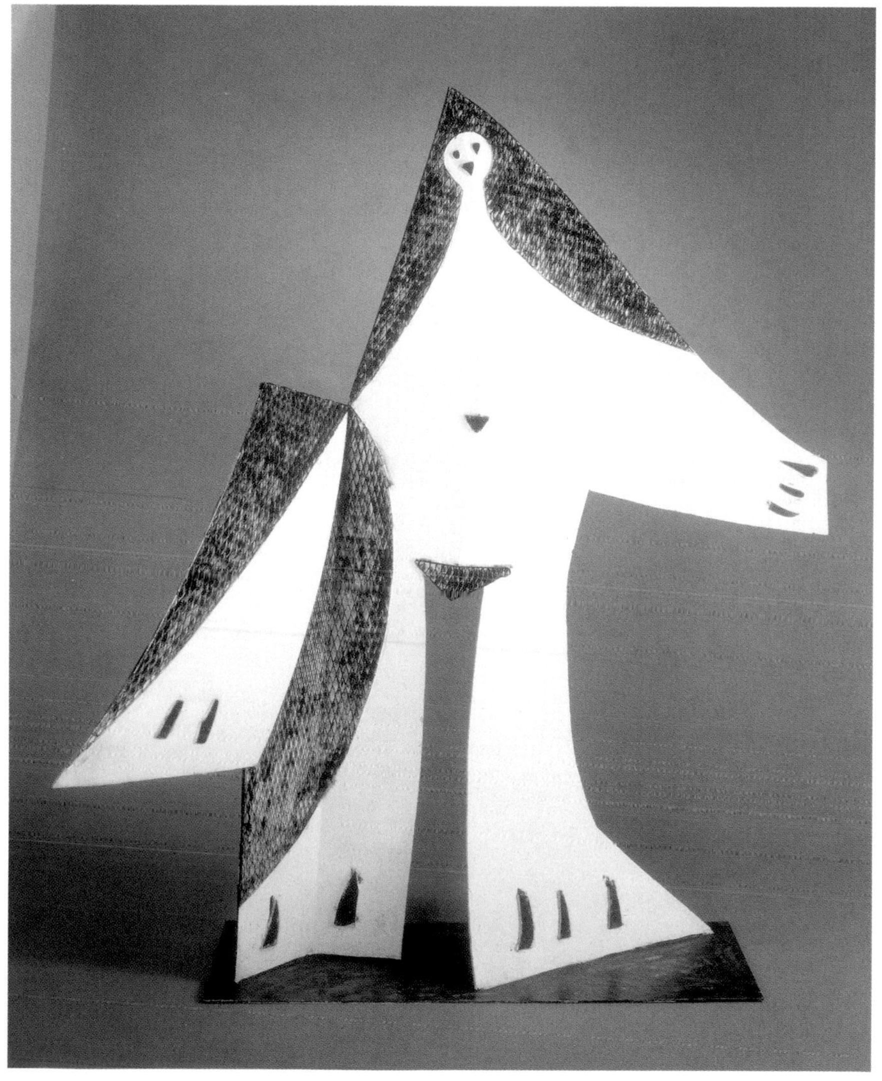

Woman in a Hat, 1963

Picasso's perception of the close relationship between painting and sculpture is perhaps nowhere as well exemplified as in this work. In January 1961, he produced an oil painting entitled *Seated Woman in a Hat*. The work represents a woman, seen in profile, wearing a chimney-shaped hat. She wears a green dress and is seated in a blue armchair, with her hands crossed and supported on one of the chair's arms. The shapes and forms of the painting correspond precisely to those of this painted sheet-metal sculpture, and only the colours of the hat, dress and armchair have been changed. This work was also produced in 1961 and, two years later, cut and assembled to form a three-dimensional sculptural object mounted on a plinth. Here, it seems, Picasso drew no distinction between the two media, effectively producing the same work as both a painting and a sculpture making the two entirely interchangeable. This easy dialogue between painting and sculpture recalls a claim made by Picasso in the 1930s, that his Cubist paintings of 1910–11 could easily have been made into corresponding sculptures.

CREATED

Mougins, Cannes or Vauvenargues

MEDIUM

Painted sheet metal

SERIES/PERIOD/MOVEMENT

Late period

SIMILAR WORKS

Woman with a Hat by Henri Matisse, 1905

Seated Woman in a Hat by Picasso, 1961

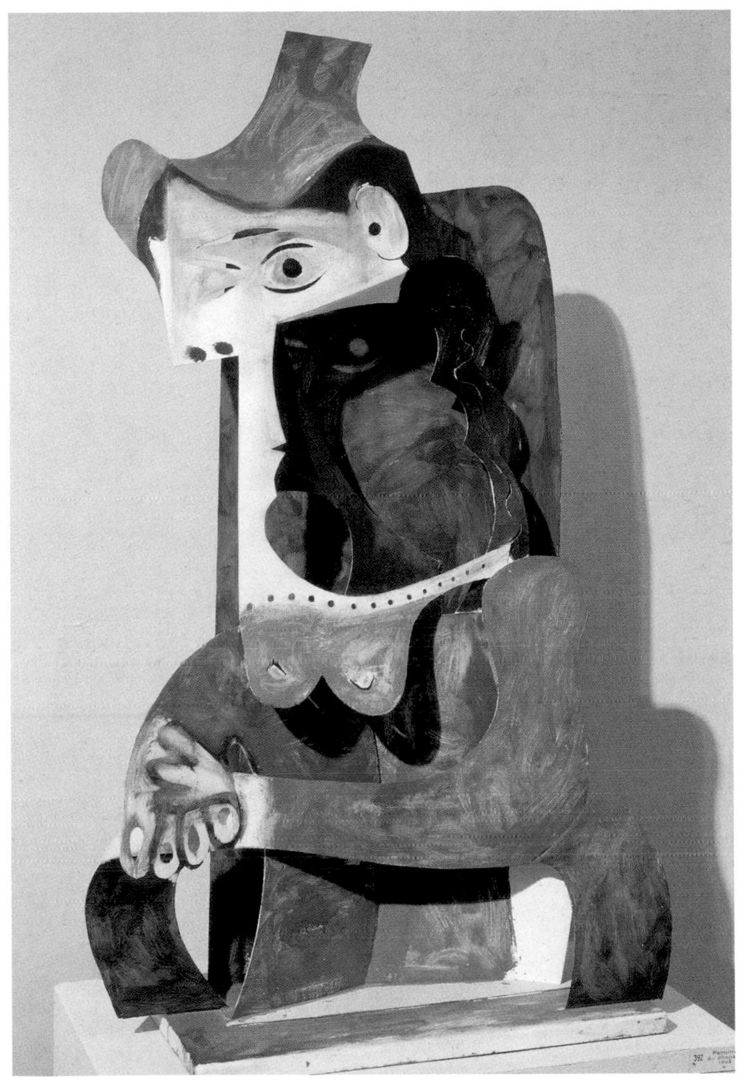

Phallic Centaur I after a work by Picasso, 1967

Amongst Picasso's numerous figurative sculptures and ceramics is a series of little-known models of centaurs produced during the 1960s. Cast in 23-carat gold by the goldsmiths Francois and Pierre Hugo, these small-scale figures, just a few inches in height, seem to be private, playful works. Here the centaur – half-horse, half-man – is reduced to a spindly form, his body and limbs constructed from thin rods that bear some resemblance to the wire constructions Picasso had made with the help of González during the 1930s. The centaur, a creature from classical mythology, is commonly represented as a warrior figure, brandishing a spear. This echoes the exaggerated phallus, shaped to suggest the neck and head of a horse, that Picasso has given the creature. Once again, Picasso draws extensively on the classicism of Ancient Greek culture, both in its use of rich ornamental gold and its depiction of the phallus as an explicit fertility symbol.

CREATED

Vauvenargues

MEDIUM

Gold

SERIES/PERIOD/MOVEMENT

Late period

SIMILAR WORKS

Pallas and the Centaur by Sandro Botticelli, *c.* 1482–83

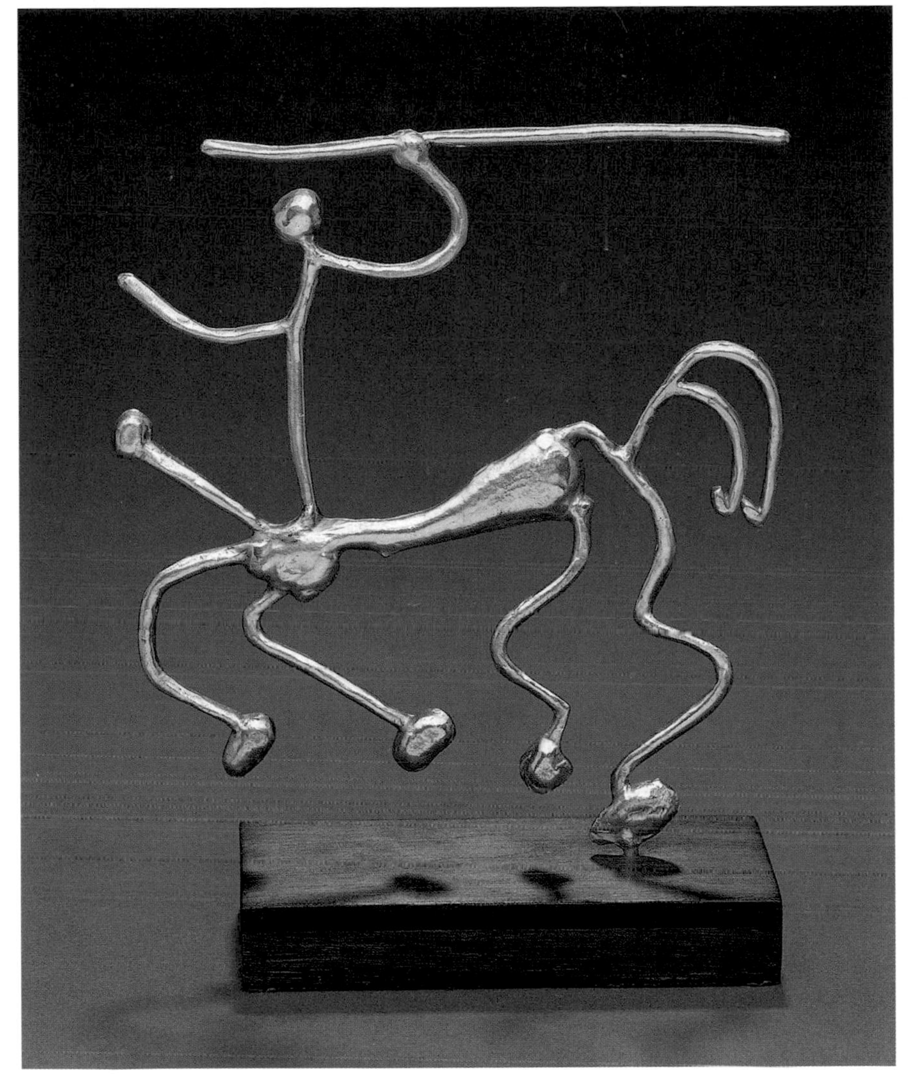

Author Biographies

Mike O'Mahony (author)

Dr Mike O'Mahony is a specialist in twentieth-century art of Europe and the United States. He studied at the Courtauld Institute and now teaches History of Art at the University of Bristol. He has lectured at the major London galleries, including Tate Britain and the Royal Academy of Arts. He is founding editor of Art on the Line, an online international arts journal. He has written and contributed articles to many publications, including *The Oxford History of Western Art*.

Pepe Karmel (foreword)

Pepe Karmel is Associate Professor in the Department of Fine Arts, New York University, prior to which he held positions as curator in the department of painting and sculpture at the Museum of Modern Art and as art critic for *The New York Times*. He worked as scriptwriter and assistant producer on the programme *New Ways of Seeing: Picasso, Braque and the Cubist Revolution*. His book, *Picasso and the Invention of Cubism*, was published by Yale University Press in 2003. He has written widely on modern and contemporary art for publications such as *Art in America*.

Picture Credits: Prelims and Introductory Matter

Pages 1 & 3: *Self-Portrait* (detail), Courtesy of Philadelphia Museum of Art, Pennsylvania, PA, USA/www.bridgeman.co.uk/© Succession Picasso/DACS 2005

Page 4: *Les Demoiselles d'Avignon*, Courtesy of Museum of Modern Art, New York, USA, Lauros/Giraudon/www.bridgeman.co.uk/© Succession Picasso/DACS 2005

Page 5 (l to r top): *Science and Charity*, Courtesy of Museo Picasso, Barcelona, Spain/www.bridgeman.co.uk/© Succession Picasso/DACS 2005; *Woman in Blue*, Courtesy of Museo Nacional Centro de Arte Reina Sofia, Madrid, Spain, Giraudon/www.bridgeman.co.uk/© Succession Picasso/DACS 2005; *Reclining Nude*, Courtesy of Private Collection/www.bridgeman.co.uk/© Succession Picasso/DACS 2005

Page 5 (l to r bottom): *Mother and Child*, Courtesy of © Fogg Art Museum, Harvard University Art Museums, USA, Bequest from the Collection of Maurice Wertheim, Class 1906/www.bridgeman.co.uk/© Succession Picasso/DACS 2005; Theatre Curtain for *Parade*, Courtesy of Private Collection, Archives Charmet/www.bridgeman.co.uk/© Succession Picasso/DACS 2005; *Circus Scene*, Courtesy of Private Collection/www.bridgeman.co.uk/© Succession Picasso/DACS 2005

Page 6 (l to r top): *Le Moulin de la Galette*, Courtesy of Solomon R. Guggenheim Museum, New York, USA/www.bridgeman.co.uk/© Succession Picasso/DACS 2005; *The Pigeons, Cannes*, Courtesy of Museo Picasso, Barcelona, Spain, Giraudon/www.bridgeman.co.uk/© Succession Picasso/DACS 2005; *Woman Lying on the Beach*, Courtesy of Private Collection, © Lefevre Fine Art Ltd, London/www.bridgeman.co.uk/© Succession Picasso/DACS 2005

Page 6 (l to r bottom): *Woman with a Guitar*, Courtesy of Private Collection, Peter Willi/www.bridgeman.co.uk/© Succession Picasso/DACS 2005; *On the Beach (Bathing)*, Courtesy of Peggy Guggenheim Foundation, Venice, Italy, Giraudon/www.bridgeman.co.uk/© Succession Picasso/DACS 2005; *Lying Nude with Head of a Man in Profile*, Courtesy of Christie's Images Ltd/© Succession Picasso/DACS 2005

Page 7 (l to r): *Two Women at a Bar*, Courtesy of Hiroshima Museum of Art, Hiroshima, Japan, Giraudon/www.bridgeman.co.uk/© Succession Picasso/DACS 2005; *Still Life with Pitcher and a Bowl of Fruit*, Courtesy of Private Collection, Giraudon/www.bridgeman.co.uk/© Succession Picasso/DACS 2005; *Weeping Woman*, Courtesy of Tate, London/© Succession Picasso/DACS 2005

Page 12: *The Bathers*, Courtesy of Musee Picasso, Paris, France/www.bridgeman.co.uk/© Succession Picasso/DACS 2005

Page 15: *Three Women at the Spring*, Courtesy of Museum of Modern Art, New York, USA/www.bridgeman.co.uk/© Succession Picasso/DACS 2005

Page 16: *Three Dancers*, Courtesy of Tate, London/© Succession Picasso/DACS 2005

Page 17: *Seated Nude*, Courtesy of Musee National d'Art Moderne, Centre Pompidou, Paris, France, Peter Willi/www.bridgeman.co.uk/© Succession Picasso/DACS 2005

Pages 18–19: *Guernica*, Courtesy of Museo Nacional Centro de Arte Reina Sofia, Madrid, Spain/www.bridgeman.co.uk/© Succession Picasso/DACS 2005

Further Reading

Baldassari, Anne et al, Picasso and Portraiture, Harry N. Abrams, 1996

Berger, John, *The Success and Failure of Picasso*, Vintage, 1993

Cowling, Elizabeth, *Picasso: Style and Meaning*, Phaidon Press, 2002

Ferrier, Jean-Louis, *Picasso*, Vilo International, 1996

Flam, Jack, *Matisse and Picasso: The Story of Their Rivavlry and Friendship*, Basic Books, 2004

Gilot, Françoise, *Life with Picasso*, Virago Press, 1990

Karmel, Pepe, *Picasso and the Invention of Cubism*, Yale University Press, 2003

Krauss, Rosalind E., *The Picasso Papers*, Thames and Hudson Ltd, 1998

Leal, Brigitte, Christine Piot, Marie-Laure Bernadac, *The Ultimate Picasso*, Harry N. Abrams, Inc., 2003

Leal, Brigitte, Maria Teresa Ocana, Valeriano Bozal, Werner Hoffman, *Picasso: From Caricature to Metamorphosis of Style*, Lund Humphries, 2003

Lemione, Serge (Ed.), *Towards Modern Art: From Puvis de Chavannes to Matisse and Picasso*, Thames and Hudson Ltd, 2002

Mailer, Norman, *Portrait of Picasso as a Young Man*, Warner Books, 1996

Martin, Russell, *Picasso's War: The Destruction of Guernica and Picasso's Masterpiece*, Scribner, 2003

O'Brian, Patrick, *Picasso: A Biography*, W.W. Norton & Company, 1994

Olivier, Fernande, *Loving Picasso: The Private Journal of Fernande Olivier*, Harry N. Abrams, 2001

Penrose, Roland, *Picasso*, Phaidon Press (Colour Library), 1992

Picasso, Claude Ruiz, Bernard Picasso, *Picasso: Painter and Sculptor in Clay*, Thames and Hudson Ltd, 1998

Picasso, Oliver Widmaier, Picasso: *The Real Family Story*, Prestel Publishing, 2004

Richardson, John, *A Life of Picasso, Vols 1 and 2*, Random House, 1991, 1996

Rubin, William, *Picasso and Braque: Pioneering Cubism*, Museum of Modern Art, New York, 1989

Stein, Gertrude, *Picasso*, Dover Publications, 1984

Todd, Jane Marie, *Conversations with Picasso*, University of Chicago Press, 2002

Walther, Ingo F., *Picasso*, Taschen, 2000

Warncke, Carsten Peter, *Picasso*, Taschen, 2003

Index by Work

Absinthe Drinker, The 121
Absinthe Drinker, The (Portrait of Angel Fernandez de Soto) 47
Acrobat, The 157, 158
After Velazquez 295
Angel Fernandez de Soto 261
Artist's Father, The 23
Asleep 349

Bather 221
Bathers 85
Bathers, The (1918) 273
Bathers, The (1956) 367
Bay at Cannes, The 253
Bottle, Cup and Newspaper 145
Bull, The 243
Bull's Head 242, 359
Bullfight 107
Bullfighting 161
Bust of a Nude 269
Bust of a Seated Woman 109

Carafe and Three Bowls 315
Charnel House, The 171, 192
Child with a Dove 35, 96
Circus Scene 159
Claude Drawing Françoise and Paloma 99
Composition with Cut Pear 329
Condor and Owl 361
Crucifixion, The 155

Dance with Veils (Nude with Drapery) 313
Death's Head 165, 166
Don Quixote 365
Dove 177
Dream, The 347

El Paseo de Colon 223
Erik Satie 77

Factory at Horta de Ebro 219
Family of Saltimbanques, The 135
First Communion 29, 30
Flautist and Child (Fatherhood) 113
Footballers 191
Four Cats Café, The 203
Menu from The Four Cats 205
Friendship 63
Frugal Repast, The 53, 130

Girl and Boy with a Goat 307
Glass of Absinthe 327
Gósol 213
Guernica 11, 16, 94, 163, 164, 170, 174, 192, 244, 350, 354, 356
Horse's Head Study for *Guernica* 355
Preparatory Drawing for *Guernica* 353
Guitar (1912–13) 323, 326, 330
Guitar (1913) 325

Head 257
Head of a Woman (1907) 311
Head of a Woman (1961) 371
Head of a Woman, Fernande 317
His Son, Paulo 275
House at Juan-les-Pins, The 237
Houses on the Hill (Horta de Ebro) 65

Joy of Life, The 173
Juan-les-Pins 233

'La Californie' at Night 251
La Celestine (Carlota Valdivia) 51

Landscape 255
Landscape (La Rue-des-Bois) 215
Landscape at Juan-les-Pins 235
Las Meninas 110, 369
Las Meninas No. I 105
Le Moulin de la Galette 207
Les Demoiselles d'Avignon 10, 11, 60, 62, 137, 138, 284
Les Misérables 131
Life 49
Lying Nude with Head of a Man in Profile 293

Man with a Sheep 167
Maria Picasso Lopez, the Artist's Mother 25
Massacre in Korea 179, 362, 364
Minotaur and Dead Mare in Front of a Cave 93
Minotauromachie 351
Monkey and her Baby 287, 242
Monument to the Spanish People who Died for France, A 175
Morning Concert, The 195
Mother and Child (c. 1901) 125
Mother and Child (1921) 274, 337
Mountains of Málaga 201

Night Fishing at Antibes 241
Notre-Dame de Paris 245
Nude from the Back 301
Nude Lying Down Beside the Sea 227

Offering, The 139
Old Guitarist, The 129
On the Beach (Bathing) 283

Paloma in Blue **97**
Paulo as a Harlequin **81**
Peasants' Repast, The **271**
Phallic Centaur I **377**
Pigeons, Cannes, The **249**
Pipes of Pan, The **277**
Portrait of a Painter, after El Greco **285**
Portrait of Ambroise Vollard **67**
Portrait of Daniel-Henry Kahnweiler **69**
Portrait of Françoise Gilot with Paloma and Claude **363**
Portrait of Gertrude Stein **55**, 56, 310
Portrait of Gustave Coquiot **123**
Portrait of Jaime Sabartés Y Gual **43**
Portrait of Madame H. P. **181**
Portrait of Marie-Thérèse **91**
Portrait of Mateu Fernandez de Soto **45**
Portrait of Maya with her Doll **95**
Portrait of Olga in an Armchair **73**
Portrait of Suzanne Bloch **133**
Portrait of the Artist's Wife, Jacqueline Kneeling **101**
Project for a Monument to Guilllaume Apollinaire **341**
Public Garden **209**

Rape of the Sabines, The **193**
Reading **345**
Reclining Nude **111**
Rooftops in Barcelona **211**

Saltimbanques, The (Harlequin and his Companion) **117**
Scenes from the Ballet *La Boutique Fantastique* **333**
Science and Charity **31**, 32
Sculptor, The **87**, 90
Seated Nude **305**
Self-Portrait (1896) **27**
Self-Portrait (1901) **39**
Self-Portrait (1901) **41**
Self-Portrait (1906) **57**
Self-Portrait (1906) **59**
Self-Portrait (1907) **61**
Self-Portrait in a Top Hat **37**, 38
Set Design for the Ballet *Pulcinella* **335**
Sketch for the Stage Curtain for *Tricorne* by Manuel de Falla **225**
Small House in a Garden **217**
Soup, The **127**
Still Life on a Piano **319**
Still Life with Chair Caning **321**
Still Life with Pitcher and Bowl of Fruit **343**
Still Life with Skull and Leeks **169**
Studio at 'La Californie', The **291**
Studio, The (1927–28) **339**
Studio, The (1955) **247**
Suite 156, L10 **197**

Theatre Curtain for *Parade* **149**
Three Dancers **83**
Three Musicians **153**
Three Women at the Spring **151**, 152
Toros y Toreros **189**
Two Figures **229**, 230
Two Nudes **309**, 336
Two Women at a Bar **299**
Two Women Running on the Beach (The Race) **231**

Vera Nemchinova and Felix Fernandez Dancing **75**
Violin **331**
Violin and Sheet Music **71**
Violin in a Café **147**
Violin, Pipe, Glass and Anchor, Souvenir of Le Havre **143**
Vive la Paix **187**

Waiting (Margot) **265**
War and Peace, in Vallauris Chapel 98, 180, **183**
'Four Corners of the World, The', from *War and Peace*, in Vallauris Chapel **185**
Weeping Woman **357**
Woman Farmer (half-length) **141**
Woman in a Hat **375**
Woman in a Red Armchair **281**
Woman in a Red Petticoat **79**
Woman in Blue **33**, 34
Woman Lying on the Beach **239**
Woman with a Chignon **119**
Woman with a Cigarette **267**
Woman with a Crow **303**, 304
Woman with a Flower **89**
Woman with a Guitar **279**
Woman with a Hat **263**
Woman with Outstretched Arms **373**
Women of Algiers, The, after Delacroix (1954) **289**
Women of Algiers, The, after Delacroix (1955) **103**

General Index

absinthe 120, 326
Abstract Expressionism 11
African masks 13, 62, 68, 136, 138, 140, 268, 310, 322
Aix-en-Provence, France 216
Alarcón, Pedro 224
Algerian crisis 102
Alicante 200
Ambassadeurs 204
Antibes 17, 172, 240, 276
Apollinaire, Guillaume 152, 340
Aragon, Louis 176
Arcimboldo, Guiseppe 286
Arles 106
Arp, Jean 282
art historians 60
Art Nouveau 202
Avril, Jane 132

Ballets Russes 72, 74, 76, 148, 222, 224, 230, 332, 334
Barcelona Universal Exhibition 222
Barcelona 16, 17, 26, 32, 42, 44, 46, 48, 50, 116, 126, 128, 136, 160, 196, 200, 202, 204, 210, 222, 260, 262
'bateau-lavoir' 52, 54, 130, 152
bathers 62, 220, 238, 272, 276, 308, 366
Bergson, Henri 146
Biarritz 78, 272
Blasco, José Ruiz (Picasso's father) 22, 24, 28, 30, 96, 112, 128, 248, 260, 262
Bloch, Henri 132
Bloch, Suzanne 132
blue period 13, 14, 40, 48, 50, 124, 128, 130, 134, 298, 300, 302, 304
Boisgeloup 86
Bonnard, Pierre 264
boxing 190
Braque, Georges 13, 64, 70, 72, 108, 142, 144, 216, 290, 318
Portuguese, The 142
Breton, André 156
Bruant, Aristide 202
bullfighting 92, 106, 160, 188, 190, 224, 242, 352

cabarets 118, 122, 124, 132, 204, 236, 324
Café la Lorraine 42
cafés 70, 76, 118, 120, 122, 124, 266, 198, 318
Cal Tampanada 212
Calder, Alexander 190
Cannes 100, 246, 250, 252, 290
film festival 252
Cap d'Antibes 84
Casagemas, Carlos 48
Casas, Ramon 202, 260
centaurs 376
ceramics 98, 360
Cervantes, Miguel de 364
Cézanne, Paul 10, 13, 62, 64, 66, 214, 216, 218, 276, 308, 314
Chateau Grimaldi 232
Chavannes, Pierre Puvis de 126, 272, 276
Shepherd's Song 276
Young Girls by the Seashore 272
Chicago 256
Chinese painting 186
cinema 60
classical mythology 84, 100, 228
classicism 150, 228, 274, 306, 376
Clouzot, Georges 17
Cocteau, Jean 74, 76, 108, 148
Cold War 13, 184, 188
collage 11, 70, 320, 358
Communism 16, 96, 170, 176, 178, 180, 188, 248, 364
constructivism 11
Coquiot, Gustave 122
Corot, Jean Baptiste Camille 278
Girl with a Mandolin 278
Cortet, Alfred 318
costume designs 74, 224, 234, 332
Courbet, Gustave 270, 284, 290
Artist's Studio, The 290
Cranach, Lucas 284
Cuban Missile Crisis 192
Cubism 10, 11, 13, 16, 60, 64, 66, 68, 72, 74, 80, 86, 102, 104, 136, 142, 144, 146, 148, 152, 168, 190, 274, 278, 284, 290, 314, 316, 318, 320, 322, 336, 338, 356, 358, 370, 374
synthetic Cubism 324, 328, 330

Dada 11
dancers 82
Daumier, Honoré 134, 364
David, Jacques-Louis 104, 192, 288
Rape of the Sabines 104, 288
De Soto, Angel Fernandez 46, 260
De Soto, Mateu Fernandez 44, 46
Degas, Edgar 196, 266, 332
Delacroix, Eugène 102, 104, 288
Women of Algiers, The 102, 104, 288
Derain, André 72
Diaghilev, Sergei 72, 222, 224, 334
Dinard 84, 226, 228, 230
Dominguin, Luis Miguel 188
doves 96, 176, 182, 184, 186, 248
Duchamp, Marcel 11

Eiffel Tower 244
El Diluvio 324
El Greco 44, 260, 266, 284
Portrait of an Artist 284
El Paseo de Colon 222
Els Quatre Gats 204
Eluard, Paul 100
Europe 202, 206, 228, 236, 240, 256
exhibitions 17, 30, 66, 78, 98, 108, 122, 126, 132, 170, 204, 216, 260, 264, 280
Expressionism 10

Fairbanks, Douglas 232
Falla, Manuel de 224
Fascism 164, 174, 352
First World Peace Congress 176
First World War 13, 68, 72, 74, 80, 148, 150, 172, 222, 224, 226, 228, 270, 274, 278
Fitzgerald, F. Scott 232
Four Cats Café 116, 202, 204, 210
France 14, 16, 52, 172, 174, 180, 216, 228, 256

French Riviera 14, 84, 226, 232, 240
Franco, Francisco 94, 106, 110, 162, 174
Fréjus 106

Gaudí, Antoni 202
Gauguin, Paul 264, 300
Gilot, Françoise 14, 96, 98, 172, 362
González, Julio 84, 340, 376
Gósol 212, 218
Gouel, Eva (Marcelle Humbert) 70
Goya, Francisco de 50, 178, 260, 292
  Executions of the Third of May, 1808 178
  Naked Maja 292
Greek art 11, 150, 276, 306, 360
Gris, Juan 278
  Woman with a Mandolin 278
Grünewald, Mathias 154
  Isenheim Altarpiece 154
Guernica 13, 154, 162, 240, 352, 356
Guilbert, Yvette 132

harlequins 14, 74, 80, 116
hatching 312
Hitler, Adolf 160
Hopkins, Anthony 17
Horta de Ebro 64, 218, 220
Hotel des Ecoles 44

Iberian sculpture 54, 56, 138, 308, 310
Ibsen, Henrik 120
Ilio, Pepe 188
Impressionism 266, 298, 328
Ingres, Jean Auguste Dominique 54, 72, 76, 150, 272, 274, 306
interior landscapes 246, 250

Jacob, Max 132, 152
jazz music 236
Joyce, James 146
Juan-les-Pins 78, 84, 232, 234, 236

Kahnweiler, Daniel-Henry 68, 148, 372
Khokhlova, Olga 14, 72, 74, 78, 80, 82, 84, 90, 94, 160, 224, 226, 280, 344
Korean War 178, 182, 186, 362

L'Estaque 216, 218
L'Humanité Dimanche 186
La Boutique Fantastique 332
'La Californie' 100, 246, 248, 250, 290
La Celestine 196
La Coruña 22, 26
La Lonja School of Art 26, 28
La Tauromaquia 106, 188
landscapes 64, 200, 212, 214, 216, 218, 232, 234, 254
Le Corbusier 338, 372
Le Havre 142
Le Journal 320
Le Nain brothers 134, 270
  Peasant's Repast, The 270
Le Train Bleu 230
Legion d'Honneur 110
Lenin Peace Prize 108
Les Lettres Français 364
lithographs 96, 176, 186, 188, 248
London 224, 332
Lopez, Maria Picasso (Picasso's mother) 24
Lopokova, Lydia 332
Lorraine, Claude 150
Louvre 56, 138, 262, 270, 284, 288, 308, 368

Maar, Dora 356
Madrid 32, 160, 200, 222, 262
Magritte, René 282
  Threatened Assassin 282
Málaga 17, 24, 30, 200
Malevich, Kasimir 11
Mañach, Pere 34, 46
Manet, Edouard 104, 134, 288
  Déjeuner sur l'herbe 104, 288
  Old Musician, The 134
Manifesto of Surrealism 156
Massine, Léonide 234, 332
Matisse, Henri 10, 100, 102, 172, 182, 190, 248, 288, 370
  Bonheur de Vivre 172
  Mme Matisse (The Green Line) 370
Médrano Circus 54, 134, 306
Mercure 76, 234
Millet, Jean François 200, 270
Minimalism 11, 256
minotaurs 14, 92, 160, 350
Mirò, Joan 156
Mistinguet 232
Modernismo 202, 210
Mondrian, Piet 11
Monte Sainte-Victoire 112
Montmartre 52, 54, 76, 118, 122, 124, 128, 130, 132, 134, 206, 266, 306, 316, 318, 322, 324, 326
Moore, Henry 282
Moulin de la Galette 206
Moulin Rouge 204
Munch, Edvard 10, 38
Musée Nationale d'Art Moderne, Paris 284
Museo Picasso, Barcelona 24, 108, 110
Museum of Ethnography, Paris 268, 310
Museum of Modern Art, New York 256
music halls 70
musical instruments 70
musketeers 294
Mystery of Picasso, The 17

Naples 222
Napoleon III 266
National Socialist Party 160, 164, 166
Neoclassicisim 11, 13, 14, 78, 80, 82, 84, 150, 152, 226, 230, 270, 280, 330, 336, 338
Neolithic art 156
Notre-Dame 244
Notre-Dame-de-Vie 254
nudes 194, 200, 226, 268, 292, 304, 308, 310, 312

Oceanic art 138
odalisques 102, 288
Olivier, Fernande 54, 70, 130, 212, 214, 316
Ozenfant, Amedée 338

Pallarès, Manuel 218
Pantheon 126
Parade 74, 76, 148

Paris International Exhibition 162, 352
Paris 13, 14, 17, 32, 34, 36, 42, 46, 48, 50, 52, 54, 56, 66, 72, 74, 76, 78, 86, 96, 98, 110, 116, 118, 122, 124, 126, 128, 130, 132, 136, 142, 148, 164, 166, 168, 170, 172, 206, 208, 210, 220, 222, 244, 262, 264, 266, 310, 358, 362
Parmelin, Hélène 180
Picasso, Claude 96, 98, 286, 362
Picasso, Maya 94
Picasso, Paloma 96, 98, 362
Picasso, Paulo 14, 78, 80, 90, 94, 160, 226, 274, 336
Pichot, Ramon 82
Pignon, Edouard 180
Poe, Edgar Allen 302
pointillism 270
Pollock, Jackson 10
Pompeii 222
Pop Art 11
Porter, Cole 236
Poussin, Nicolas 150, 192, 306
Massacre of the Innocents 192
Prado 32, 94, 260, 262, 368
primitivism 138, 140
printmaking 350
prostitutes 36, 38, 118, 122, 124, 136, 298
Proust, Marcel 146
Pulcinella 334
Purism 338
Putman, Marie-Louise 140

Raynal, Maurice 100
Rembrandt 26, 196, 294
Renaissance, the 10, 64
Renoir, Pierre Auguste 66, 206
Resistance, the 164, 166, 174
Roman art 11
Rome 184, 222
Romeu, Pere 204
Roque, Jacqueline 100, 102, 108
rose period 13, 74, 304, 306, 308
Rousseau, Henri 190, 272
Football Players 190, 272
Royal Academy of San Fernando 32
Rue des Grands-Augustins 244
Rue-des-Bois 140, 214, 216, 218
Rusiñol, Santiago 202

Sabartés, Jaime 42, 44
Saint-Lazare prison 124, 126, 136
Sala Parés gallery, Barcelona 204
Salon d'Autumne 134
Salon of the Liberation 170
saltimbanques 116, 134
San Sebastien 160
Satie, Erik 76, 234
Saussure, Ferdinand de 144
sculpture 13, 17, 86, 90, 108, 164, 166, 190, 242, 316, 322, 326, 340, 342, 358, 366, 370, 374
Second World War 11, 13, 96, 164, 166, 174, 180, 242, 244
Seine, River 52, 244
self-portraits 14, 26, 36, 38, 56, 58, 60
Semiotics 144
Shchukin, Sergei 58
Soviet Union 176
Spain 16, 32, 42, 56, 92, 94, 104, 106, 110, 116, 154, 160, 174, 222, 250, 322
Spanish Civil War 13, 94, 154, 162, 358
St Malo 226
St Raphael 84
stage designs 74, 224, 234, 332
Stein, Gertrude 10, 54, 58, 256
Stein, Leo 10
still lifes 200, 314, 318, 320, 326, 328, 342
Surrealism 11, 13, 88, 156, 158, 280, 282, 286
Surviving Picasso 17
Symbolism 13, 264, 276, 298
syphilis 128, 136

Tate Gallery, London 11
Toledo 160
Toros y Toreros 106, 188
Toulouse-Lautrec, Henri de 32, 118, 132, 204, 206, 260, 264
Tricorne 224, 332
Trocadero, Paris 138
Turner Prize 11

Uhde, Wilhelm 58
UNESCO building 108
United States of America 16, 108, 178, 180

Valdivia, Carlota 50, 128, 196
Valencia 200
Valentino, Rudolf 232
Vallauris 98, 182, 284, 242, 360, 364
Chapel 98, 182, 184
Van Gogh, Vincent 40, 262, 264
Self-Portrait with Bandaged Ear 40
Vauvenargues 112, 250
Velazquez, Diego 50, 104, 242, 262, 288, 290, 294, 368
Las Meninas 104, 242, 288, 290, 368
Villa Chêne 236
Vollard Suite 92
Vollard, Ambroise 36, 66, 68, 92
Vuillard, Edouard 208, 264

Walter, Marie-Thérèse 14, 88, 90, 94, 344, 346, 348, 356
Watteau, Jean-Antoine 134
World Peace Congress 96

Zola, Emile 120